Yamada-kun AND THE Seven Witches

8

MIKI YOSHIKAWA

TWITCH

TWITCH

TURN

Urara Shiraishi

A second-year at Suzaku High School and president of the Supernatural Studies Club. She's known as the "Switch Witch" and switches bodies with the person whom she kisses. Her smile, which she shows from time to time, is so cute that it should be illegal.

Ryu Yamada

A second-year at Suzaku High School and part of the Supernatural Studies Club. He's loathed by his schoolmates for some reason. He's known as the "Copy Guy" and possesses the ability to copy the power of whichever witch he kisses.

Kentaro Tsubaki

A second-year at Suzaku High School and part of the Supernatural Studies Club. He is both scholarly and a good fighter, and he used to live abroad. However, he's also an odd fellow who fries up some tempura when he starts to feel lonely.

Miyabi Itou

A second-year at Suzaku High School and part of the Supernatural Studies Club. She's the only member of the club who's into the occult. She's surprisingly popular with boys.

Toranosuke Miyamura

A second-year at Suzaku High School. He's the vice-president of the Supernatural Studies Club and Student Council. The polar opposite of Yamada, he's the most popular kid in school. He's very curious and sharp, but his perverted streak is a problem.

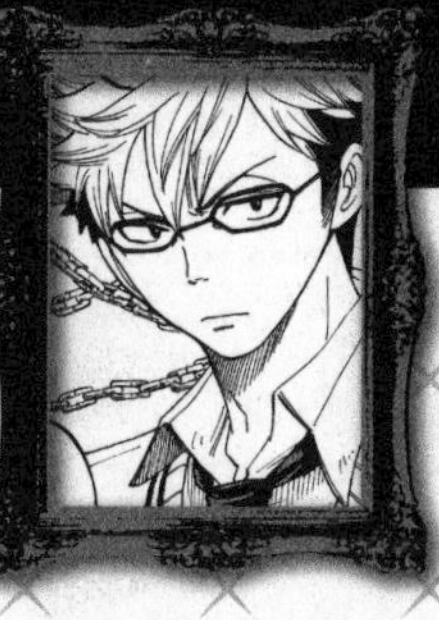

Ushio Igarashi

A second-year at Suzaku High School. He is the loyal minion of the cunning Odagiri. He was Yamada's friend in junior high.

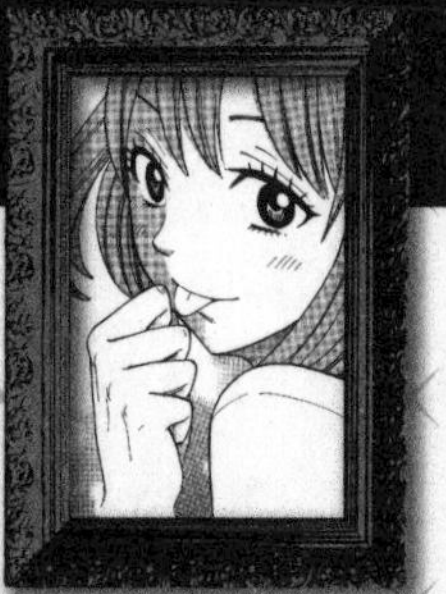

Nene Odagiri

A second-year at Suzaku High School. She shares the position of Student Council vice-president with Miyamura. She is known as the "Charm Witch" and makes the person whom she kisses fall in love with her.

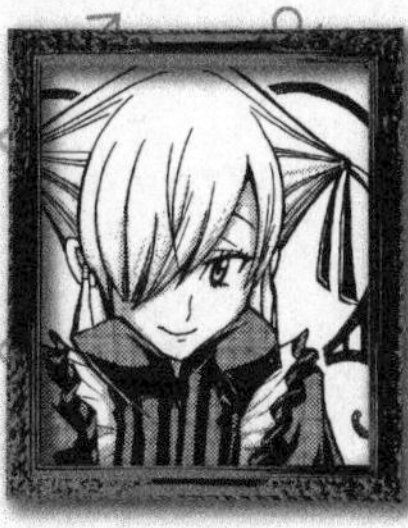

Noa Takigawa

A first-year at Suzaku High School. A little rascal who is infatuated with Yamada. She is known as the "Retrocognition Witch" and by way of dreams can see the past trauma of whomever she kisses.

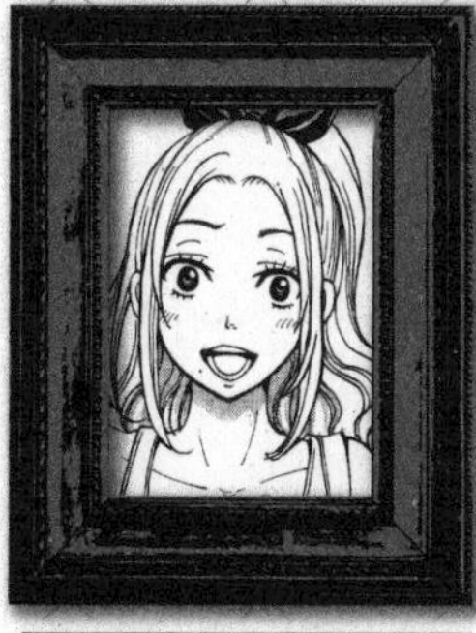

Maria Sarushima

A second-year at Suzaku High School. She's a kissing-fiend who used to live abroad. She is known as the "Prediction Witch" and can see the future from the perspective of the person whom she kisses.

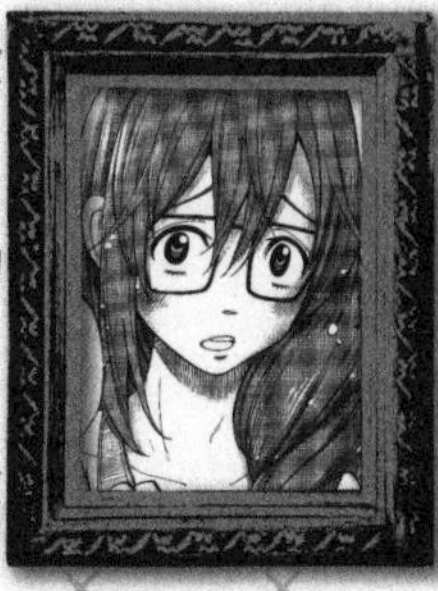

Meiko Otsuka

A second-year at Suzaku High School and member of the Manga Studies Club. She is known as the "Thought Witch" and can perform telepathic communication with the person whom she kisses.

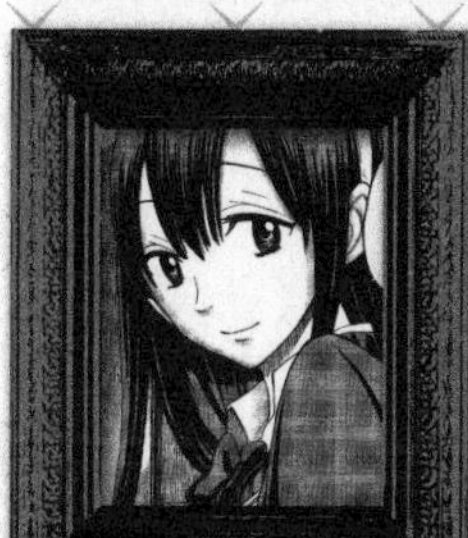

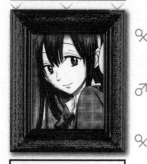

Mikoto Asuka

A third-year at Suzaku High School and vice president of the Student Council. She loves the Student Council president and is super sadistic! She used to be the "Invisible Witch" but had her power erased by Tamaki.

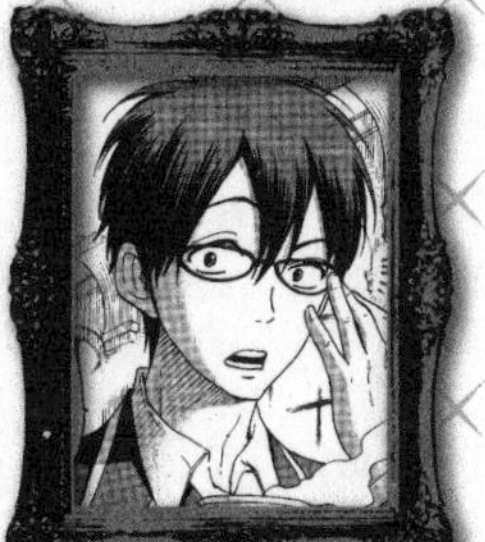

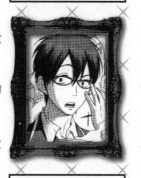

Haruma Yamazaki

A third-year at Suzaku High School and president of the Student Council. He's a crafty guy who holds many secrets. And he has a dirty mind.

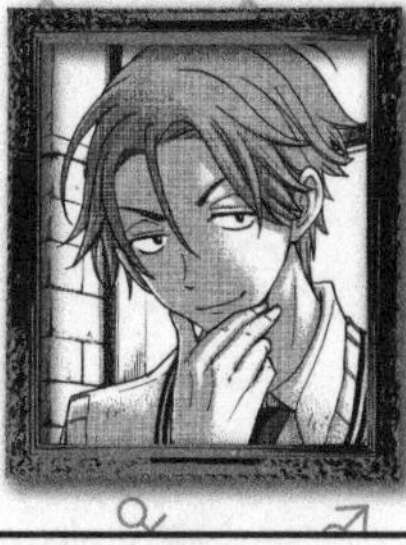

Shinichi Tamaki

A second-year at Suzaku High School. A guy with an attitude who's aiming to be the next Student Council president. He's known as the "Capture Guy" and steals the power of the witch whom he kisses. He currently possesses the ability to turn invisible.

CONTENTS

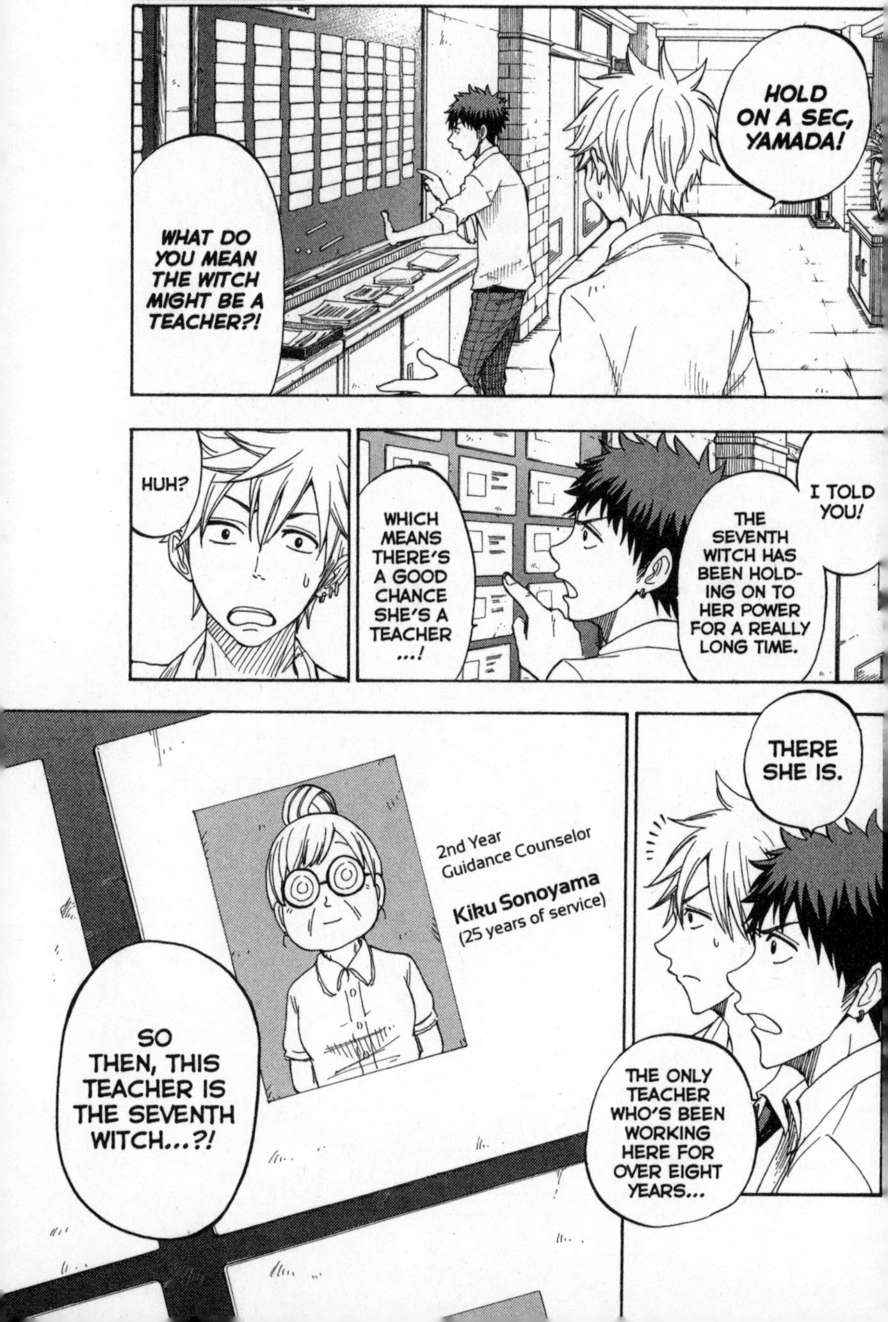
HOLD ON A SEC, YAMADA!
WHAT DO YOU MEAN THE WITCH MIGHT BE A TEACHER?!
I TOLD YOU!
THE SEVENTH WITCH HAS BEEN HOLDING ON TO HER POWER FOR A REALLY LONG TIME.
WHICH MEANS THERE'S A GOOD CHANCE SHE'S A TEACHER ...!
HUH?
THERE SHE IS.
THE ONLY TEACHER WHO'S BEEN WORKING HERE FOR OVER EIGHT YEARS...
2nd Year Guidance Counselor
Kiku Sonoyama
(25 years of service)
SO THEN, THIS TEACHER IS THE SEVENTH WITCH...?!

CHAPTER 61: Just lemme kiss you!

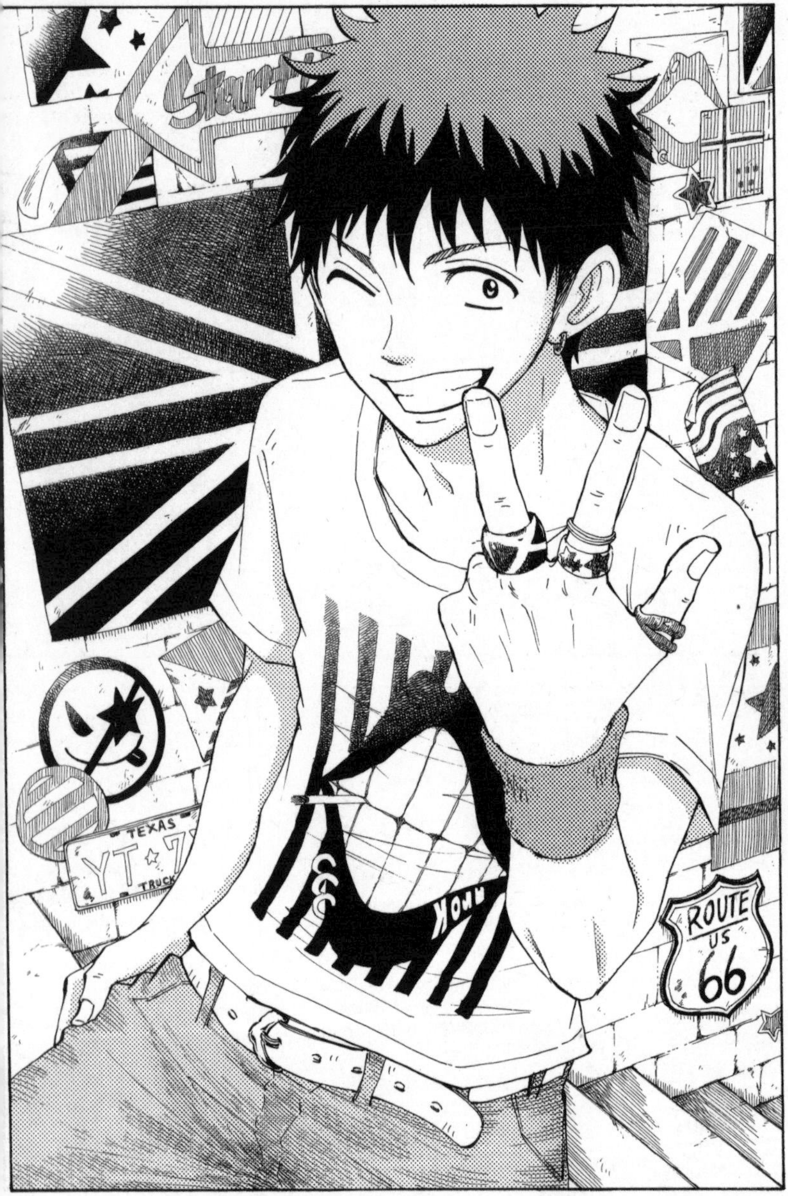
TEXAS
TRUCK
ROUTE
US
66

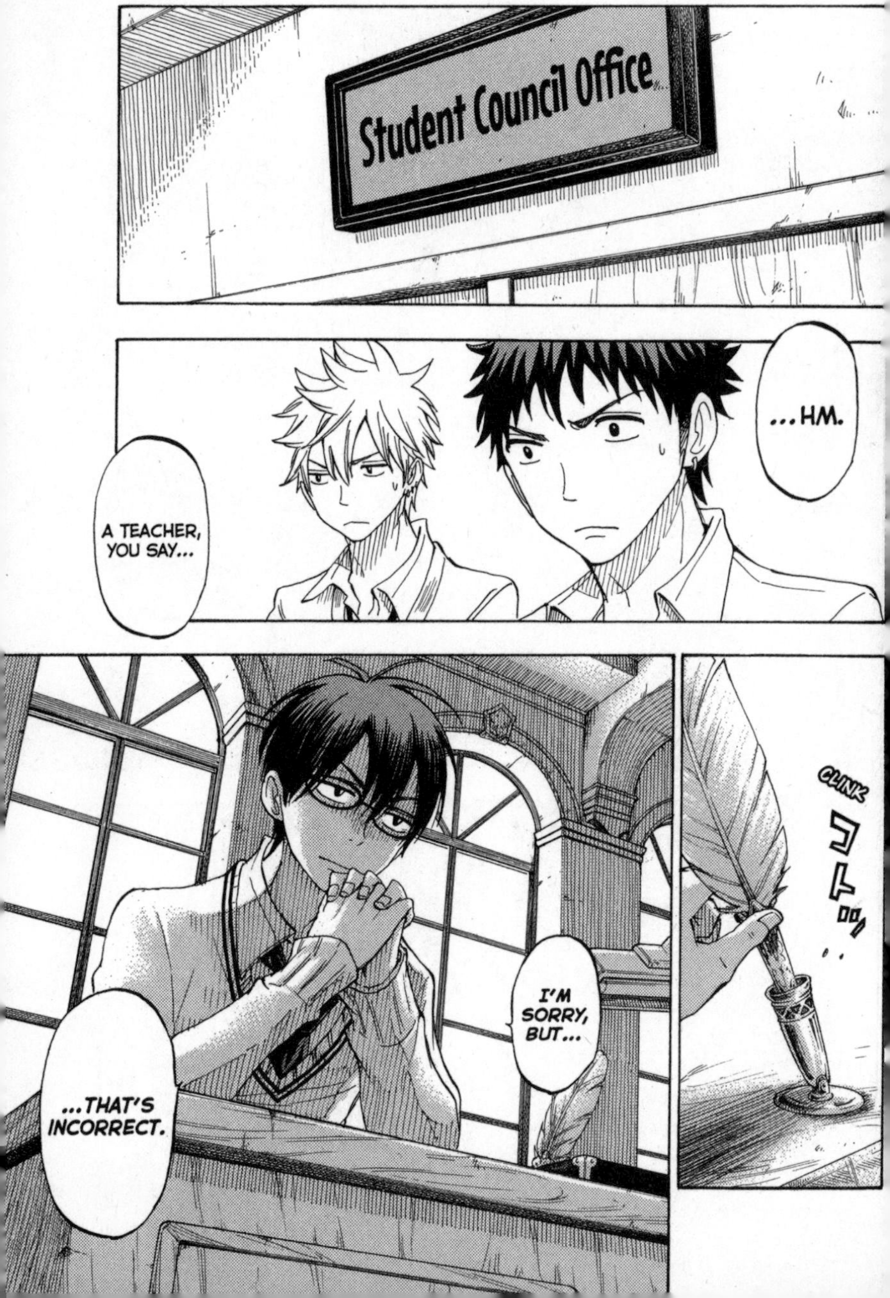
Student Council Office
...HM.
A TEACHER, YOU SAY...
CLINK
コトッ
I'M SORRY, BUT...
...THAT'S INCORRECT.

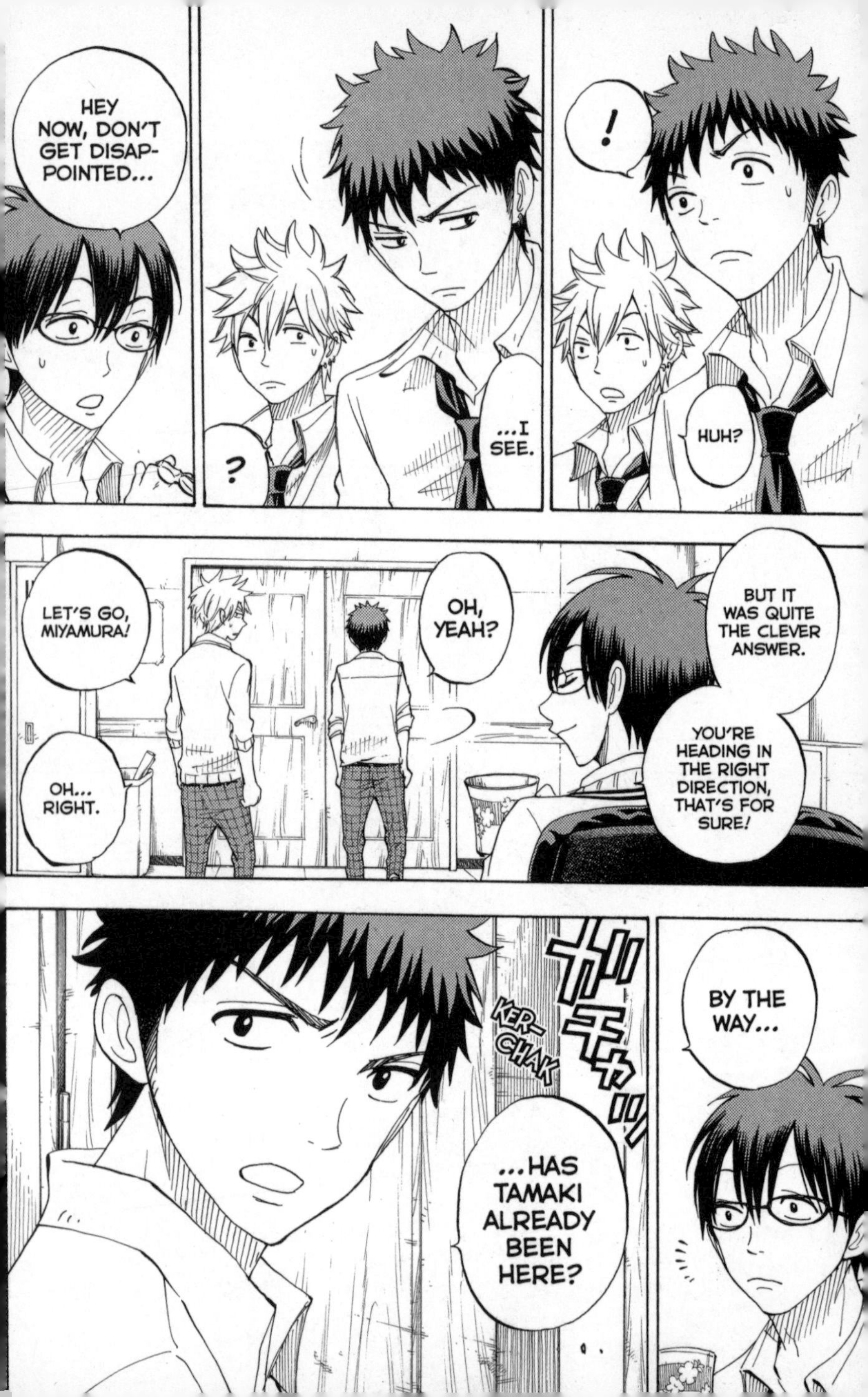
!
HUH?
...I SEE.
?
HEY NOW, DON'T GET DISAP-POINTED...
BUT IT WAS QUITE THE CLEVER ANSWER.
YOU'RE HEADING IN THE RIGHT DIRECTION, THAT'S FOR SURE!
OH, YEAH?
LET'S GO, MIYAMURA!
OH... RIGHT.
BY THE WAY...
KER-CHAK
...HAS TAMAKI ALREADY BEEN HERE?

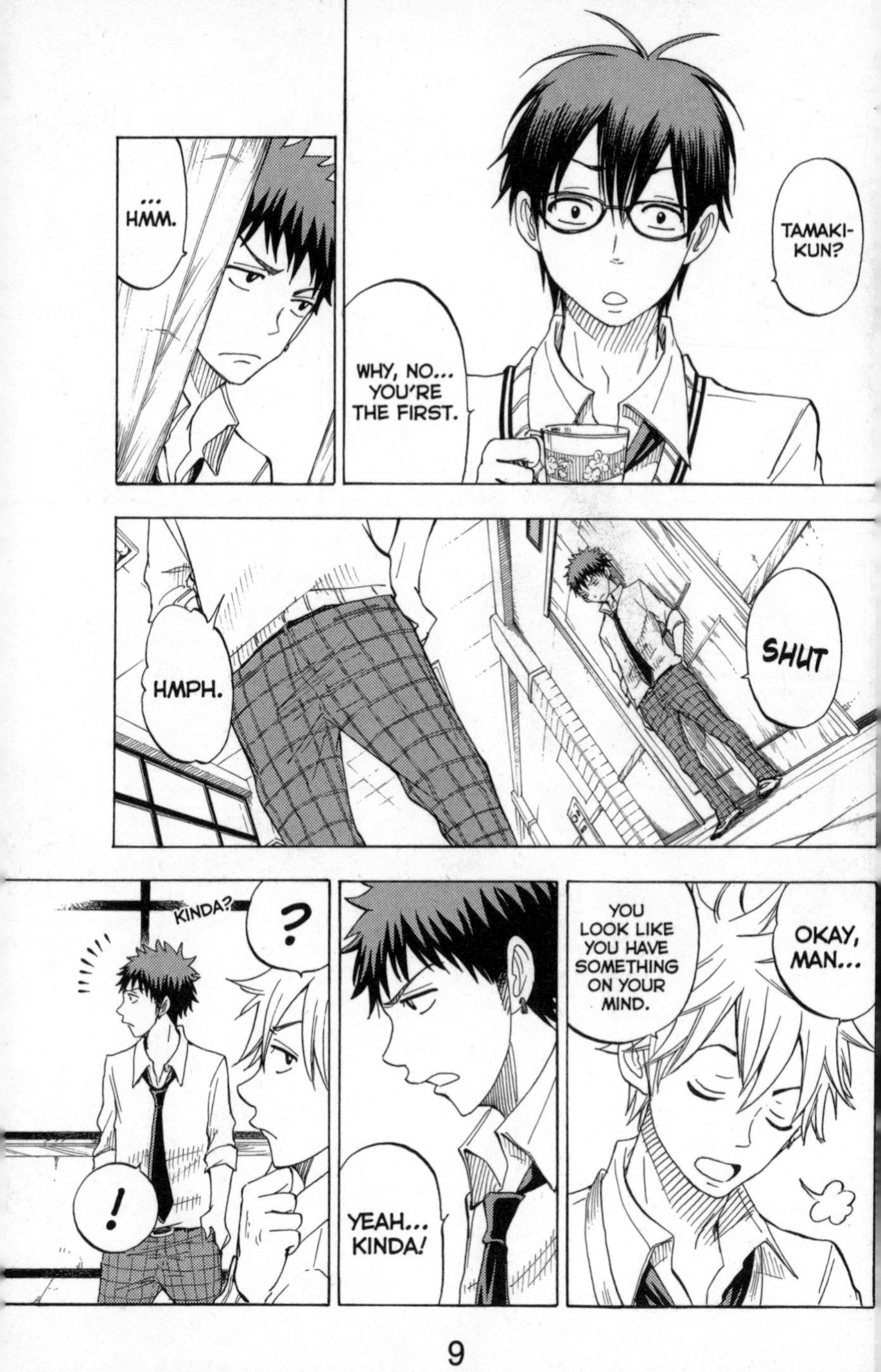
TAMAKI-KUN?
WHY, NO... YOU'RE THE FIRST.
... HMM.
SHUT
HMPH.
OKAY, MAN...
YOU LOOK LIKE YOU HAVE SOMETHING ON YOUR MIND.
YEAH... KINDA!
?
KINDA?
!

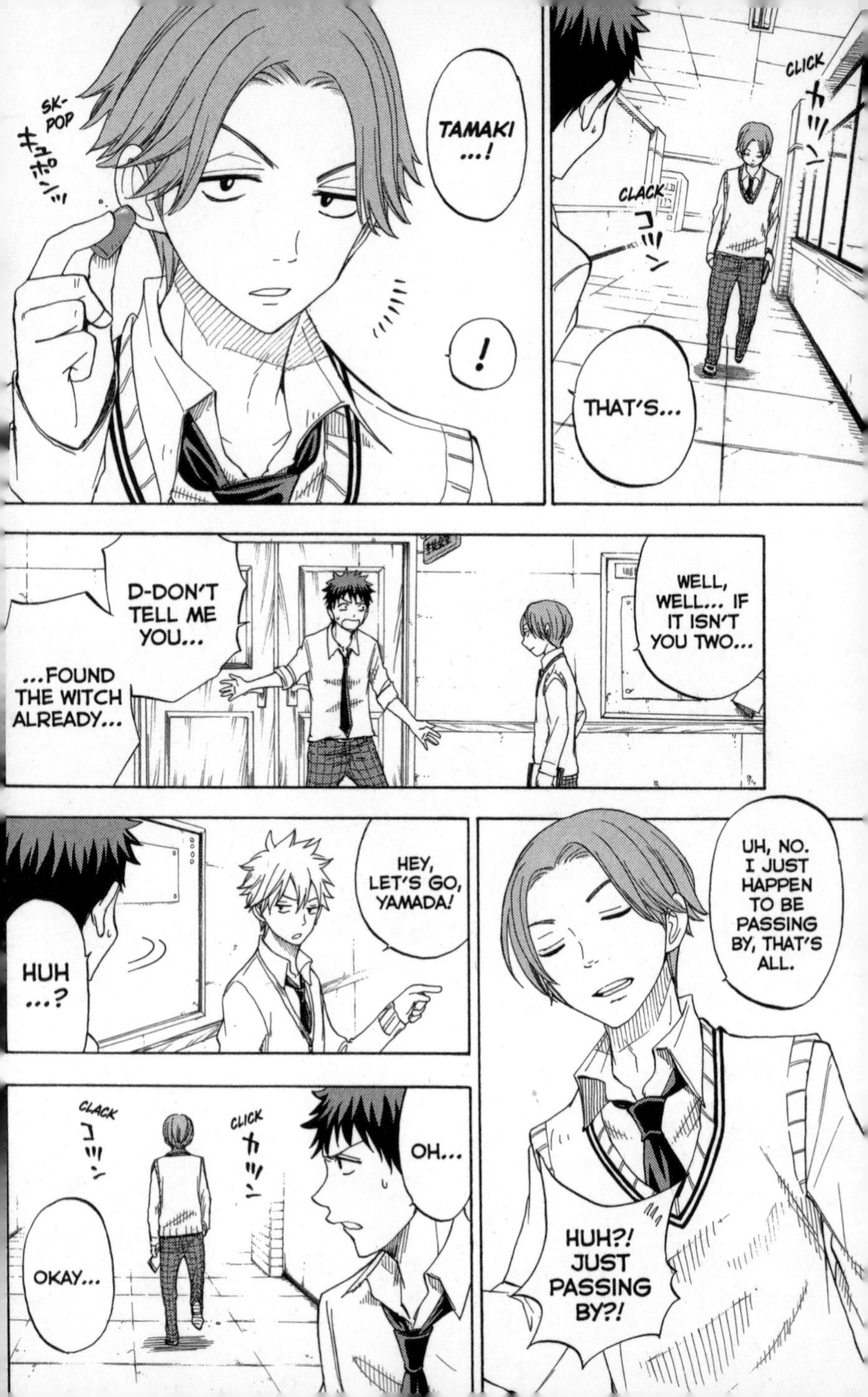

CLICK
カッ
CLACK
コッ
THAT'S...
TAMAKI ...!
!
SK-POP
キュポンッ
WELL, WELL... IF IT ISN'T YOU TWO...
D-DON'T TELL ME YOU...
...FOUND THE WITCH ALREADY...
UH, NO. I JUST HAPPEN TO BE PASSING BY, THAT'S ALL.
HUH?! JUST PASSING BY?!
HEY, LET'S GO, YAMADA!
HUH ...?
OH...
CLICK
カッ
CLACK
コッ
OKAY...

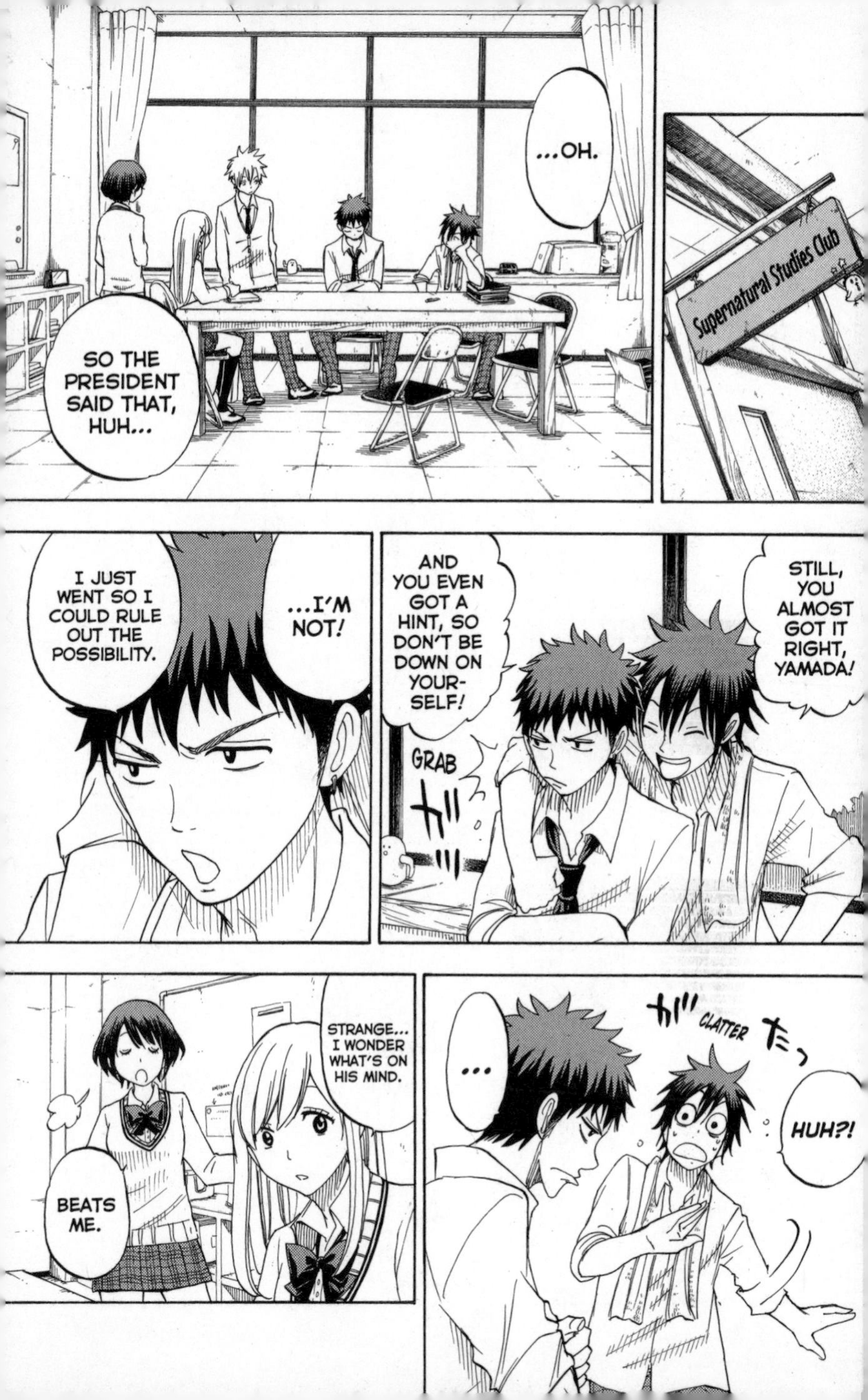
Supernatural Studies Club
...OH.
SO THE PRESIDENT SAID THAT, HUH...
STILL, YOU ALMOST GOT IT RIGHT, YAMADA!
AND YOU EVEN GOT A HINT, SO DON'T BE DOWN ON YOURSELF!
GRAB
...I'M NOT!
I JUST WENT SO I COULD RULE OUT THE POSSIBILITY.
CLATTER
HUH?!
...
STRANGE... I WONDER WHAT'S ON HIS MIND.
BEATS ME.

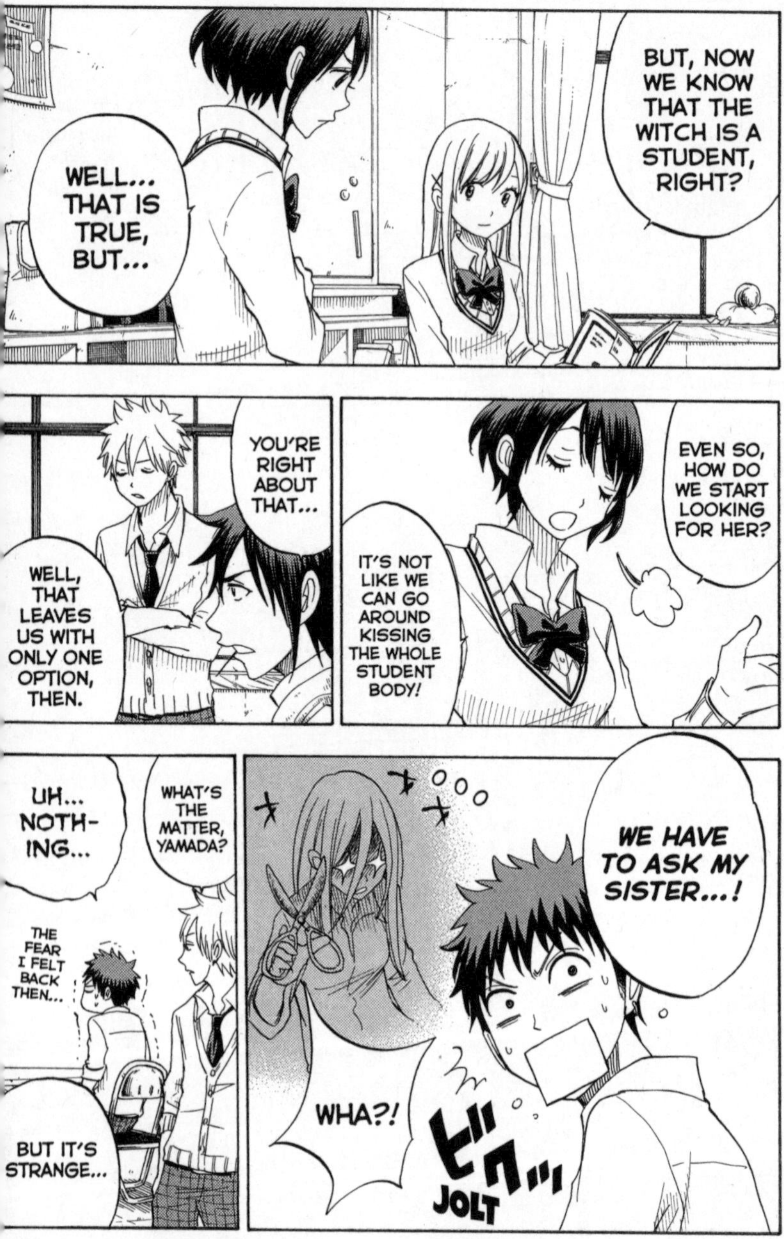
BUT, NOW WE KNOW THAT THE WITCH IS A STUDENT, RIGHT?
WELL... THAT IS TRUE, BUT...
EVEN SO, HOW DO WE START LOOKING FOR HER?
IT'S NOT LIKE WE CAN GO AROUND KISSING THE WHOLE STUDENT BODY!
YOU'RE RIGHT ABOUT THAT...
WELL, THAT LEAVES US WITH ONLY ONE OPTION, THEN.
WE HAVE TO ASK MY SISTER...!
WHA?!
JOLT
WHAT'S THE MATTER, YAMADA?
UH... NOTHING...
THE FEAR I FELT BACK THEN...
BUT IT'S STRANGE...

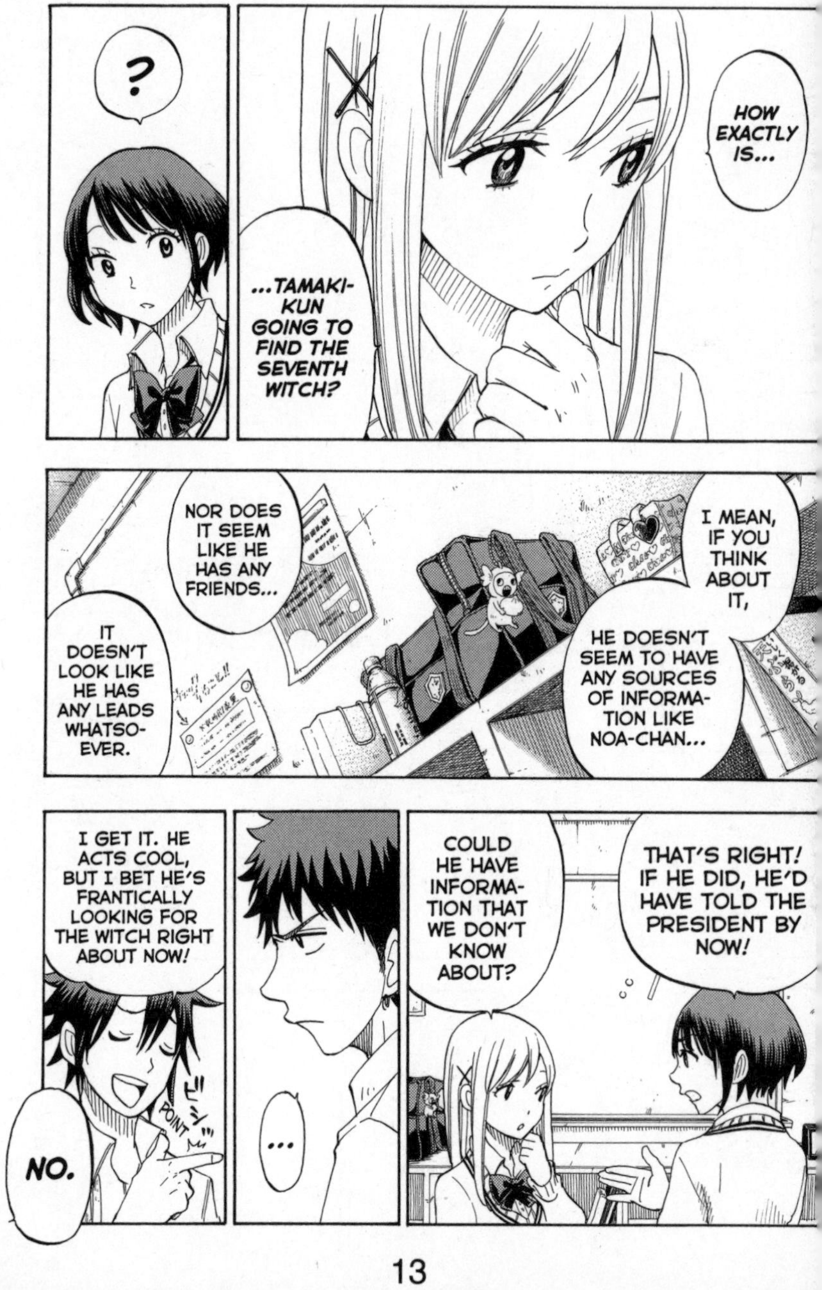
HOW EXACTLY IS...
...TAMAKI-KUN GOING TO FIND THE SEVENTH WITCH?
?
I MEAN, IF YOU THINK ABOUT IT,
HE DOESN'T SEEM TO HAVE ANY SOURCES OF INFORMATION LIKE NOA-CHAN...
NOR DOES IT SEEM LIKE HE HAS ANY FRIENDS...
IT DOESN'T LOOK LIKE HE HAS ANY LEADS WHATSOEVER.
THAT'S RIGHT! IF HE DID, HE'D HAVE TOLD THE PRESIDENT BY NOW!
COULD HE HAVE INFORMATION THAT WE DON'T KNOW ABOUT?
...
I GET IT. HE ACTS COOL, BUT I BET HE'S FRANTICALLY LOOKING FOR THE WITCH RIGHT ABOUT NOW!
POINT
NO.

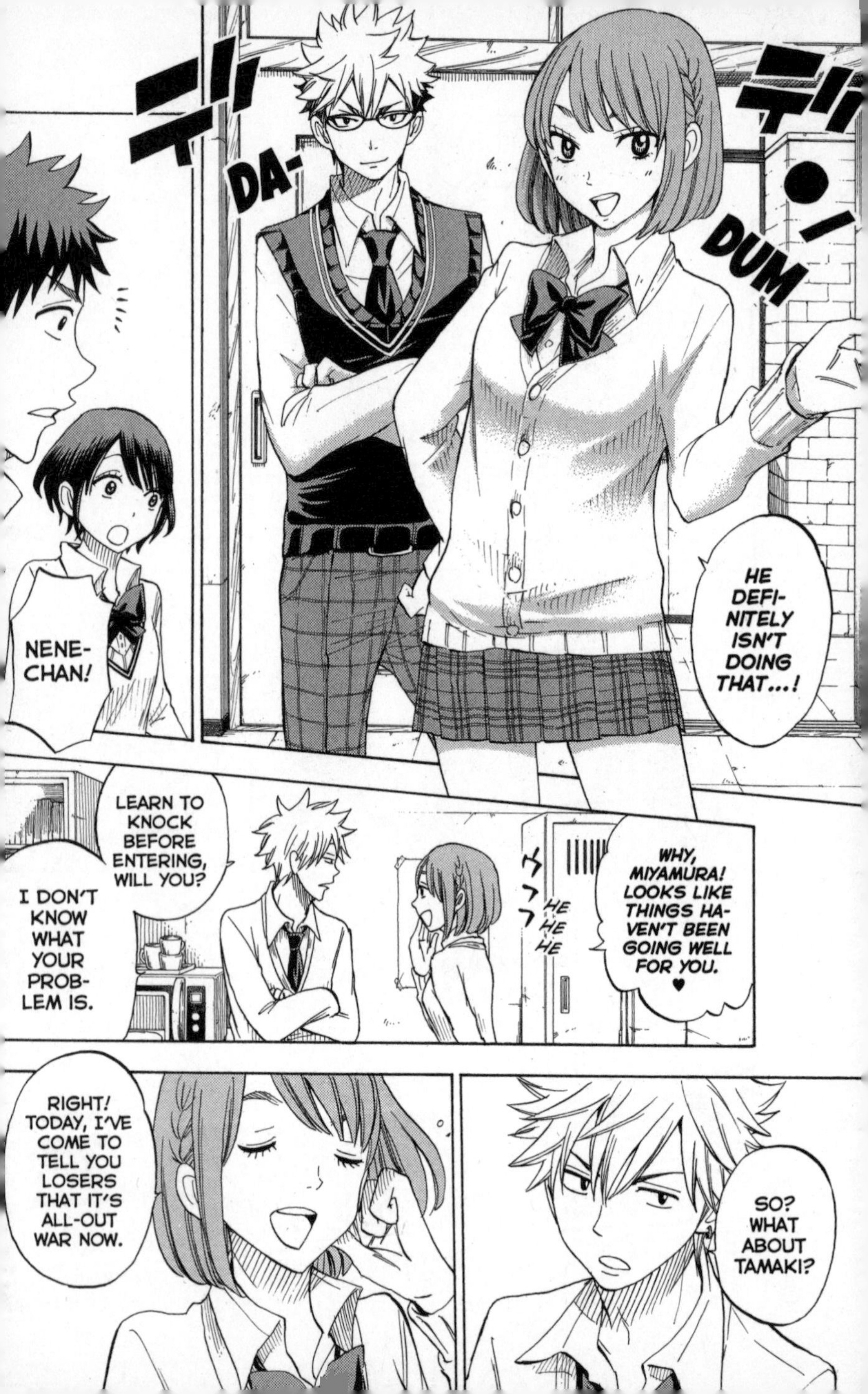
DA-
DUM
HE DEFINITELY ISN'T DOING THAT...!
NENE-CHAN!
WHY, MIYAMURA! LOOKS LIKE THINGS HAVEN'T BEEN GOING WELL FOR YOU. ♥
HE HE HE
LEARN TO KNOCK BEFORE ENTERING, WILL YOU?
I DON'T KNOW WHAT YOUR PROBLEM IS.
SO? WHAT ABOUT TAMAKI?
RIGHT! TODAY, I'VE COME TO TELL YOU LOSERS THAT IT'S ALL-OUT WAR NOW.

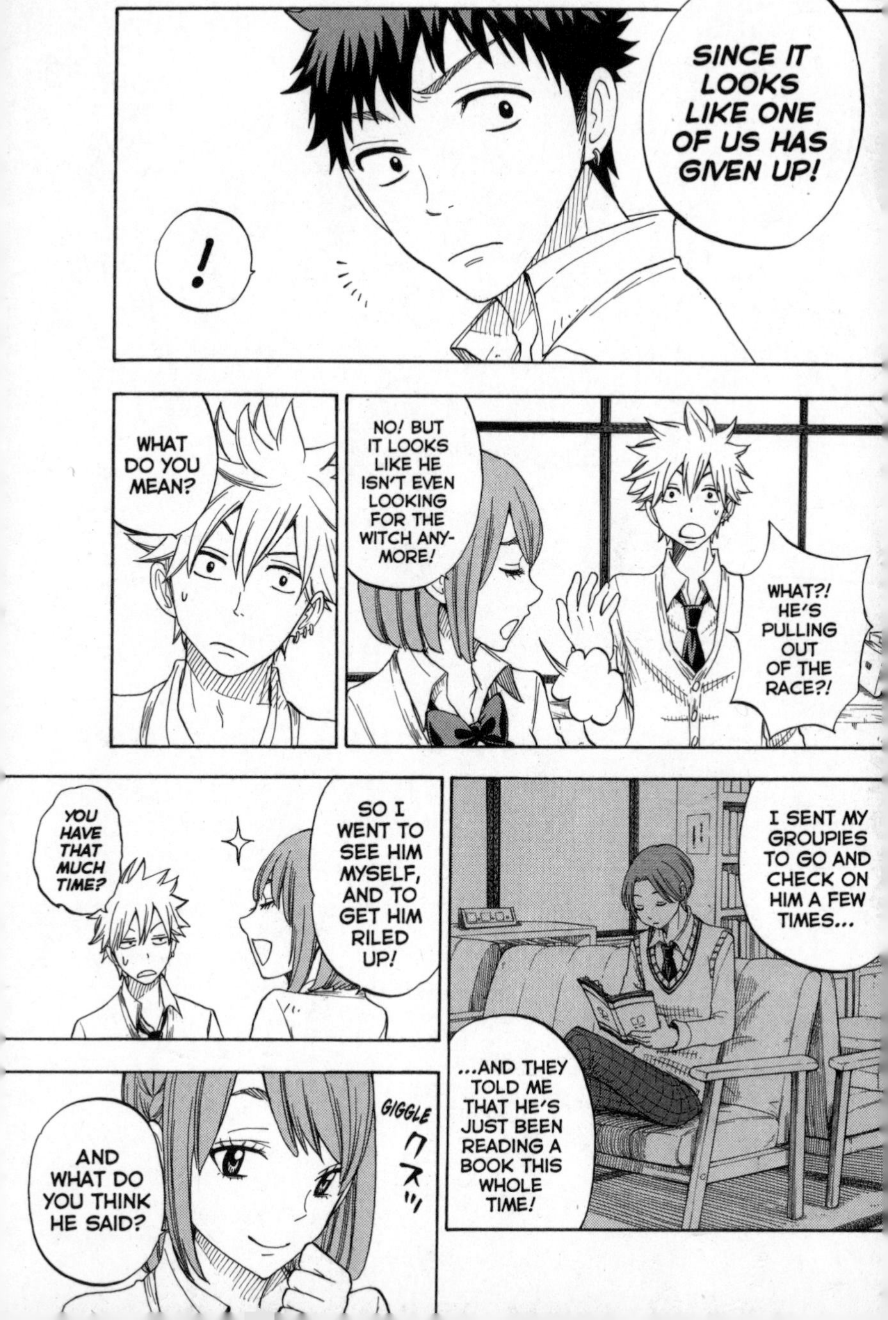
SINCE IT LOOKS LIKE ONE OF US HAS GIVEN UP!
!
WHAT?! HE'S PULLING OUT OF THE RACE?!
NO! BUT IT LOOKS LIKE HE ISN'T EVEN LOOKING FOR THE WITCH ANY-MORE!
WHAT DO YOU MEAN?
I SENT MY GROUPIES TO GO AND CHECK ON HIM A FEW TIMES...
...AND THEY TOLD ME THAT HE'S JUST BEEN READING A BOOK THIS WHOLE TIME!
SO I WENT TO SEE HIM MYSELF, AND TO GET HIM RILED UP!
YOU HAVE THAT MUCH TIME?
GIGGLE
AND WHAT DO YOU THINK HE SAID?

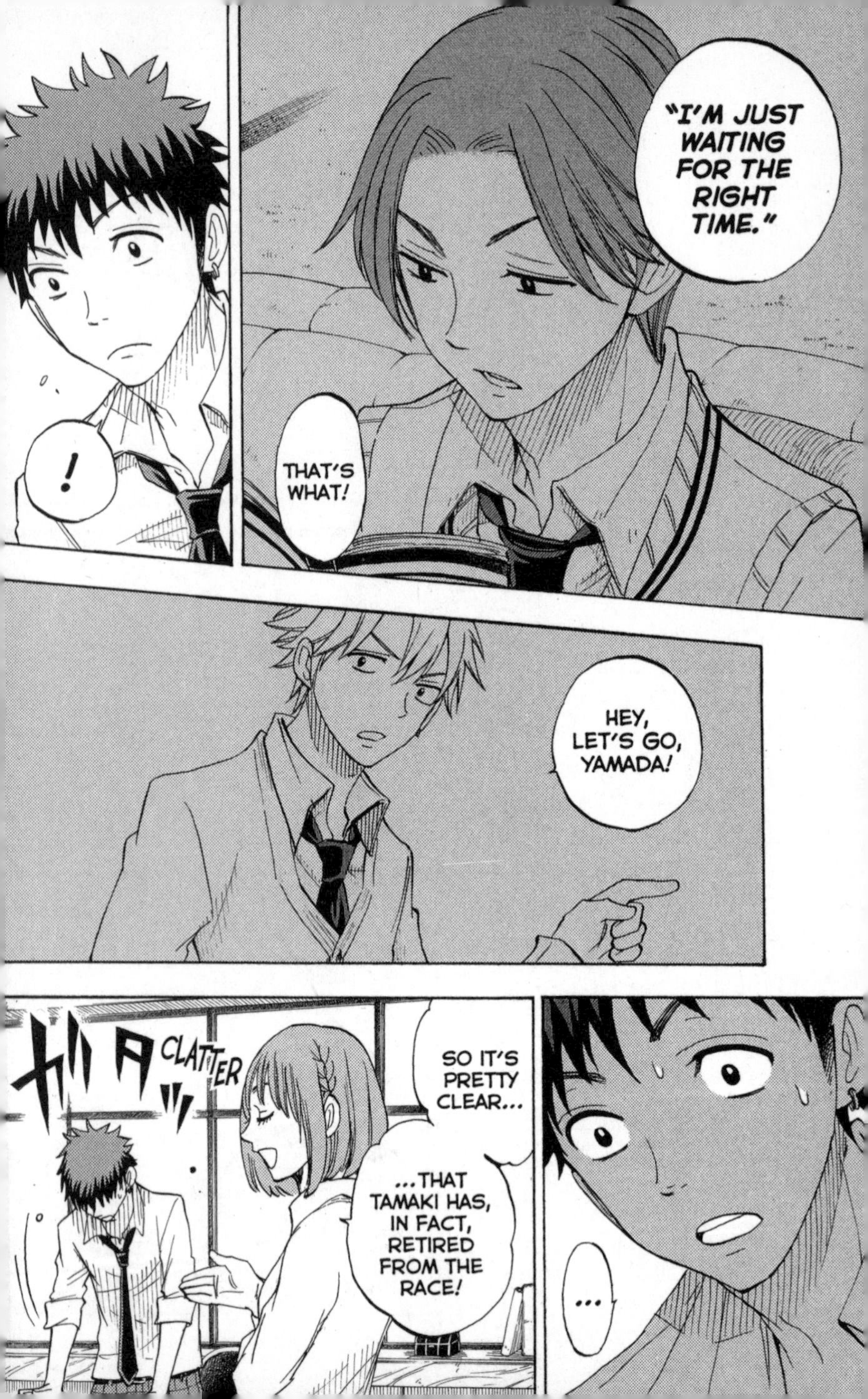
"I'M JUST WAITING FOR THE RIGHT TIME."
THAT'S WHAT!
!
HEY, LET'S GO, YAMADA!
...
SO IT'S PRETTY CLEAR...
...THAT TAMAKI HAS, IN FACT, RETIRED FROM THE RACE!
CLATTER

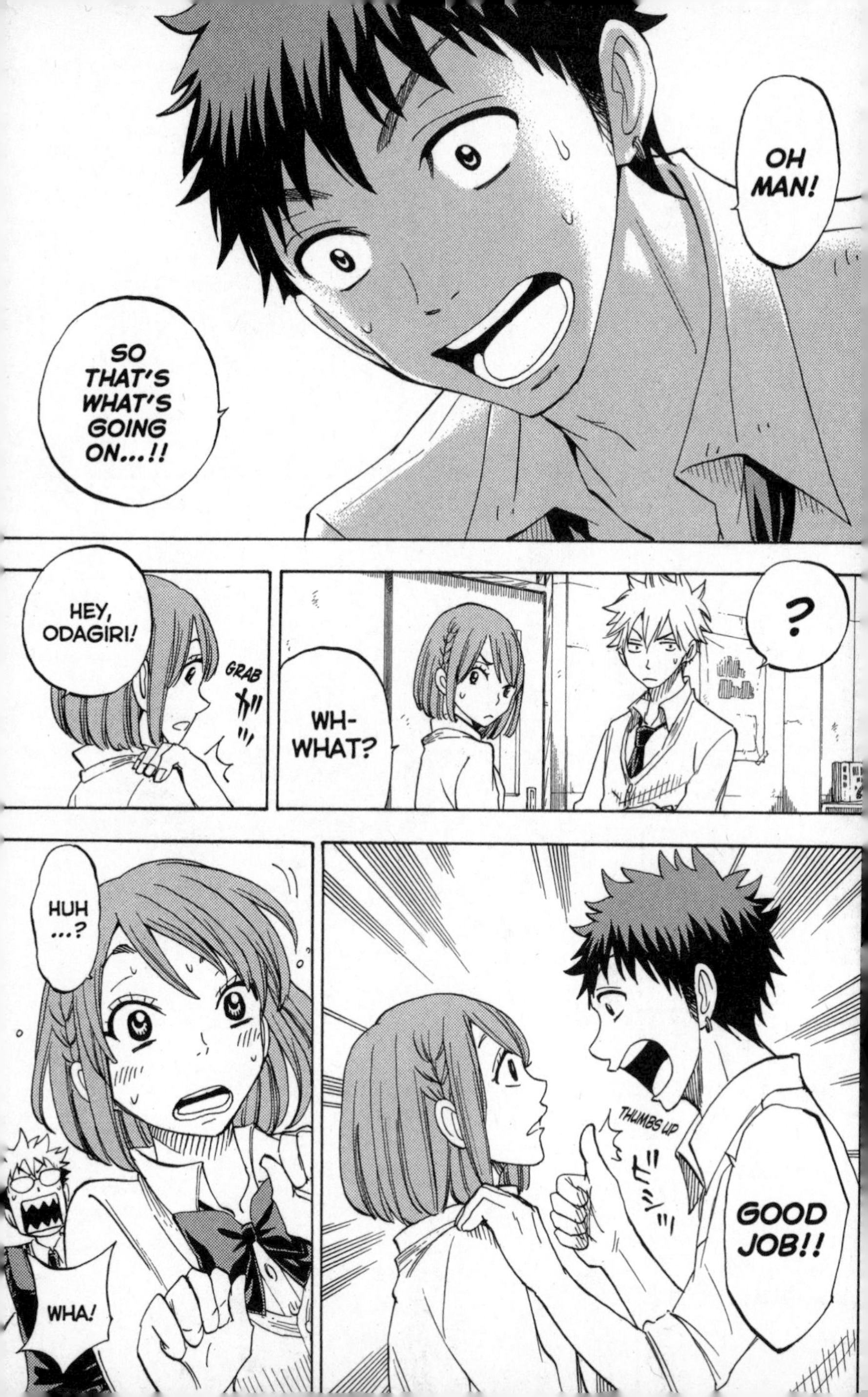
OH MAN!
SO THAT'S WHAT'S GOING ON...!!
?
WH-WHAT?
HEY, ODAGIRI!
GRAB
THUMBS UP
GOOD JOB!!
HUH ...?
WHA!

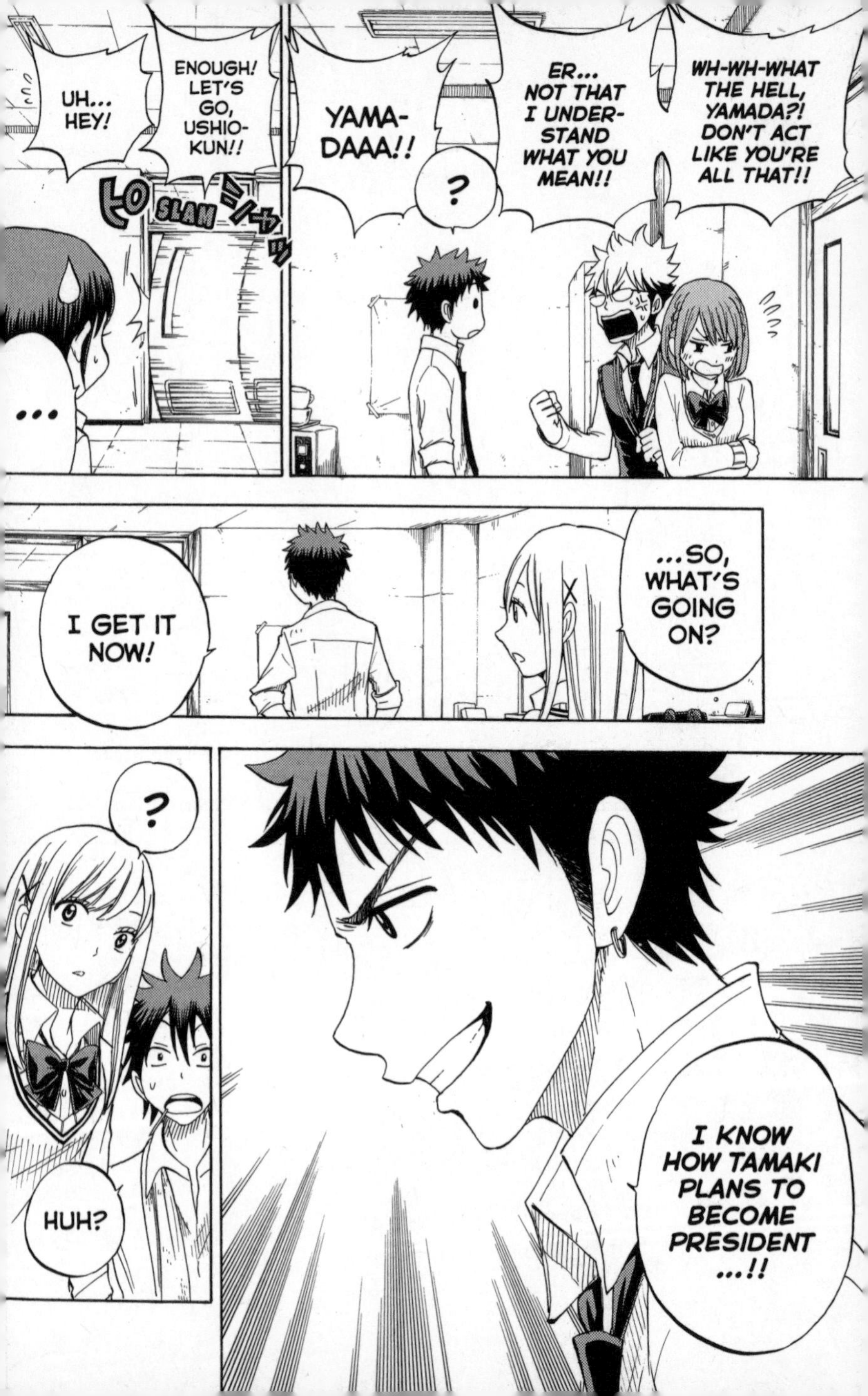
WH-WH-WHAT THE HELL, YAMADA?! DON'T ACT LIKE YOU'RE ALL THAT!!
ER... NOT THAT I UNDER-STAND WHAT YOU MEAN!!
YAMA-DAAA!!
?
ENOUGH! LET'S GO, USHIO-KUN!!
SLAM
UH... HEY!
...
...SO, WHAT'S GOING ON?
I GET IT NOW!
I KNOW HOW TAMAKI PLANS TO BECOME PRESIDENT ...!!
?
HUH?

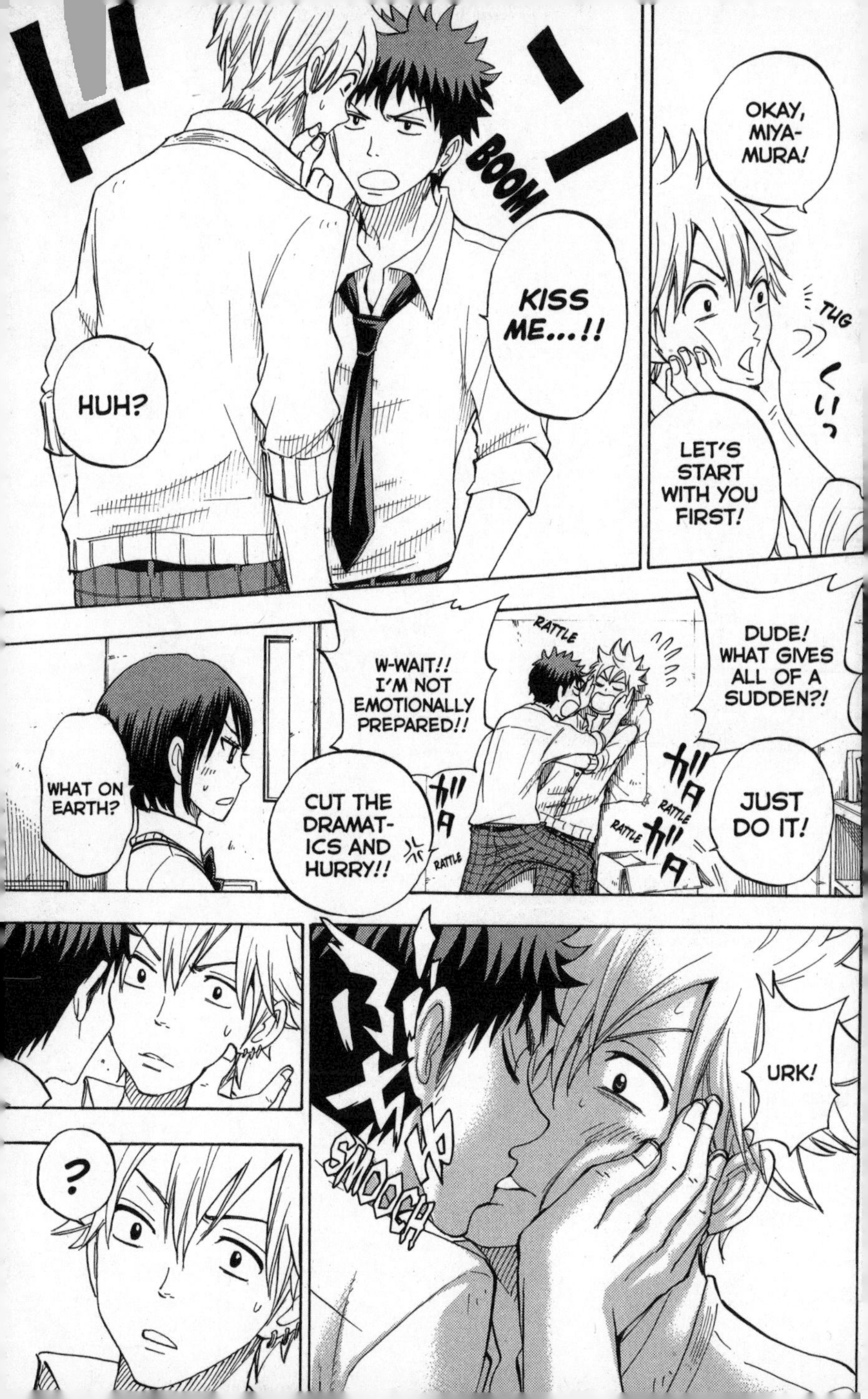
OKAY, MIYA-MURA!
TUG
LET'S START WITH YOU FIRST!
BOOM
KISS ME...!!
HUH?
DUDE! WHAT GIVES ALL OF A SUDDEN?!
RATTLE
W-WAIT!! I'M NOT EMOTIONALLY PREPARED!!
JUST DO IT!
RATTLE
RATTLE
CUT THE DRAMAT-ICS AND HURRY!!
RATTLE
WHAT ON EARTH?
URK!
SMOOCH
?

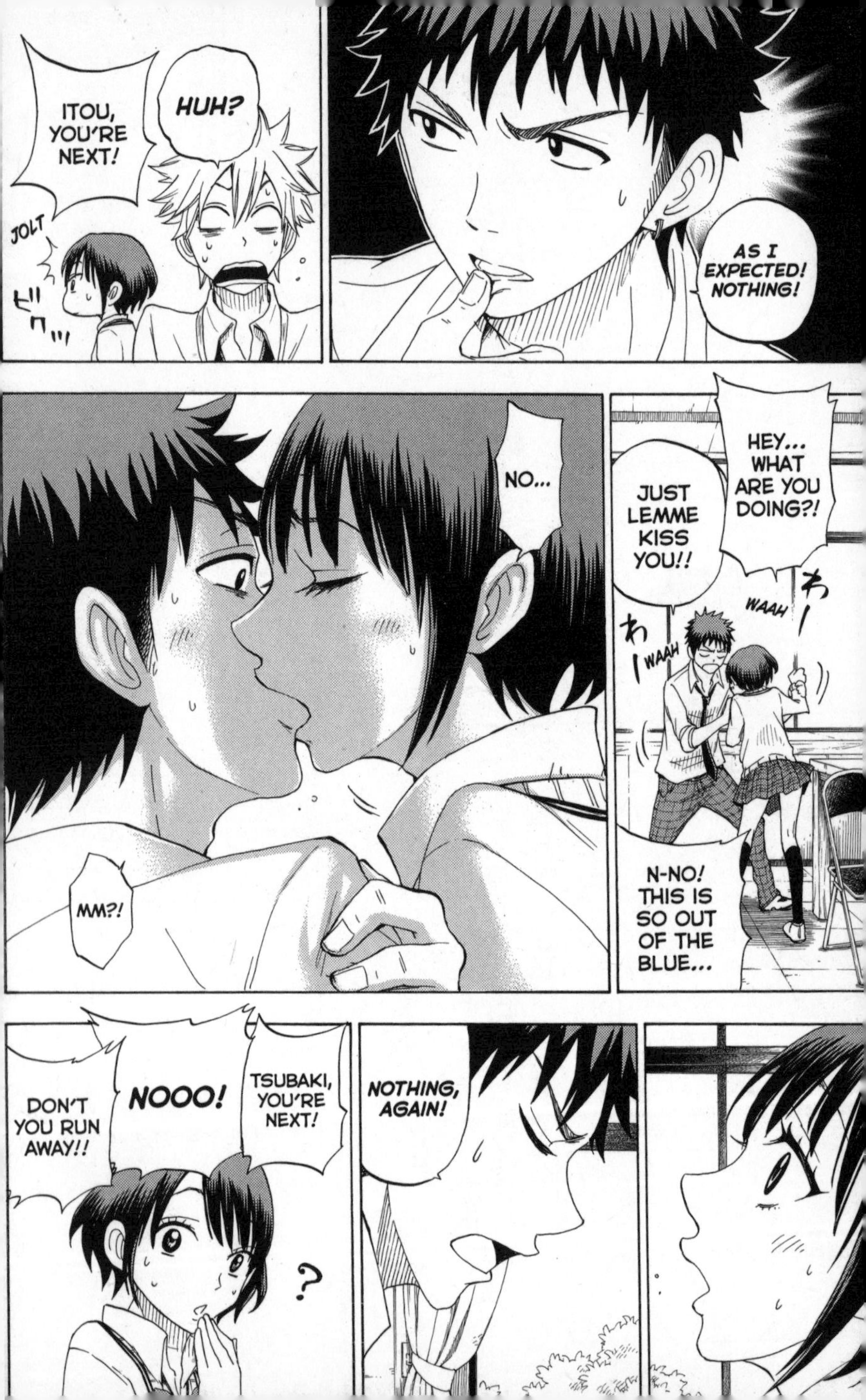

AS I EXPECTED! NOTHING!
ITOU, YOU'RE NEXT!
HUH?
JOLT
ビクッ
HEY... WHAT ARE YOU DOING?!
JUST LEMME KISS YOU!!
わー
WAAH
わー
WAAH
N-NO! THIS IS SO OUT OF THE BLUE...
NO...
MM?!
NOTHING, AGAIN!
TSUBAKI, YOU'RE NEXT!
NOOO!
DON'T YOU RUN AWAY!!
?

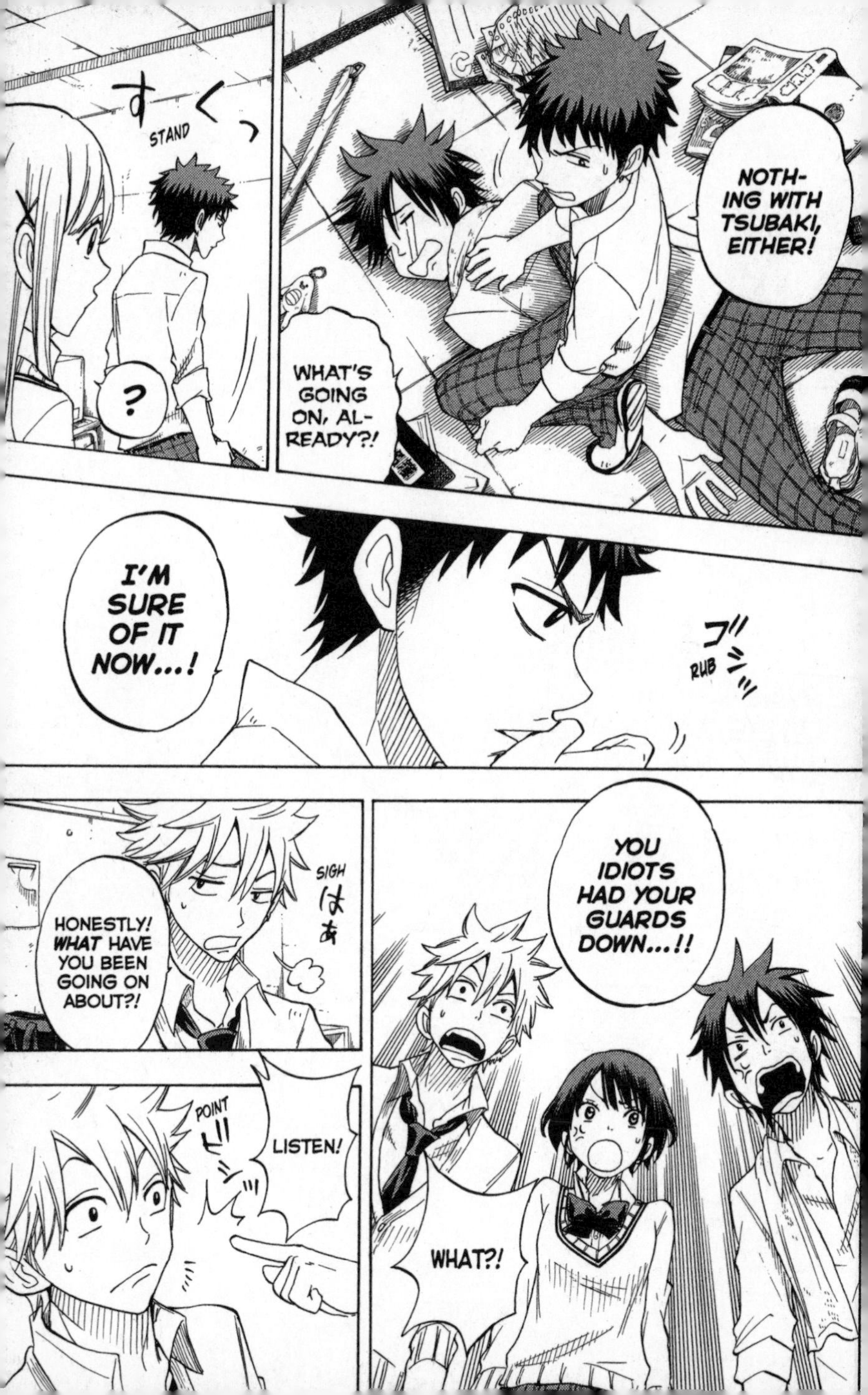
NOTHING WITH TSUBAKI, EITHER!
WHAT'S GOING ON, ALREADY?!
すくっ
STAND
?
RUB
I'M SURE OF IT NOW...!
YOU IDIOTS HAD YOUR GUARDS DOWN...!!
WHAT?!
SIGH
はあ
HONESTLY! *WHAT* HAVE YOU BEEN GOING ON ABOUT?!
LISTEN!
POINT

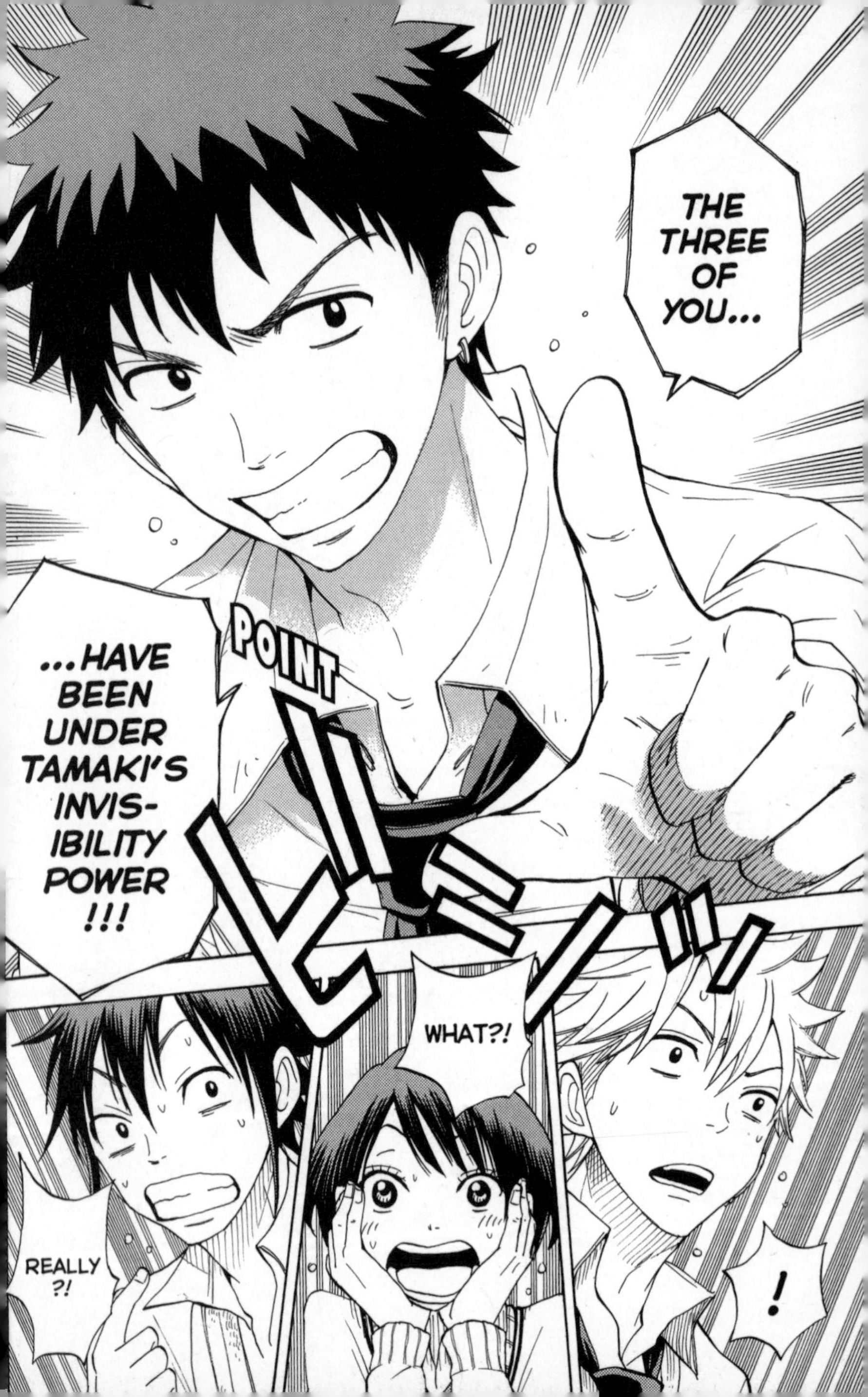
THE THREE OF YOU...
...HAVE BEEN UNDER TAMAKI'S INVISIBILITY POWER!!!
POINT
!
WHAT?!
REALLY?!

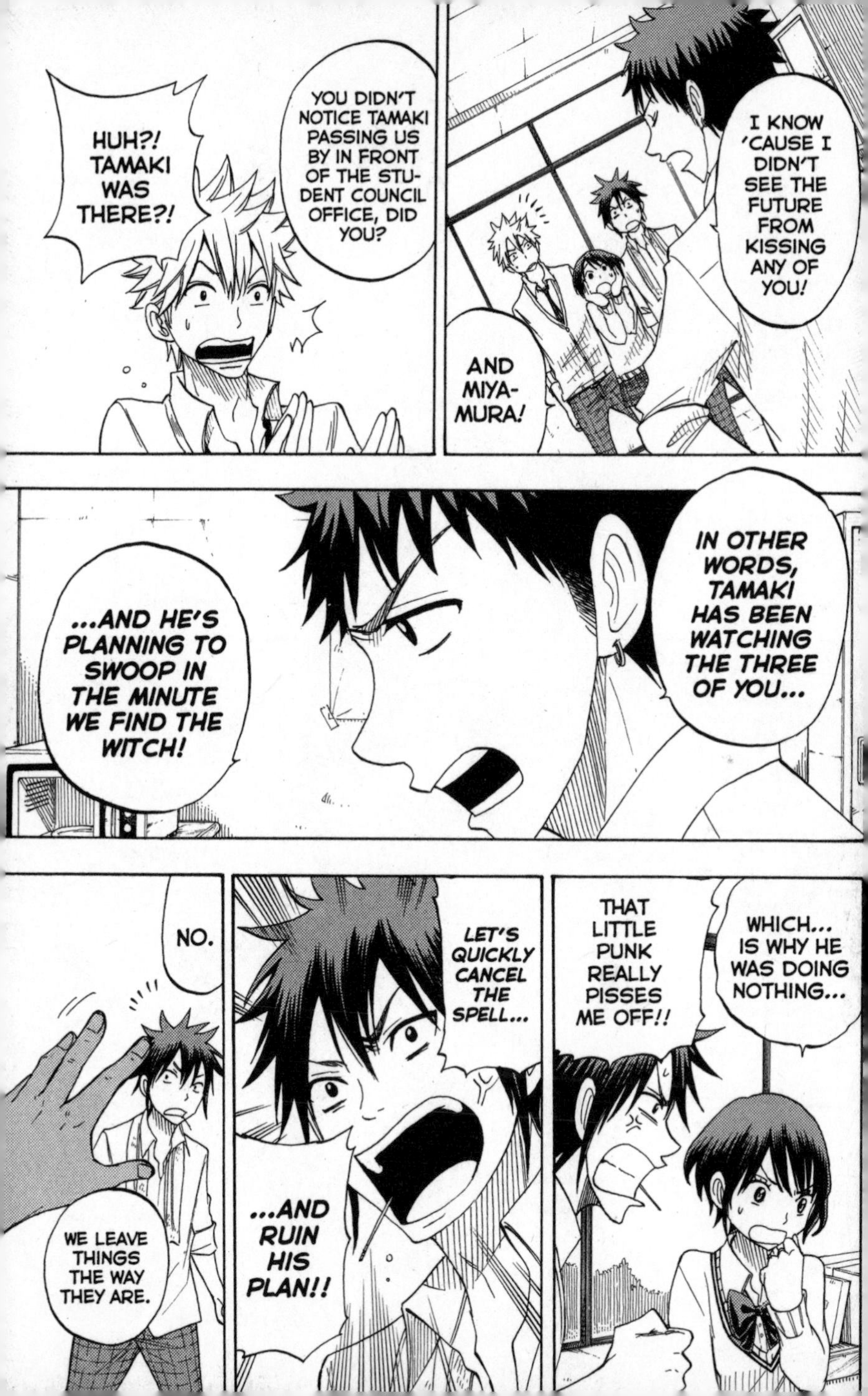
I KNOW 'CAUSE I DIDN'T SEE THE FUTURE FROM KISSING ANY OF YOU!
AND MIYAMURA!
YOU DIDN'T NOTICE TAMAKI PASSING US BY IN FRONT OF THE STUDENT COUNCIL OFFICE, DID YOU?
HUH?! TAMAKI WAS THERE?!
IN OTHER WORDS, TAMAKI HAS BEEN WATCHING THE THREE OF YOU...
...AND HE'S PLANNING TO SWOOP IN THE MINUTE WE FIND THE WITCH!
WHICH... IS WHY HE WAS DOING NOTHING...
THAT LITTLE PUNK REALLY PISSES ME OFF!!
LET'S QUICKLY CANCEL THE SPELL...
...AND RUIN HIS PLAN!!
NO.
WE LEAVE THINGS THE WAY THEY ARE.

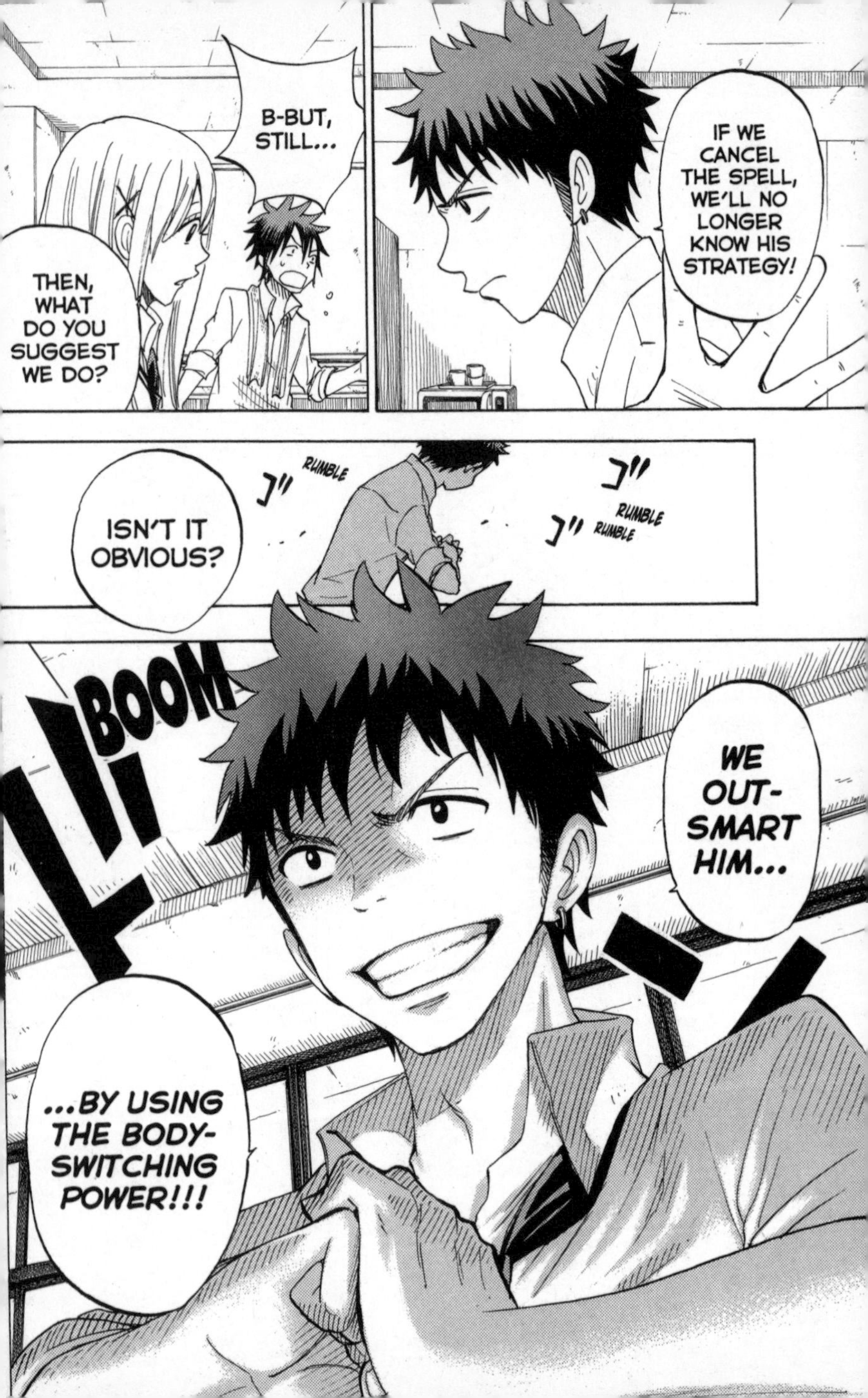
IF WE CANCEL THE SPELL, WE'LL NO LONGER KNOW HIS STRATEGY!
B-BUT, STILL...
THEN, WHAT DO YOU SUGGEST WE DO?
RUMBLE
RUMBLE
RUMBLE
ISN'T IT OBVIOUS?
WE OUT-SMART HIM...
BOOM
...BY USING THE BODY-SWITCHING POWER!!!

CHAPTER 62: I don't ever want to see you look that way again!

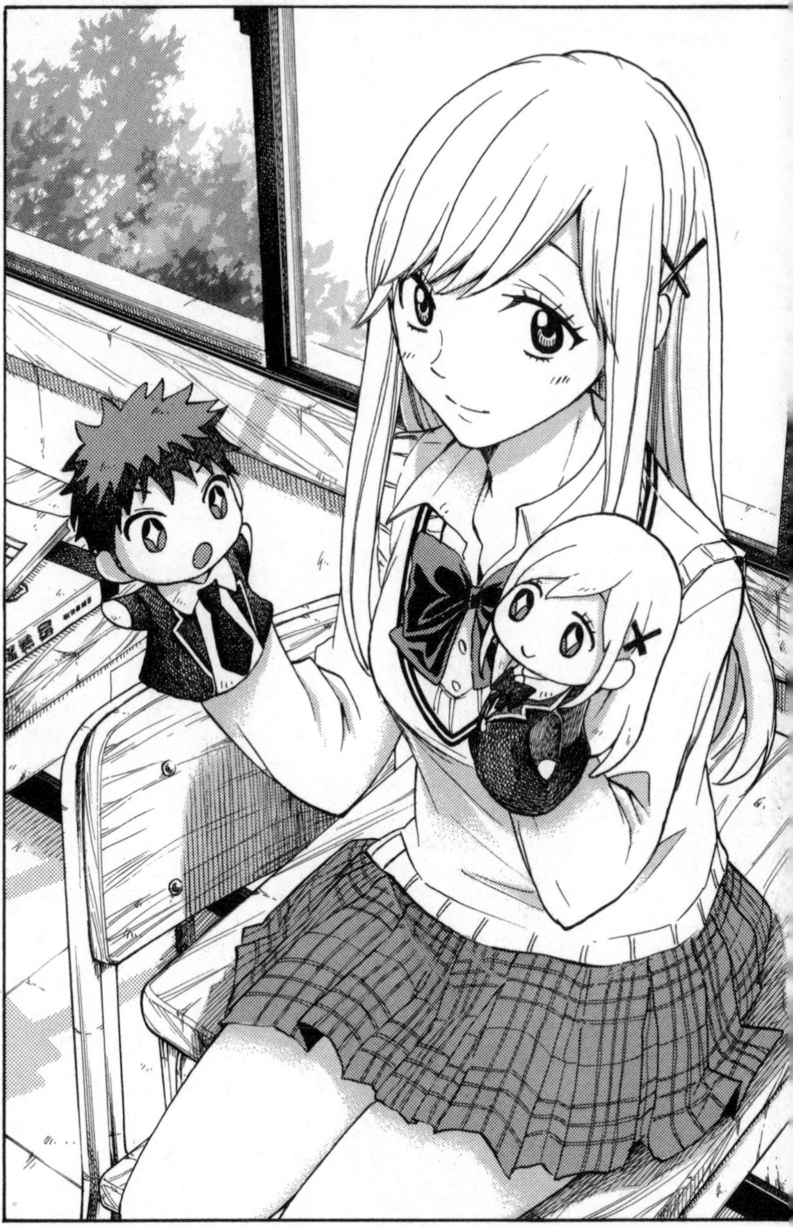

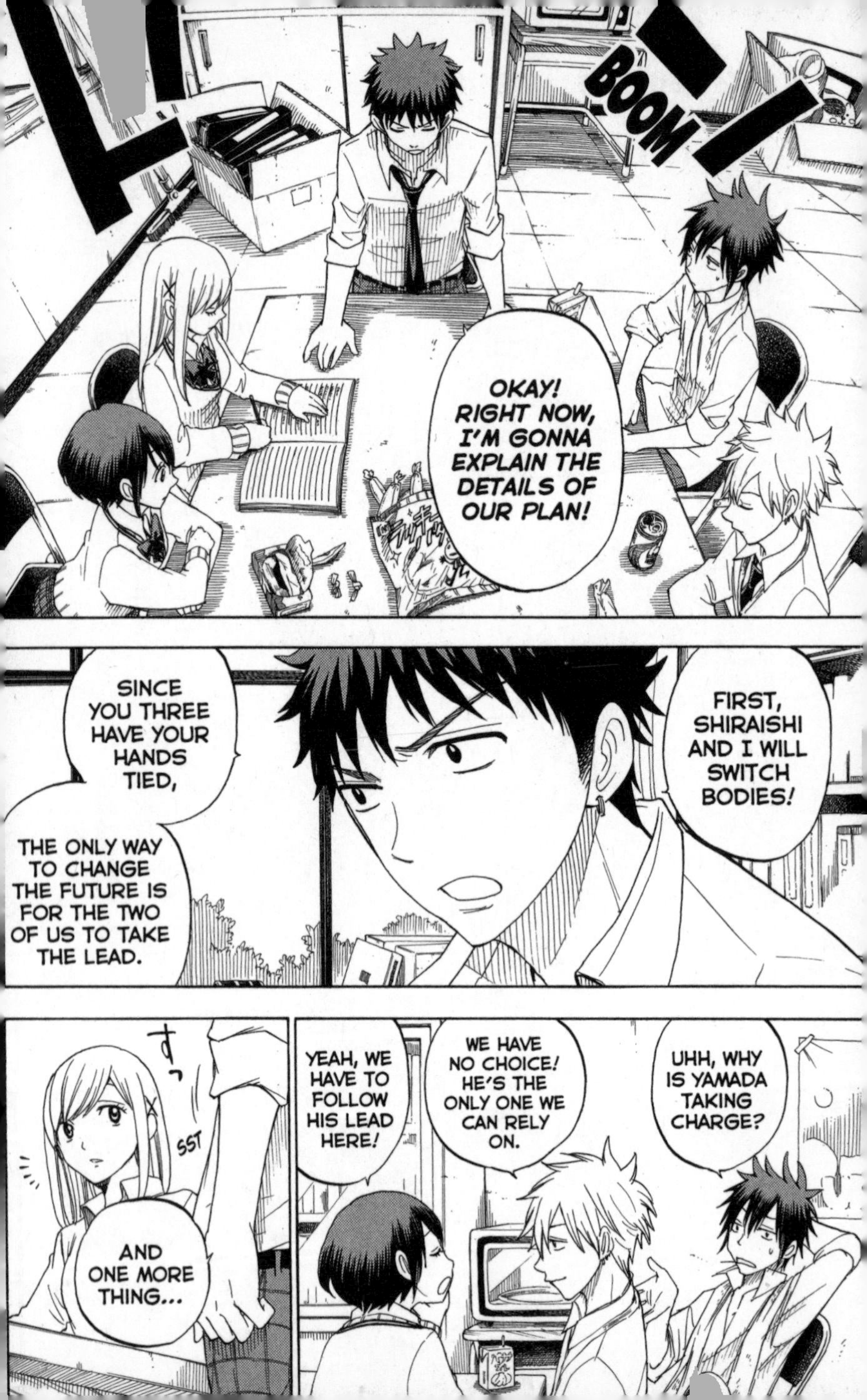
BOOM
OKAY! RIGHT NOW, I'M GONNA EXPLAIN THE DETAILS OF OUR PLAN!
FIRST, SHIRAISHI AND I WILL SWITCH BODIES!
SINCE YOU THREE HAVE YOUR HANDS TIED,
THE ONLY WAY TO CHANGE THE FUTURE IS FOR THE TWO OF US TO TAKE THE LEAD.
UHH, WHY IS YAMADA TAKING CHARGE?
WE HAVE NO CHOICE! HE'S THE ONLY ONE WE CAN RELY ON.
YEAH, WE HAVE TO FOLLOW HIS LEAD HERE!
すっ
SST
AND ONE MORE THING...

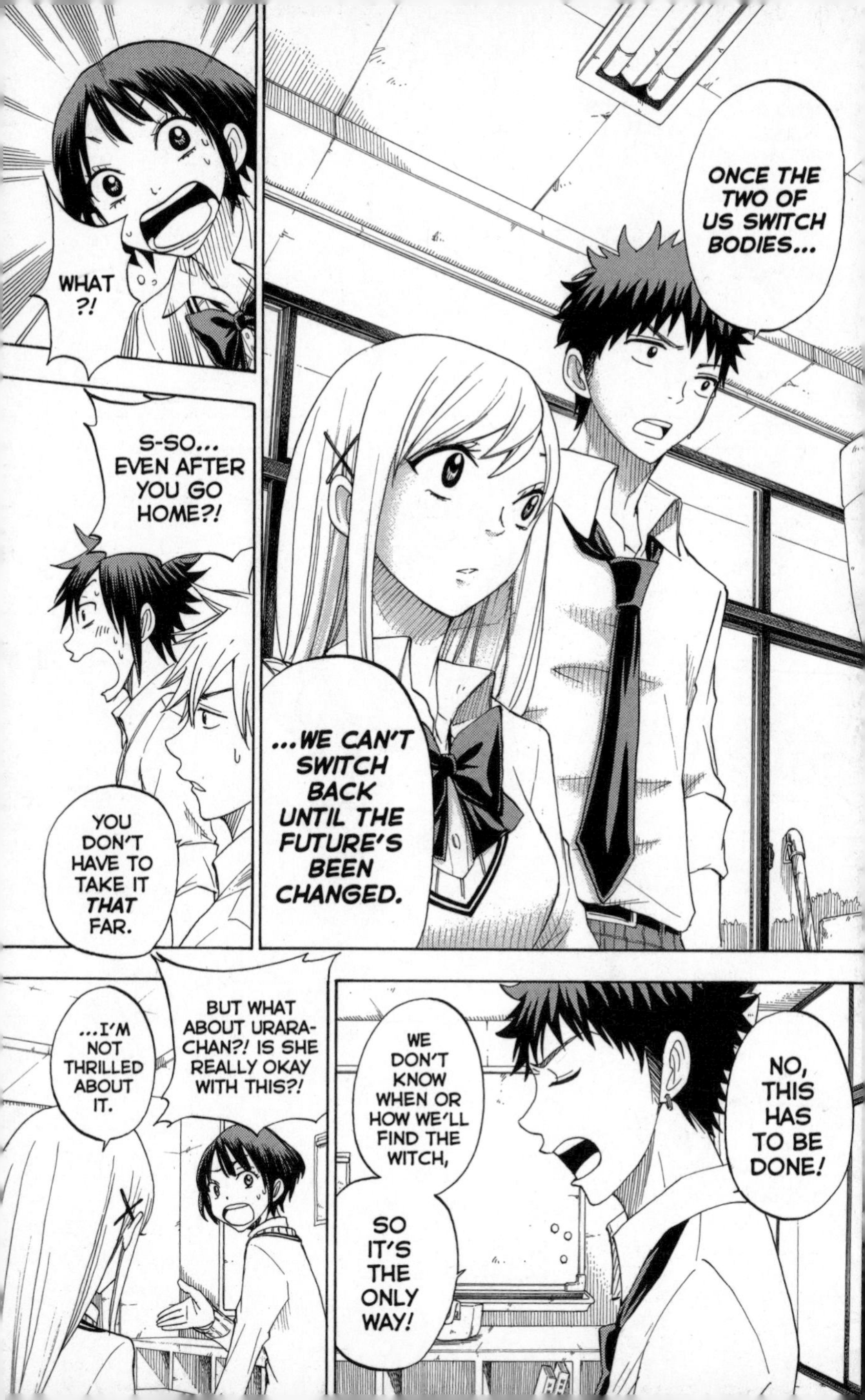
ONCE THE TWO OF US SWITCH BODIES...
...WE CAN'T SWITCH BACK UNTIL THE FUTURE'S BEEN CHANGED.
WHAT?!
S-SO... EVEN AFTER YOU GO HOME?!
YOU DON'T HAVE TO TAKE IT *THAT* FAR.
NO, THIS HAS TO BE DONE!
WE DON'T KNOW WHEN OR HOW WE'LL FIND THE WITCH,
SO IT'S THE ONLY WAY!
BUT WHAT ABOUT URARA-CHAN?! IS SHE REALLY OKAY WITH THIS?!
...I'M NOT THRILLED ABOUT IT.

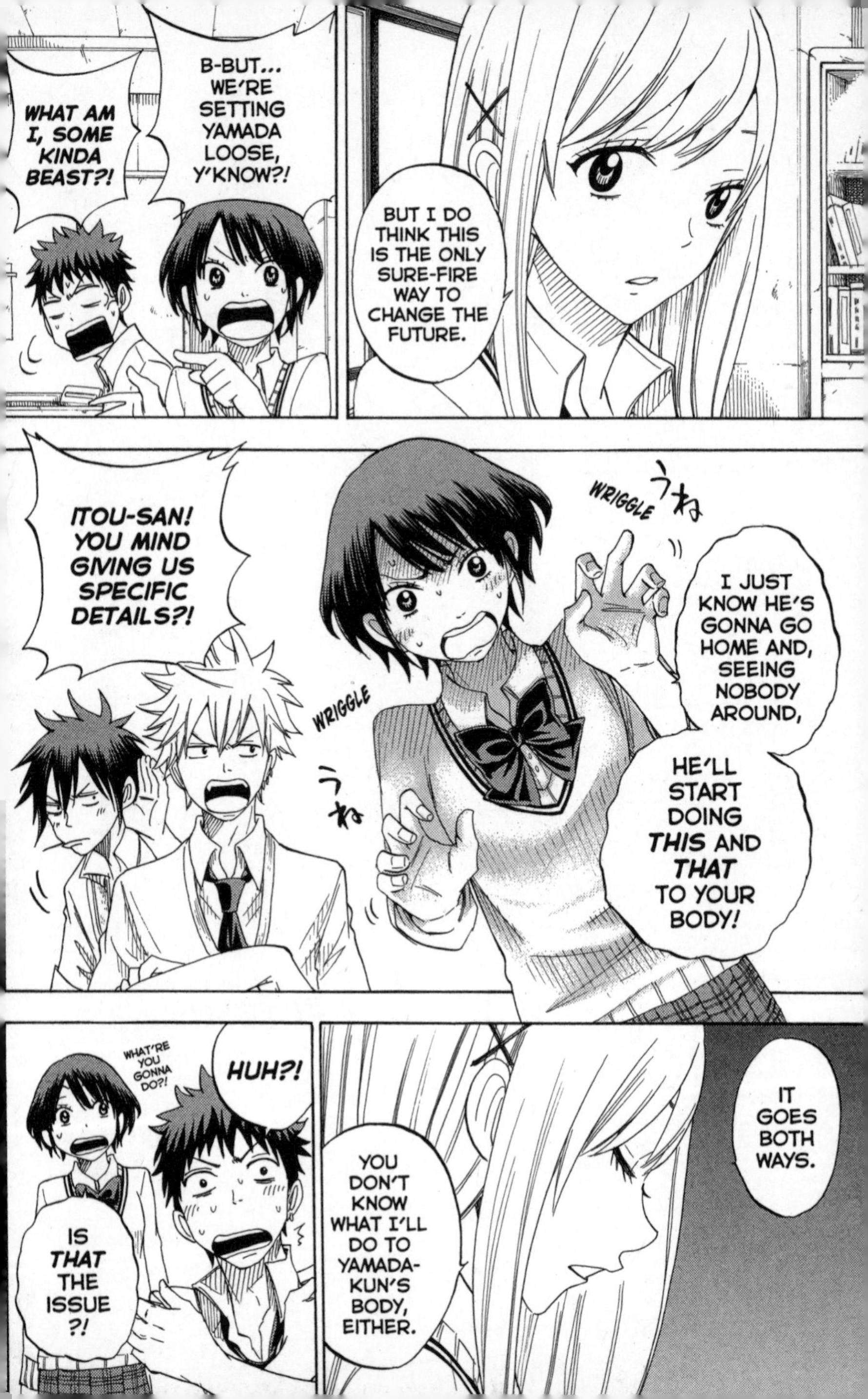
BUT I DO THINK THIS IS THE ONLY SURE-FIRE WAY TO CHANGE THE FUTURE.
B-BUT... WE'RE SETTING YAMADA LOOSE, Y'KNOW?!
WHAT AM I, SOME KINDA BEAST?!
WRIGGLE
うね
I JUST KNOW HE'S GONNA GO HOME AND, SEEING NOBODY AROUND,
HE'LL START DOING THIS AND THAT TO YOUR BODY!
ITOU-SAN! YOU MIND GIVING US SPECIFIC DETAILS?!
WRIGGLE
うね
IT GOES BOTH WAYS.
YOU DON'T KNOW WHAT I'LL DO TO YAMADA-KUN'S BODY, EITHER.
HUH?!
WHAT'RE YOU GONNA DO?!
IS THAT THE ISSUE ?!

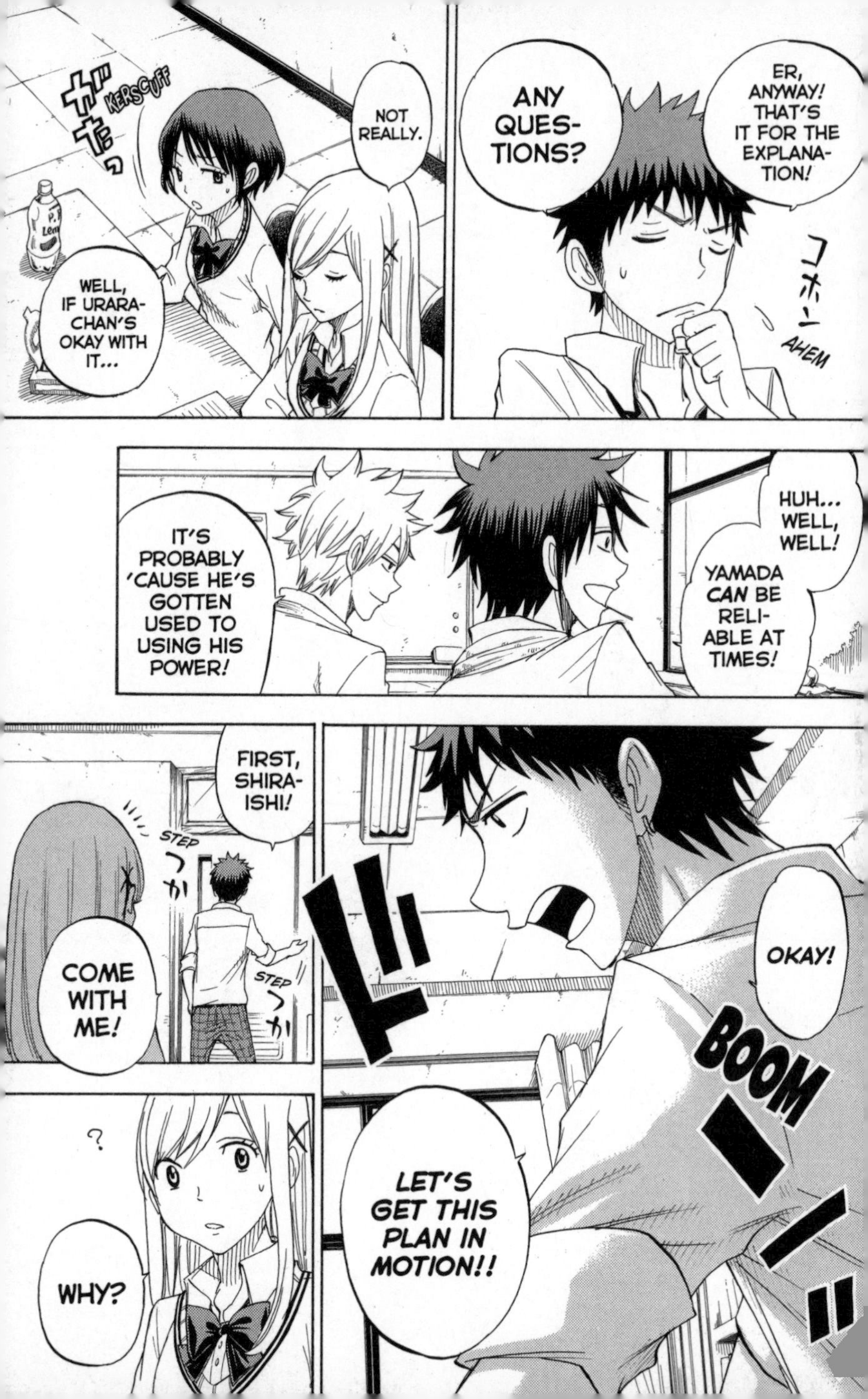
ER, ANYWAY! THAT'S IT FOR THE EXPLANATION!
AHEM
ANY QUESTIONS?
NOT REALLY.
KERSCUFF
WELL, IF URARA-CHAN'S OKAY WITH IT...
HUH... WELL, WELL! YAMADA CAN BE RELIABLE AT TIMES!
IT'S PROBABLY 'CAUSE HE'S GOTTEN USED TO USING HIS POWER!
OKAY!
BOOM
LET'S GET THIS PLAN IN MOTION!!
FIRST, SHIRAISHI!
STEP
STEP
COME WITH ME!
?
WHY?

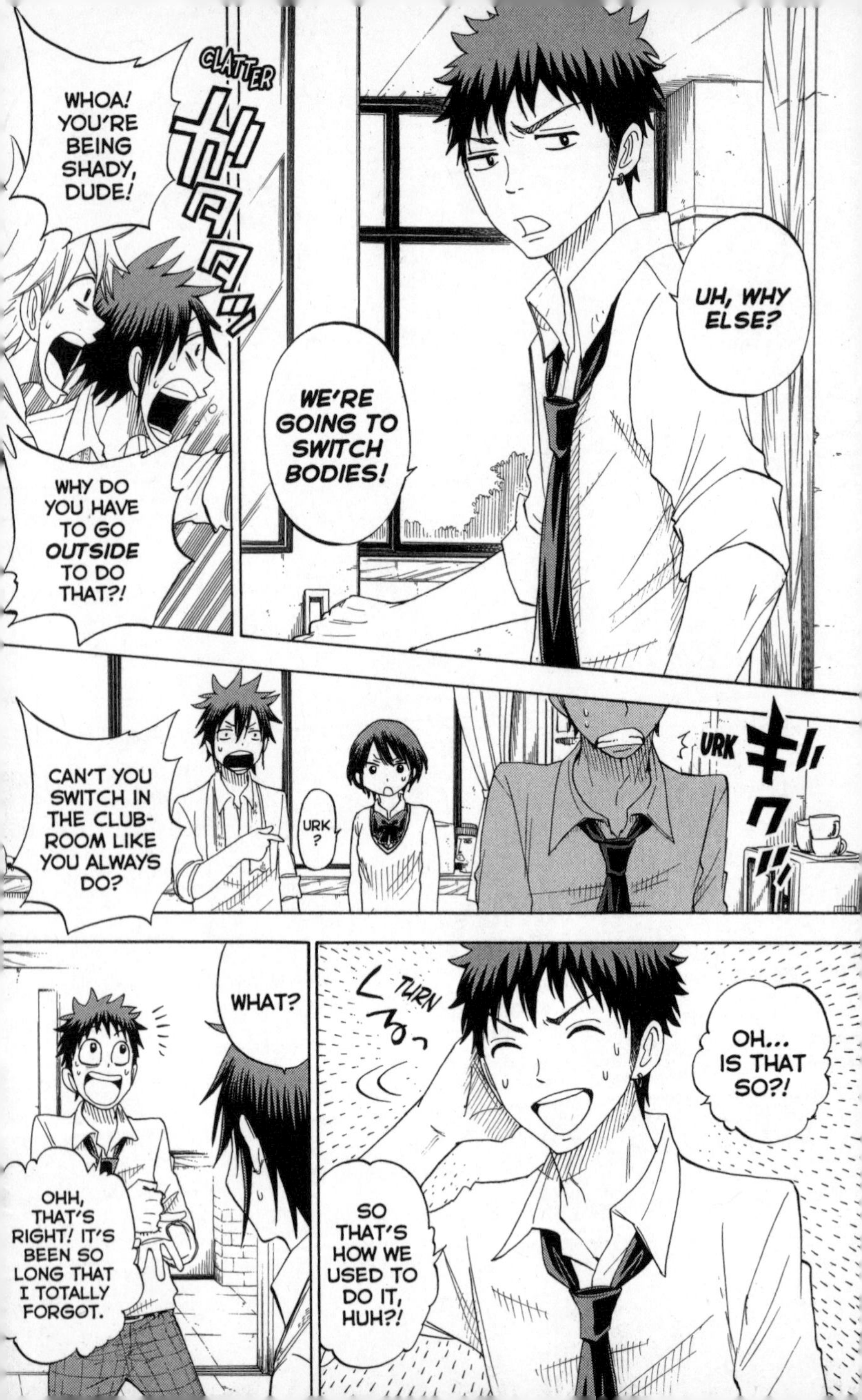
UH, WHY ELSE?
WE'RE GOING TO SWITCH BODIES!
CLATTER
WHOA! YOU'RE BEING SHADY, DUDE!
WHY DO YOU HAVE TO GO *OUTSIDE* TO DO THAT?!
URK
URK?
CAN'T YOU SWITCH IN THE CLUB-ROOM LIKE YOU ALWAYS DO?
TURN
OH... IS THAT SO?!
SO THAT'S HOW WE USED TO DO IT, HUH?!
WHAT?
OHH, THAT'S RIGHT! IT'S BEEN SO LONG THAT I TOTALLY FORGOT.

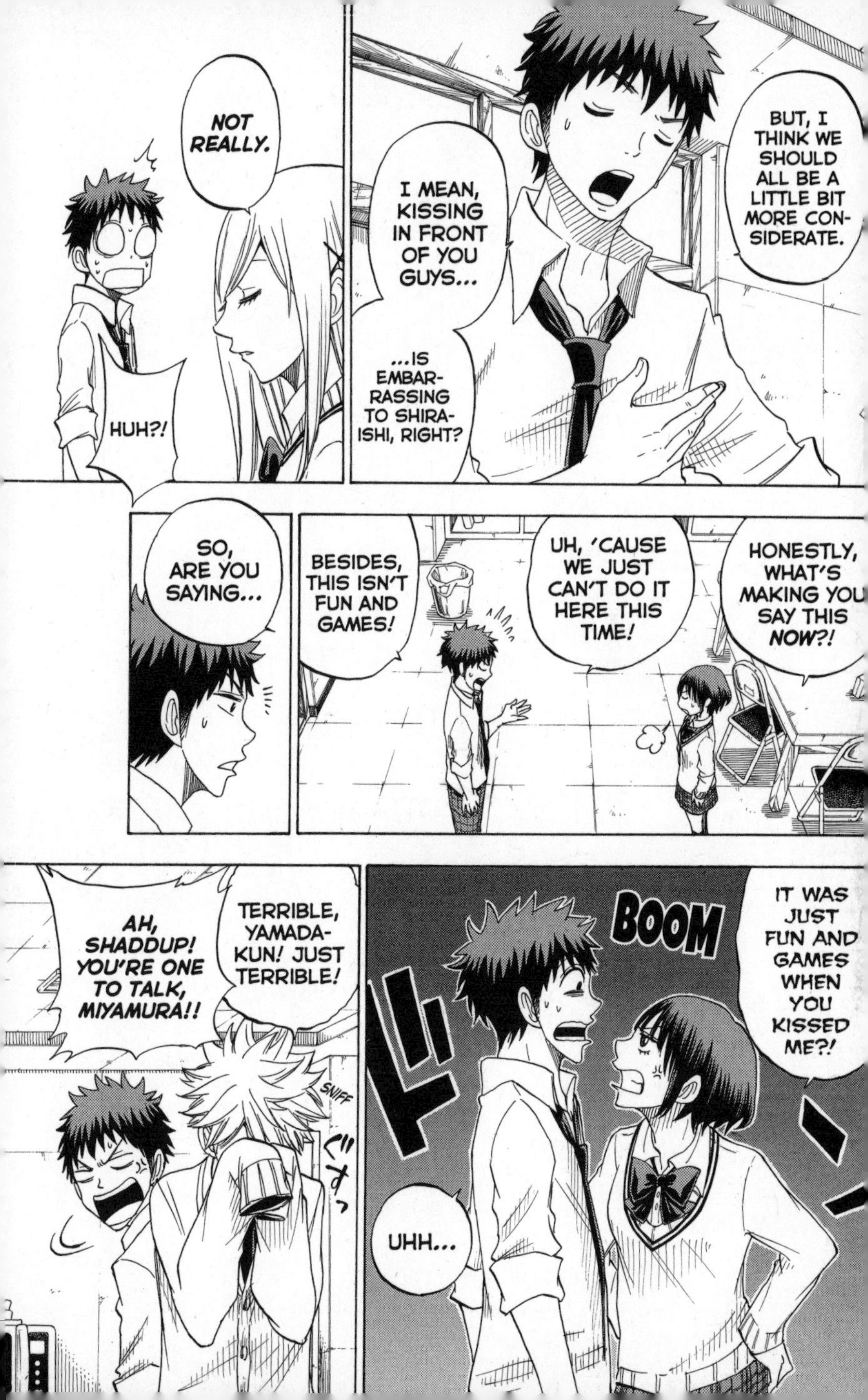
BUT, I THINK WE SHOULD ALL BE A LITTLE BIT MORE CONSIDERATE.
I MEAN, KISSING IN FRONT OF YOU GUYS...
...IS EMBARRASSING TO SHIRAISHI, RIGHT?
NOT REALLY.
HUH?!
HONESTLY, WHAT'S MAKING YOU SAY THIS NOW?!
UH, 'CAUSE WE JUST CAN'T DO IT HERE THIS TIME!
BESIDES, THIS ISN'T FUN AND GAMES!
SO, ARE YOU SAYING...
IT WAS JUST FUN AND GAMES WHEN YOU KISSED ME?!
BOOM
UHH...
TERRIBLE, YAMADA-KUN! JUST TERRIBLE!
AH, SHADDUP! YOU'RE ONE TO TALK, MIYAMURA!!
SNIFF
ぐすっ

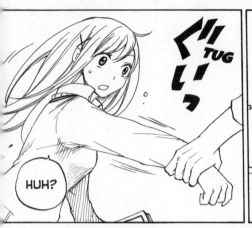

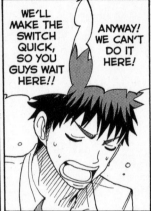

ANYWAY! WE CAN'T DO IT HERE!
WE'LL MAKE THE SWITCH QUICK, SO YOU GUYS WAIT HERE!!
ぐいっ
TUG
HUH?
SLAM
HEY...
...
SOME-THING'S UP, ALL RIGHT!
WHAT'S GOTTEN INTO HIM?!
GRIN GRIN
ニヤニヤ

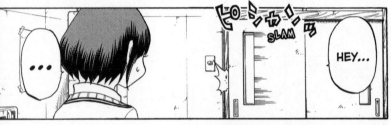

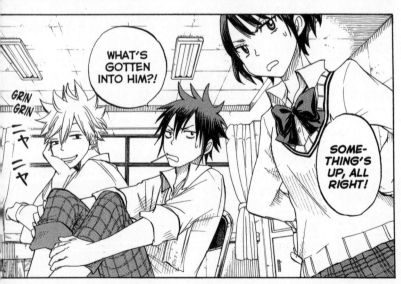

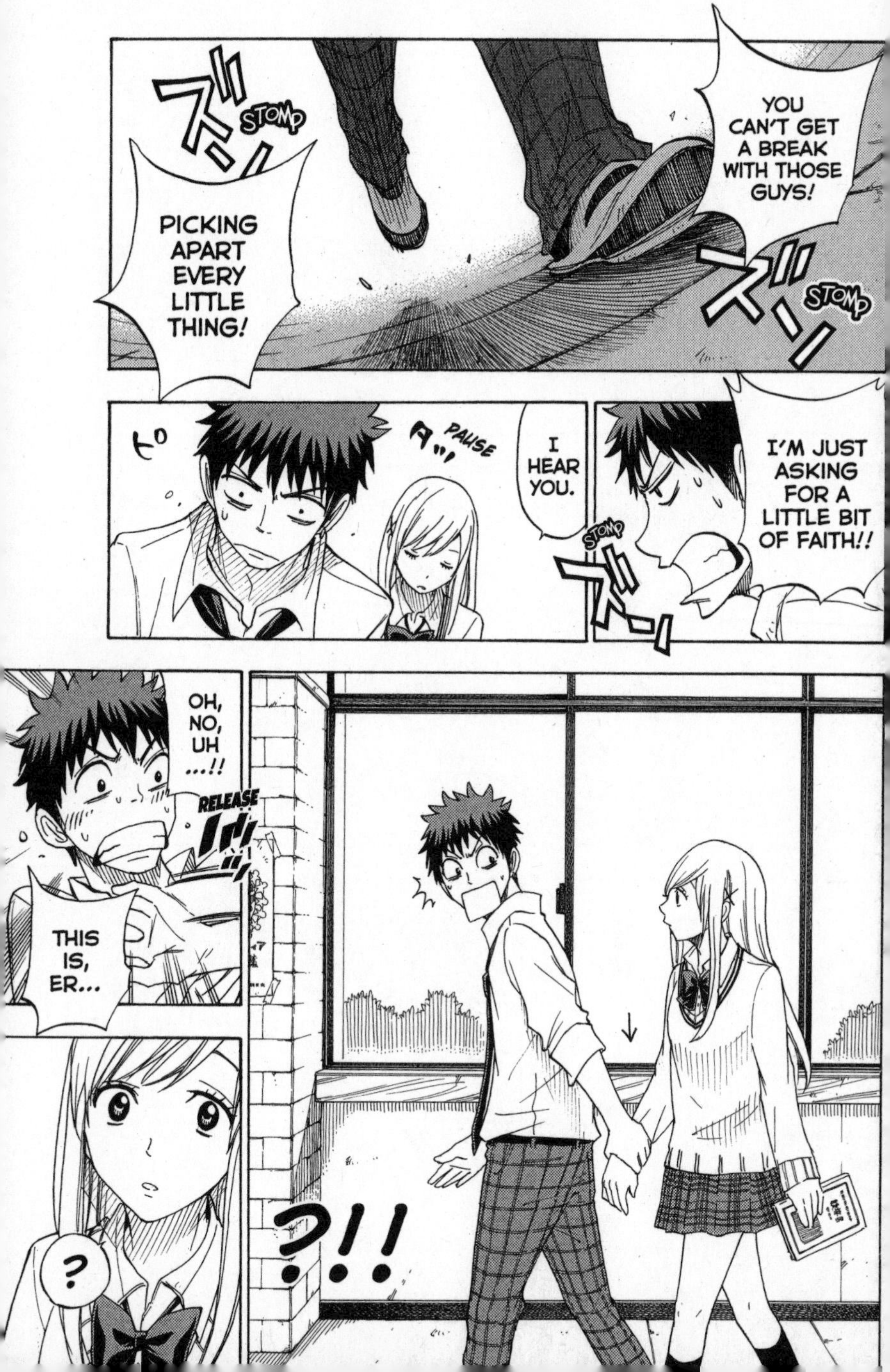
YOU CAN'T GET A BREAK WITH THOSE GUYS!
STOMP
STOMP
PICKING APART EVERY LITTLE THING!
I'M JUST ASKING FOR A LITTLE BIT OF FAITH!!
STOMP
I HEAR YOU.
PAUSE
?!!
OH, NO, UH ...!!
RELEASE
THIS IS, ER...
?

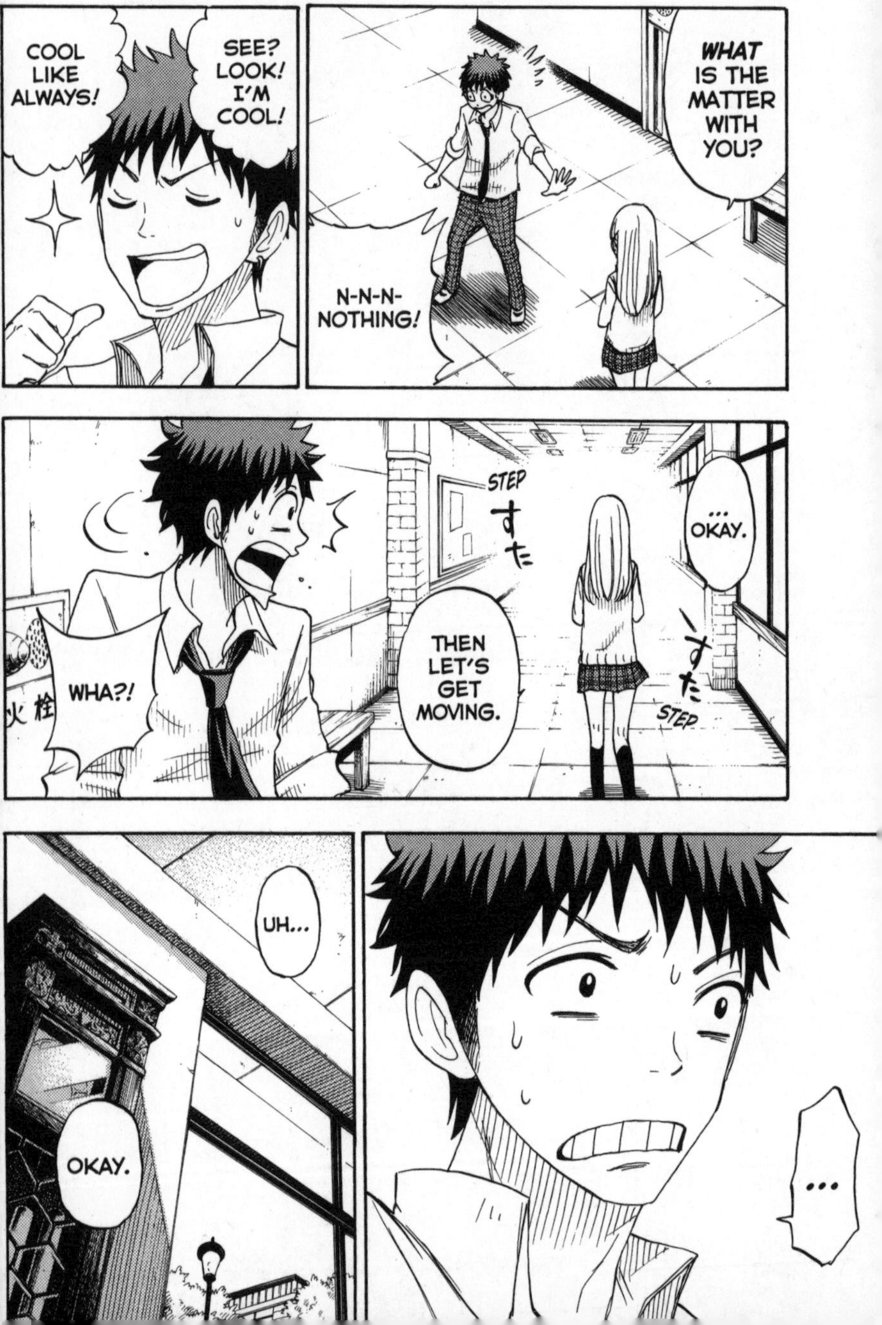
WHAT IS THE MATTER WITH YOU?
N-N-N-NOTHING!
SEE? LOOK! I'M COOL!
COOL LIKE ALWAYS!
... OKAY.
STEP すた
すた STEP
THEN LET'S GET MOVING.
WHA?!
火栓
...
UH...
OKAY.

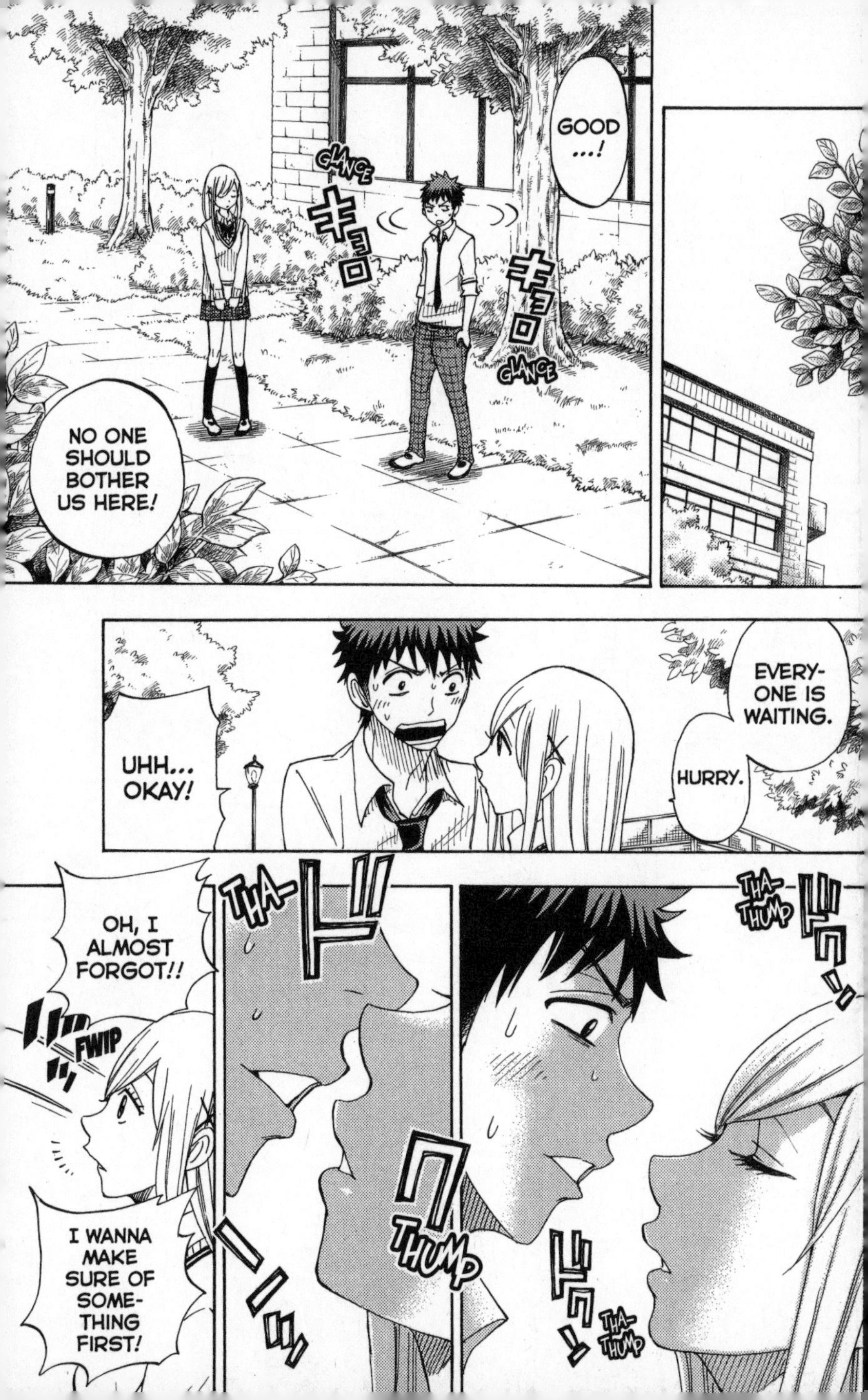

GOOD...!
GLANCE
GLANCE
NO ONE SHOULD BOTHER US HERE!
EVERY-ONE IS WAITING.
HURRY.
UHH... OKAY!
THA-THUMP
THA-THUMP
THA-
THUMP
OH, I ALMOST FORGOT!!
FWIP
I WANNA MAKE SURE OF SOME-THING FIRST!

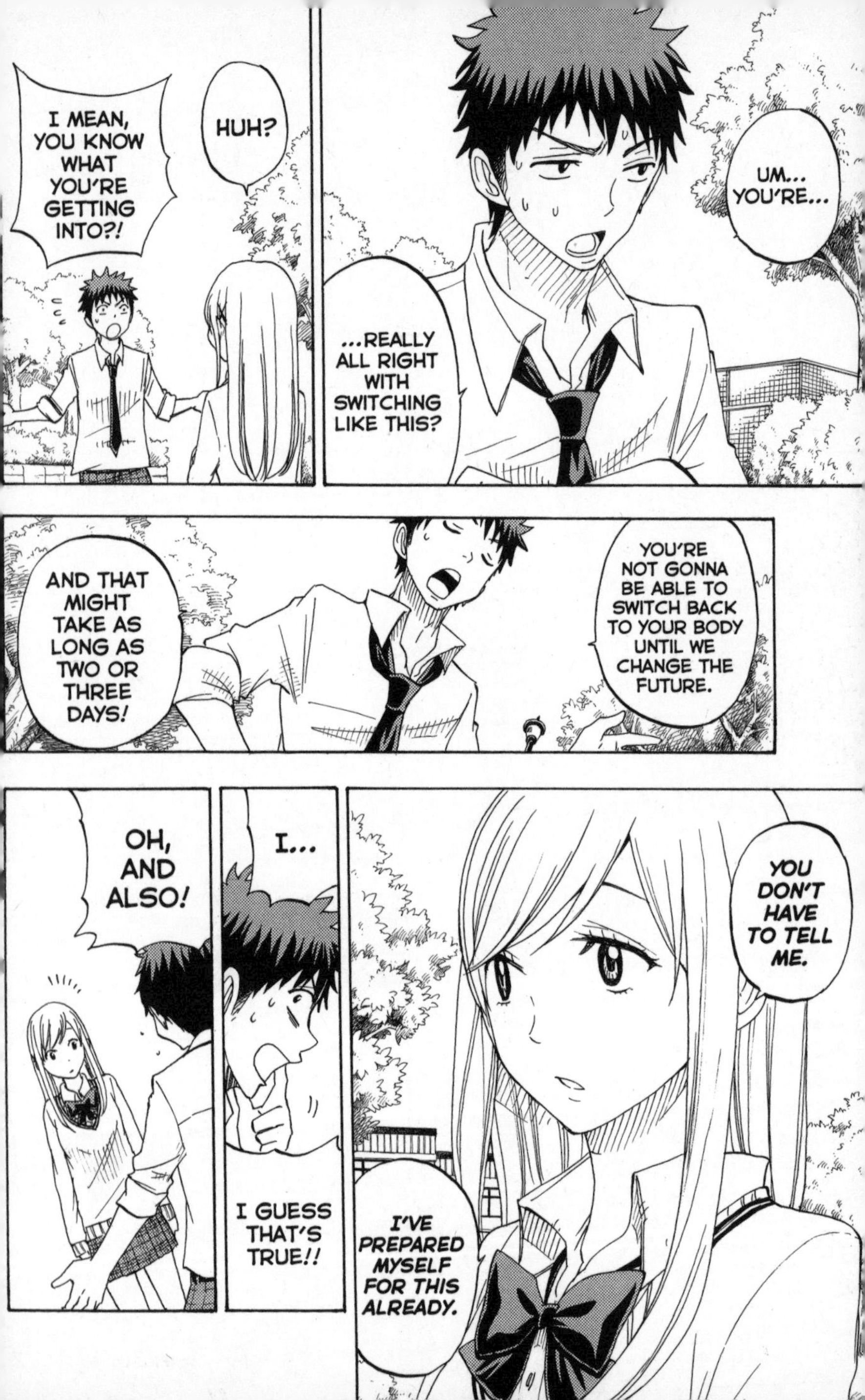
UM... YOU'RE...
...REALLY ALL RIGHT WITH SWITCHING LIKE THIS?
HUH?
I MEAN, YOU KNOW WHAT YOU'RE GETTING INTO?!
YOU'RE NOT GONNA BE ABLE TO SWITCH BACK TO YOUR BODY UNTIL WE CHANGE THE FUTURE.
AND THAT MIGHT TAKE AS LONG AS TWO OR THREE DAYS!
YOU DON'T HAVE TO TELL ME.
I'VE PREPARED MYSELF FOR THIS ALREADY.
I...
I GUESS THAT'S TRUE!!
OH, AND ALSO!

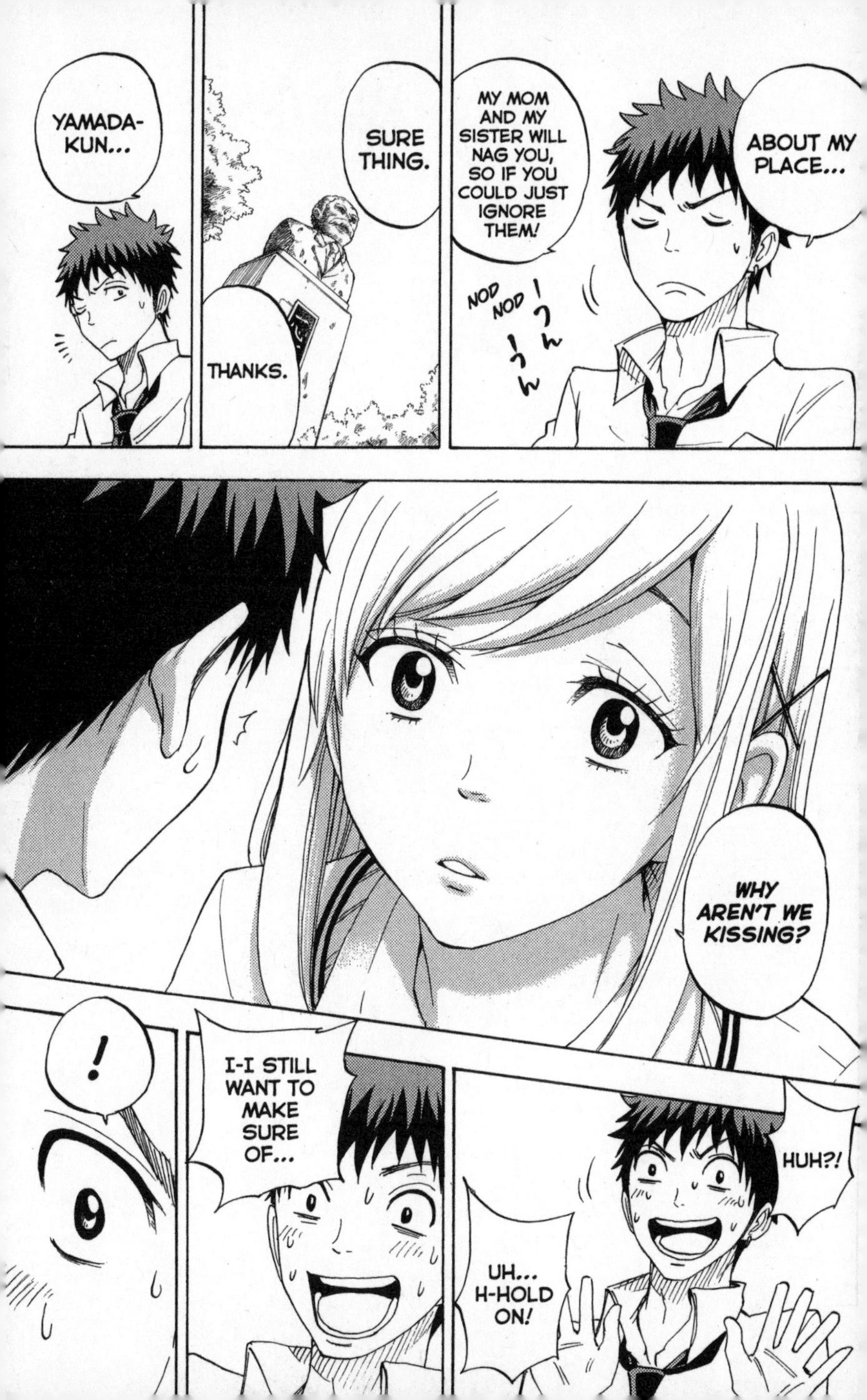
ABOUT MY PLACE...
MY MOM AND MY SISTER WILL NAG YOU, SO IF YOU COULD JUST IGNORE THEM!
NOD NOD
うん うん
SURE THING.
THANKS.
YAMADA-KUN...
WHY AREN'T WE KISSING?
HUH?!
UH... H-HOLD ON!
I-I STILL WANT TO MAKE SURE OF...
!

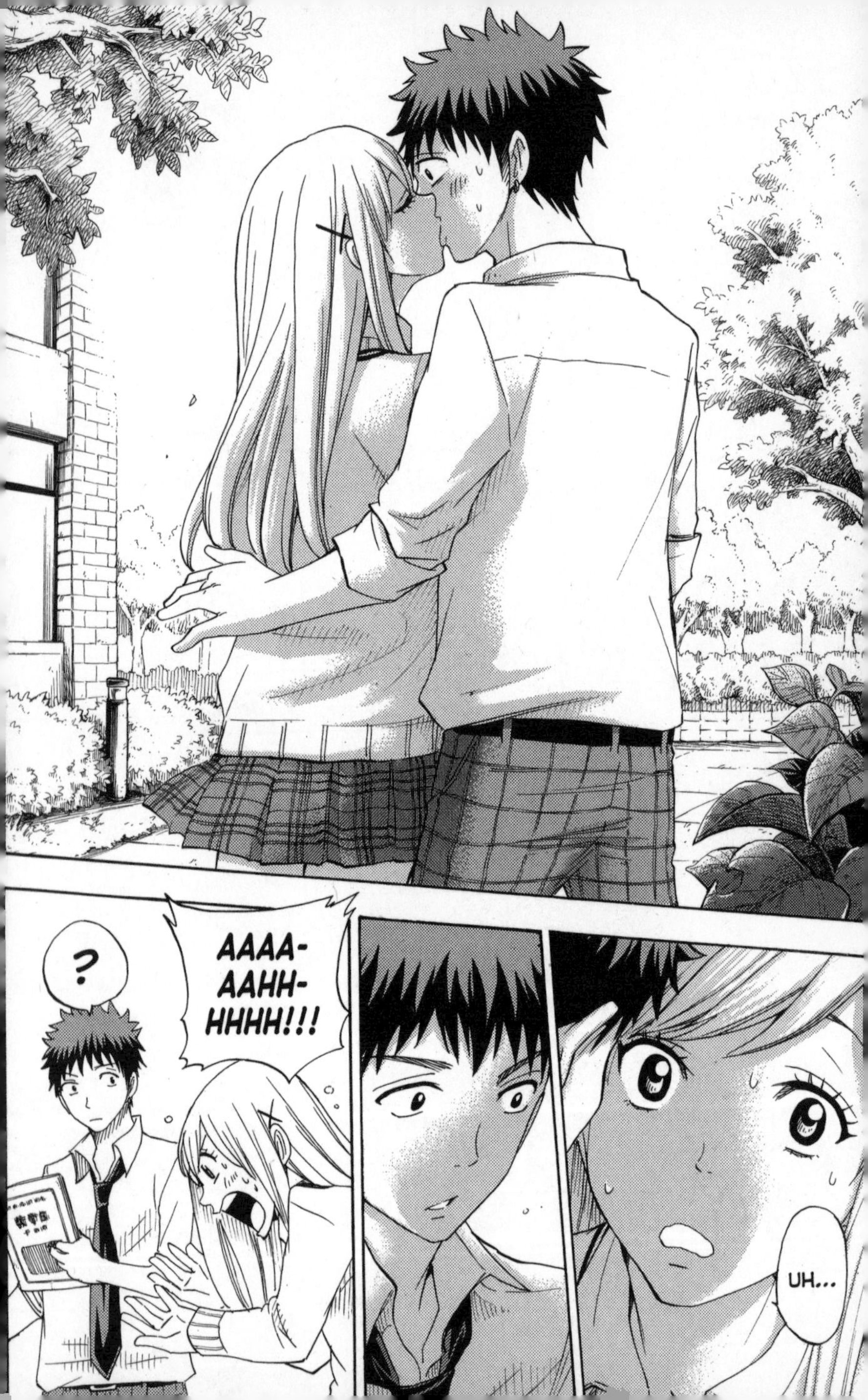
UH...
AAAA-AAHH-HHHH!!!
?

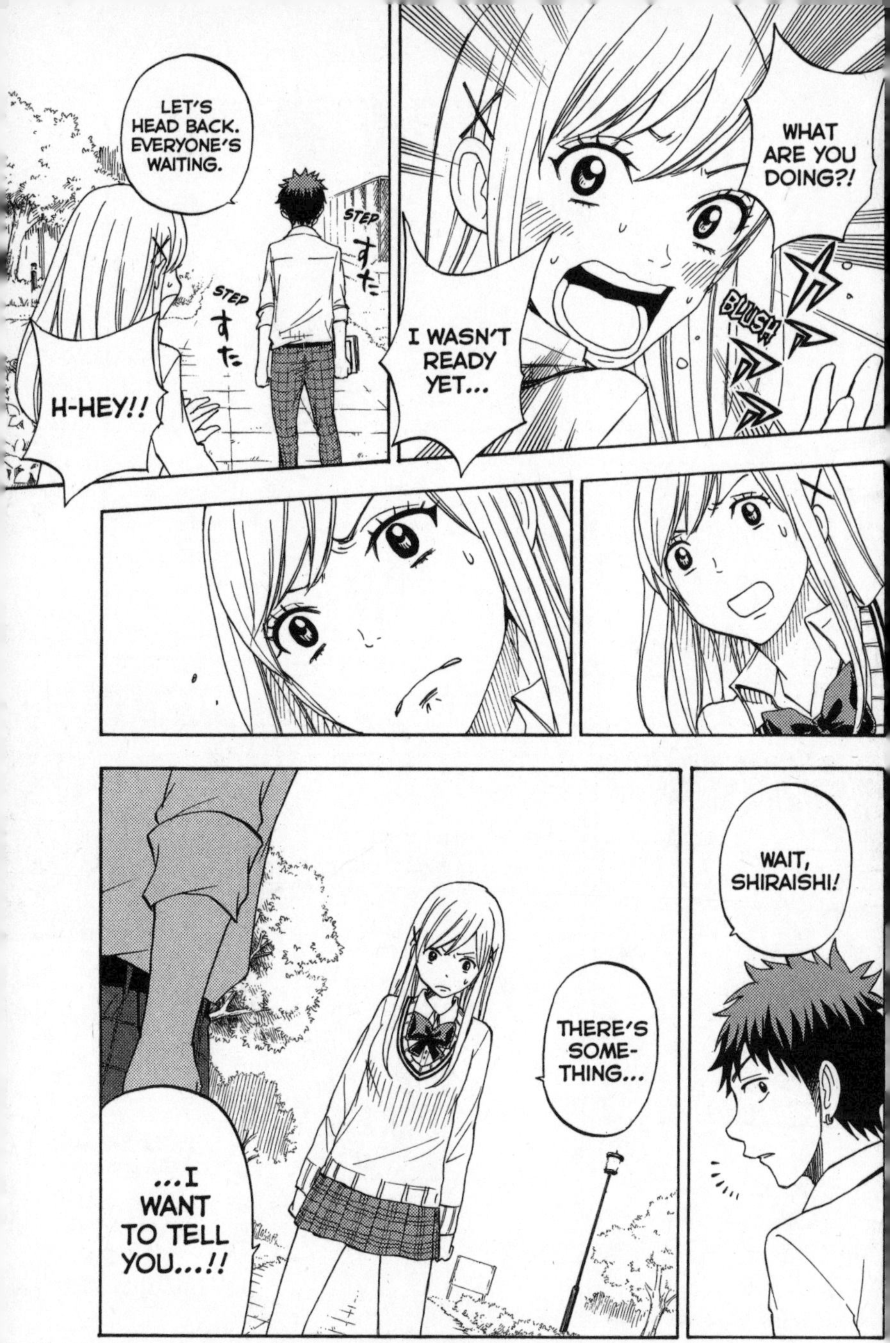
WHAT ARE YOU DOING?!
BLUSH
I WASN'T READY YET...
LET'S HEAD BACK. EVERYONE'S WAITING.
STEP すた
STEP すた
H-HEY!!
WAIT, SHIRAISHI!
THERE'S SOME-THING...
...I WANT TO TELL YOU...!!

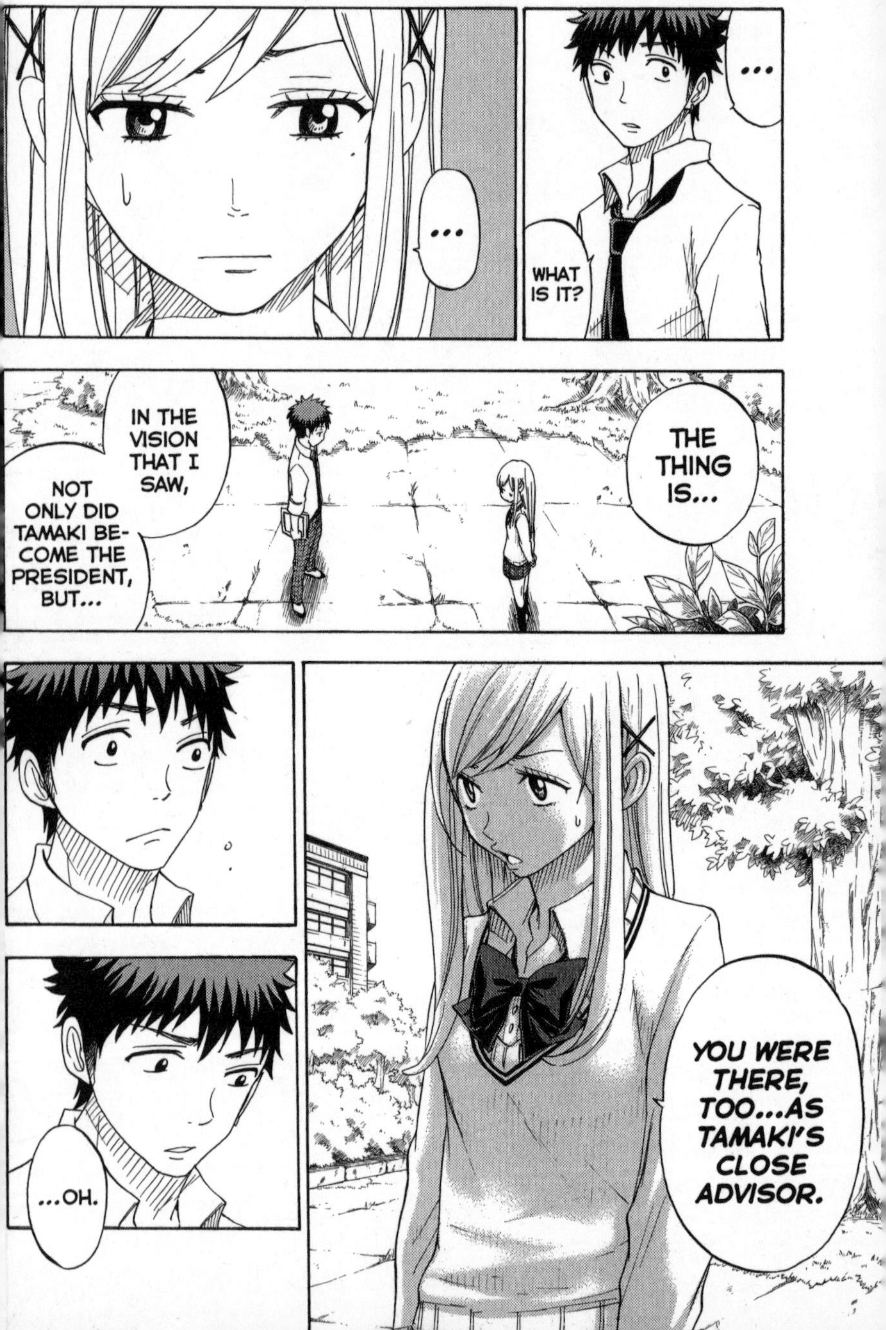
...
WHAT IS IT?
...
THE THING IS...
IN THE VISION THAT I SAW,
NOT ONLY DID TAMAKI BE-COME THE PRESIDENT, BUT...
YOU WERE THERE, TOO...AS TAMAKI'S CLOSE ADVISOR.
...OH.

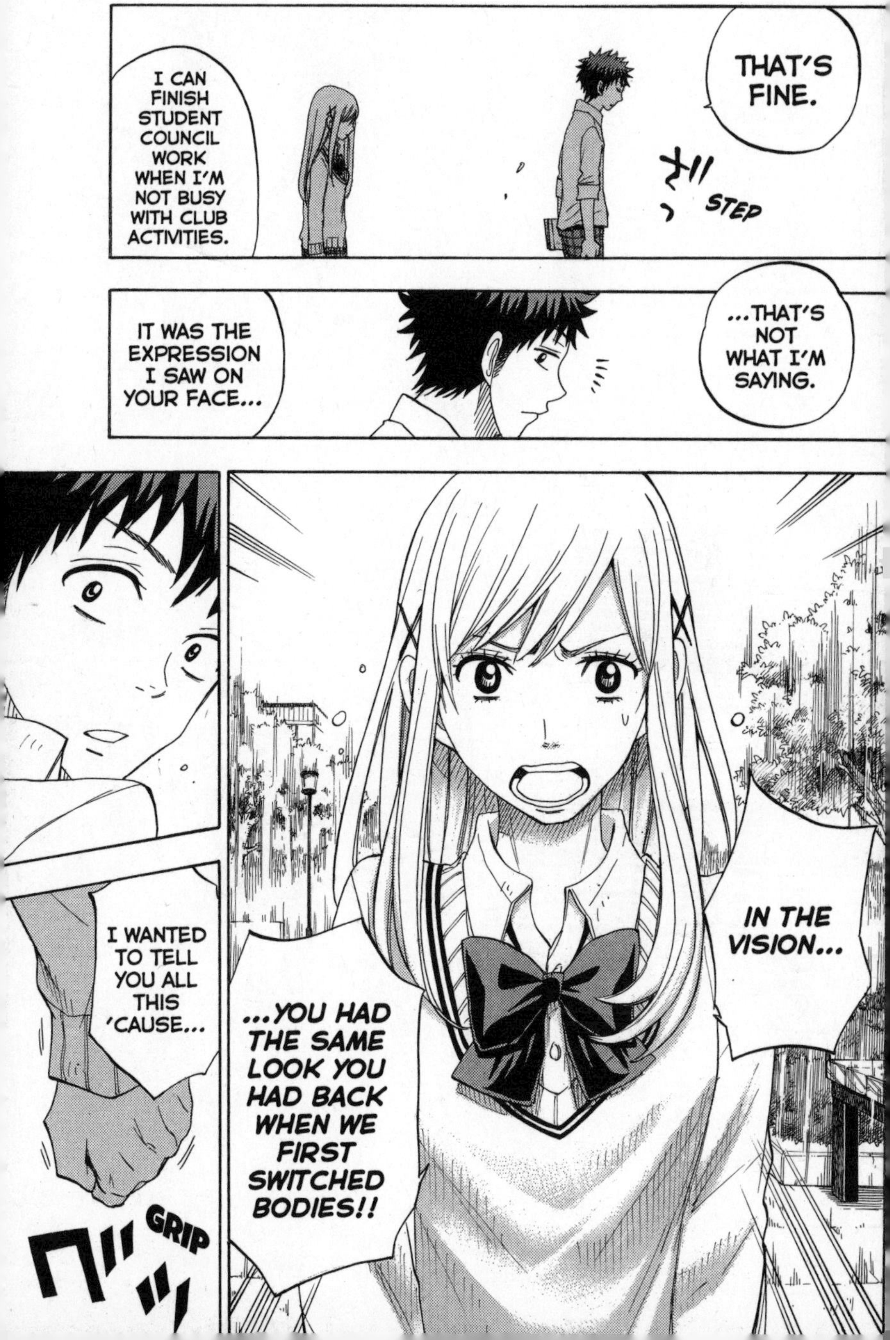
THAT'S FINE.
STEP
I CAN FINISH STUDENT COUNCIL WORK WHEN I'M NOT BUSY WITH CLUB ACTIVITIES.
...THAT'S NOT WHAT I'M SAYING.
IT WAS THE EXPRESSION I SAW ON YOUR FACE...
IN THE VISION...
...YOU HAD THE SAME LOOK YOU HAD BACK WHEN WE FIRST SWITCHED BODIES!!
I WANTED TO TELL YOU ALL THIS 'CAUSE...
GRIP

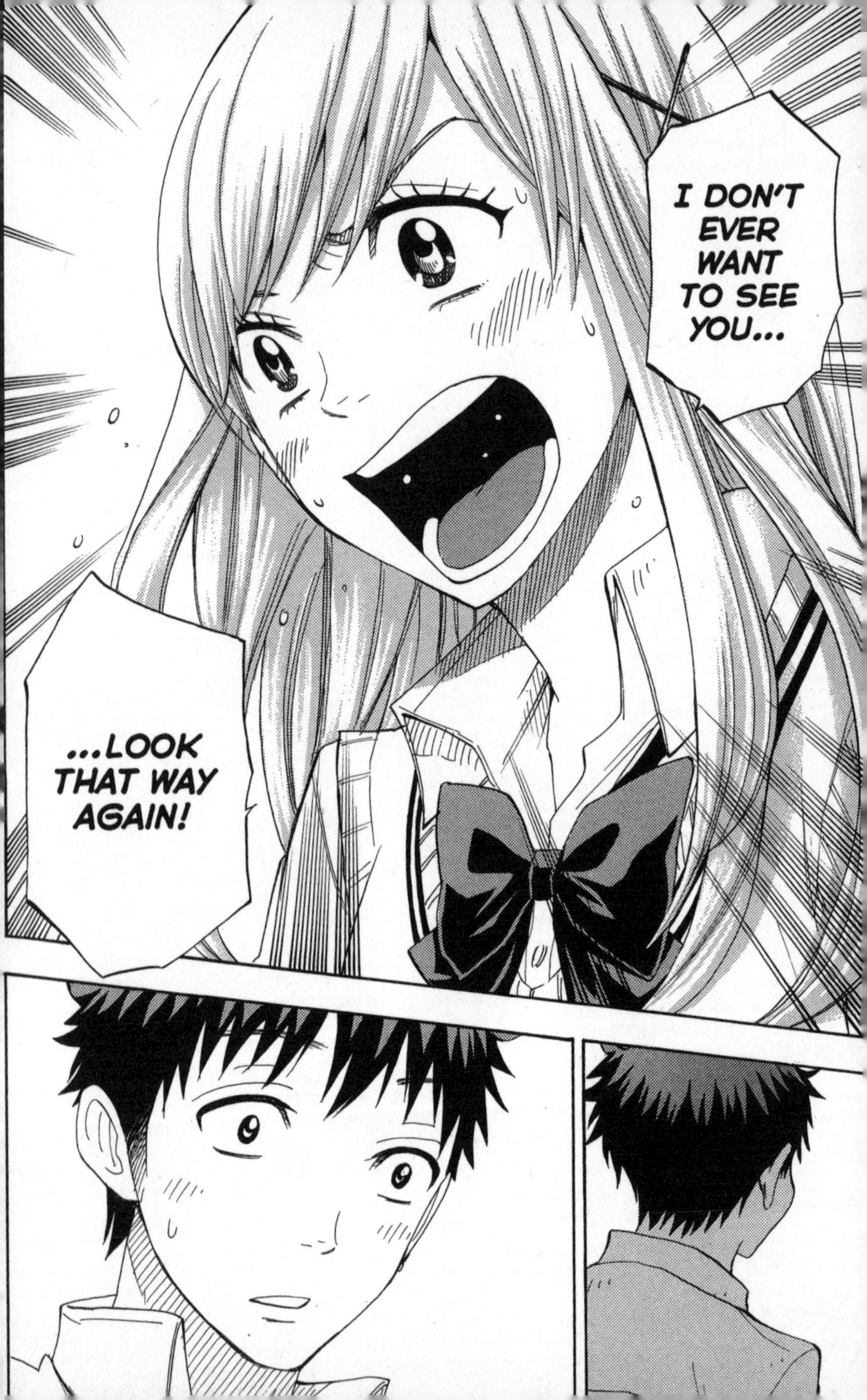
I DON'T EVER WANT TO SEE YOU...
...LOOK THAT WAY AGAIN!

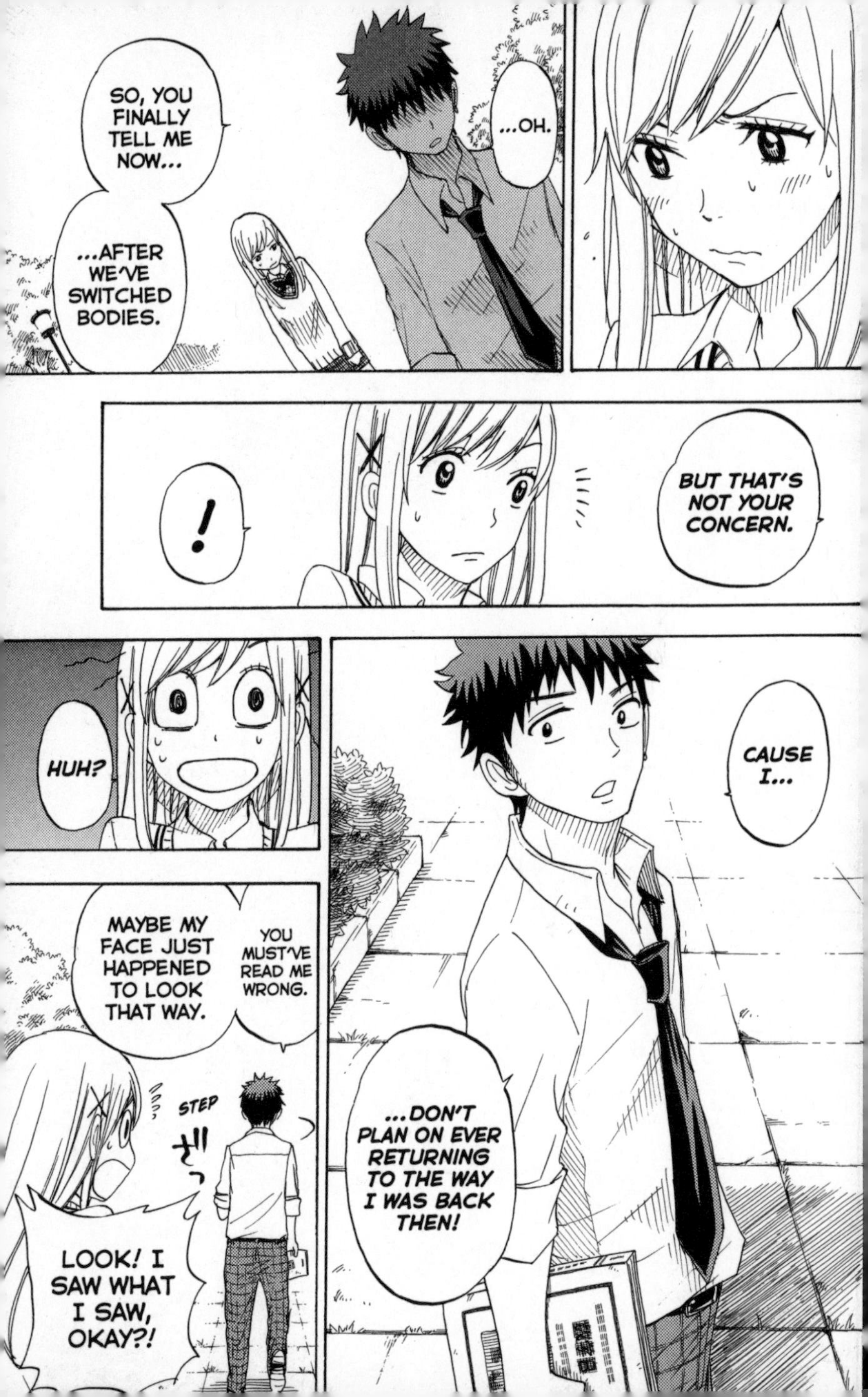
...OH.
SO, YOU FINALLY TELL ME NOW...
...AFTER WE'VE SWITCHED BODIES.
BUT THAT'S NOT YOUR CONCERN.
!
CAUSE I...
...DON'T PLAN ON EVER RETURNING TO THE WAY I WAS BACK THEN!
HUH?
YOU MUST'VE READ ME WRONG.
MAYBE MY FACE JUST HAPPENED TO LOOK THAT WAY.
STEP
LOOK! I SAW WHAT I SAW, OKAY?!

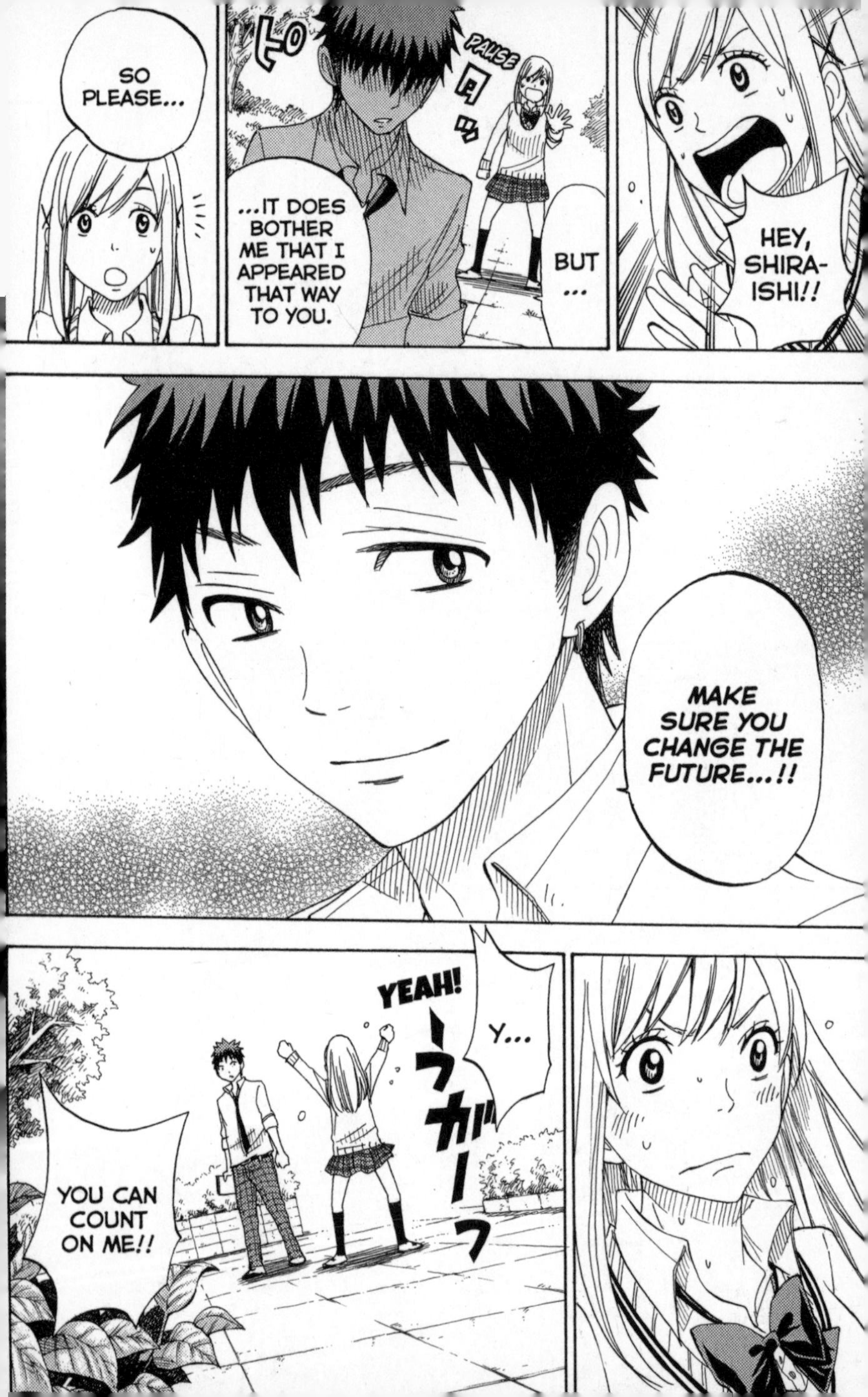
HEY, SHIRA-ISHI!!
PAUSE
BUT ...
...IT DOES BOTHER ME THAT I APPEARED THAT WAY TO YOU.
SO PLEASE...
MAKE SURE YOU CHANGE THE FUTURE...!!
Y...
YEAH!
YOU CAN COUNT ON ME!!

CHAPTER 63: Shriek!

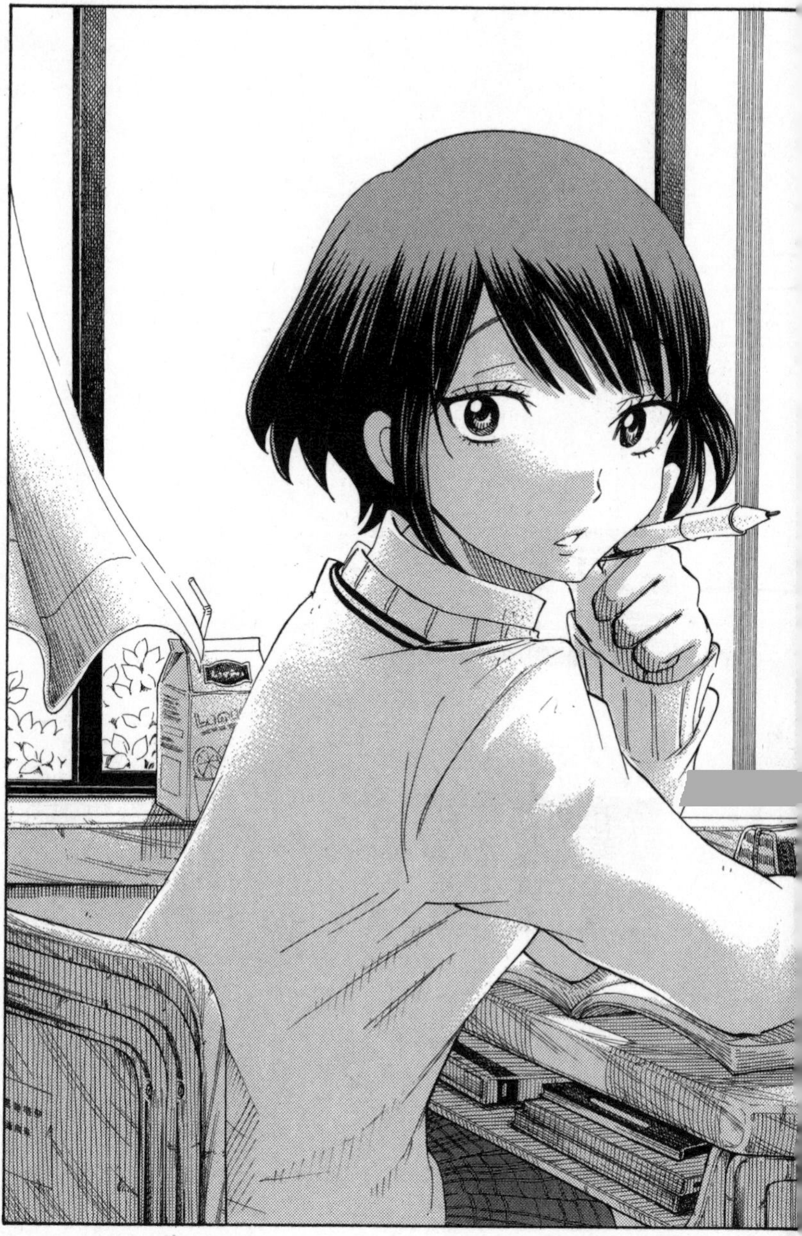

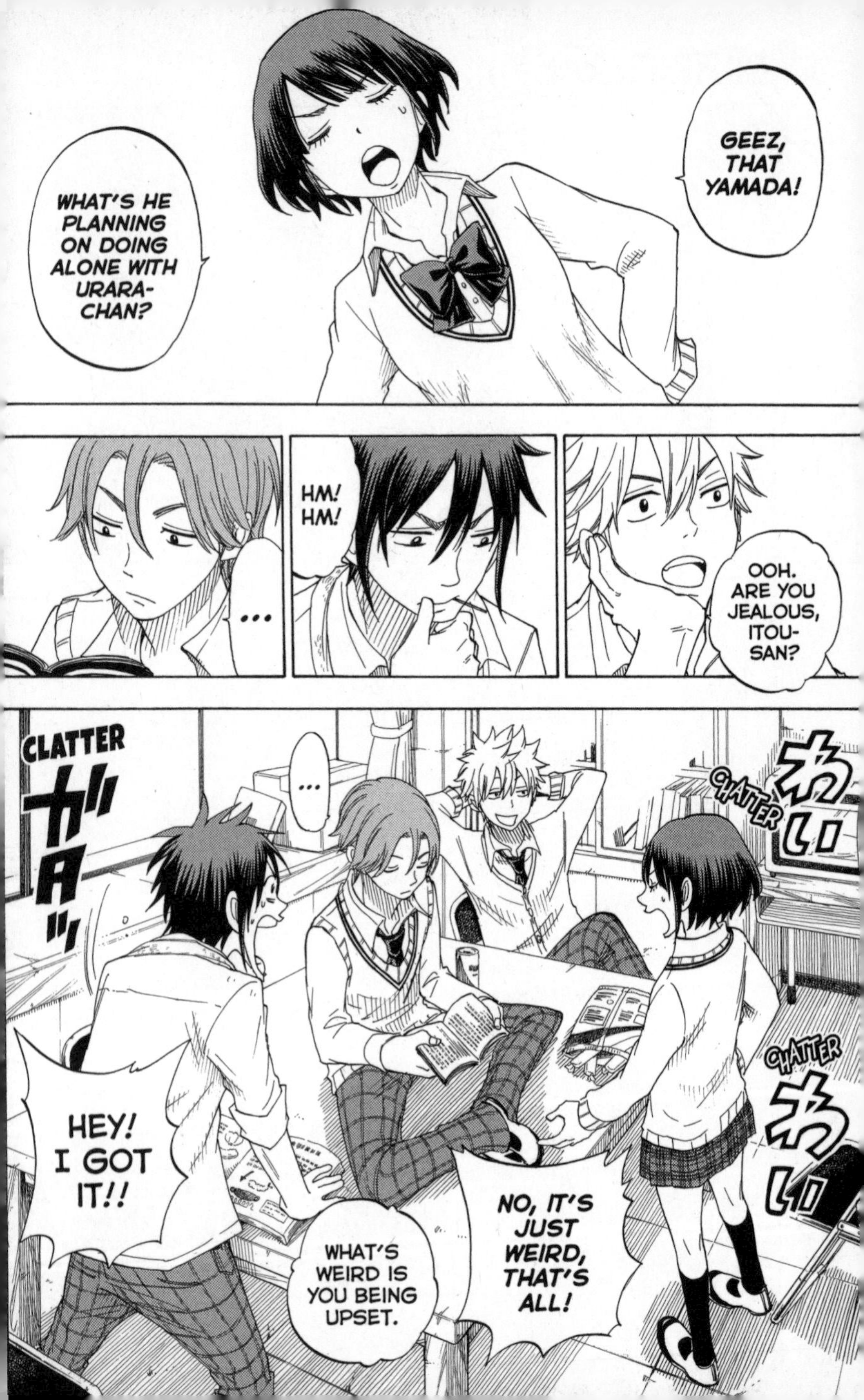
GEEZ, THAT YAMADA!
WHAT'S HE PLANNING ON DOING ALONE WITH URARA-CHAN?
OOH. ARE YOU JEALOUS, ITOU-SAN?
HM! HM!
...
CHATTER
わい
...
CLATTER
ガタッ
CHATTER
わい
NO, IT'S JUST WEIRD, THAT'S ALL!
WHAT'S WEIRD IS YOU BEING UPSET.
HEY! I GOT IT!!

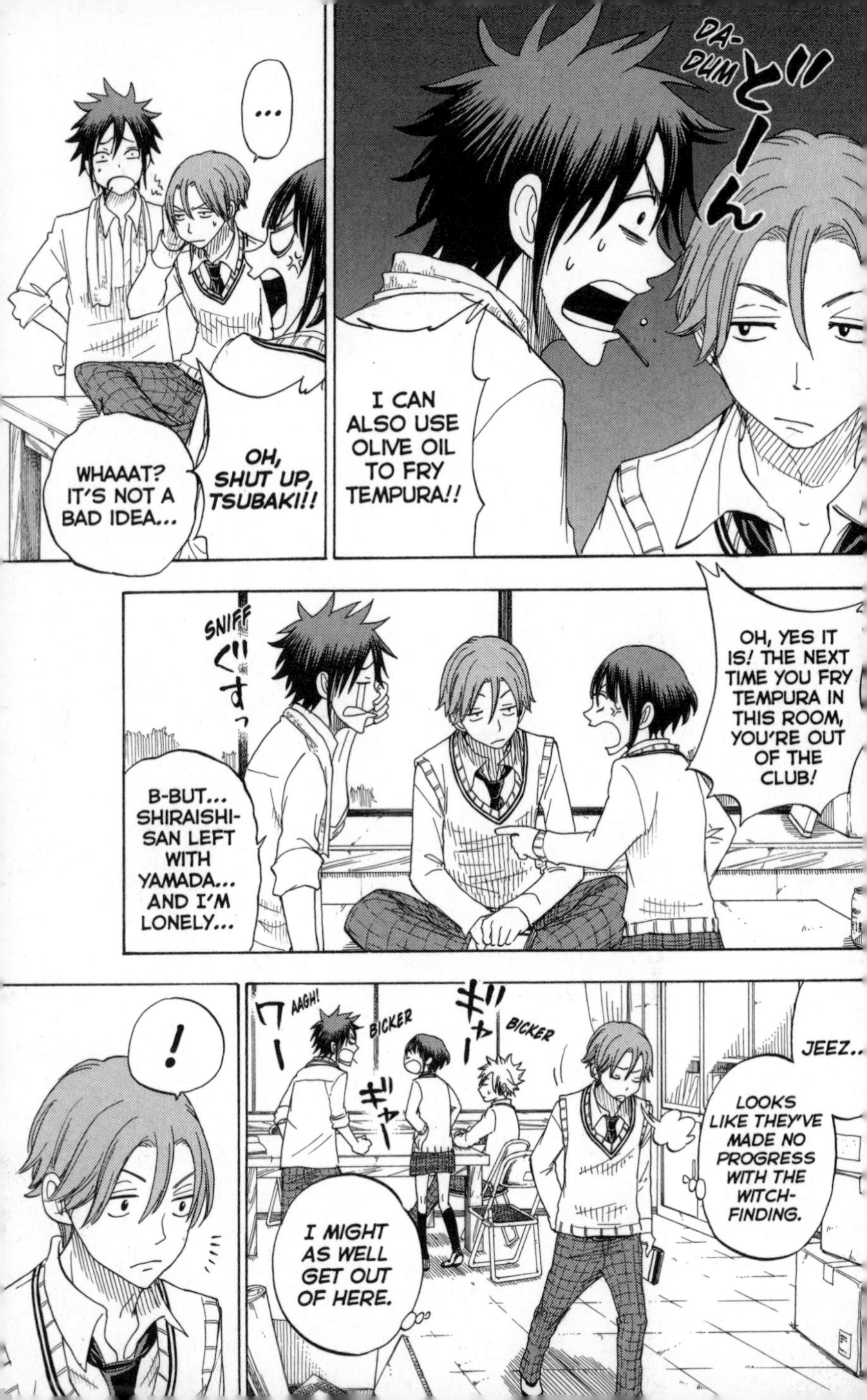
DA-DUM
I CAN ALSO USE OLIVE OIL TO FRY TEMPURA!!
...
OH, SHUT UP, TSUBAKI!!
WHAAAT? IT'S NOT A BAD IDEA...
OH, YES IT IS! THE NEXT TIME YOU FRY TEMPURA IN THIS ROOM, YOU'RE OUT OF THE CLUB!
SNIFF
B-BUT... SHIRAISHI-SAN LEFT WITH YAMADA... AND I'M LONELY...
JEEZ..
LOOKS LIKE THEY'VE MADE NO PROGRESS WITH THE WITCH-FINDING.
BICKER
BICKER
AAGH!
I MIGHT AS WELL GET OUT OF HERE.
!

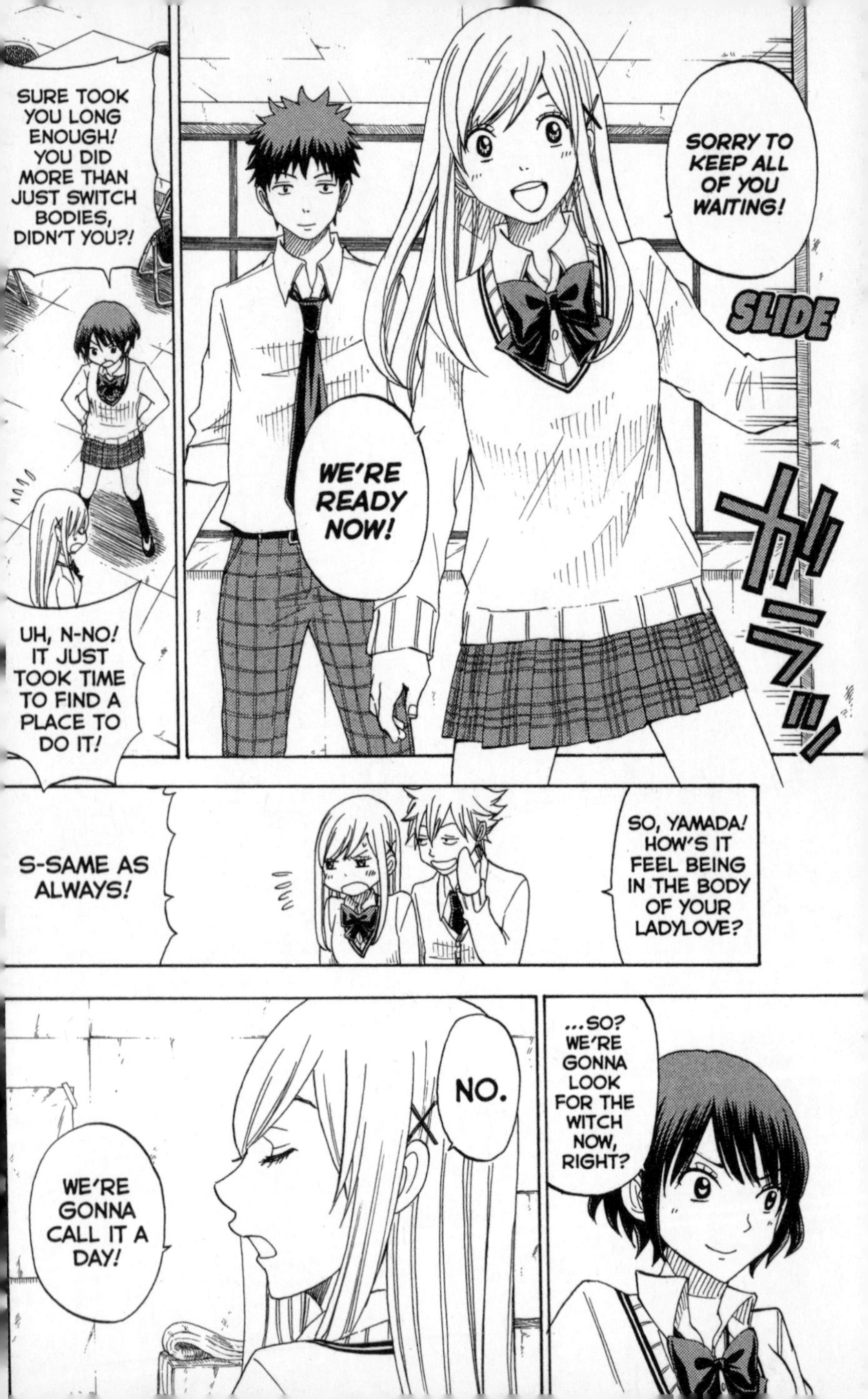
SORRY TO KEEP ALL OF YOU WAITING!
SLIDE
ガラッ
WE'RE READY NOW!
SURE TOOK YOU LONG ENOUGH! YOU DID MORE THAN JUST SWITCH BODIES, DIDN'T YOU?!
UH, N-NO! IT JUST TOOK TIME TO FIND A PLACE TO DO IT!
SO, YAMADA! HOW'S IT FEEL BEING IN THE BODY OF YOUR LADYLOVE?
S-SAME AS ALWAYS!
...SO? WE'RE GONNA LOOK FOR THE WITCH NOW, RIGHT?
NO.
WE'RE GONNA CALL IT A DAY!

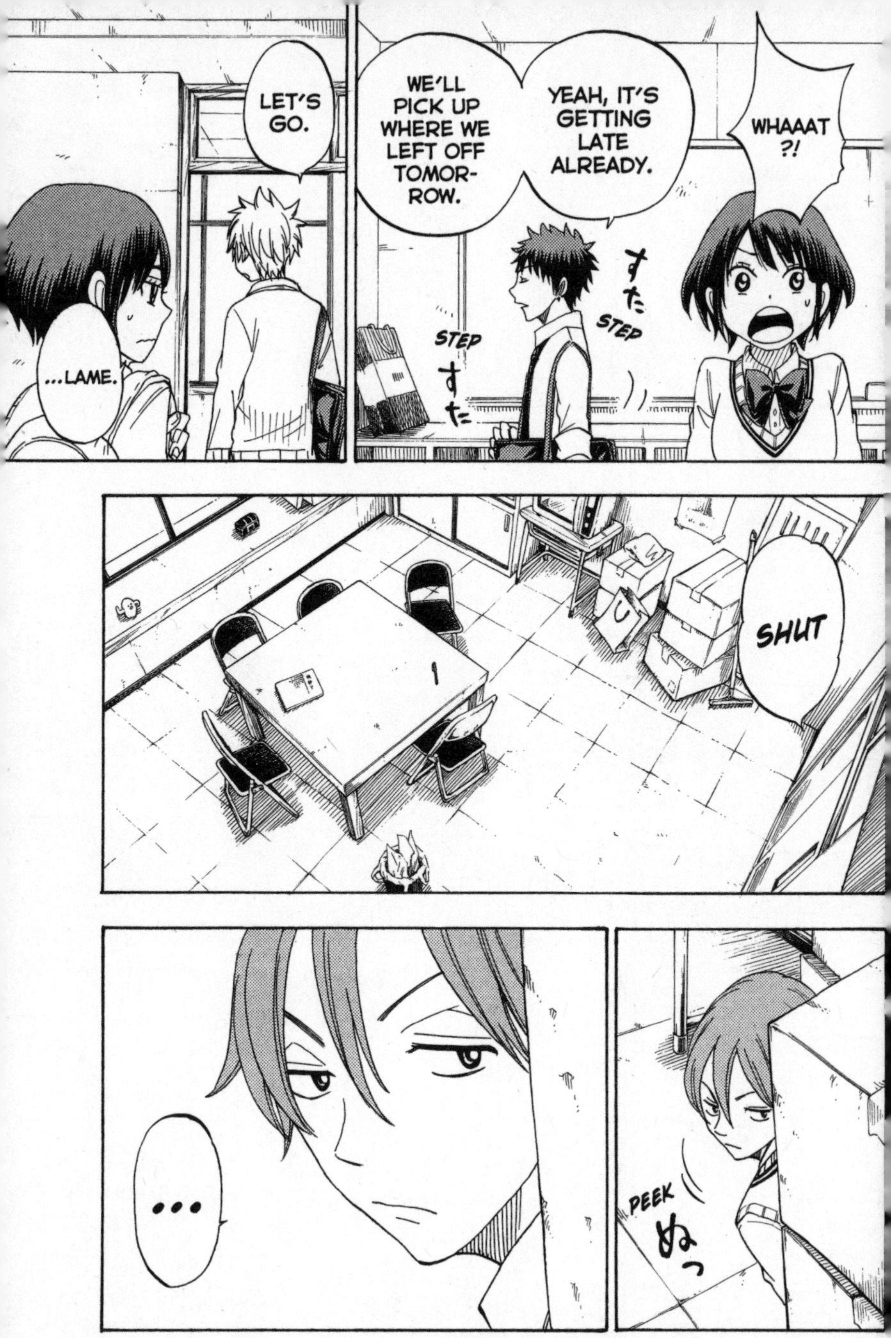
WHAAAT?!
YEAH, IT'S GETTING LATE ALREADY.
WE'LL PICK UP WHERE WE LEFT OFF TOMOR-ROW.
すた
STEP
STEP
すた
LET'S GO.
...LAME.
SHUT
PEEK
ぬっ
...

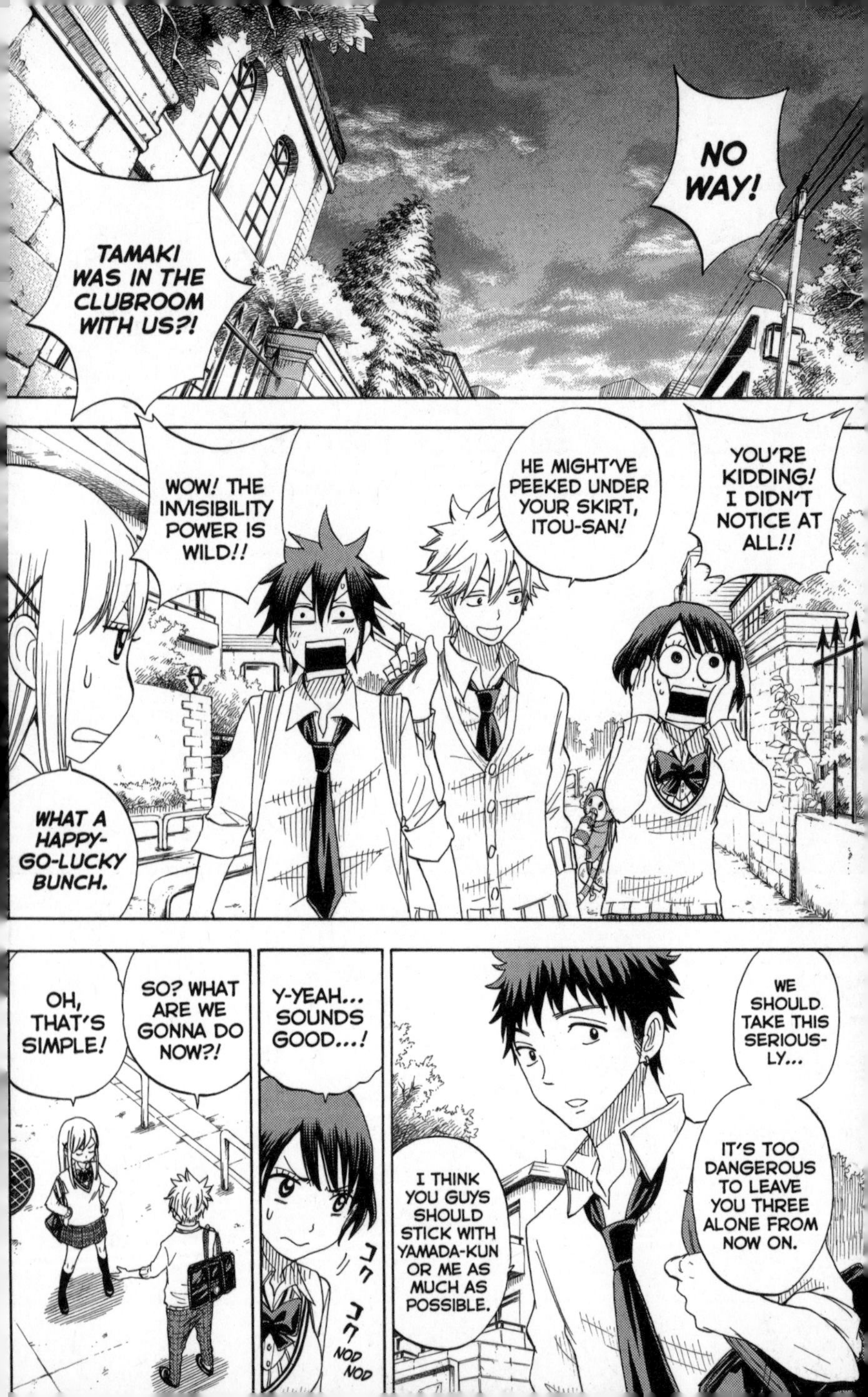
NO WAY!
TAMAKI WAS IN THE CLUBROOM WITH US?!
YOU'RE KIDDING! I DIDN'T NOTICE AT ALL!!
HE MIGHT'VE PEEKED UNDER YOUR SKIRT, ITOU-SAN!
WOW! THE INVISIBILITY POWER IS WILD!!
WHAT A HAPPY-GO-LUCKY BUNCH.
WE SHOULD TAKE THIS SERIOUS-LY...
IT'S TOO DANGEROUS TO LEAVE YOU THREE ALONE FROM NOW ON.
I THINK YOU GUYS SHOULD STICK WITH YAMADA-KUN OR ME AS MUCH AS POSSIBLE.
Y-YEAH... SOUNDS GOOD...!
コク コク
NOD NOD
SO? WHAT ARE WE GONNA DO NOW?!
OH, THAT'S SIMPLE!

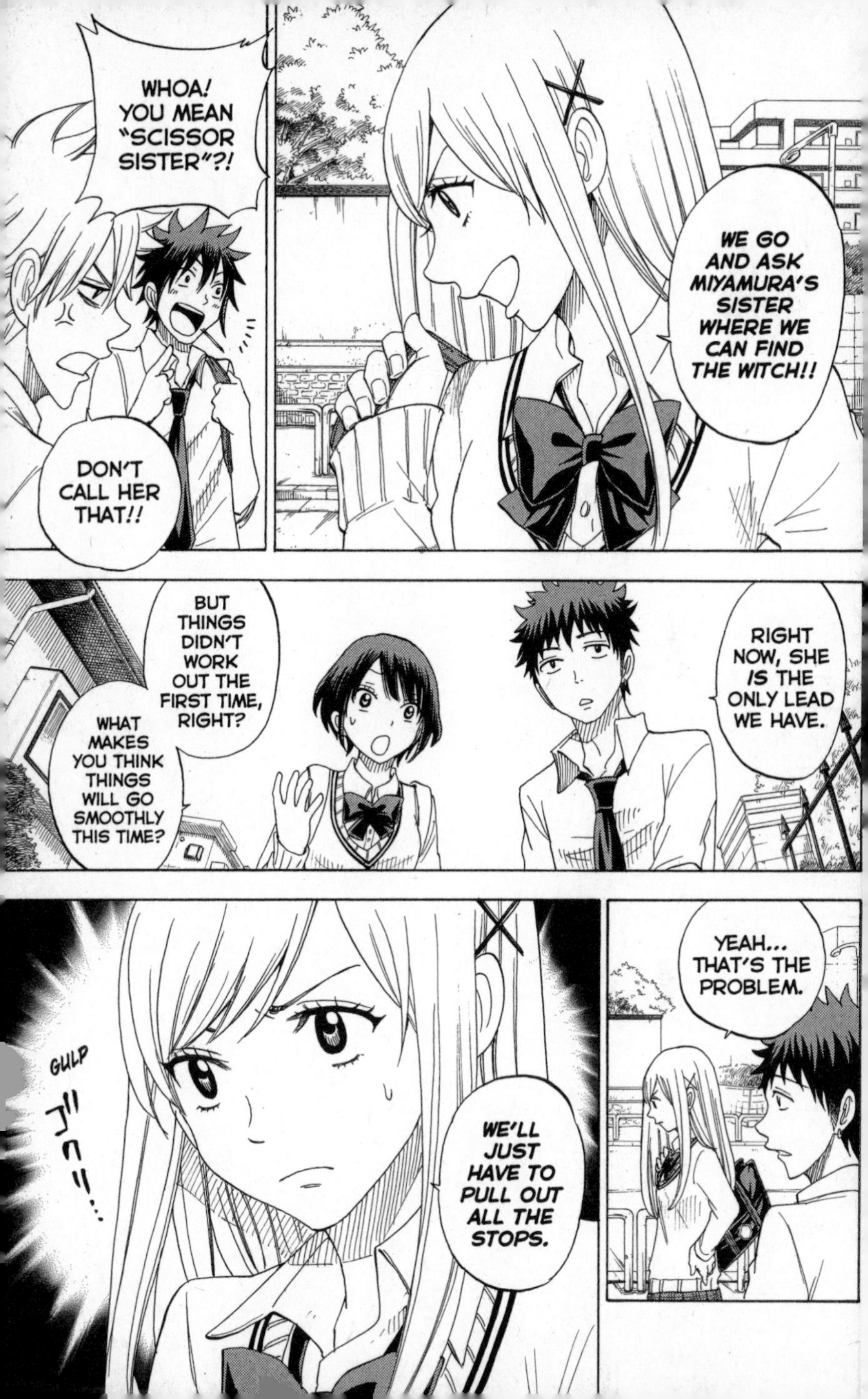
WE GO AND ASK MIYAMURA'S SISTER WHERE WE CAN FIND THE WITCH!!
WHOA! YOU MEAN "SCISSOR SISTER"?!
DON'T CALL HER THAT!!
RIGHT NOW, SHE *IS* THE ONLY LEAD WE HAVE.
BUT THINGS DIDN'T WORK OUT THE FIRST TIME, RIGHT?
WHAT MAKES YOU THINK THINGS WILL GO SMOOTHLY THIS TIME?
YEAH... THAT'S THE PROBLEM.
WE'LL JUST HAVE TO PULL OUT ALL THE STOPS.
GULP
ゴクリ…

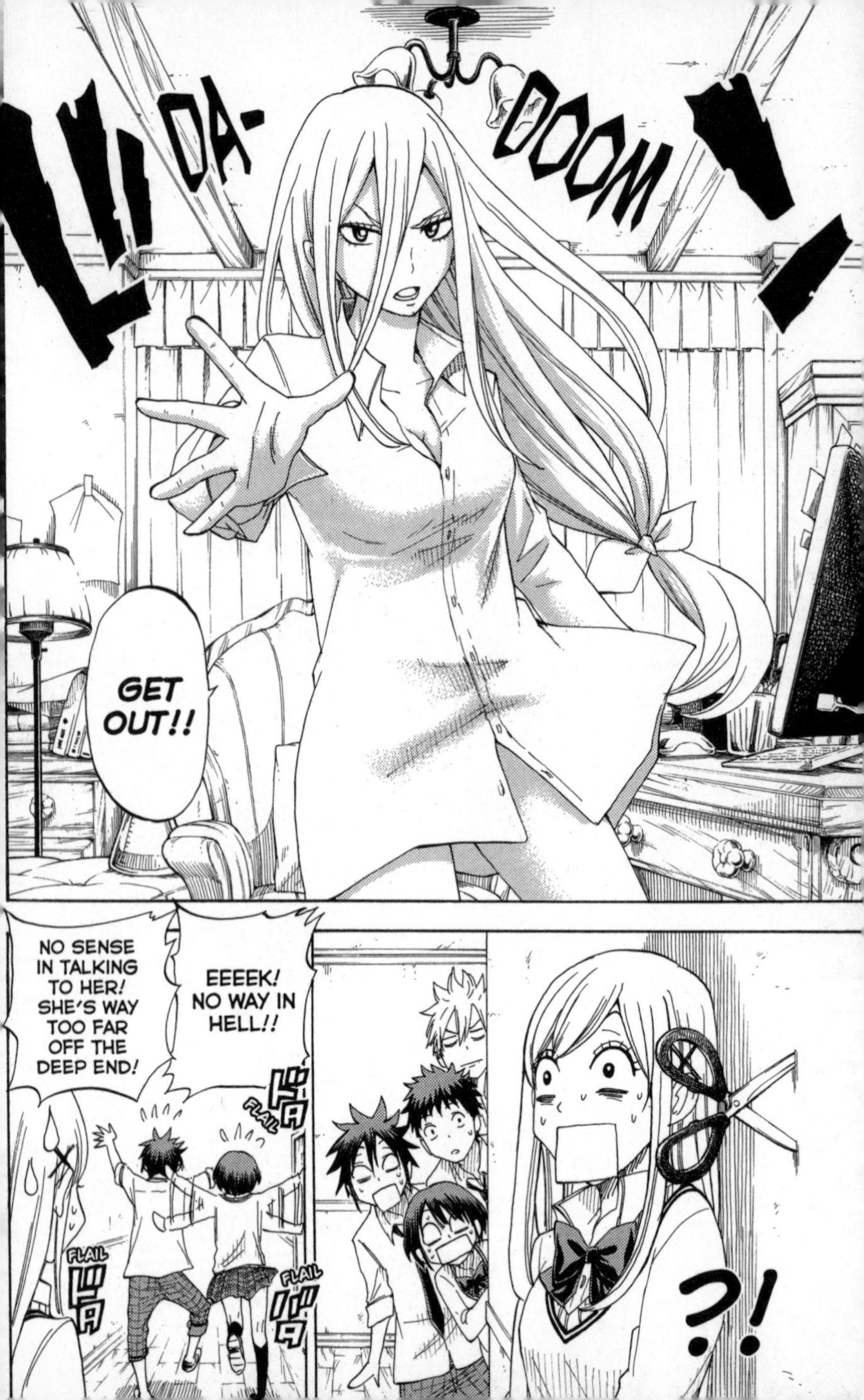
DA-
DOOM
GET OUT!!
?!
EEEEK! NO WAY IN HELL!!
NO SENSE IN TALKING TO HER! SHE'S WAY TOO FAR OFF THE DEEP END!
FLAIL
FLAIL
FLAIL

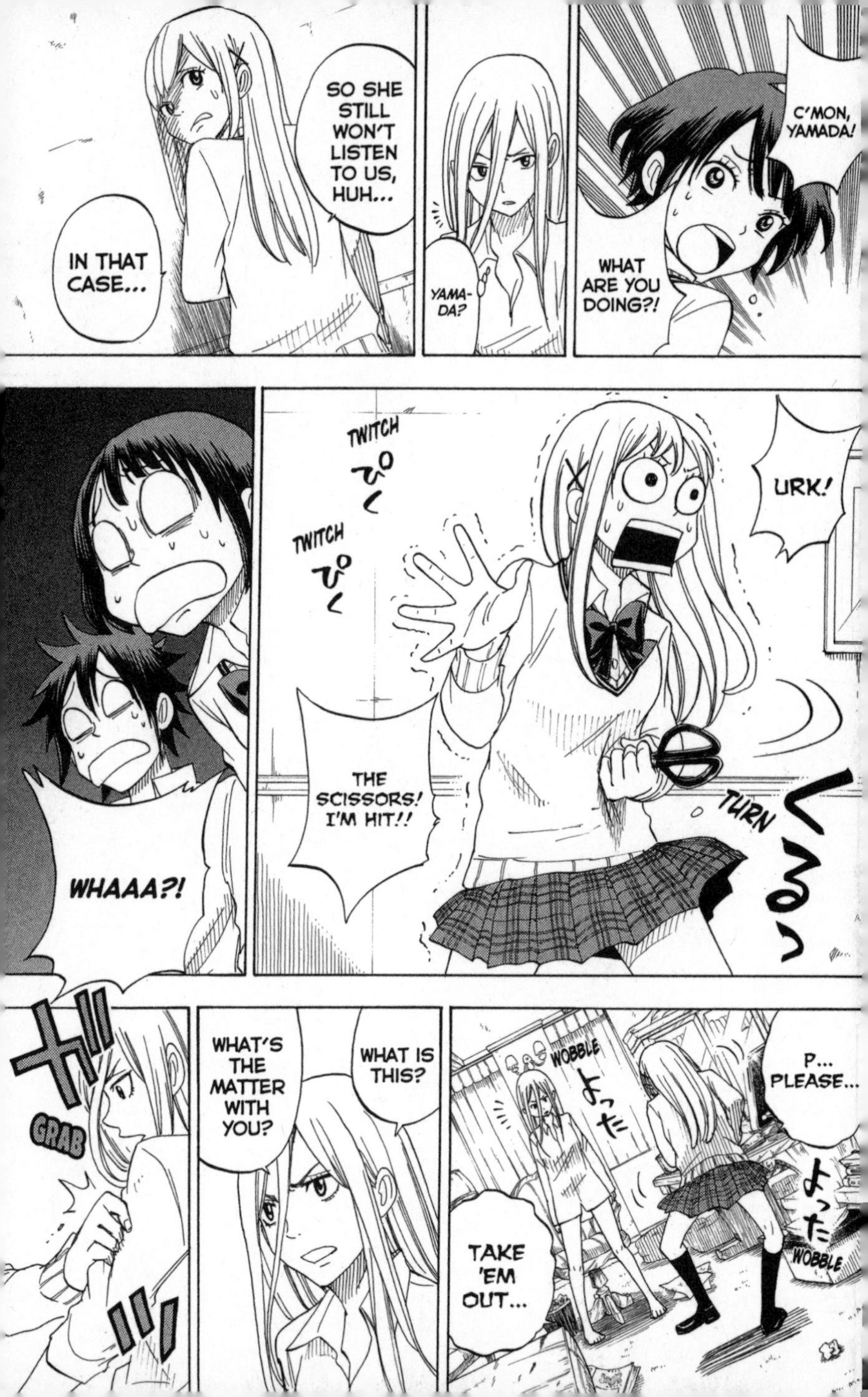
C'MON, YAMADA!
WHAT ARE YOU DOING?!
YAMA-DA?
SO SHE STILL WON'T LISTEN TO US, HUH...
IN THAT CASE...
URK!
TWITCH
ぴく
TWITCH
ぴく
TURN
くるっ
THE SCISSORS! I'M HIT!!
WHAAA?!
P... PLEASE...
WOBBLE
よった
よった
WOBBLE
TAKE 'EM OUT...
WHAT IS THIS?
WHAT'S THE MATTER WITH YOU?
GRAB

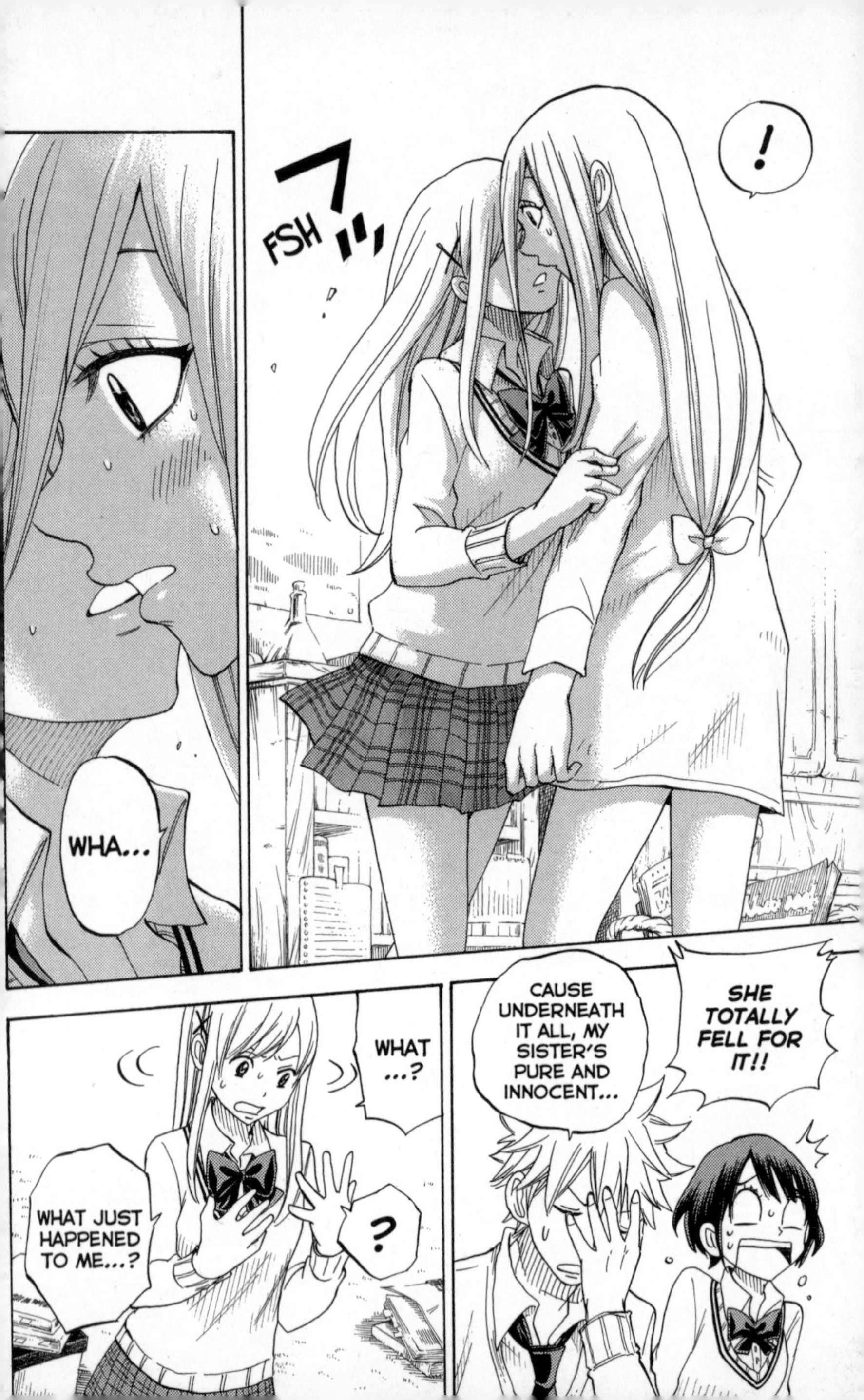
!
FSH
WHA...
SHE TOTALLY FELL FOR IT!!
CAUSE UNDERNEATH IT ALL, MY SISTER'S PURE AND INNOCENT...
WHAT ...?
?
WHAT JUST HAPPENED TO ME...?

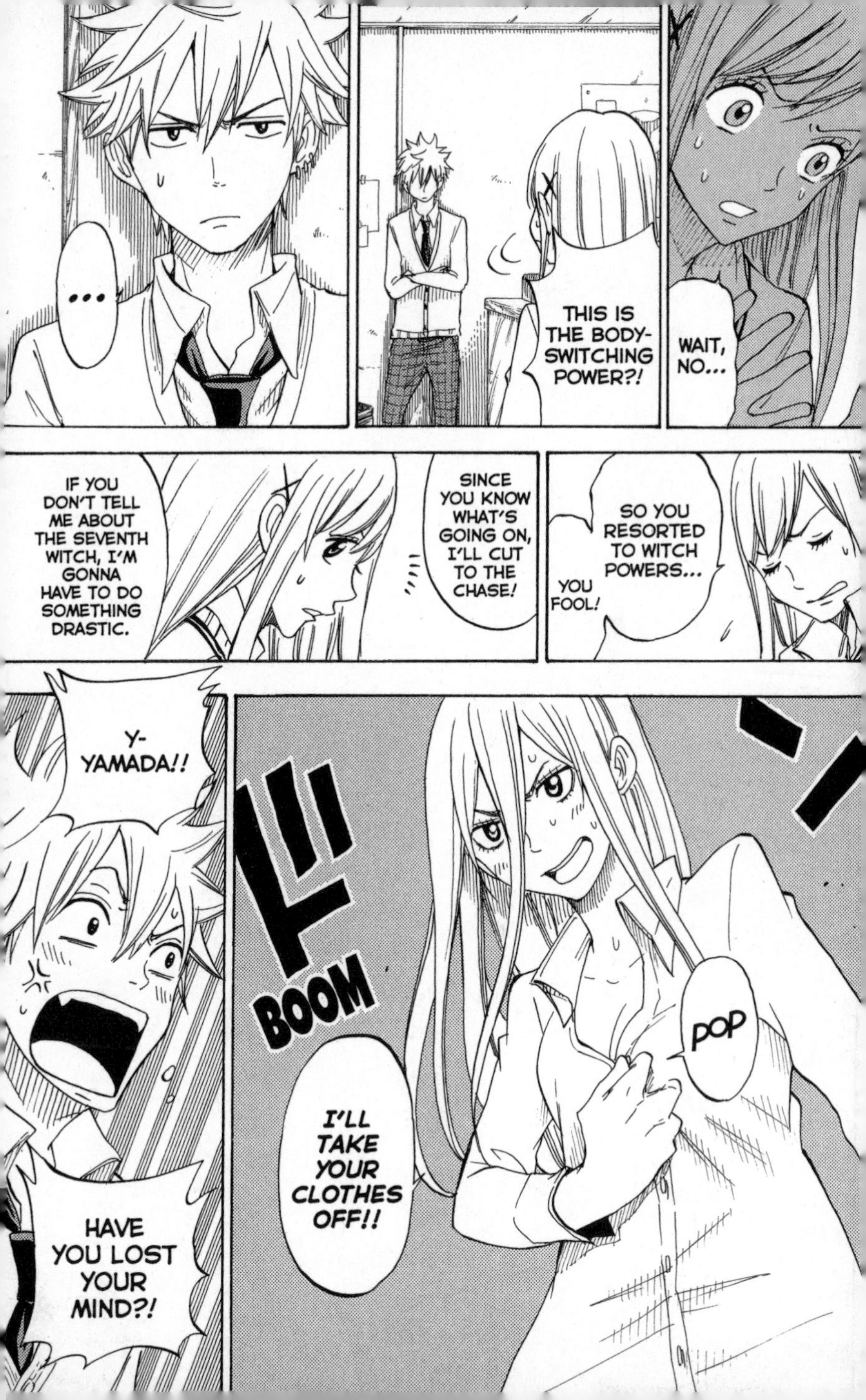
WAIT, NO...
THIS IS THE BODY-SWITCHING POWER?!
...
SO YOU RESORTED TO WITCH POWERS...
YOU FOOL!
SINCE YOU KNOW WHAT'S GOING ON, I'LL CUT TO THE CHASE!
IF YOU DON'T TELL ME ABOUT THE SEVENTH WITCH, I'M GONNA HAVE TO DO SOMETHING DRASTIC.
BOOM
POP
I'LL TAKE YOUR CLOTHES OFF!!
Y-YAMADA!!
HAVE YOU LOST YOUR MIND?!

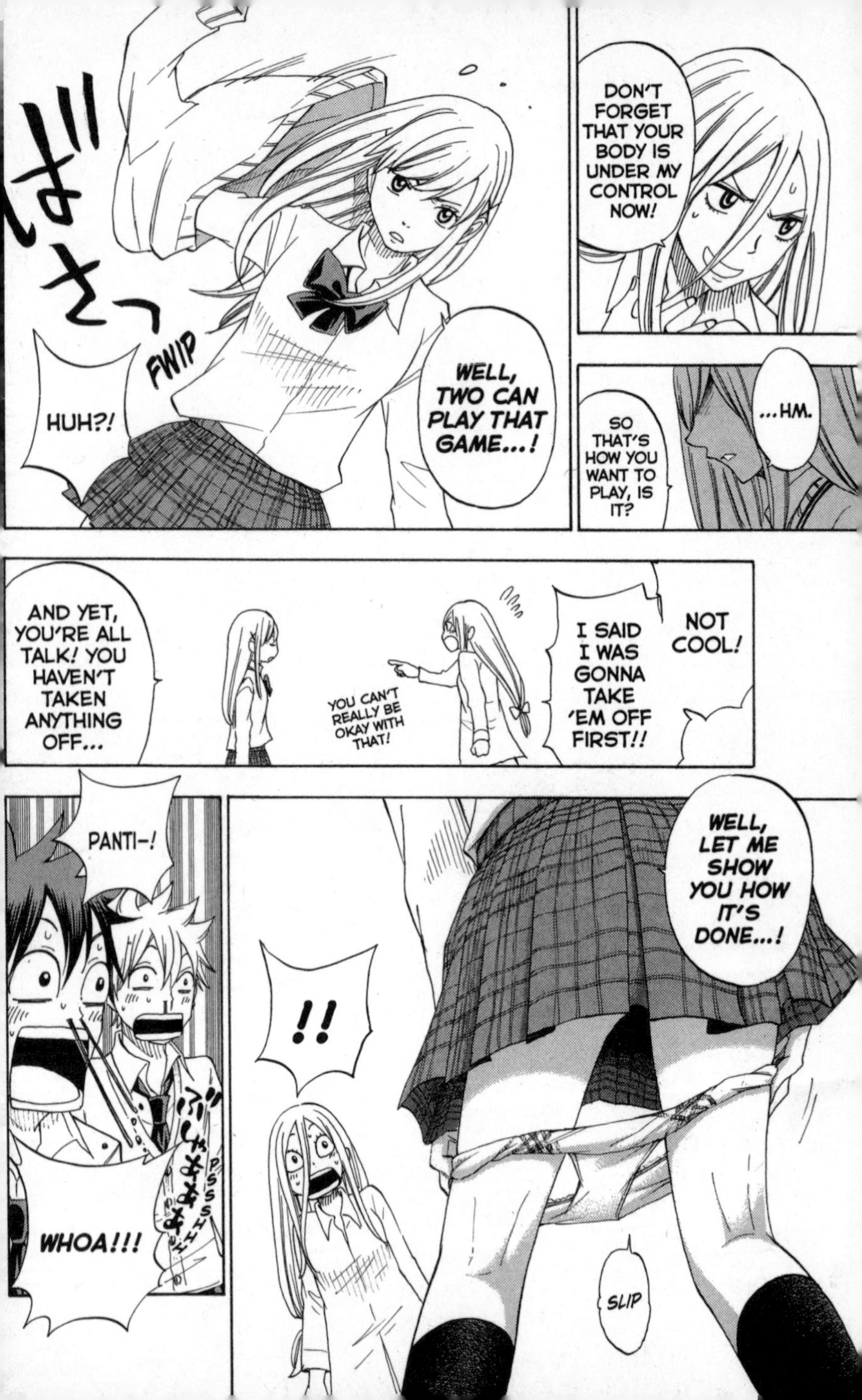
DON'T FORGET THAT YOUR BODY IS UNDER MY CONTROL NOW!
...HM.
SO THAT'S HOW YOU WANT TO PLAY, IS IT?
WELL, TWO CAN PLAY THAT GAME...!
ばさっ
FWIP
HUH?!
NOT COOL!
I SAID I WAS GONNA TAKE 'EM OFF FIRST!!
YOU CAN'T REALLY BE OKAY WITH THAT!
AND YET, YOU'RE ALL TALK! YOU HAVEN'T TAKEN ANYTHING OFF...
WELL, LET ME SHOW YOU HOW IT'S DONE...!
!!
SLIP
PANTI-!
PSSSHHH
WHOA!!!

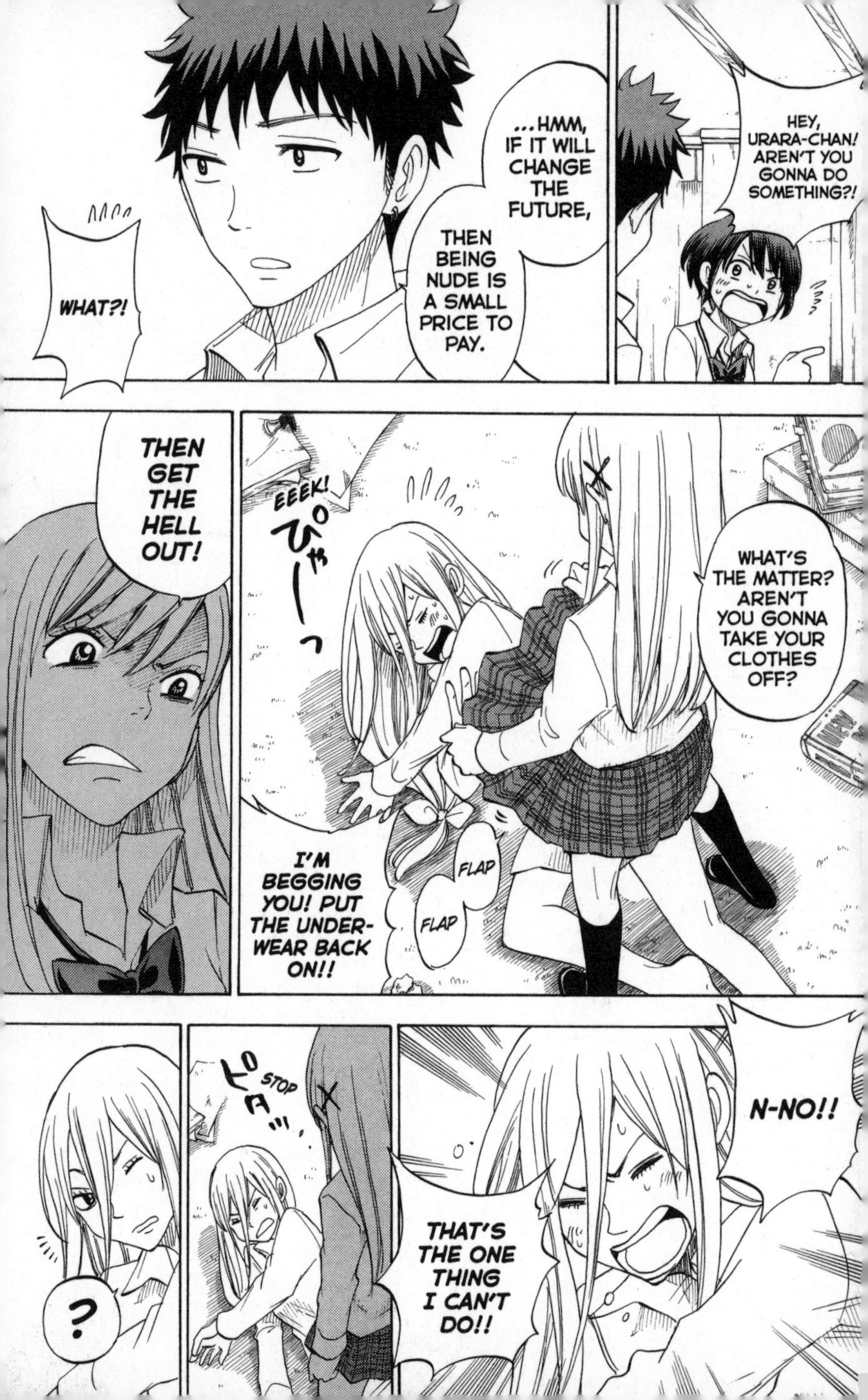
HEY, URARA-CHAN! AREN'T YOU GONNA DO SOMETHING?!
...HMM, IF IT WILL CHANGE THE FUTURE,
THEN BEING NUDE IS A SMALL PRICE TO PAY.
WHAT?!
WHAT'S THE MATTER? AREN'T YOU GONNA TAKE YOUR CLOTHES OFF?
EEEK!
ぴゃーっ
FLAP
FLAP
I'M BEGGING YOU! PUT THE UNDER-WEAR BACK ON!!
THEN GET THE HELL OUT!
N-NO!!
THAT'S THE ONE THING I CAN'T DO!!
ピタッ
STOP
?

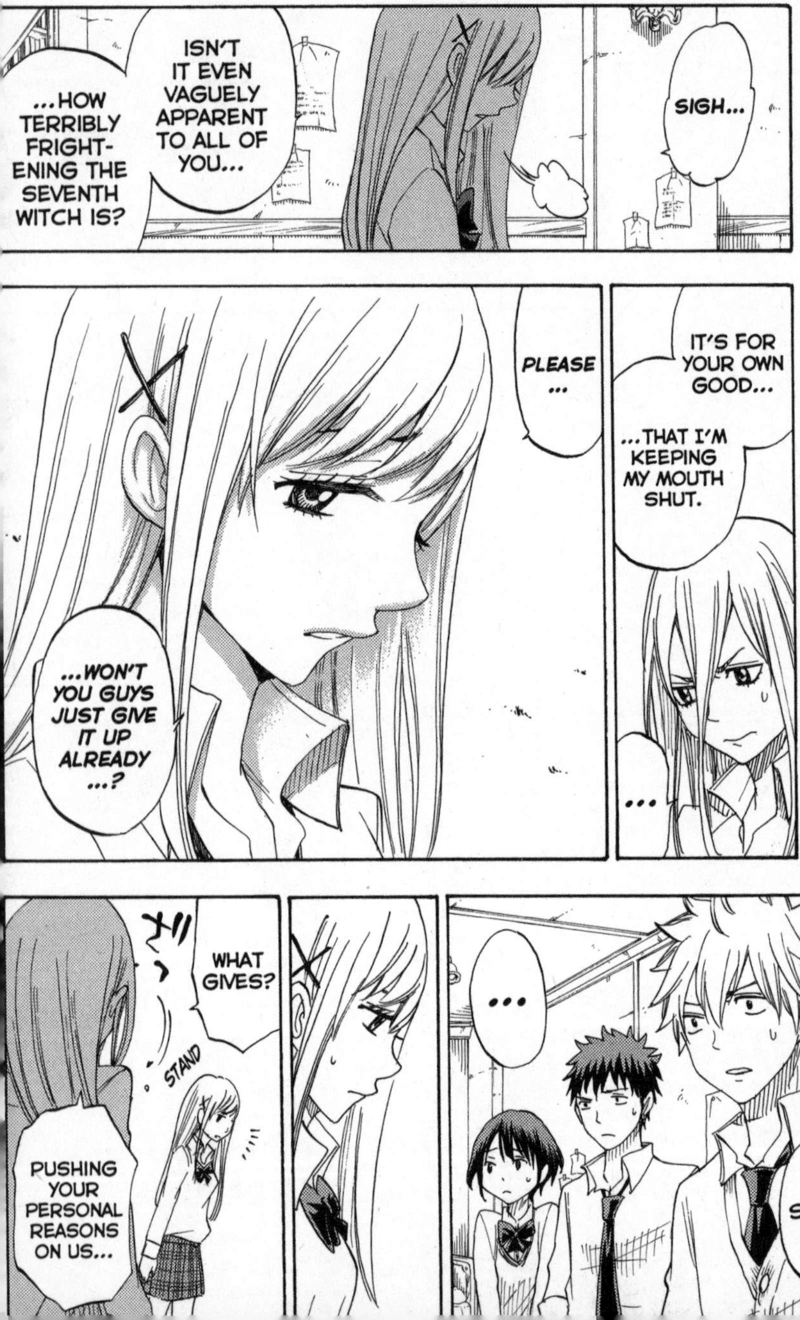
SIGH...
ISN'T IT EVEN VAGUELY APPARENT TO ALL OF YOU...
...HOW TERRIBLY FRIGHT-ENING THE SEVENTH WITCH IS?
IT'S FOR YOUR OWN GOOD...
...THAT I'M KEEPING MY MOUTH SHUT.
...
PLEASE ...
...WON'T YOU GUYS JUST GIVE IT UP ALREADY ...?
...
SIS...
WHAT GIVES?
STAND
PUSHING YOUR PERSONAL REASONS ON US...

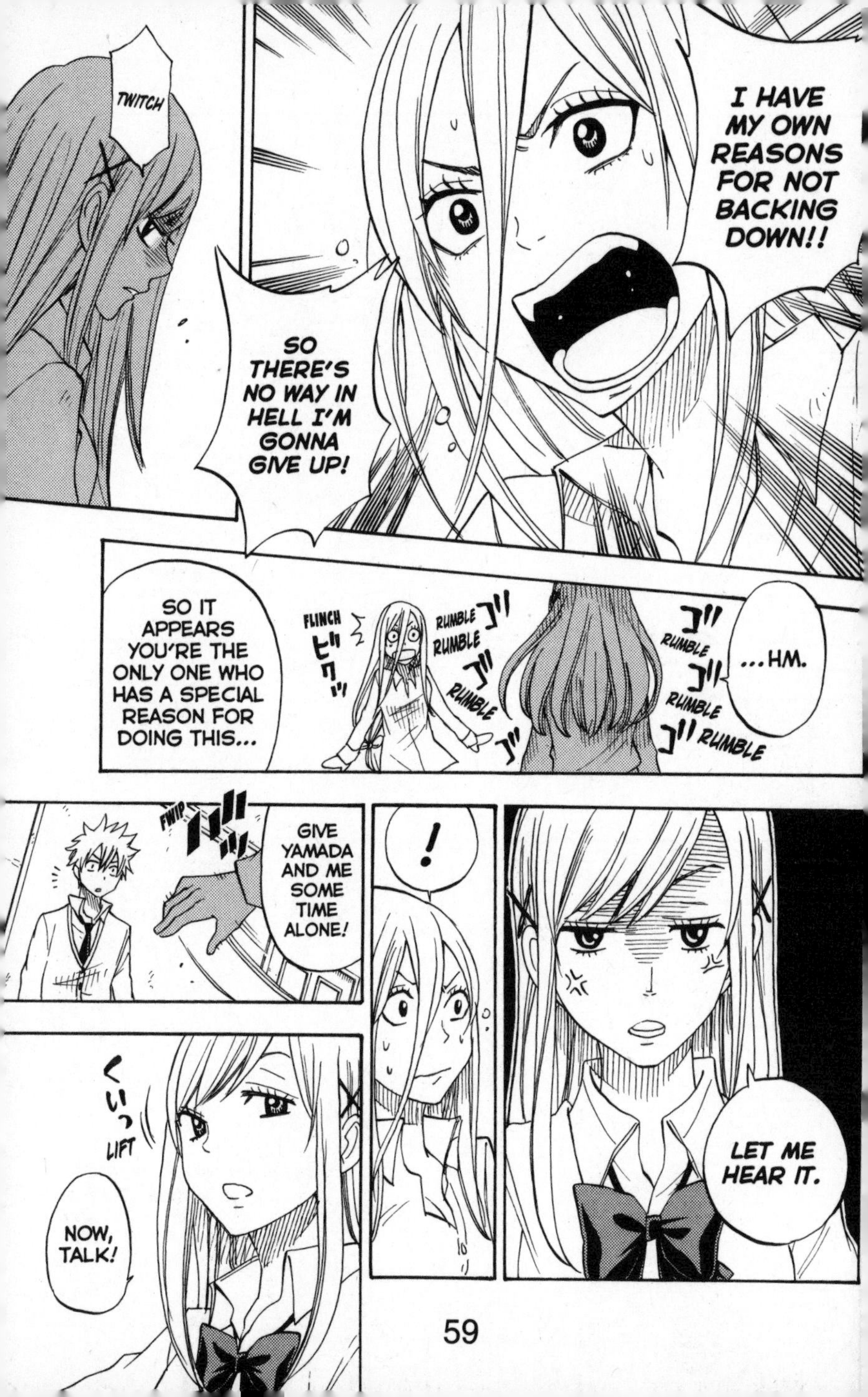
I HAVE MY OWN REASONS FOR NOT BACKING DOWN!!
SO THERE'S NO WAY IN HELL I'M GONNA GIVE UP!
TWITCH
...HM.
RUMBLE
RUMBLE
RUMBLE
RUMBLE
RUMBLE
RUMBLE
FLINCH
SO IT APPEARS YOU'RE THE ONLY ONE WHO HAS A SPECIAL REASON FOR DOING THIS...
LET ME HEAR IT.
!
GIVE YAMADA AND ME SOME TIME ALONE!
FWIP
LIFT
NOW, TALK!

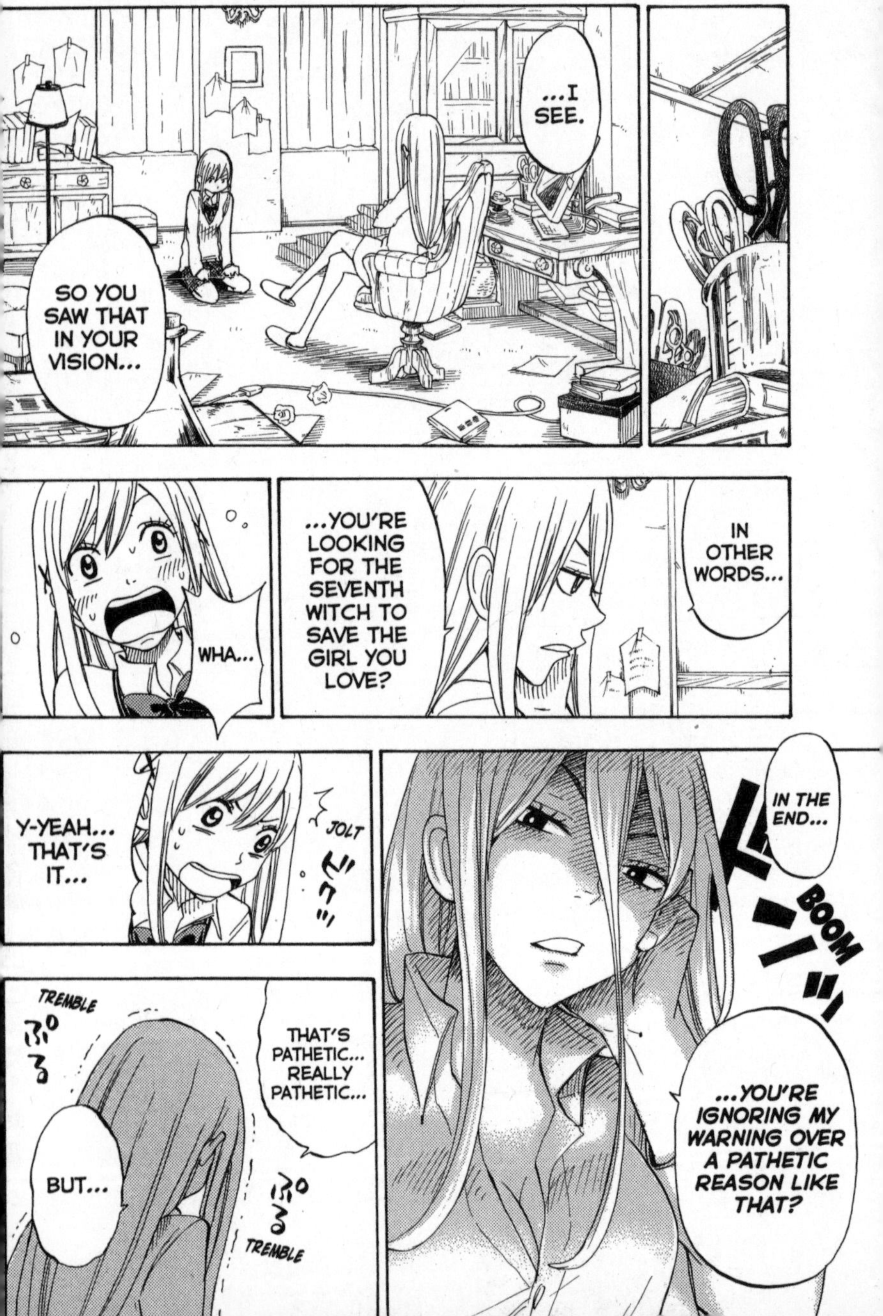
...I SEE.
SO YOU SAW THAT IN YOUR VISION...
IN OTHER WORDS...
...YOU'RE LOOKING FOR THE SEVENTH WITCH TO SAVE THE GIRL YOU LOVE?
WHA...
IN THE END...
BOOM
...YOU'RE IGNORING MY WARNING OVER A PATHETIC REASON LIKE THAT?
JOLT
Y-YEAH... THAT'S IT...
THAT'S PATHETIC... REALLY PATHETIC...
TREMBLE
BUT...
TREMBLE

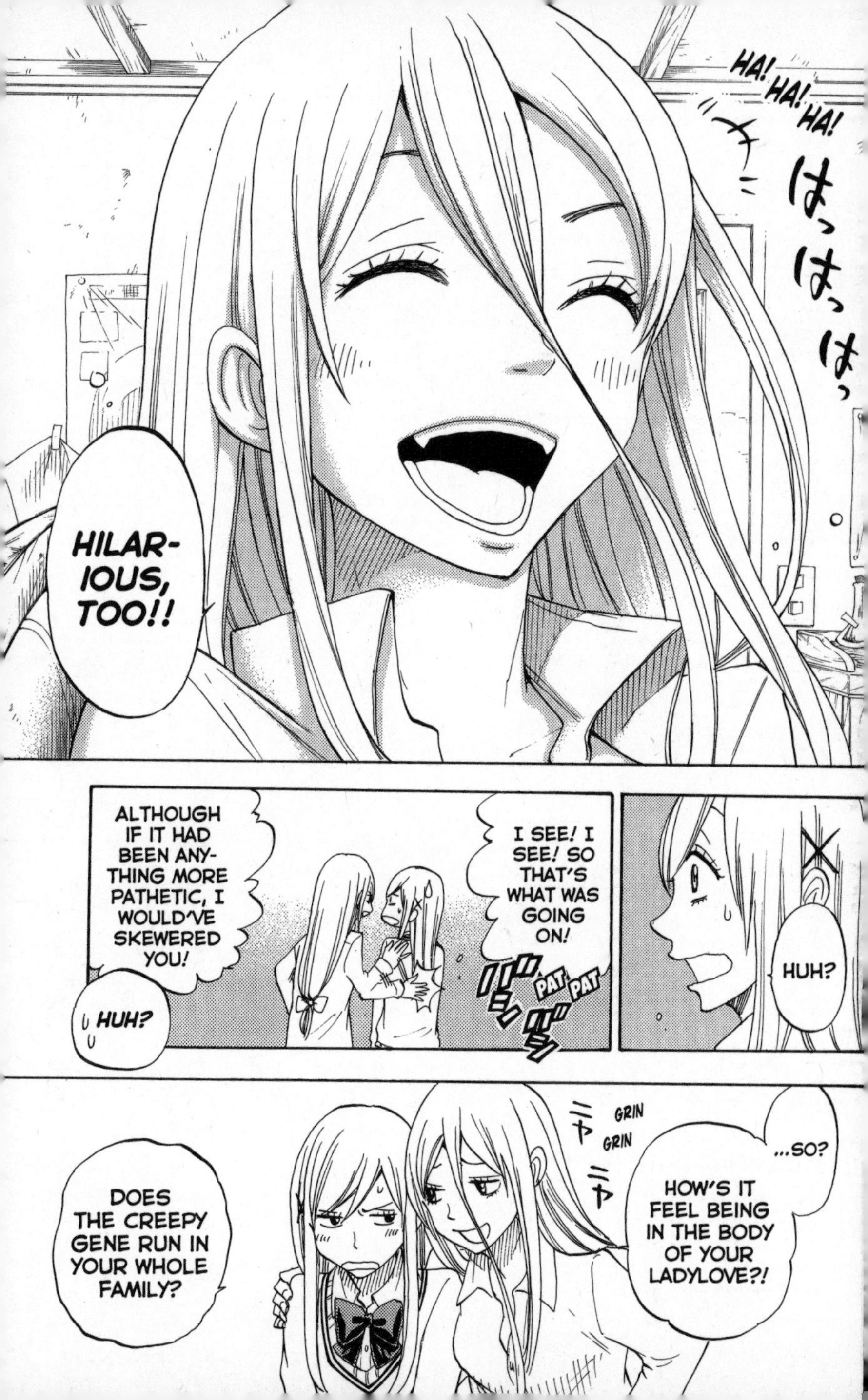
HA! HA! HA!
はっはっはっ
HILARIOUS, TOO!!
HUH?
I SEE! I SEE! SO THAT'S WHAT WAS GOING ON!
PAT PAT
ALTHOUGH IF IT HAD BEEN ANYTHING MORE PATHETIC, I WOULD'VE SKEWERED YOU!
HUH?
...SO?
HOW'S IT FEEL BEING IN THE BODY OF YOUR LADYLOVE?!
ニヤ ニヤ
GRIN GRIN
DOES THE CREEPY GENE RUN IN YOUR WHOLE FAMILY?

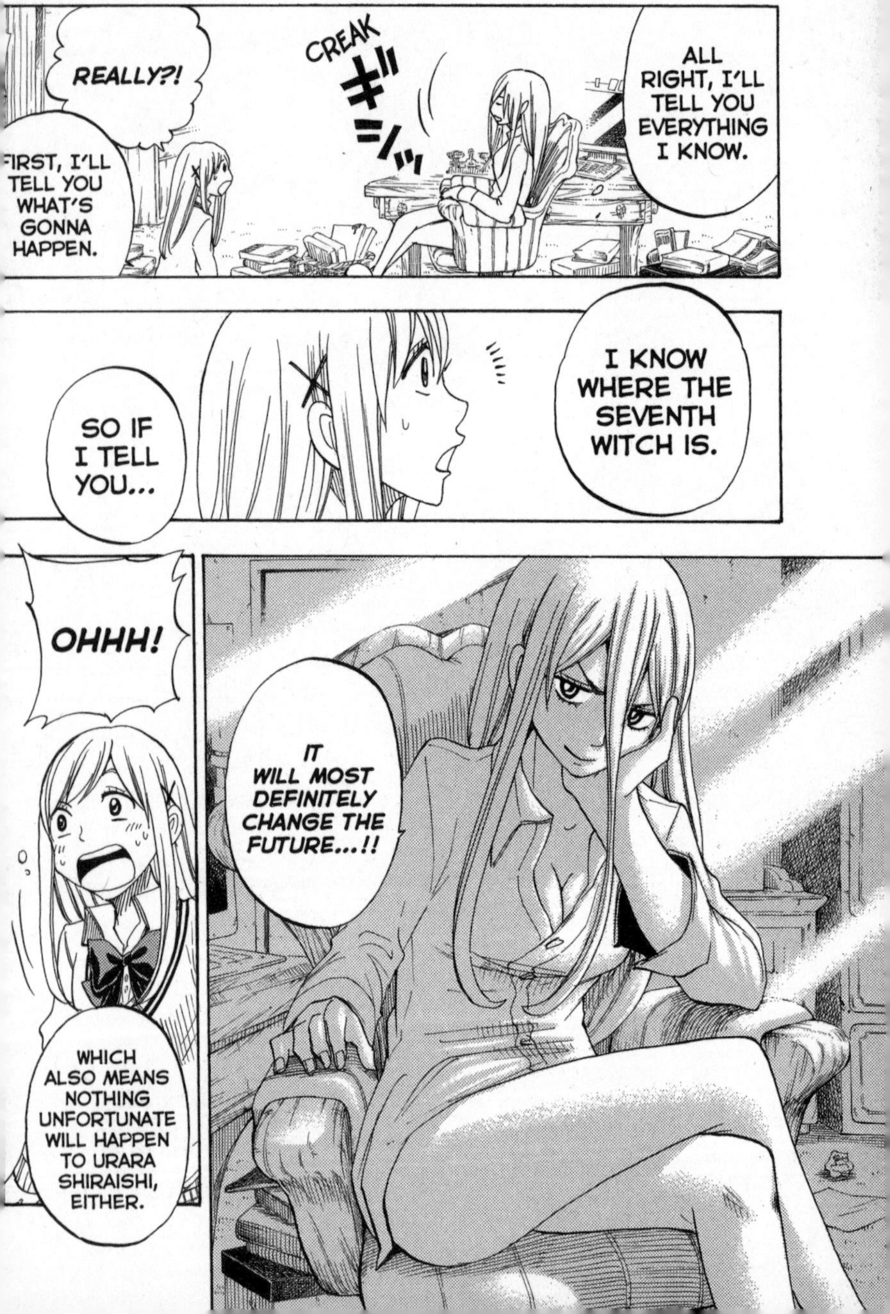
ALL RIGHT, I'LL TELL YOU EVERYTHING I KNOW.
CREAK
ギシッ
REALLY?!
FIRST, I'LL TELL YOU WHAT'S GONNA HAPPEN.
I KNOW WHERE THE SEVENTH WITCH IS.
SO IF I TELL YOU...
IT WILL MOST DEFINITELY CHANGE THE FUTURE...!!
OHHH!
WHICH ALSO MEANS NOTHING UNFORTUNATE WILL HAPPEN TO URARA SHIRAISHI, EITHER.

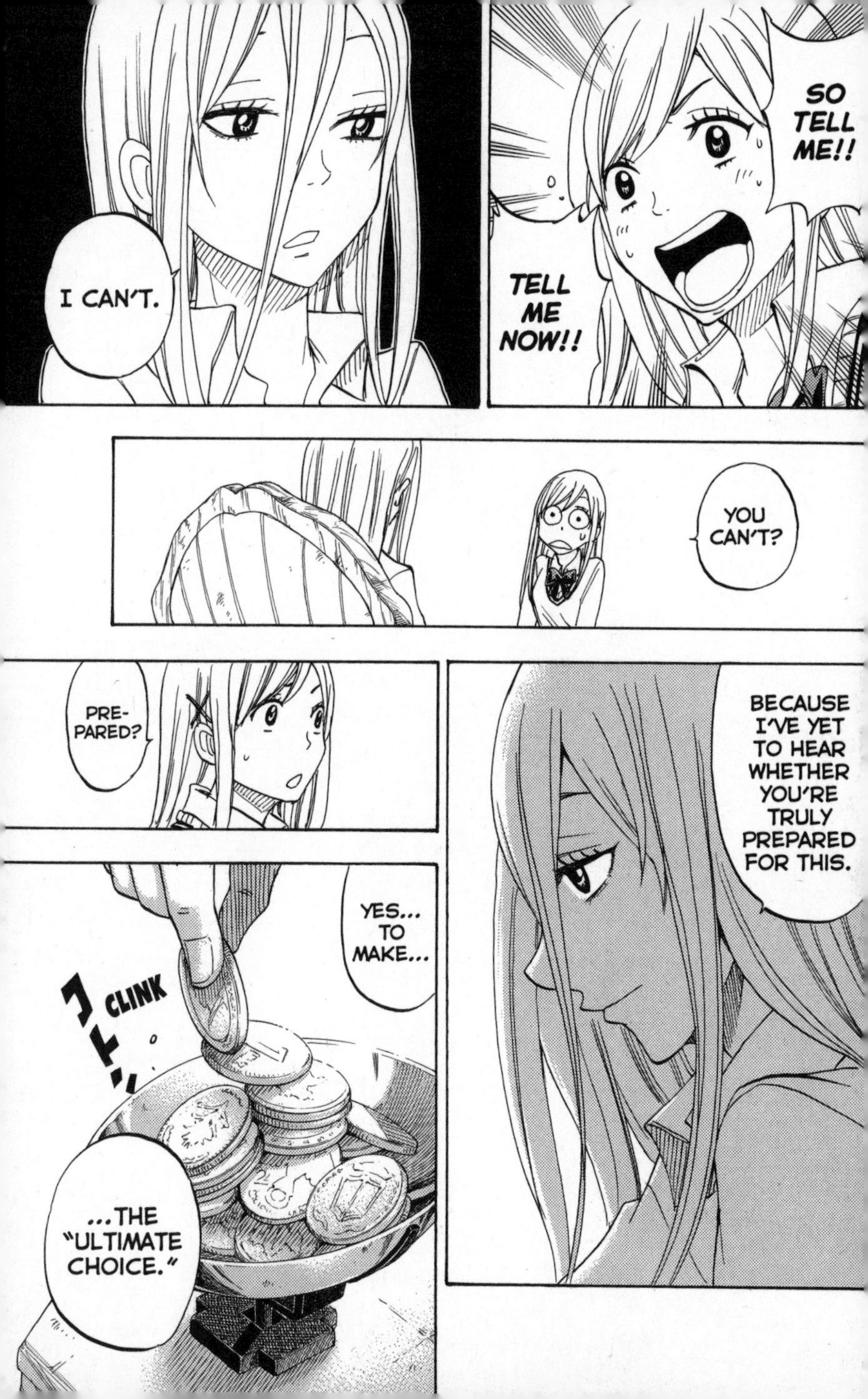
SO TELL ME!!
TELL ME NOW!!
I CAN'T.
YOU CAN'T?
BECAUSE I'VE YET TO HEAR WHETHER YOU'RE TRULY PREPARED FOR THIS.
PRE-PARED?
YES... TO MAKE...
CLINK
...THE "ULTIMATE CHOICE."

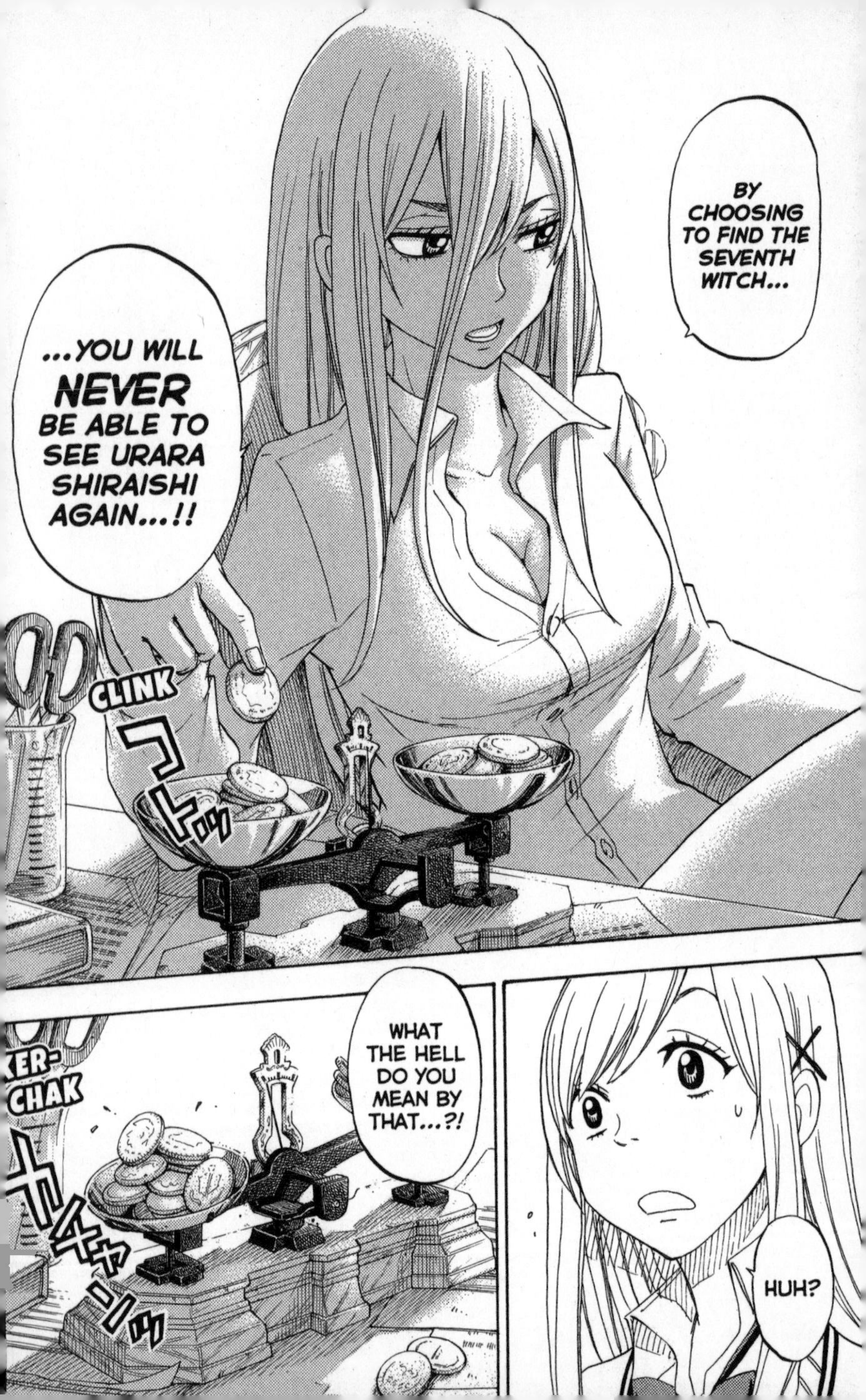
BY CHOOSING TO FIND THE SEVENTH WITCH...
...YOU WILL NEVER BE ABLE TO SEE URARA SHIRAISHI AGAIN...!!
CLINK
コトッ
HUH?
WHAT THE HELL DO YOU MEAN BY THAT...?!
KER-CHAK

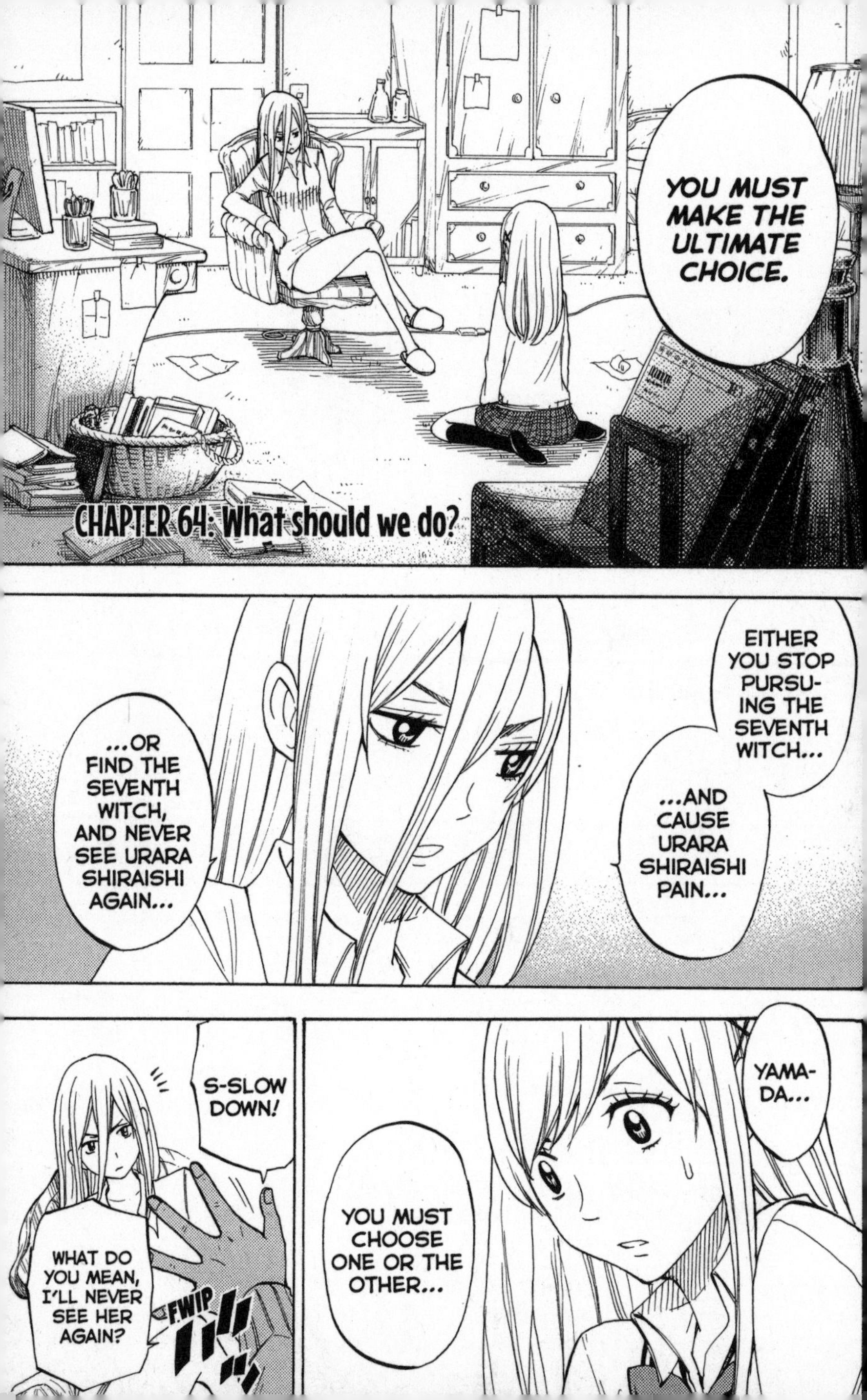
YOU MUST MAKE THE ULTIMATE CHOICE.
CHAPTER 64: What should we do?
EITHER YOU STOP PURSUING THE SEVENTH WITCH...
...AND CAUSE URARA SHIRAISHI PAIN...
...OR FIND THE SEVENTH WITCH, AND NEVER SEE URARA SHIRAISHI AGAIN...
YAMADA...
YOU MUST CHOOSE ONE OR THE OTHER...
S-SLOW DOWN!
FWIP
WHAT DO YOU MEAN, I'LL NEVER SEE HER AGAIN?

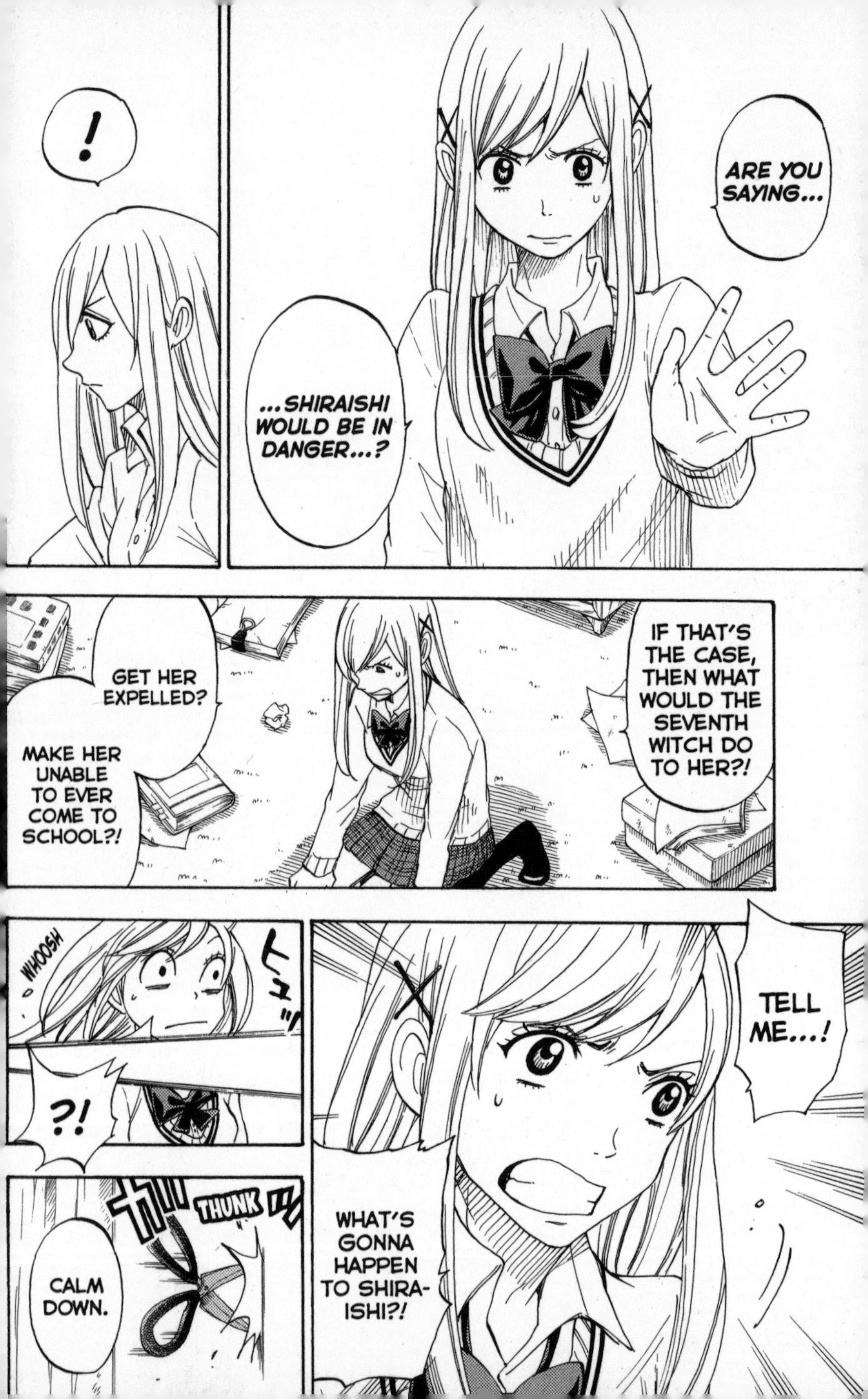
ARE YOU SAYING...
...SHIRAISHI WOULD BE IN DANGER...?
!
IF THAT'S THE CASE, THEN WHAT WOULD THE SEVENTH WITCH DO TO HER?!
GET HER EXPELLED?
MAKE HER UNABLE TO EVER COME TO SCHOOL?!
TELL ME...!
WHAT'S GONNA HAPPEN TO SHIRA-ISHI?!
WHOOSH
?!
THUNK
CALM DOWN.

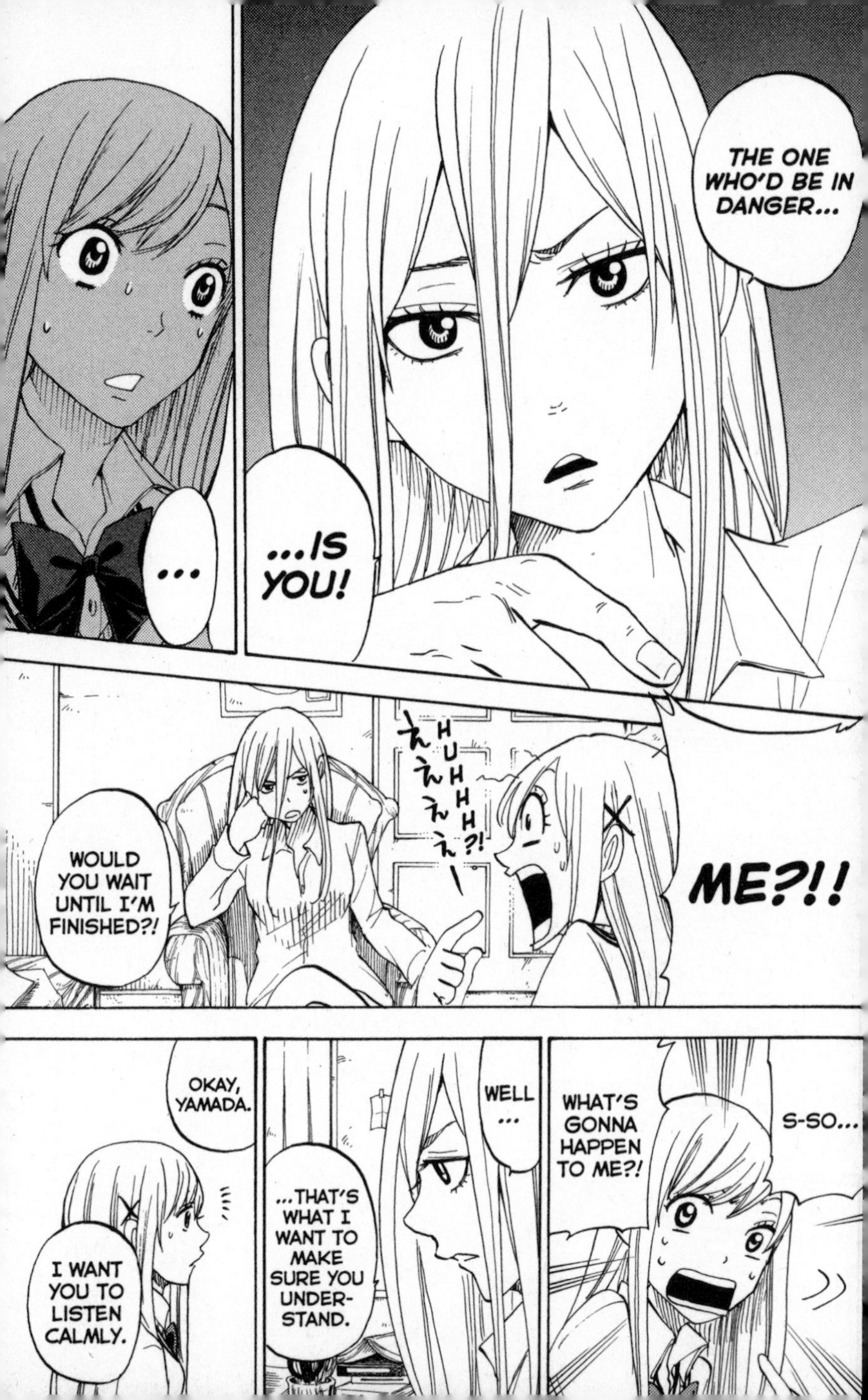
THE ONE WHO'D BE IN DANGER...
...IS YOU!
...
ME?!!
えええええー
HUHHHH?!
WOULD YOU WAIT UNTIL I'M FINISHED?!
S-SO...
WHAT'S GONNA HAPPEN TO ME?!
WELL...
...THAT'S WHAT I WANT TO MAKE SURE YOU UNDER-STAND.
OKAY, YAMADA.
I WANT YOU TO LISTEN CALMLY.

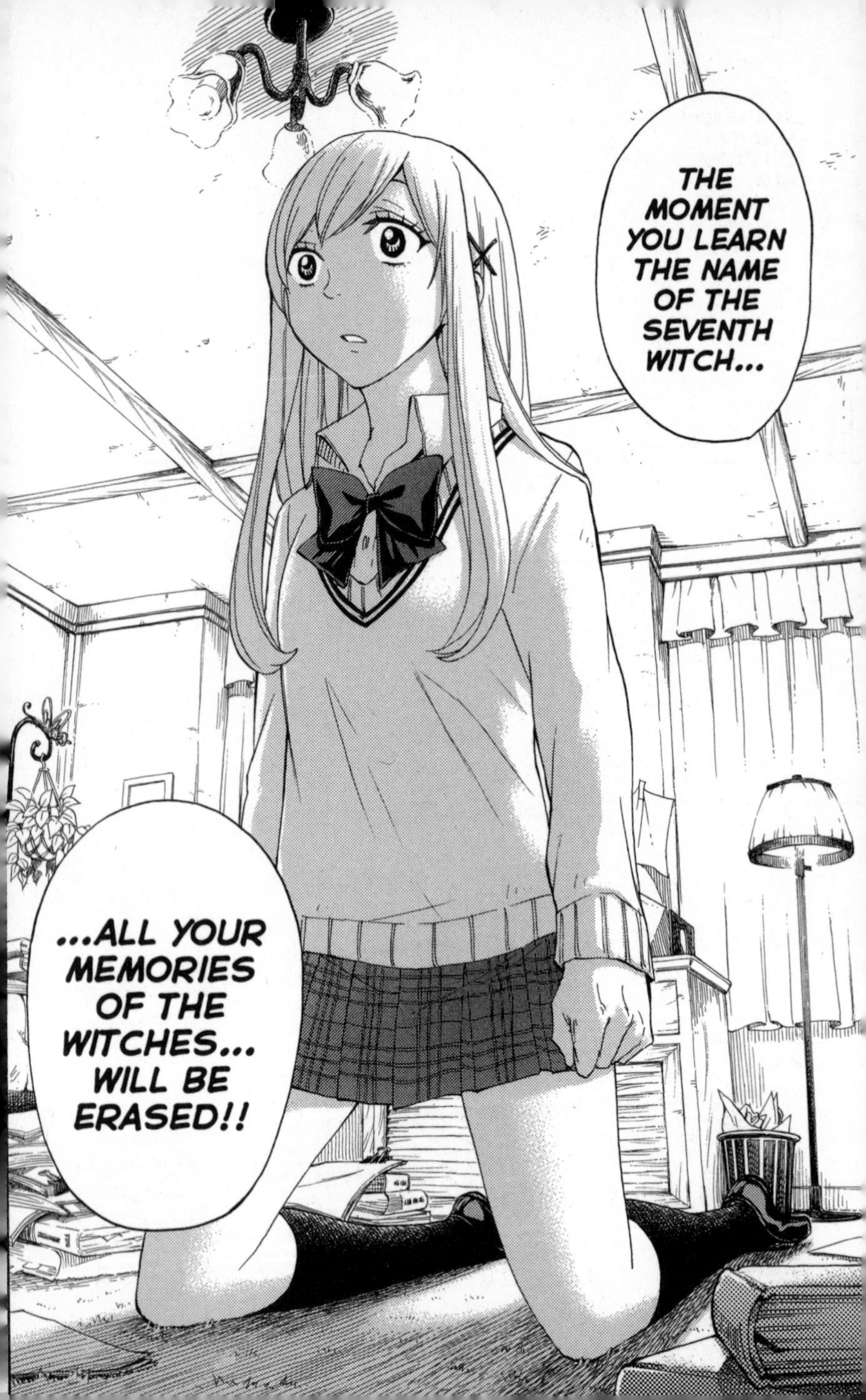
THE MOMENT YOU LEARN THE NAME OF THE SEVENTH WITCH...
...ALL YOUR MEMORIES OF THE WITCHES... WILL BE ERASED!!

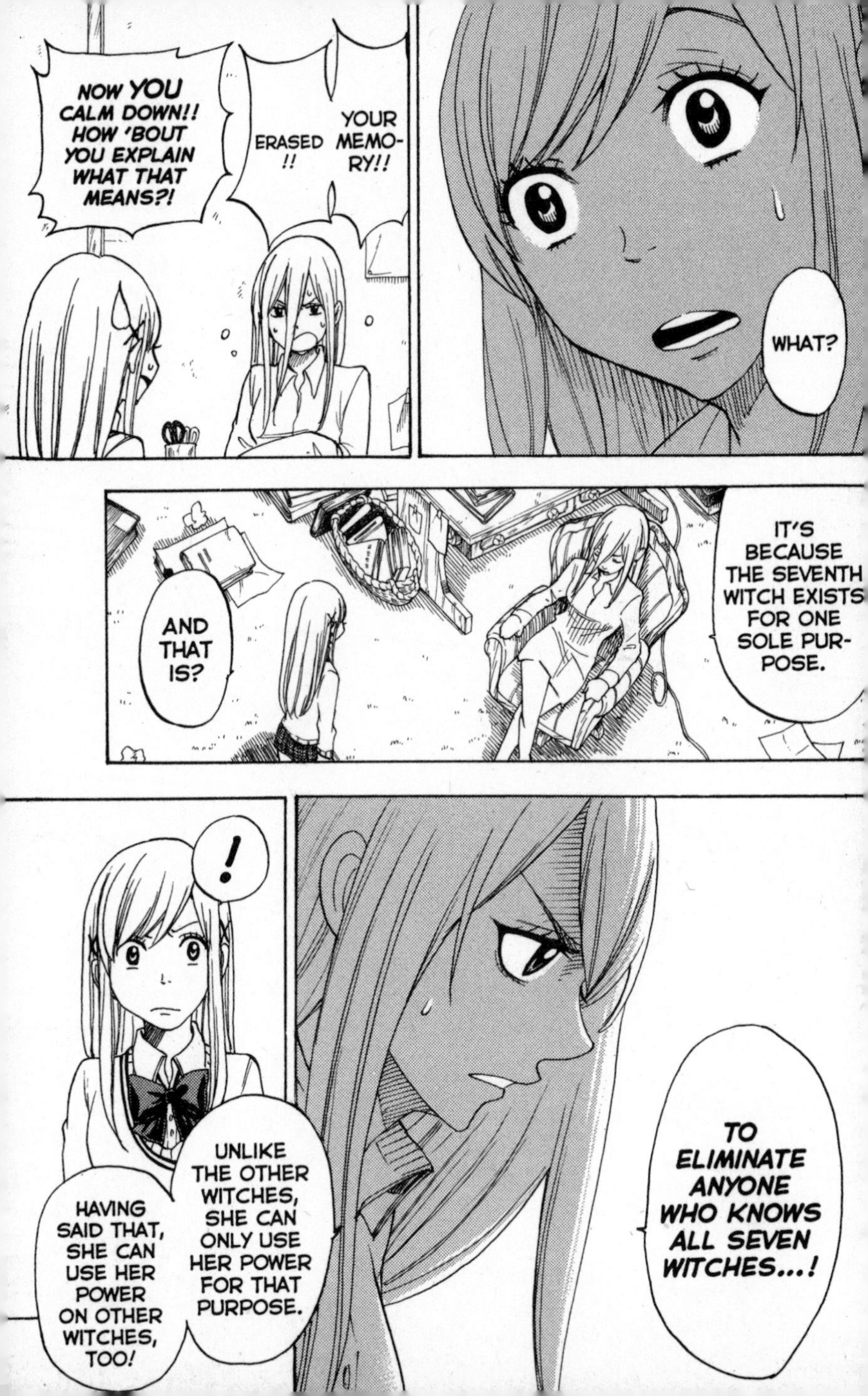
WHAT?
YOUR MEMORY!!
ERASED!!
NOW YOU CALM DOWN!! HOW 'BOUT YOU EXPLAIN WHAT THAT MEANS?!
IT'S BECAUSE THE SEVENTH WITCH EXISTS FOR ONE SOLE PURPOSE.
AND THAT IS?
TO ELIMINATE ANYONE WHO KNOWS ALL SEVEN WITCHES...!
!
UNLIKE THE OTHER WITCHES, SHE CAN ONLY USE HER POWER FOR THAT PURPOSE.
HAVING SAID THAT, SHE CAN USE HER POWER ON OTHER WITCHES, TOO!

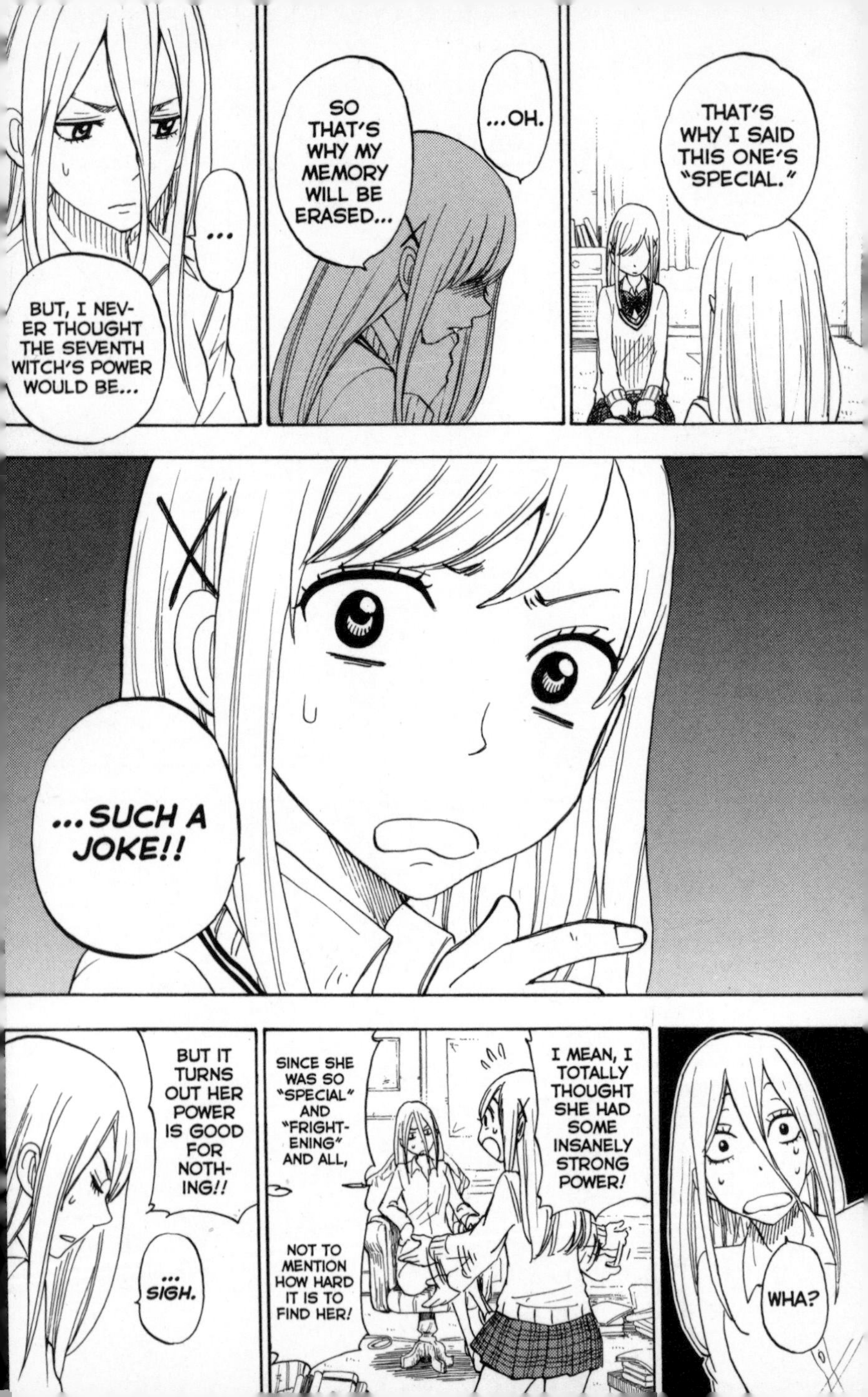
THAT'S WHY I SAID THIS ONE'S "SPECIAL."
...OH.
SO THAT'S WHY MY MEMORY WILL BE ERASED...
...
BUT, I NEVER THOUGHT THE SEVENTH WITCH'S POWER WOULD BE...
...SUCH A JOKE!!
WHA?
I MEAN, I TOTALLY THOUGHT SHE HAD SOME INSANELY STRONG POWER!
SINCE SHE WAS SO "SPECIAL" AND "FRIGHTENING" AND ALL,
NOT TO MENTION HOW HARD IT IS TO FIND HER!
BUT IT TURNS OUT HER POWER IS GOOD FOR NOTHING!!
...SIGH.

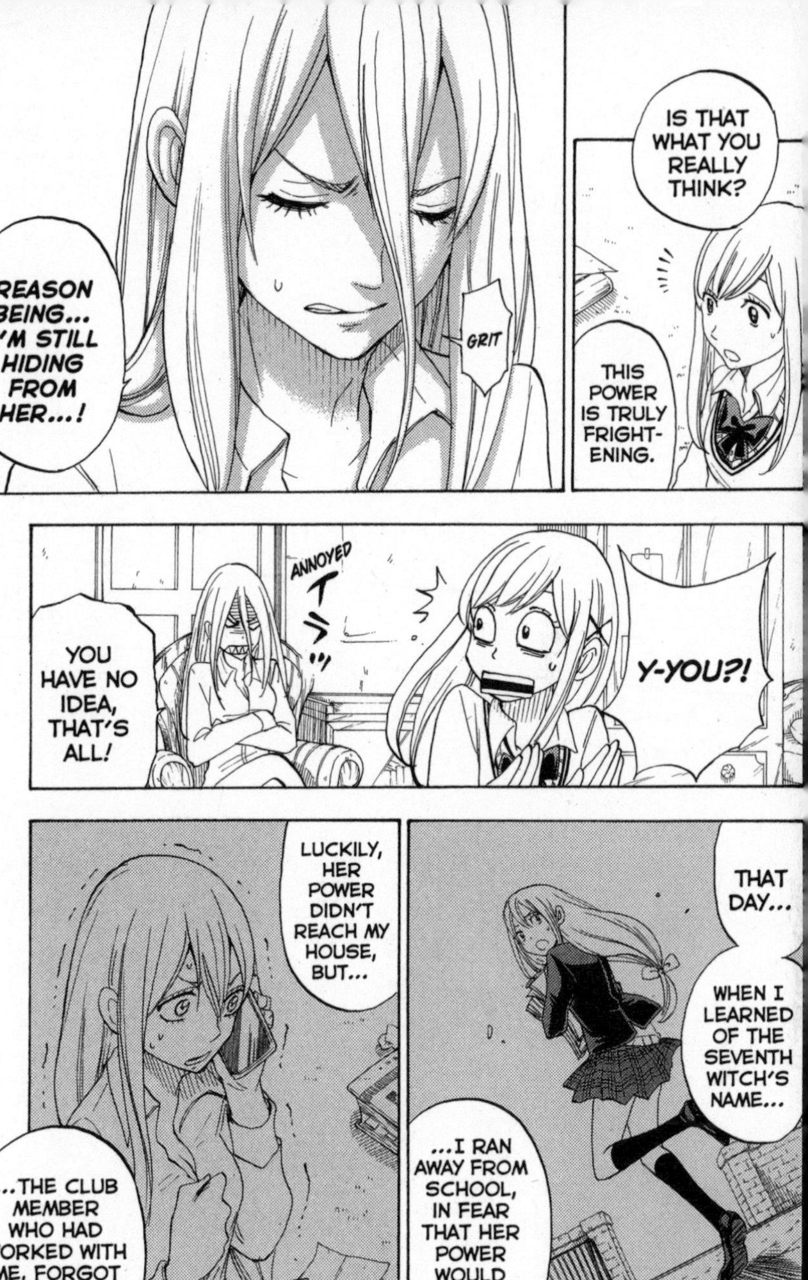
IS THAT WHAT YOU REALLY THINK?
THIS POWER IS TRULY FRIGHT-ENING.
GRIT
REASON BEING... I'M STILL HIDING FROM HER...!
Y-YOU?!
ANNOYED
YOU HAVE NO IDEA, THAT'S ALL!
THAT DAY...
WHEN I LEARNED OF THE SEVENTH WITCH'S NAME...
...I RAN AWAY FROM SCHOOL, IN FEAR THAT HER POWER WOULD GET ME.
LUCKILY, HER POWER DIDN'T REACH MY HOUSE, BUT...
...THE CLUB MEMBER WHO HAD WORKED WITH ME, FORGOT EVERYTHING ABOUT THE WITCHES.

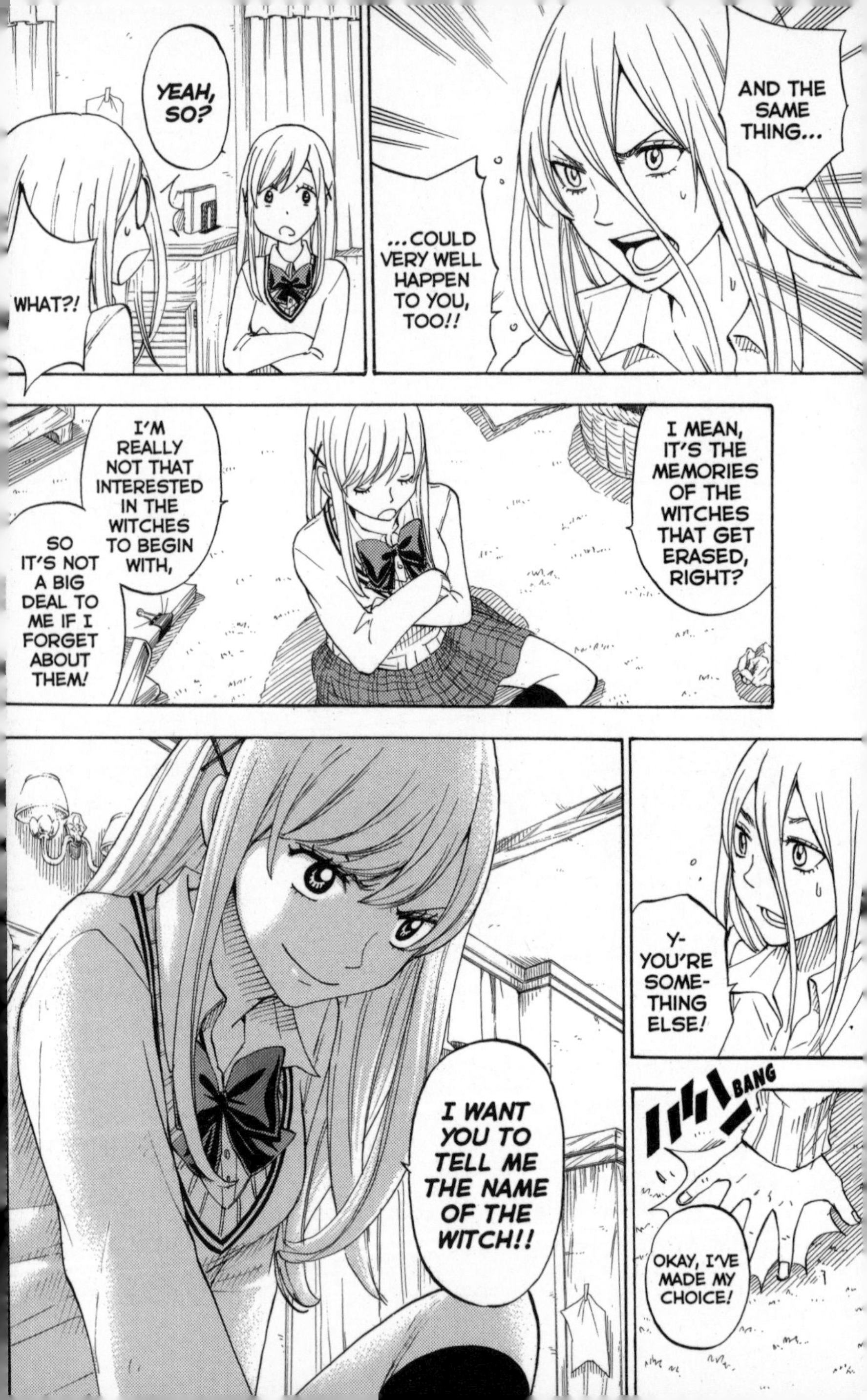
AND THE SAME THING...
...COULD VERY WELL HAPPEN TO YOU, TOO!!
YEAH, SO?
WHAT?!
I MEAN, IT'S THE MEMORIES OF THE WITCHES THAT GET ERASED, RIGHT?
I'M REALLY NOT THAT INTERESTED IN THE WITCHES TO BEGIN WITH,
SO IT'S NOT A BIG DEAL TO ME IF I FORGET ABOUT THEM!
Y- YOU'RE SOME-THING ELSE!
BANG
OKAY, I'VE MADE MY CHOICE!
I WANT YOU TO TELL ME THE NAME OF THE WITCH!!

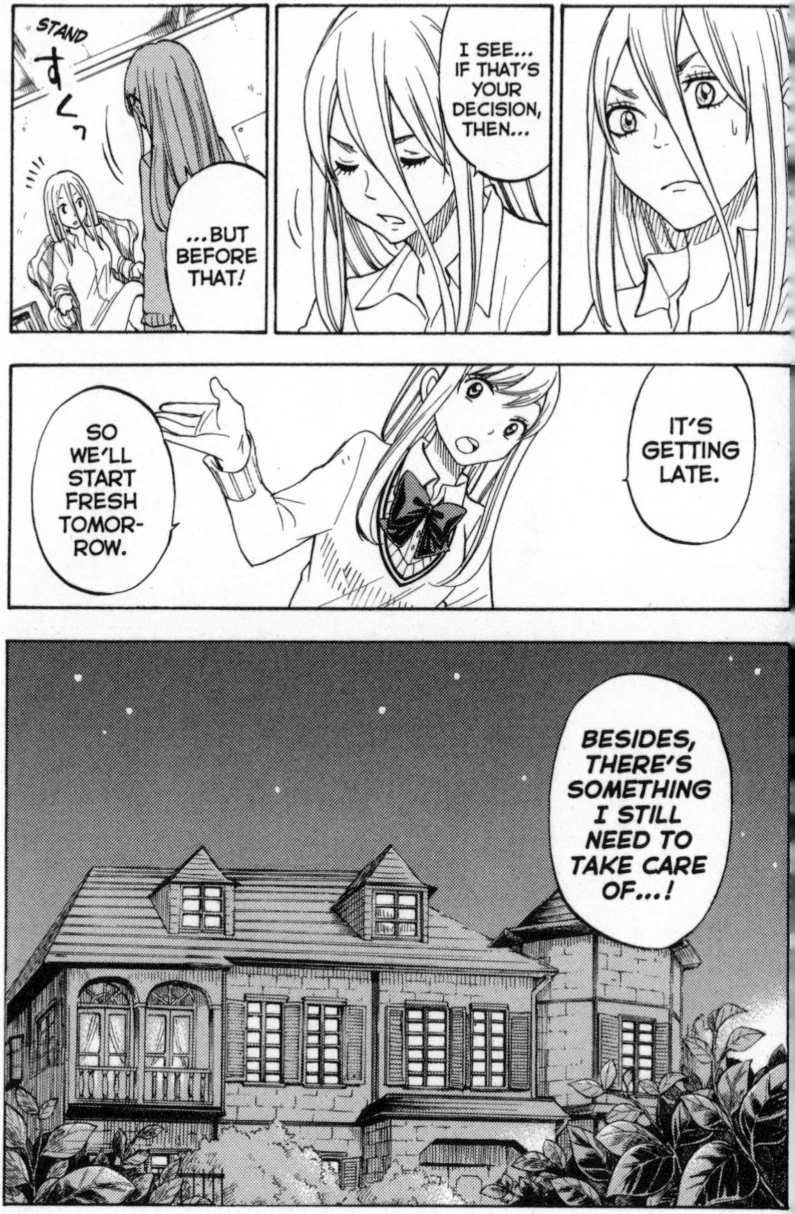
I SEE... IF THAT'S YOUR DECISION, THEN...
STAND
すくっ
...BUT BEFORE THAT!
IT'S GETTING LATE.
SO WE'LL START FRESH TOMOR-ROW.
BESIDES, THERE'S SOMETHING I STILL NEED TO TAKE CARE OF...!

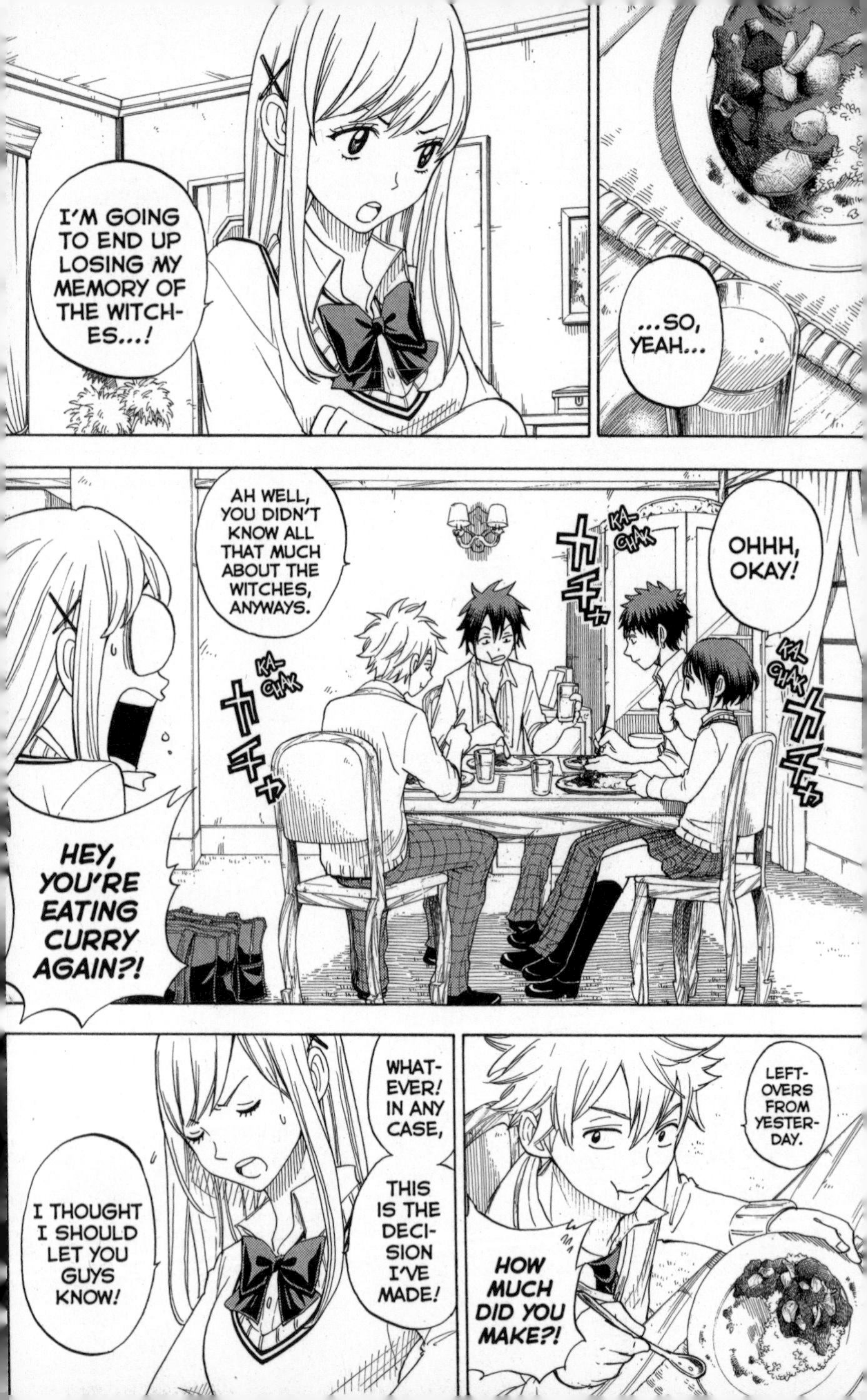
...SO, YEAH...
I'M GOING TO END UP LOSING MY MEMORY OF THE WITCHES...!
OHHH, OKAY!
KA-CHAK
KA-CHAK
AH WELL, YOU DIDN'T KNOW ALL THAT MUCH ABOUT THE WITCHES, ANYWAYS.
KA-CHAK
HEY, YOU'RE EATING CURRY AGAIN?!
LEFT-OVERS FROM YESTER-DAY.
HOW MUCH DID YOU MAKE?!
WHAT-EVER! IN ANY CASE,
THIS IS THE DECISION I'VE MADE!
I THOUGHT I SHOULD LET YOU GUYS KNOW!

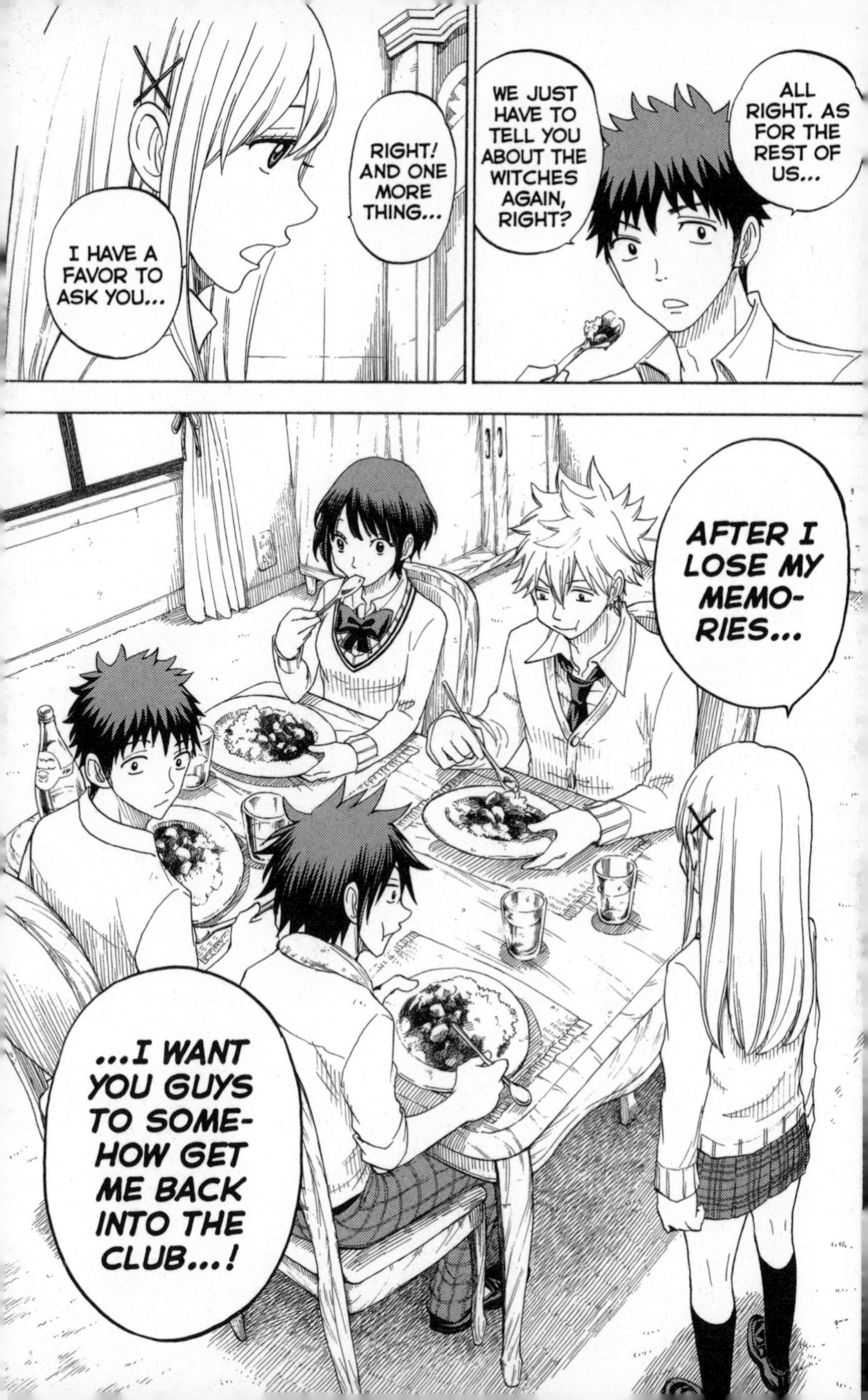
ALL RIGHT. AS FOR THE REST OF US...
WE JUST HAVE TO TELL YOU ABOUT THE WITCHES AGAIN, RIGHT?
RIGHT! AND ONE MORE THING...
I HAVE A FAVOR TO ASK YOU...
AFTER I LOSE MY MEMO-RIES...
...I WANT YOU GUYS TO SOME-HOW GET ME BACK INTO THE CLUB...!

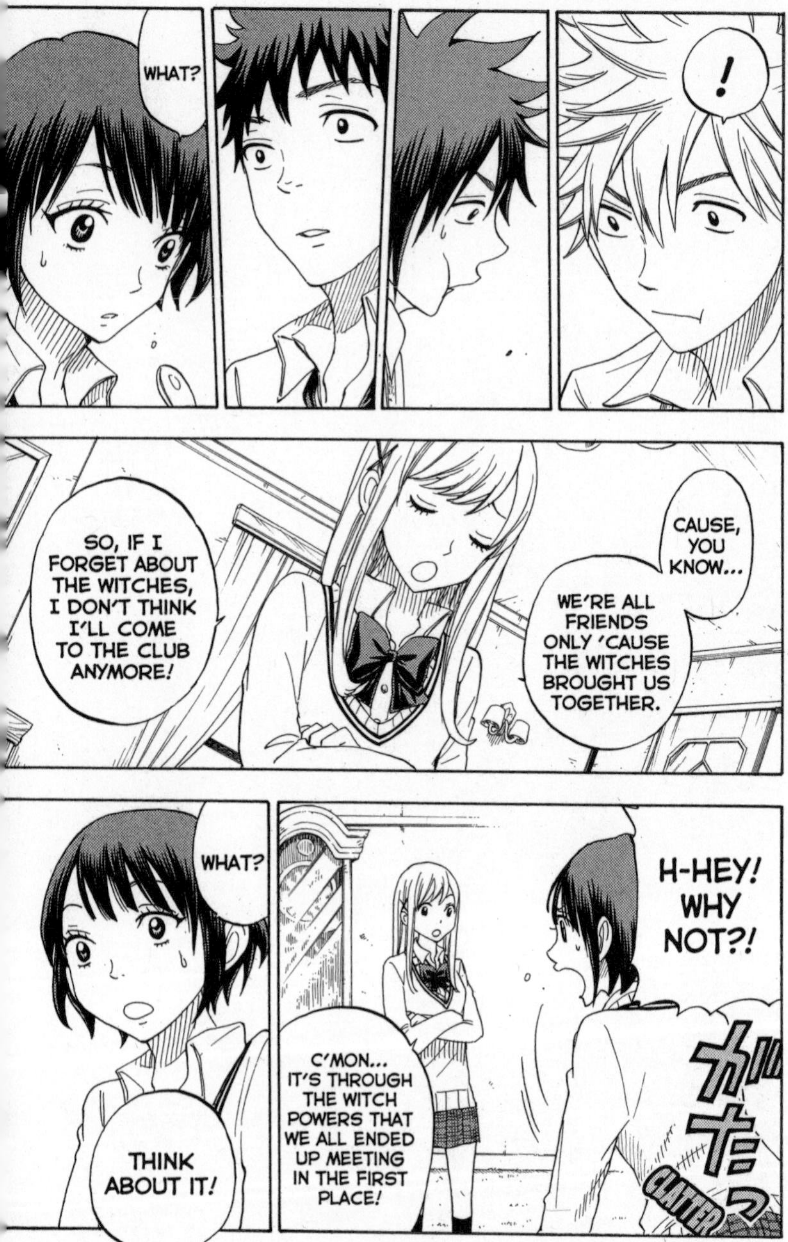
!
WHAT?
CAUSE, YOU KNOW...
WE'RE ALL FRIENDS ONLY 'CAUSE THE WITCHES BROUGHT US TOGETHER.
SO, IF I FORGET ABOUT THE WITCHES, I DON'T THINK I'LL COME TO THE CLUB ANYMORE!
H-HEY! WHY NOT?!
CLATTER
C'MON... IT'S THROUGH THE WITCH POWERS THAT WE ALL ENDED UP MEETING IN THE FIRST PLACE!
WHAT?
THINK ABOUT IT!

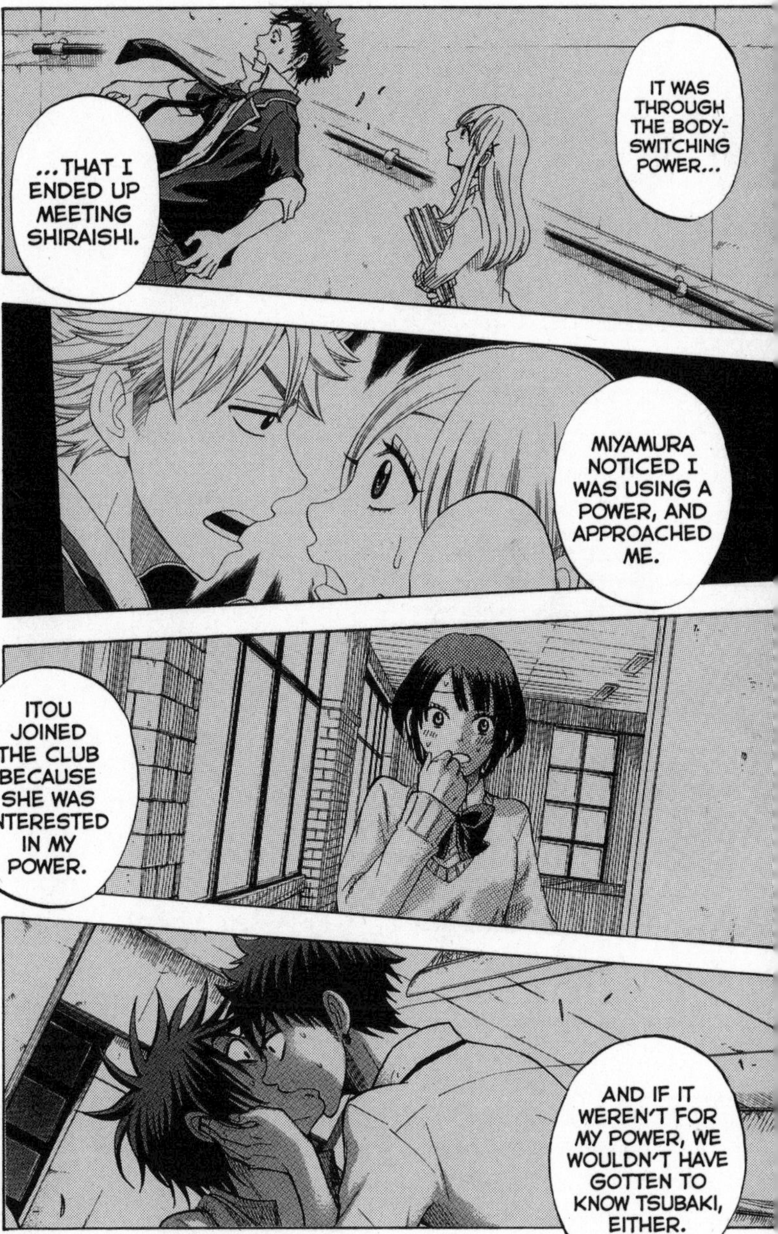
IT WAS THROUGH THE BODY-SWITCHING POWER...
...THAT I ENDED UP MEETING SHIRAISHI.
MIYAMURA NOTICED I WAS USING A POWER, AND APPROACHED ME.
ITOU JOINED THE CLUB BECAUSE SHE WAS INTERESTED IN MY POWER.
AND IF IT WEREN'T FOR MY POWER, WE WOULDN'T HAVE GOTTEN TO KNOW TSUBAKI, EITHER.

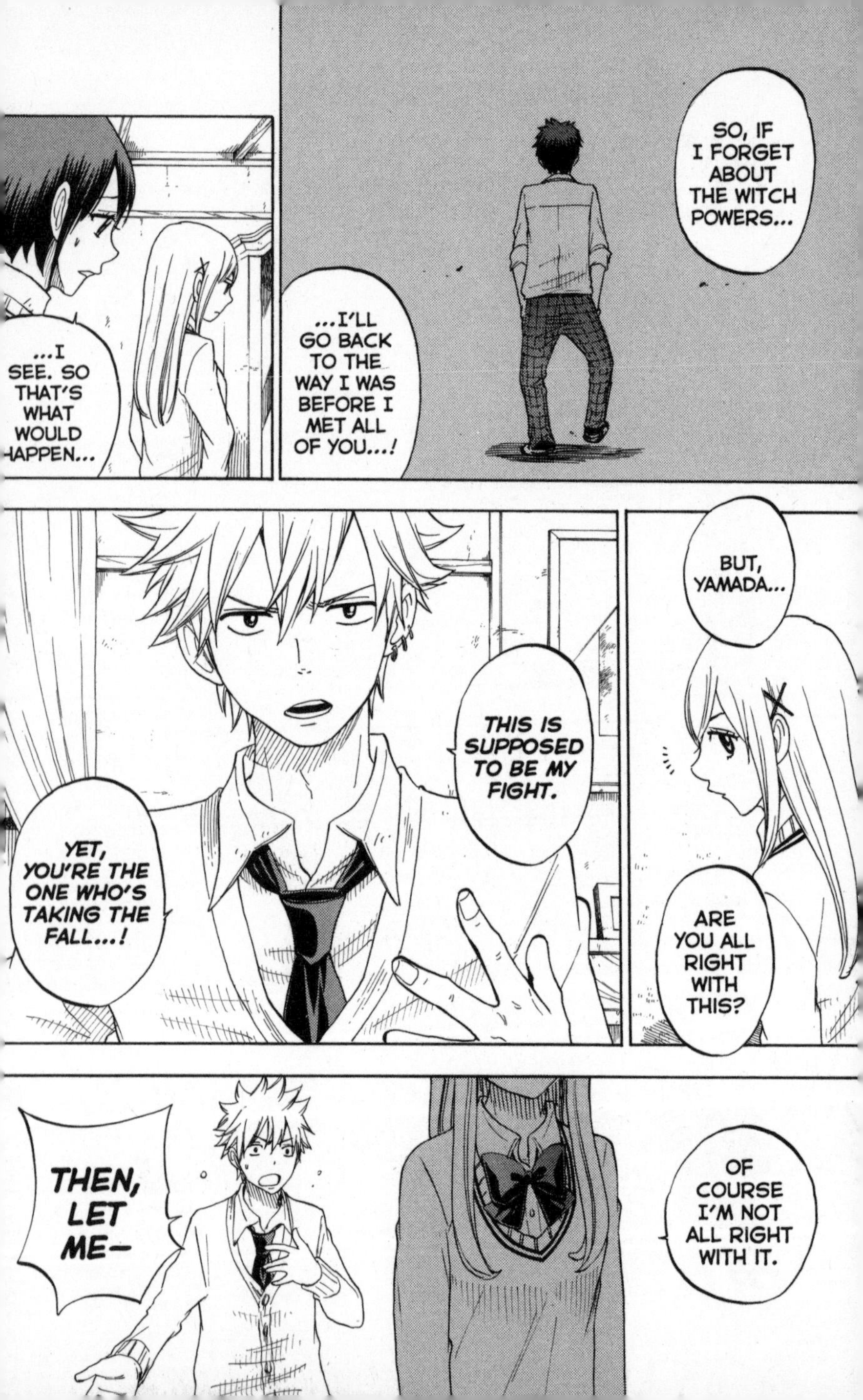
SO, IF I FORGET ABOUT THE WITCH POWERS...
...I'LL GO BACK TO THE WAY I WAS BEFORE I MET ALL OF YOU...!
...I SEE. SO THAT'S WHAT WOULD HAPPEN...
BUT, YAMADA...
ARE YOU ALL RIGHT WITH THIS?
THIS IS SUPPOSED TO BE MY FIGHT.
YET, YOU'RE THE ONE WHO'S TAKING THE FALL...!
OF COURSE I'M NOT ALL RIGHT WITH IT.
THEN, LET ME—

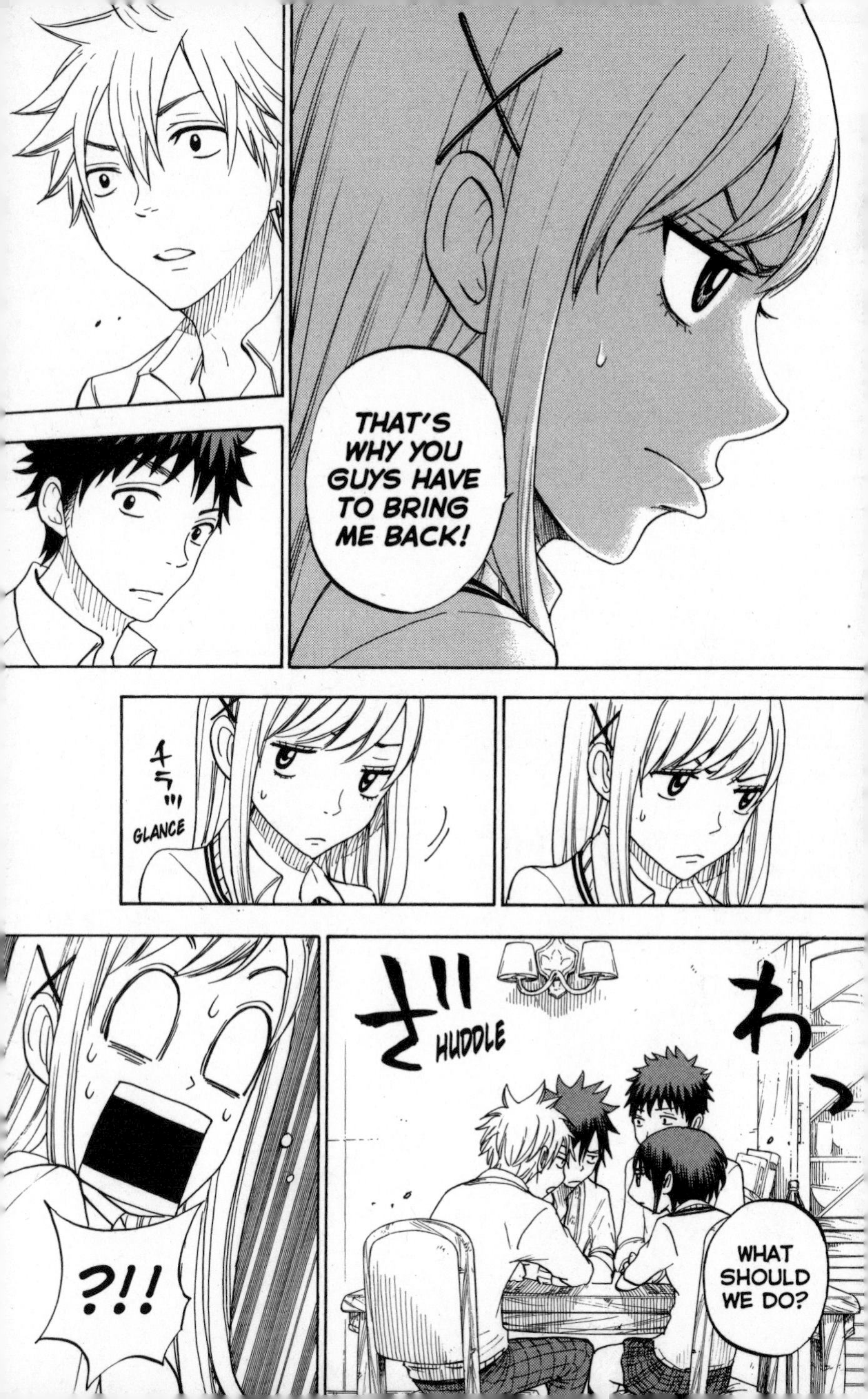
THAT'S WHY YOU GUYS HAVE TO BRING ME BACK!
チラッ
GLANCE
わっ
ざ
HUDDLE
WHAT SHOULD WE DO?
?!!

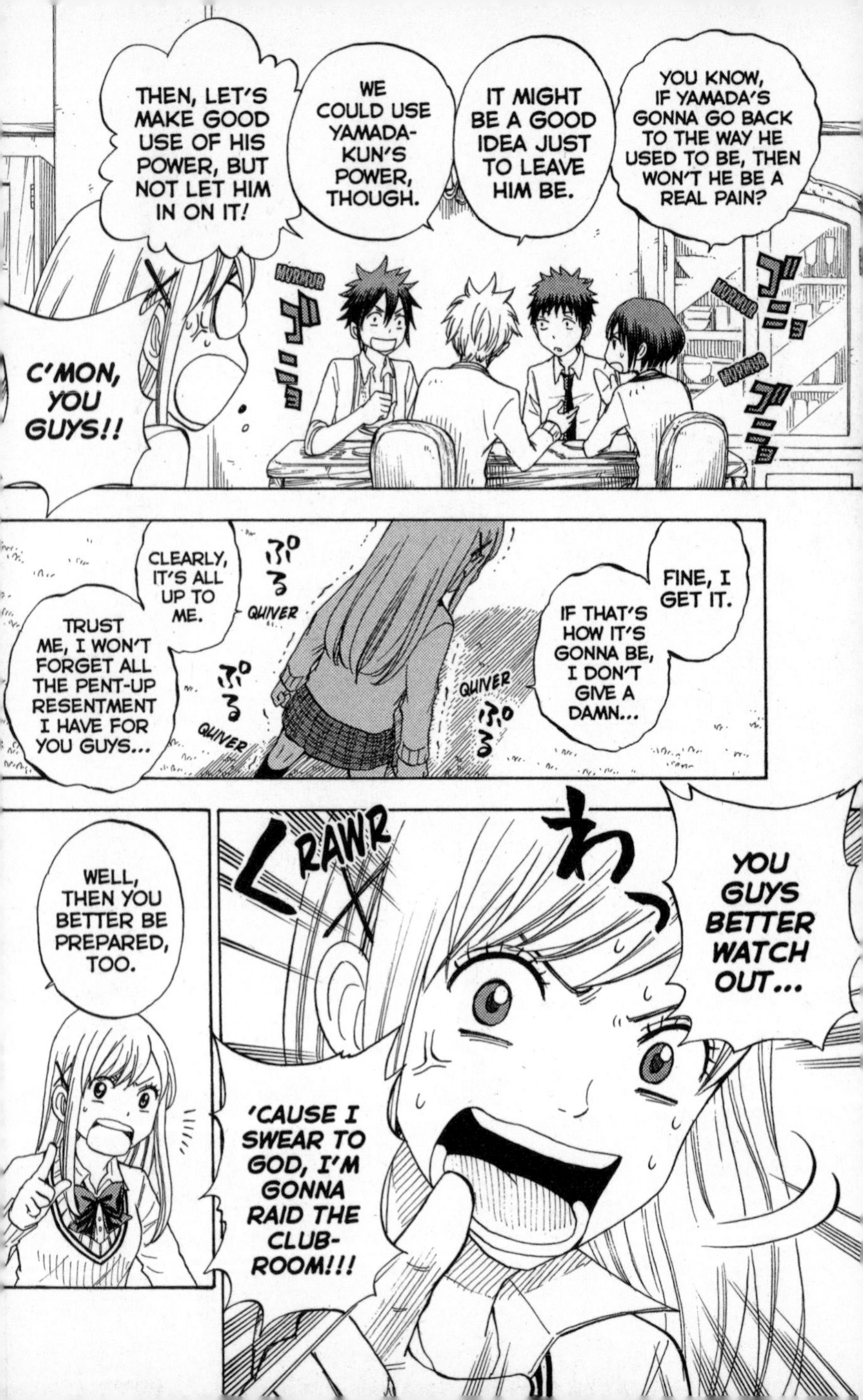
YOU KNOW, IF YAMADA'S GONNA GO BACK TO THE WAY HE USED TO BE, THEN WON'T HE BE A REAL PAIN?
IT MIGHT BE A GOOD IDEA JUST TO LEAVE HIM BE.
WE COULD USE YAMADA-KUN'S POWER, THOUGH.
THEN, LET'S MAKE GOOD USE OF HIS POWER, BUT NOT LET HIM IN ON IT!
MURMUR ゴニョ
MURMUR ゴニョ
MURMUR ゴニョ
C'MON, YOU GUYS!!
FINE, I GET IT.
IF THAT'S HOW IT'S GONNA BE, I DON'T GIVE A DAMN...
QUIVER ぷる
QUIVER ぷる
QUIVER ぷる
CLEARLY, IT'S ALL UP TO ME.
TRUST ME, I WON'T FORGET ALL THE PENT-UP RESENTMENT I HAVE FOR YOU GUYS...
わっ RAWR
YOU GUYS BETTER WATCH OUT...
'CAUSE I SWEAR TO GOD, I'M GONNA RAID THE CLUB-ROOM!!!
WELL, THEN YOU BETTER BE PREPARED, TOO.

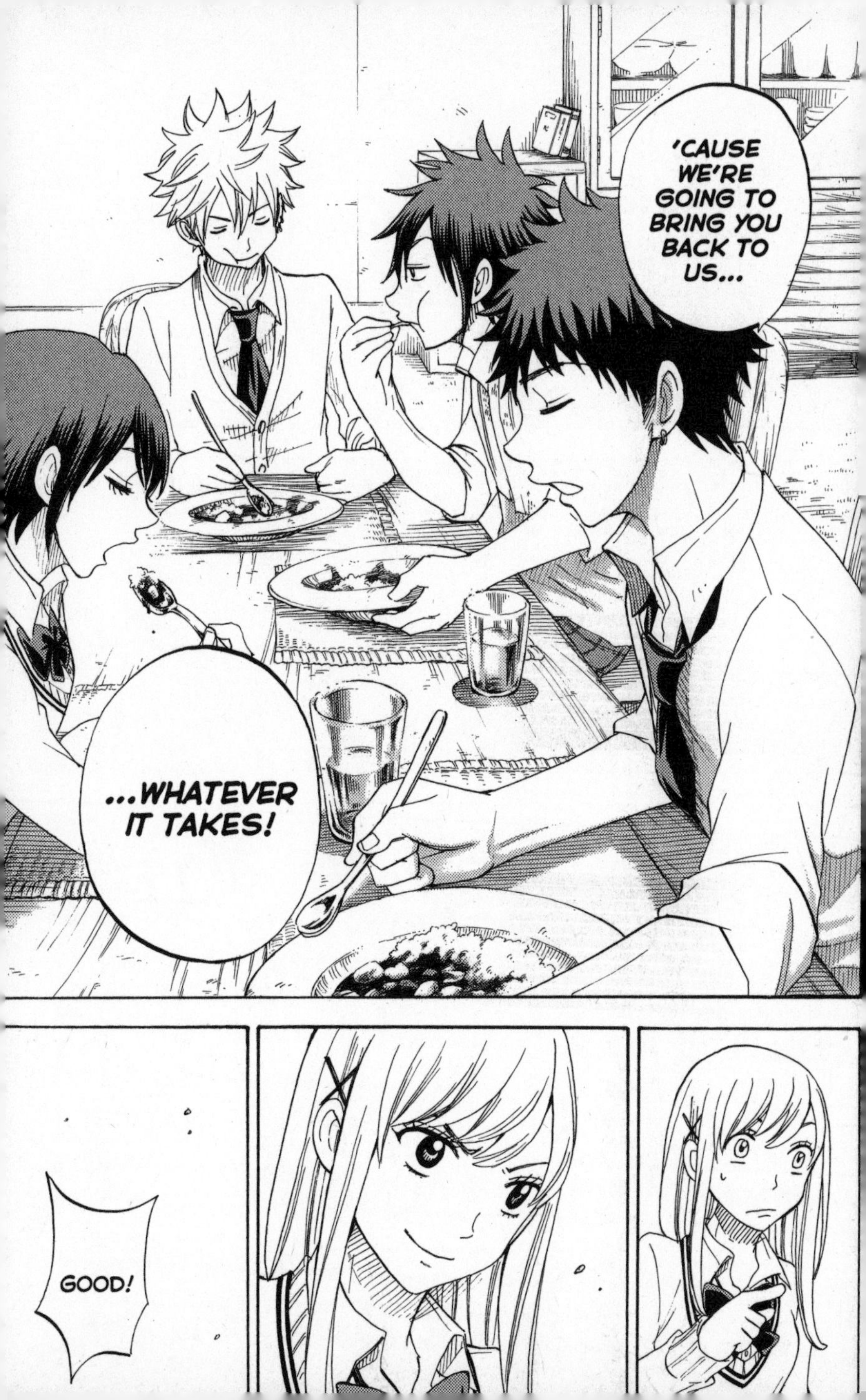
'CAUSE WE'RE GOING TO BRING YOU BACK TO US...
...WHATEVER IT TAKES!
GOOD!

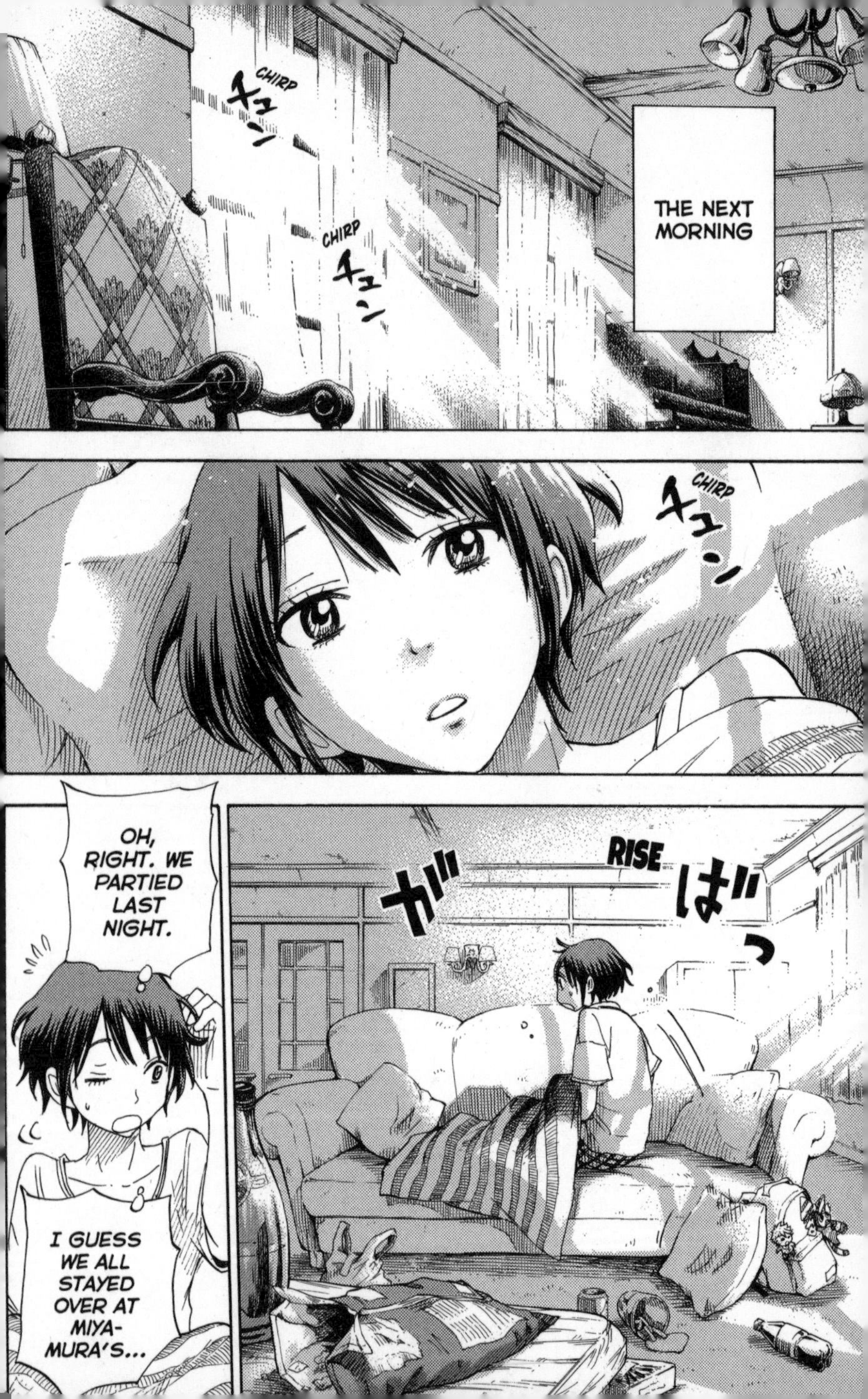
THE NEXT MORNING
CHIRP
チュン
CHIRP
チュン
CHIRP
チュン
RISE
ガばっ
OH, RIGHT. WE PARTIED LAST NIGHT.
I GUESS WE ALL STAYED OVER AT MIYA-MURA'S...

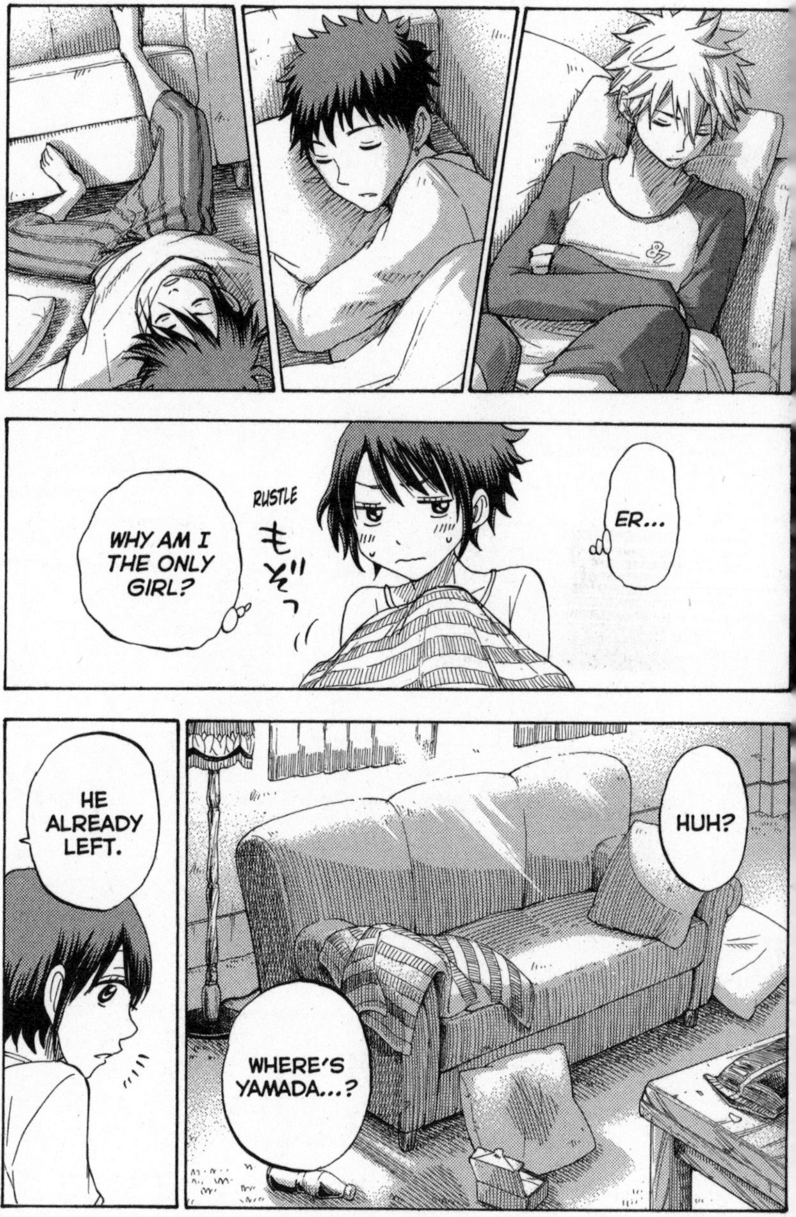
ER...
RUSTLE
もぞっ
WHY AM I THE ONLY GIRL?
HUH?
WHERE'S YAMADA...?
HE ALREADY LEFT.

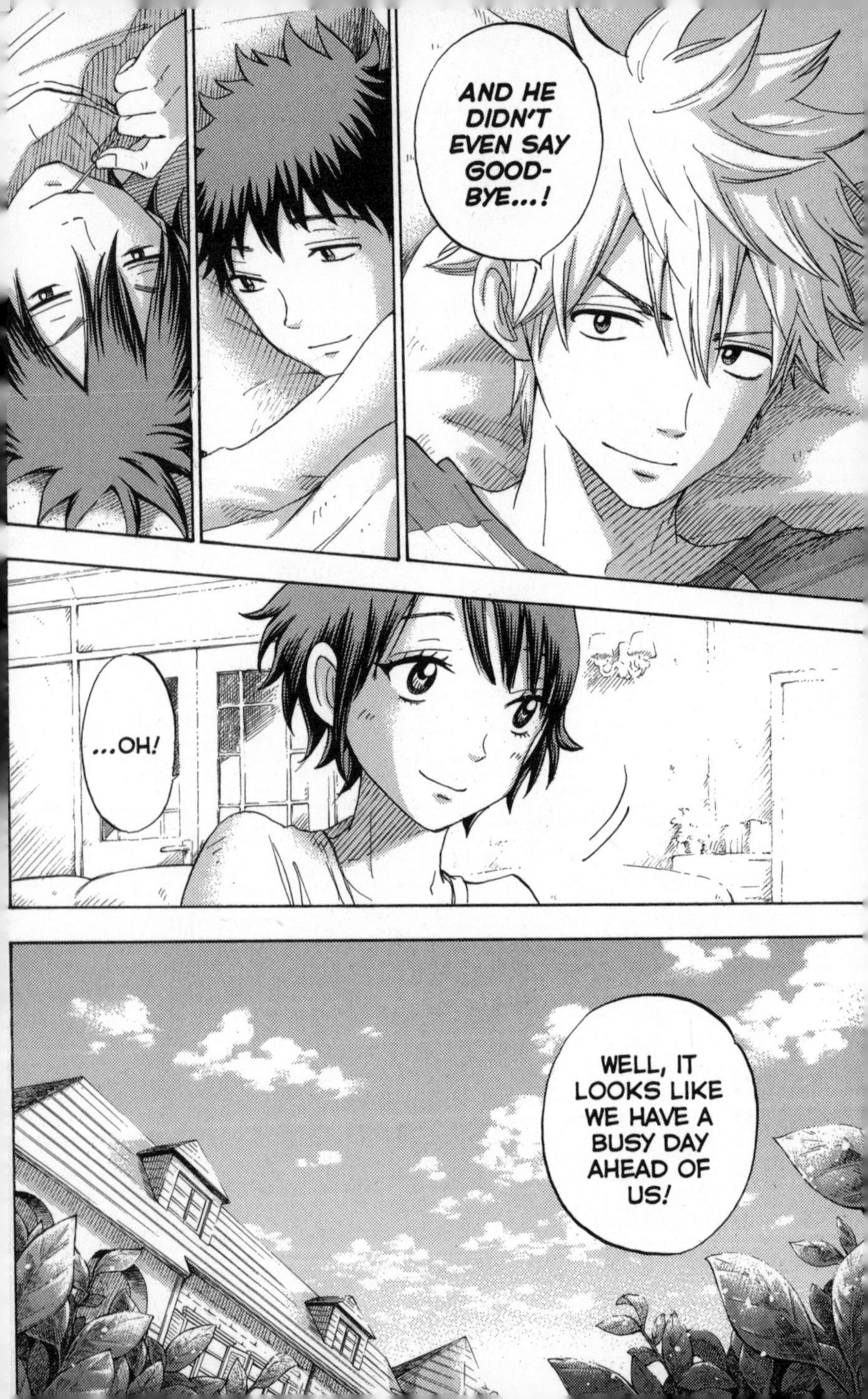
AND HE DIDN'T EVEN SAY GOOD-BYE...!
...OH!
WELL, IT LOOKS LIKE WE HAVE A BUSY DAY AHEAD OF US!

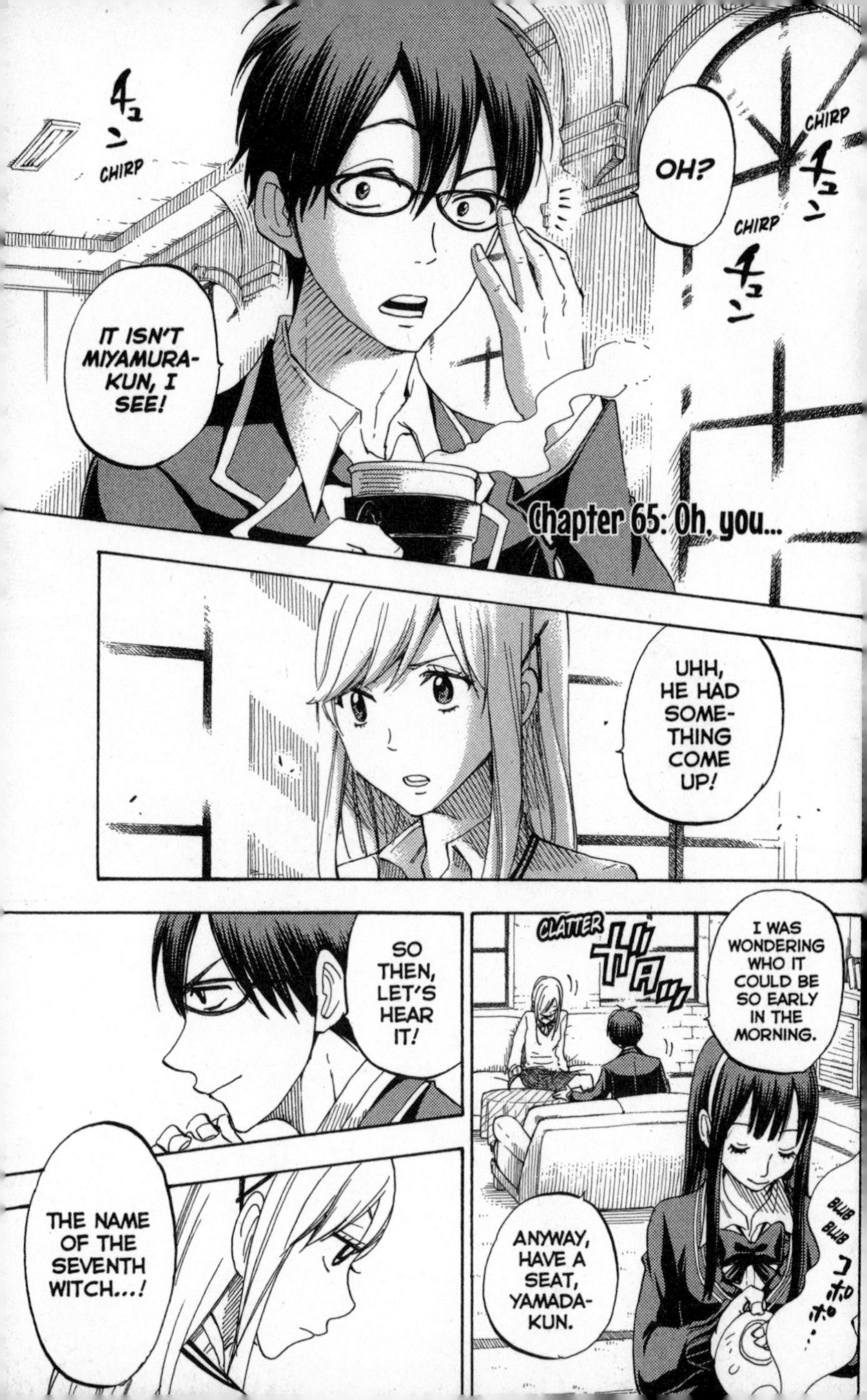

CHIRP
チュン
CHIRP
チュン
OH?
チュン
CHIRP
IT ISN'T MIYAMURA-KUN, I SEE!
Chapter 65: Oh, you...
UHH, HE HAD SOME-THING COME UP!
I WAS WONDERING WHO IT COULD BE SO EARLY IN THE MORNING.
CLATTER
ガタッ
ANYWAY, HAVE A SEAT, YAMADA-KUN.
BLUB BLUB
コポポ…
SO THEN, LET'S HEAR IT!
THE NAME OF THE SEVENTH WITCH...!

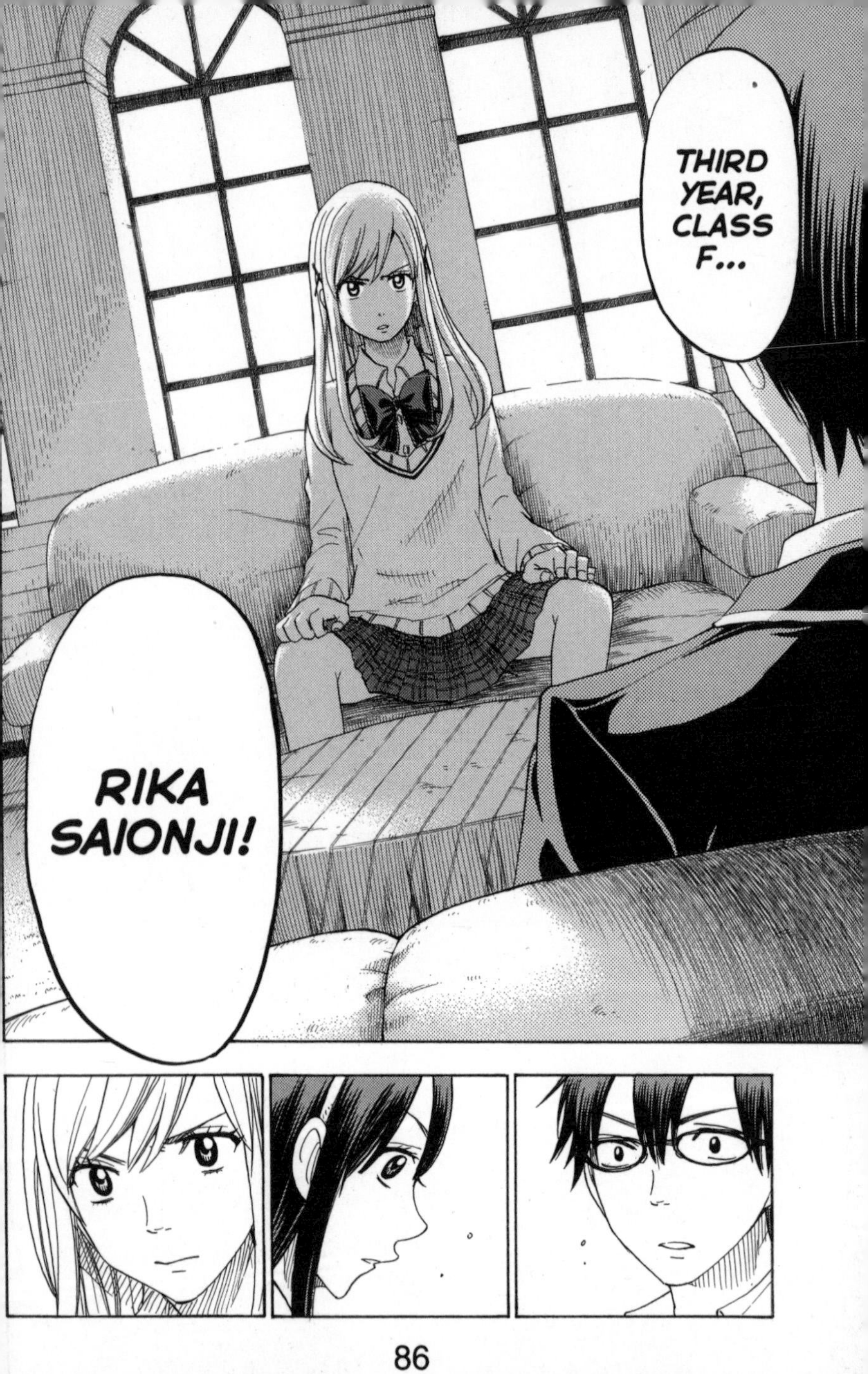
THIRD YEAR, CLASS F...
RIKA SAIONJI!

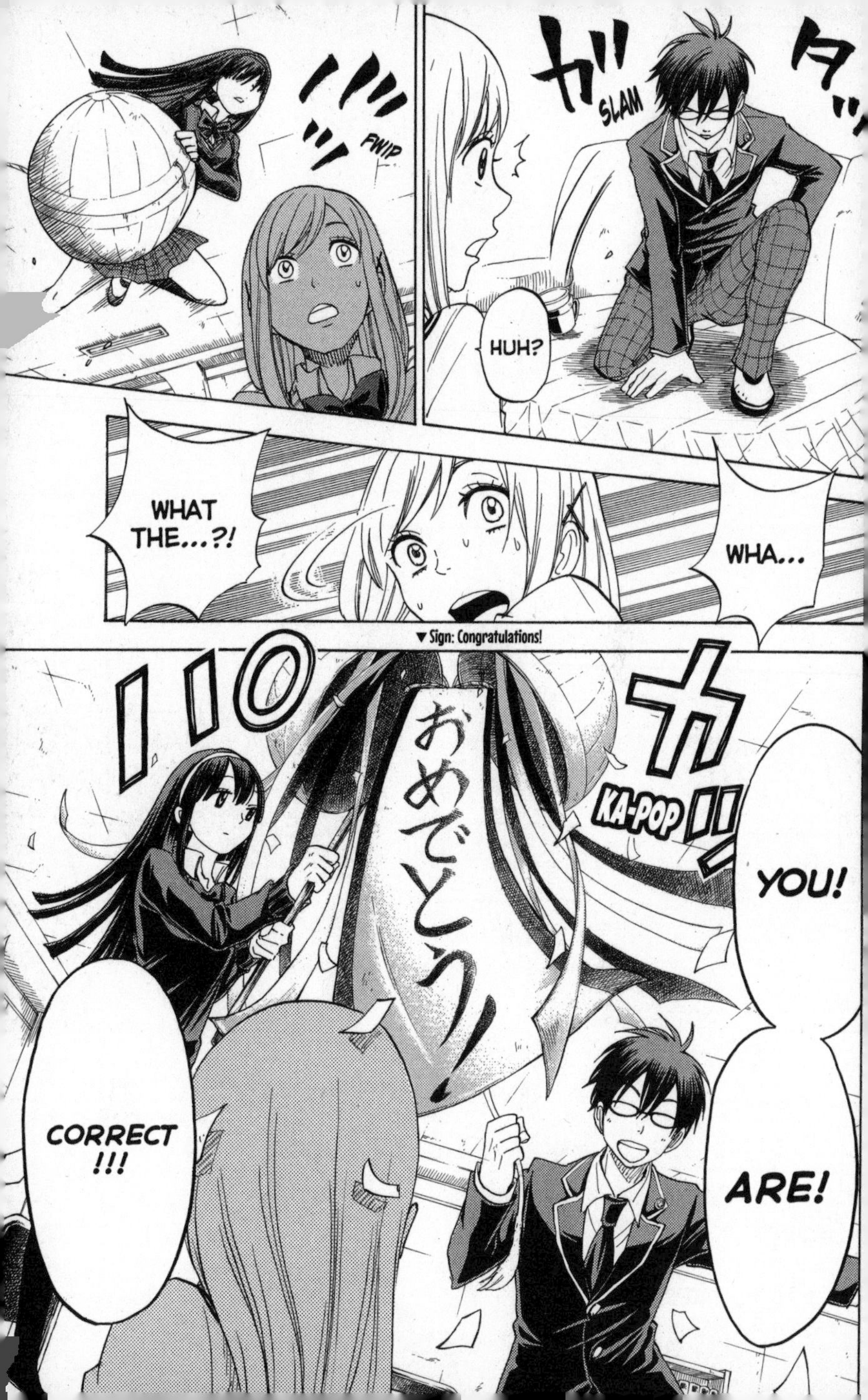
SLAM
HUH?
FWIP
WHA...
WHAT THE...?!
▼Sign: Congratulations!
KA-POP
おめでとう!
YOU!
ARE!
CORRECT
!!!

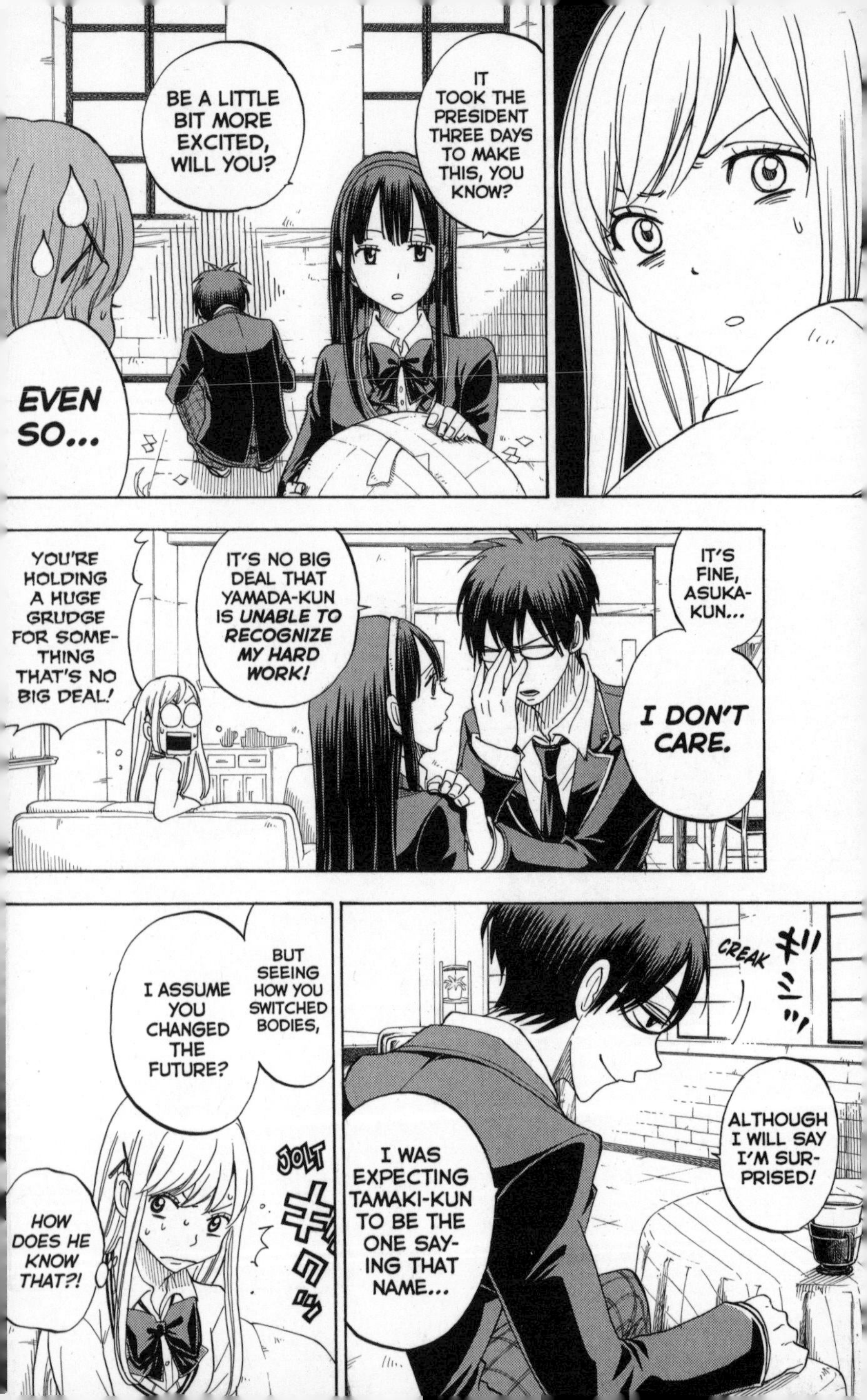
IT TOOK THE PRESIDENT THREE DAYS TO MAKE THIS, YOU KNOW?
BE A LITTLE BIT MORE EXCITED, WILL YOU?
EVEN SO...
IT'S FINE, ASUKA-KUN...
I DON'T CARE.
IT'S NO BIG DEAL THAT YAMADA-KUN IS UNABLE TO RECOGNIZE MY HARD WORK!
YOU'RE HOLDING A HUGE GRUDGE FOR SOMETHING THAT'S NO BIG DEAL!
CREAK
ALTHOUGH I WILL SAY I'M SURPRISED!
I WAS EXPECTING TAMAKI-KUN TO BE THE ONE SAYING THAT NAME...
BUT SEEING HOW YOU SWITCHED BODIES,
I ASSUME YOU CHANGED THE FUTURE?
JOLT
HOW DOES HE KNOW THAT?!

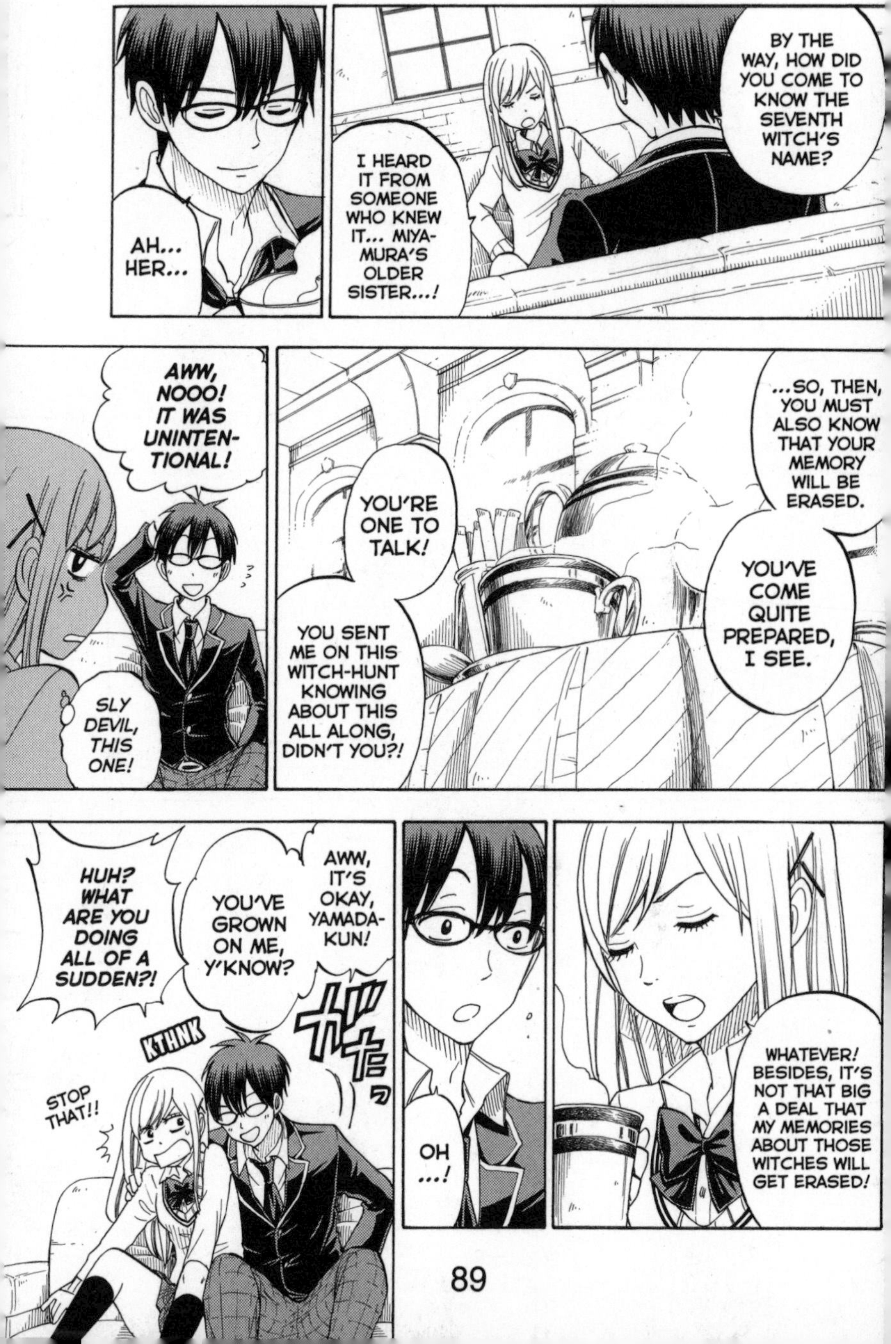
BY THE WAY, HOW DID YOU COME TO KNOW THE SEVENTH WITCH'S NAME?
I HEARD IT FROM SOMEONE WHO KNEW IT... MIYA-MURA'S OLDER SISTER...!
AH... HER...
...SO, THEN, YOU MUST ALSO KNOW THAT YOUR MEMORY WILL BE ERASED.
YOU'VE COME QUITE PREPARED, I SEE.
YOU'RE ONE TO TALK!
YOU SENT ME ON THIS WITCH-HUNT KNOWING ABOUT THIS ALL ALONG, DIDN'T YOU?!
AWW, NOOO! IT WAS UNINTEN-TIONAL!
SLY DEVIL, THIS ONE!
WHATEVER! BESIDES, IT'S NOT THAT BIG A DEAL THAT MY MEMORIES ABOUT THOSE WITCHES WILL GET ERASED!
OH ...!
AWW, IT'S OKAY, YAMADA-KUN!
YOU'VE GROWN ON ME, Y'KNOW?
HUH? WHAT ARE YOU DOING ALL OF A SUDDEN?!
KTHNK
STOP THAT!!

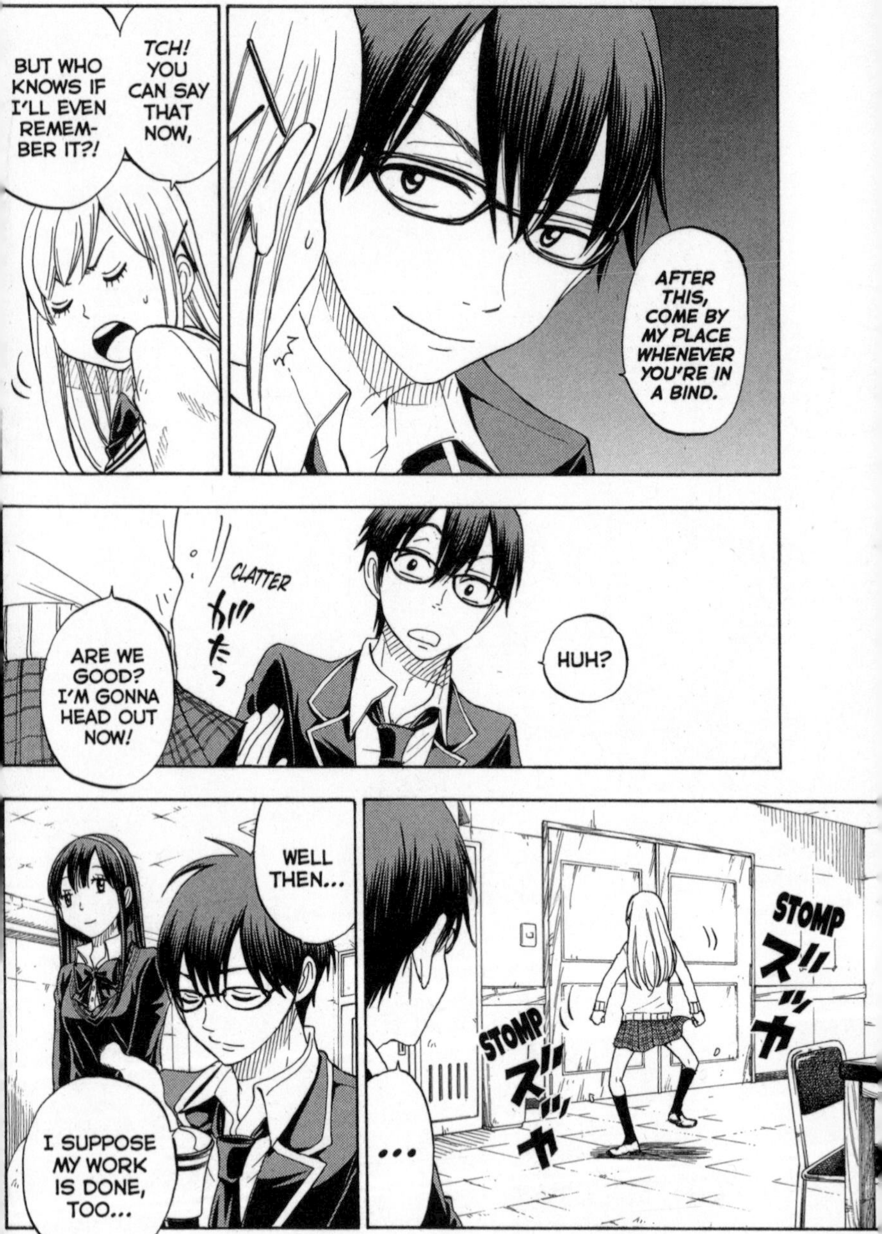
AFTER THIS, COME BY MY PLACE WHENEVER YOU'RE IN A BIND.
TCH! YOU CAN SAY THAT NOW,
BUT WHO KNOWS IF I'LL EVEN REMEM-BER IT?!
CLATTER
がたっ
HUH?
ARE WE GOOD? I'M GONNA HEAD OUT NOW!
STOMP
STOMP
...
WELL THEN...
I SUPPOSE MY WORK IS DONE, TOO...

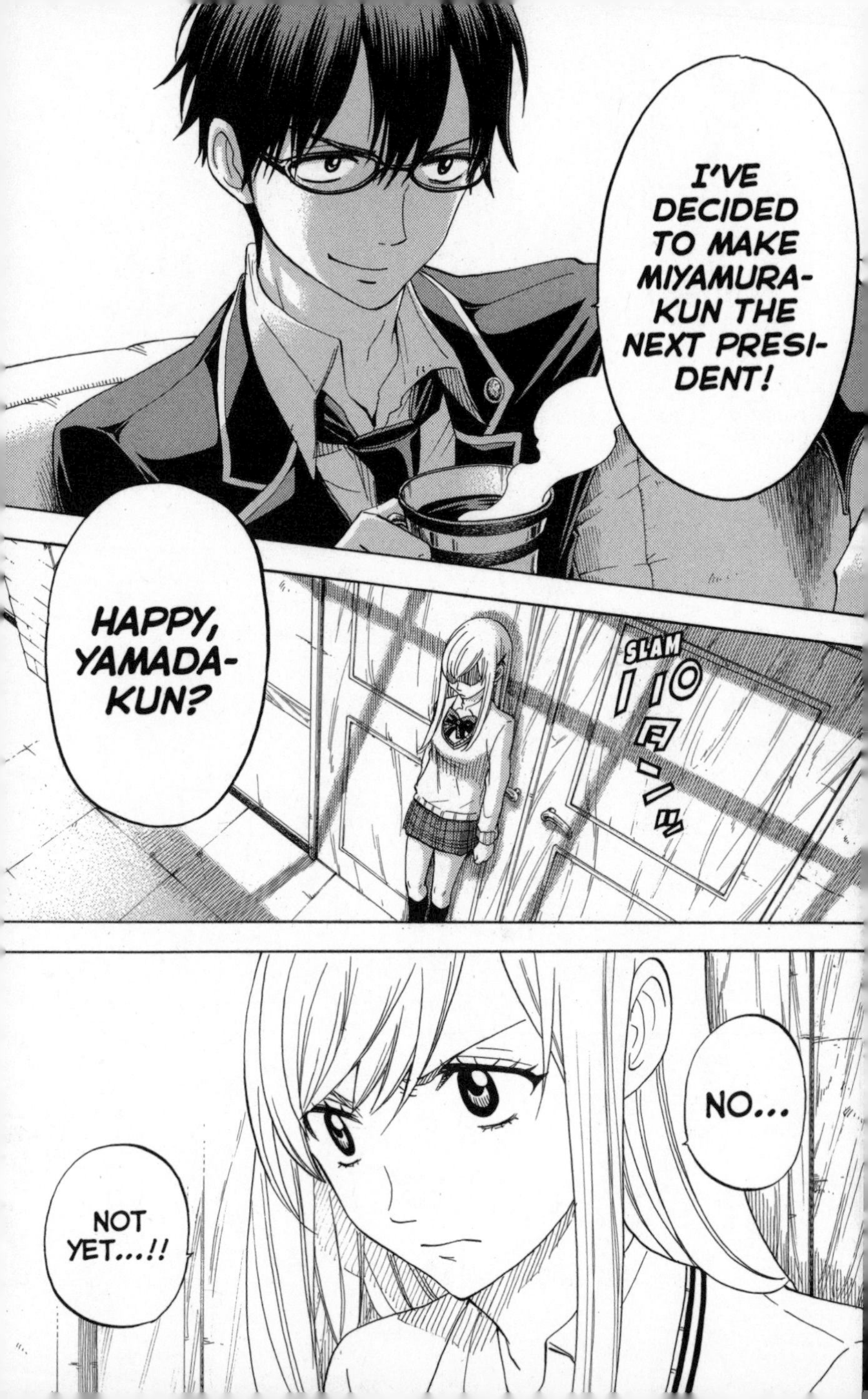
I'VE DECIDED TO MAKE MIYAMURA-KUN THE NEXT PRESI-DENT!
HAPPY, YAMADA-KUN?
SLAM
NO...
NOT YET...!!

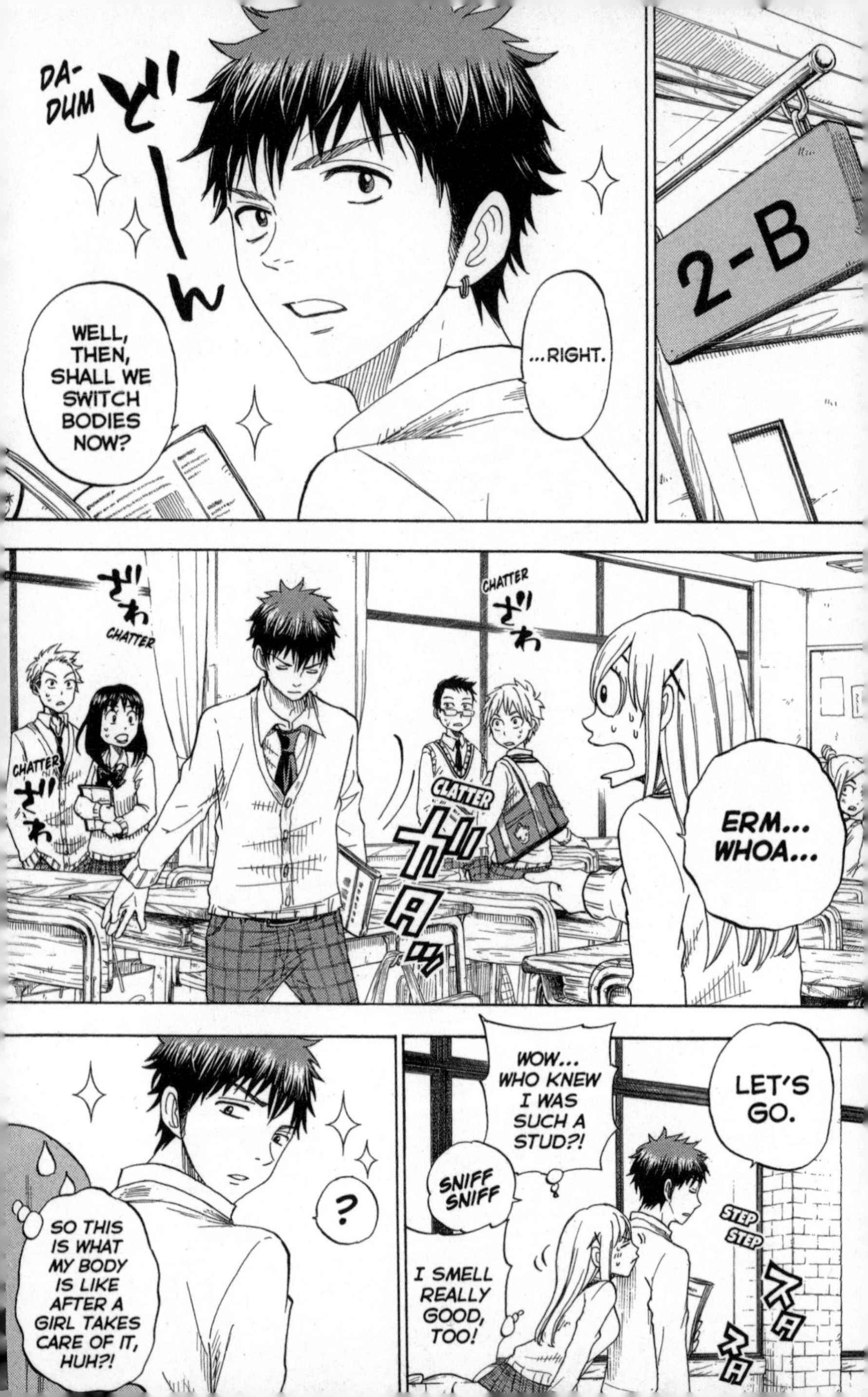
2-B
DA-DUM
...RIGHT.
WELL, THEN, SHALL WE SWITCH BODIES NOW?
CHATTER
ERM... WHOA...
CLATTER
CHATTER
CHATTER
LET'S GO.
WOW... WHO KNEW I WAS SUCH A STUD?!
SNIFF SNIFF
STEP STEP
I SMELL REALLY GOOD, TOO!
?
SO THIS IS WHAT MY BODY IS LIKE AFTER A GIRL TAKES CARE OF IT, HUH?!

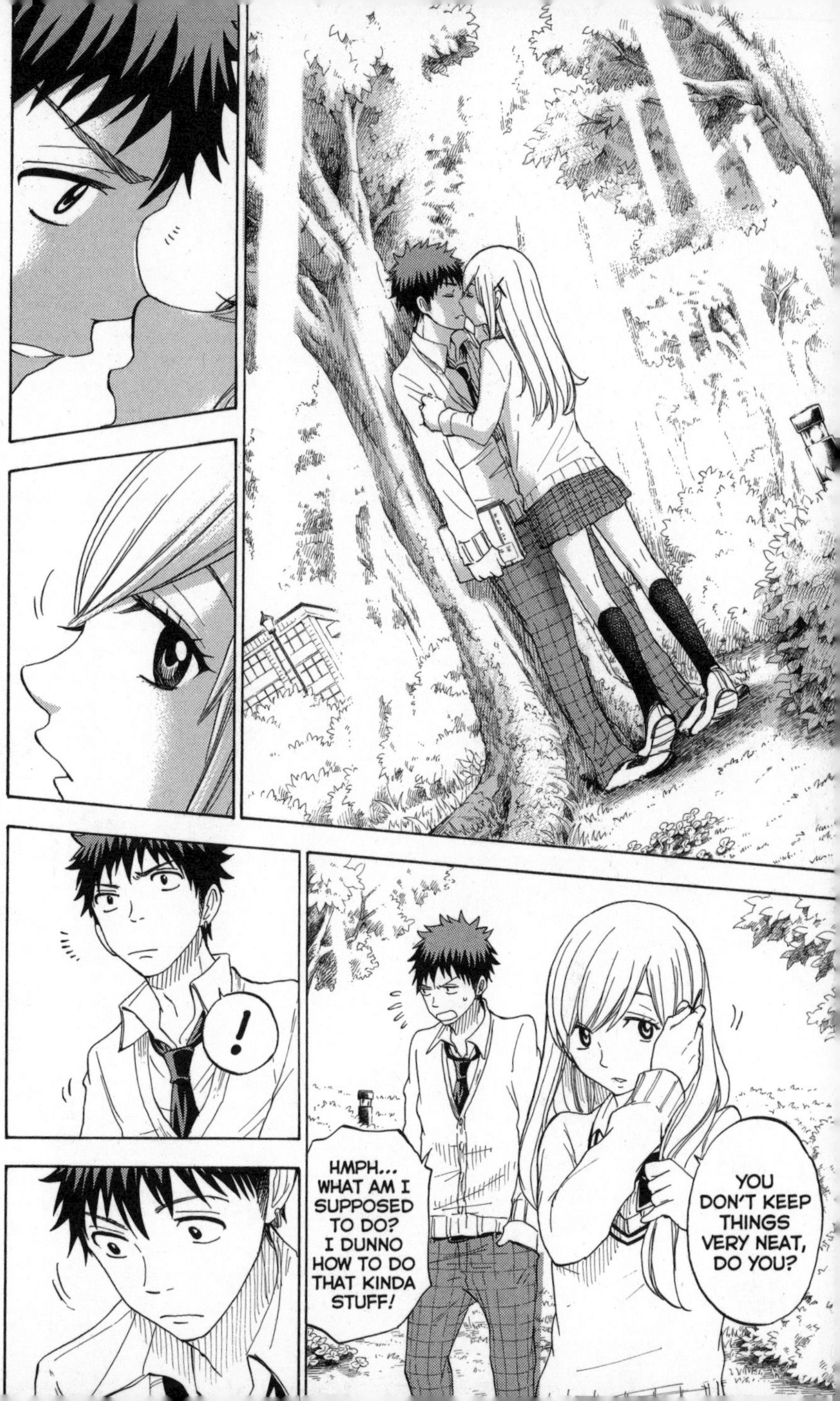
YOU DON'T KEEP THINGS VERY NEAT, DO YOU?
HMPH... WHAT AM I SUPPOSED TO DO? I DUNNO HOW TO DO THAT KINDA STUFF!
!

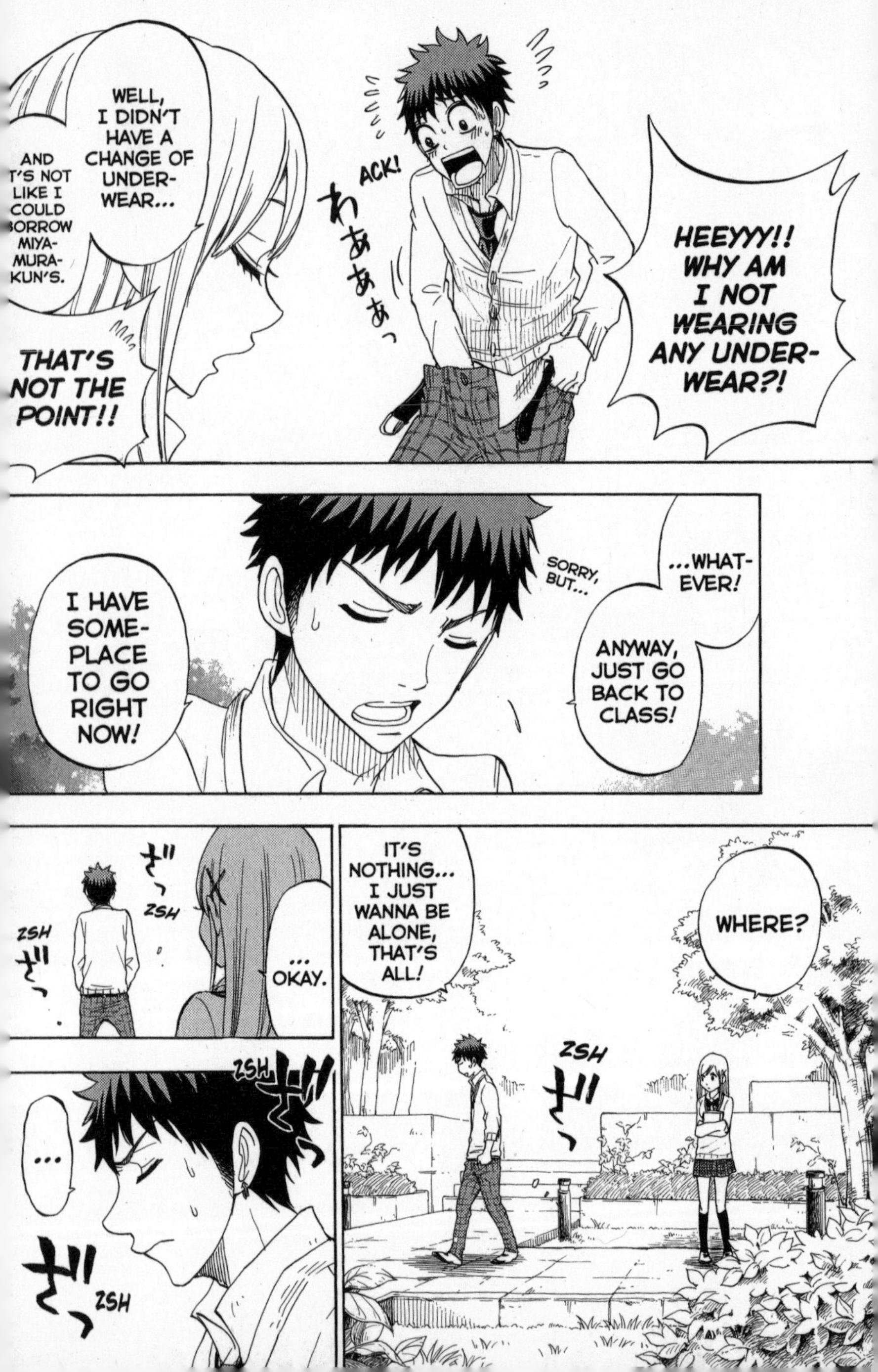
HEEYYY!! WHY AM I NOT WEARING ANY UNDER-WEAR?!
ACK!
わあああっ
WELL, I DIDN'T HAVE A CHANGE OF UNDER-WEAR...
AND IT'S NOT LIKE I COULD BORROW MIYA-MURA-KUN'S.
THAT'S NOT THE POINT!!
...WHAT-EVER!
SORRY, BUT...
ANYWAY, JUST GO BACK TO CLASS!
I HAVE SOME-PLACE TO GO RIGHT NOW!
WHERE?
IT'S NOTHING... I JUST WANNA BE ALONE, THAT'S ALL!
ZSH
ざっ
ざっ
ZSH
...OKAY.
ZSH
ざっ
ZSH
ざっ
...
ざっ
ZSH

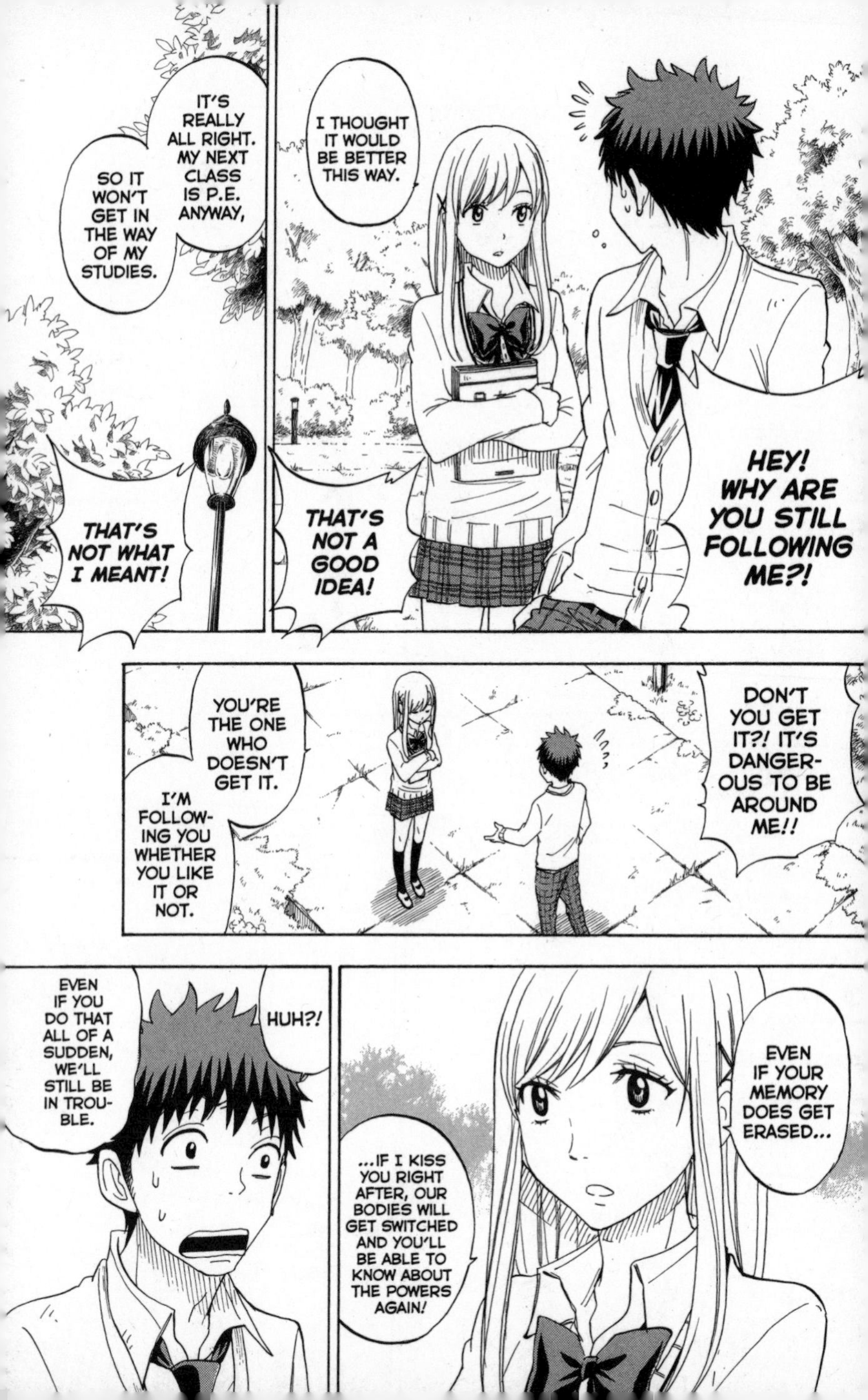
HEY! WHY ARE YOU STILL FOLLOWING ME?!
I THOUGHT IT WOULD BE BETTER THIS WAY.
THAT'S NOT A GOOD IDEA!
IT'S REALLY ALL RIGHT. MY NEXT CLASS IS P.E. ANYWAY,
SO IT WON'T GET IN THE WAY OF MY STUDIES.
THAT'S NOT WHAT I MEANT!
DON'T YOU GET IT?! IT'S DANGER-OUS TO BE AROUND ME!!
YOU'RE THE ONE WHO DOESN'T GET IT.
I'M FOLLOW-ING YOU WHETHER YOU LIKE IT OR NOT.
EVEN IF YOUR MEMORY DOES GET ERASED...
...IF I KISS YOU RIGHT AFTER, OUR BODIES WILL GET SWITCHED AND YOU'LL BE ABLE TO KNOW ABOUT THE POWERS AGAIN!
HUH?!
EVEN IF YOU DO THAT ALL OF A SUDDEN, WE'LL STILL BE IN TROU-BLE.

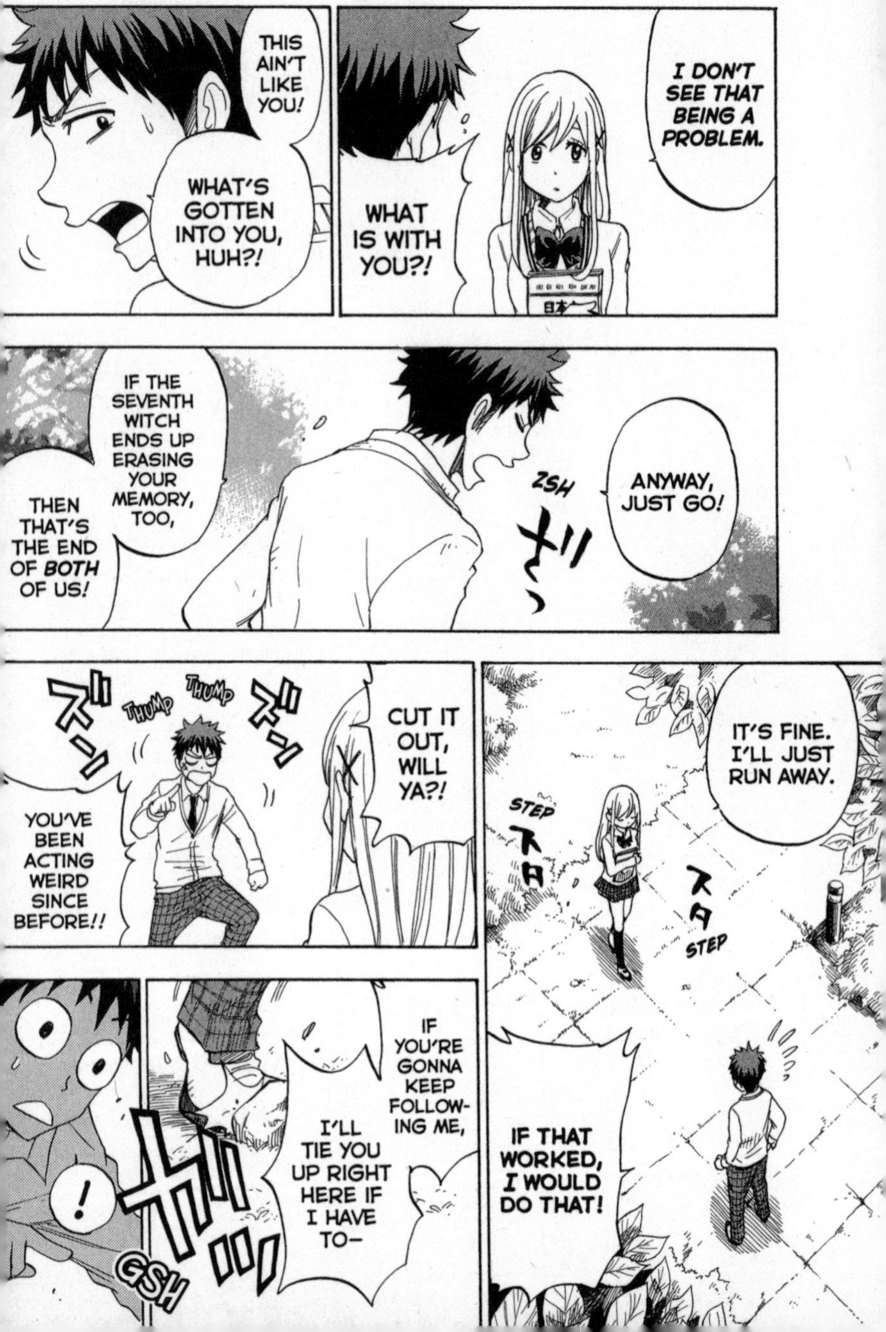
I DON'T SEE THAT BEING A PROBLEM.
WHAT IS WITH YOU?!
THIS AIN'T LIKE YOU!
WHAT'S GOTTEN INTO YOU, HUH?!
ANYWAY, JUST GO!
ZSH
IF THE SEVENTH WITCH ENDS UP ERASING YOUR MEMORY, TOO,
THEN THAT'S THE END OF *BOTH* OF US!
IT'S FINE. I'LL JUST RUN AWAY.
STEP
STEP
IF THAT WORKED, *I* WOULD DO THAT!
CUT IT OUT, WILL YA?!
THUMP
THUMP
YOU'VE BEEN ACTING WEIRD SINCE BEFORE!!
IF YOU'RE GONNA KEEP FOLLOW-ING ME,
I'LL TIE YOU UP RIGHT HERE IF I HAVE TO—
GSH
!

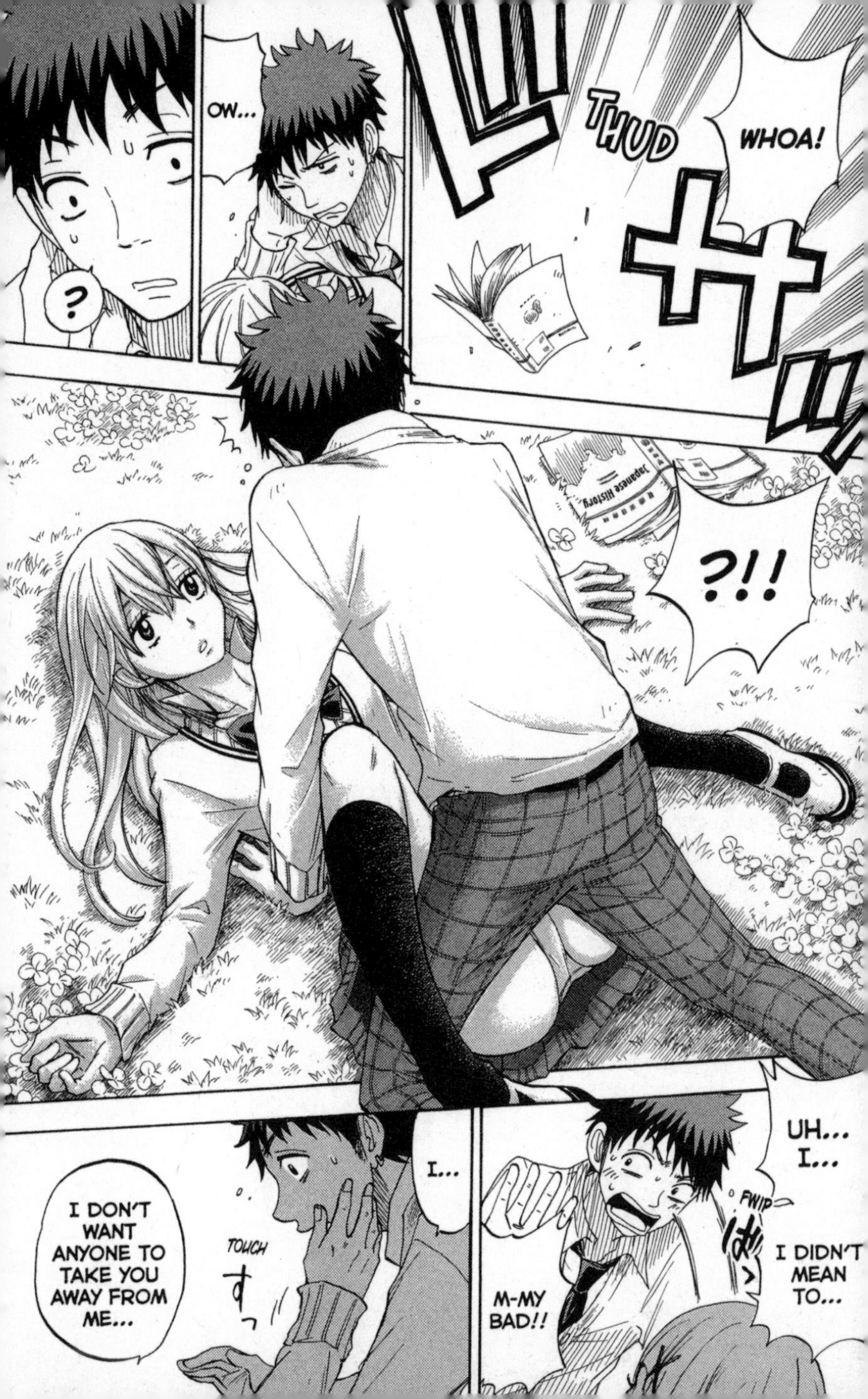

WHOA!
THUD
OW...
?
?!!
UH... I...
FWIP
I DIDN'T MEAN TO...
M-MY BAD!!
I...
TOUCH
すっ
I DON'T WANT ANYONE TO TAKE YOU AWAY FROM ME...

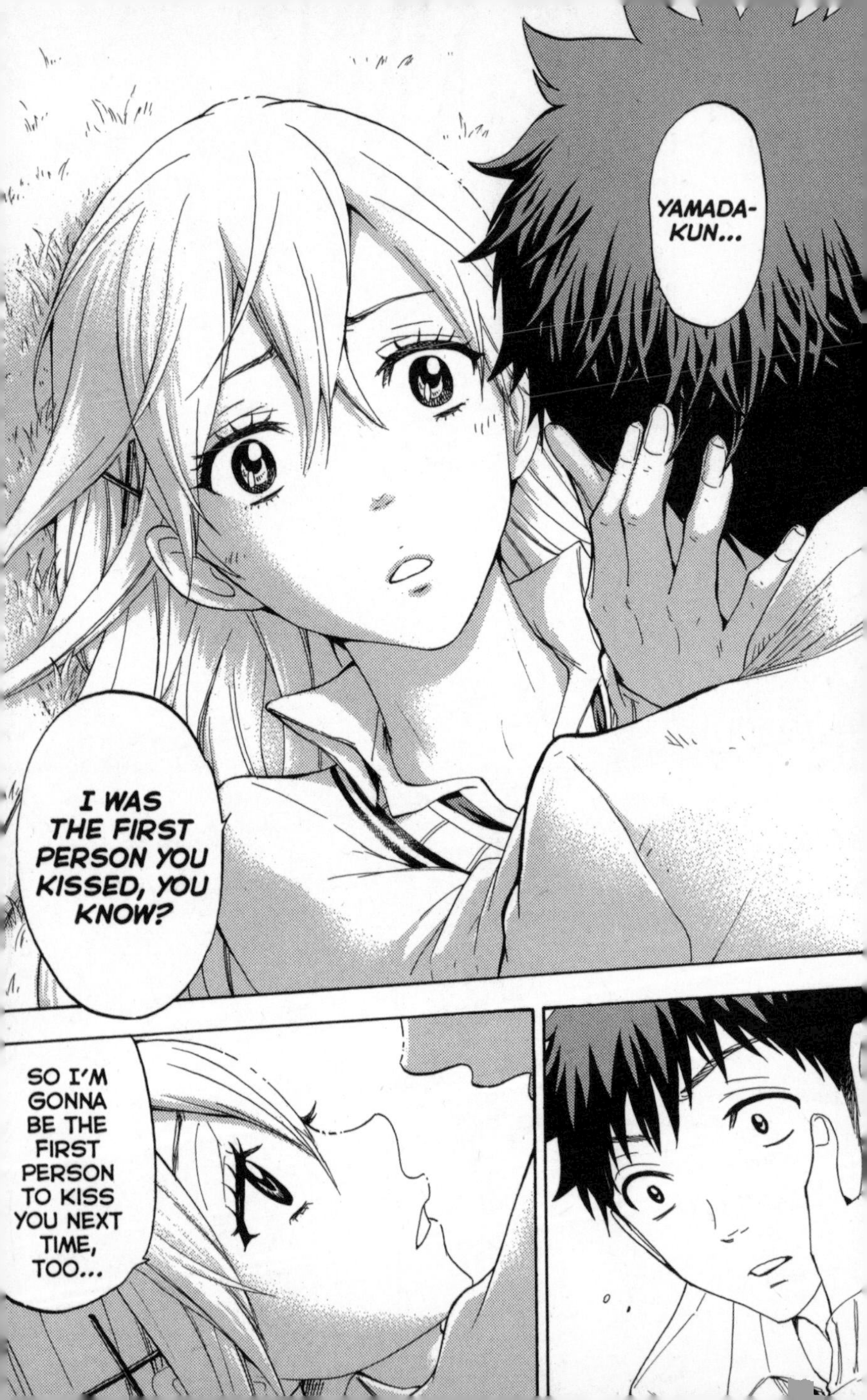
YAMADA-KUN...
I WAS THE FIRST PERSON YOU KISSED, YOU KNOW?
SO I'M GONNA BE THE FIRST PERSON TO KISS YOU NEXT TIME, TOO...

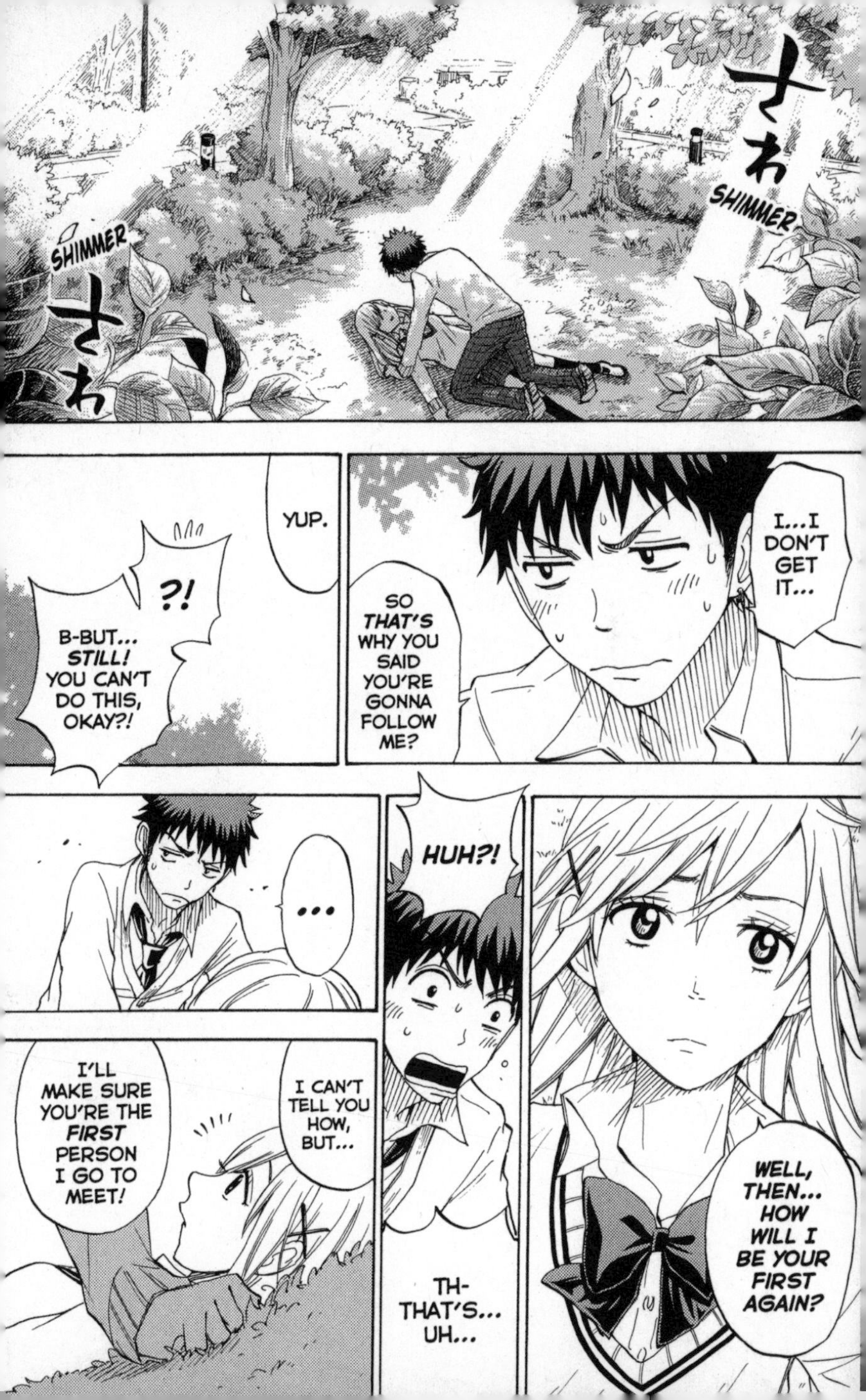
さわ
SHIMMER
SHIMMER
さわ
I...I DON'T GET IT...
SO THAT'S WHY YOU SAID YOU'RE GONNA FOLLOW ME?
YUP.
?!
B-BUT... STILL! YOU CAN'T DO THIS, OKAY?!
WELL, THEN... HOW WILL I BE YOUR FIRST AGAIN?
HUH?!
TH- THAT'S... UH...
...
I CAN'T TELL YOU HOW, BUT...
I'LL MAKE SURE YOU'RE THE FIRST PERSON I GO TO MEET!

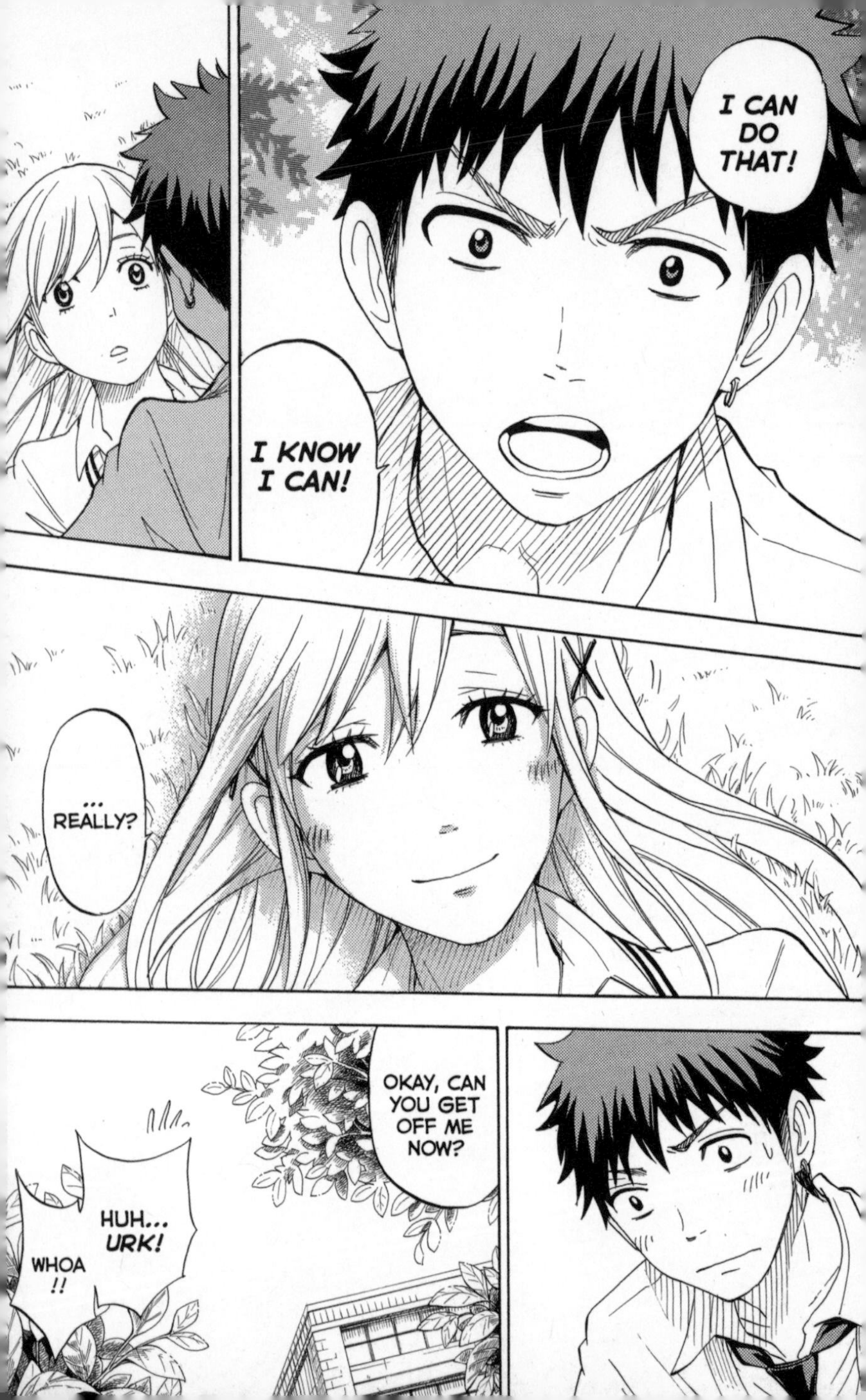
I CAN DO THAT!
I KNOW I CAN!
... REALLY?
OKAY, CAN YOU GET OFF ME NOW?
HUH... URK!
WHOA !!

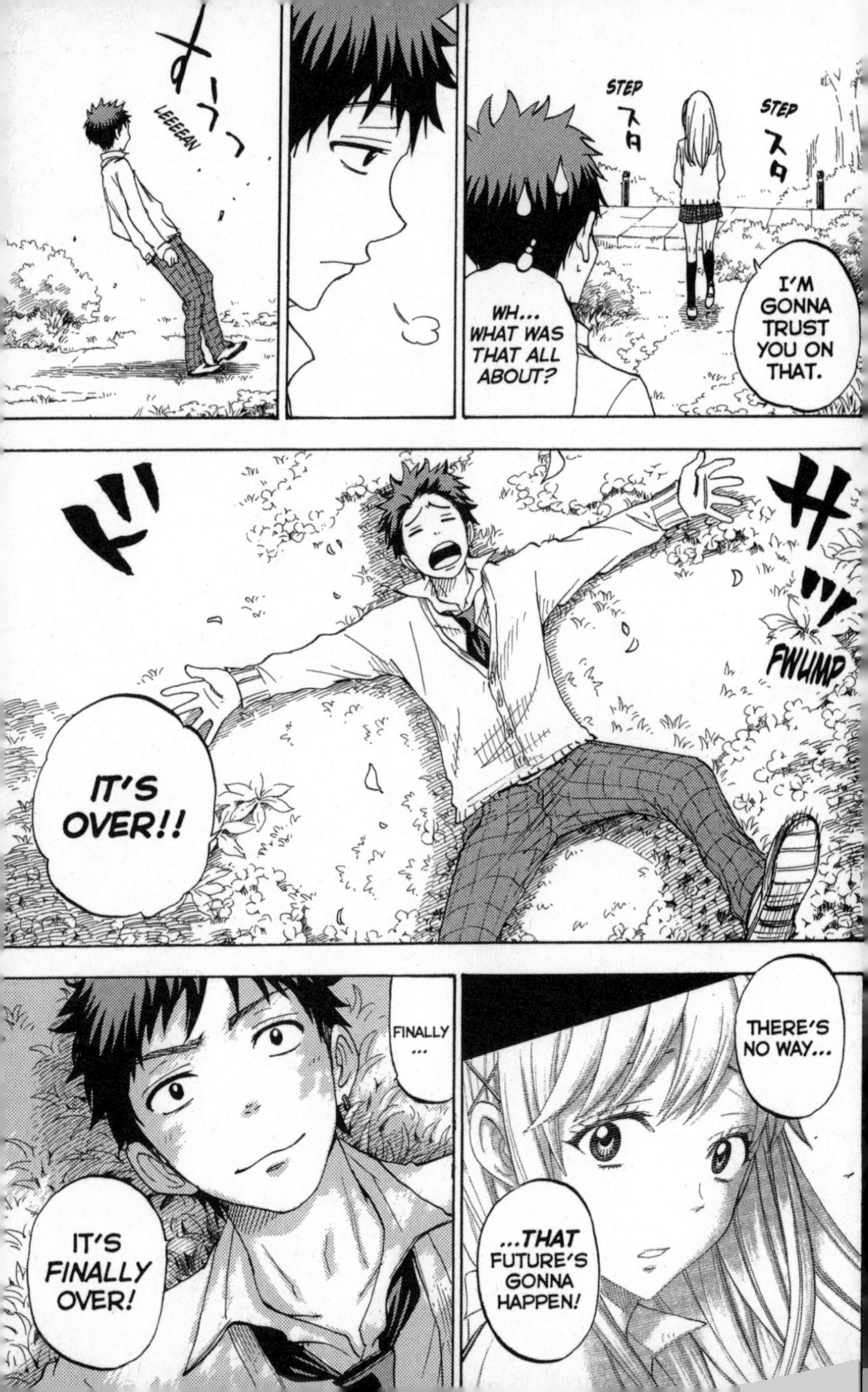
STEP
スタ
STEP
スタ
I'M GONNA TRUST YOU ON THAT.
WH... WHAT WAS THAT ALL ABOUT?
LEEEEAN
FWUMP
IT'S OVER!!
THERE'S NO WAY...
...THAT FUTURE'S GONNA HAPPEN!
FINALLY...
IT'S FINALLY OVER!

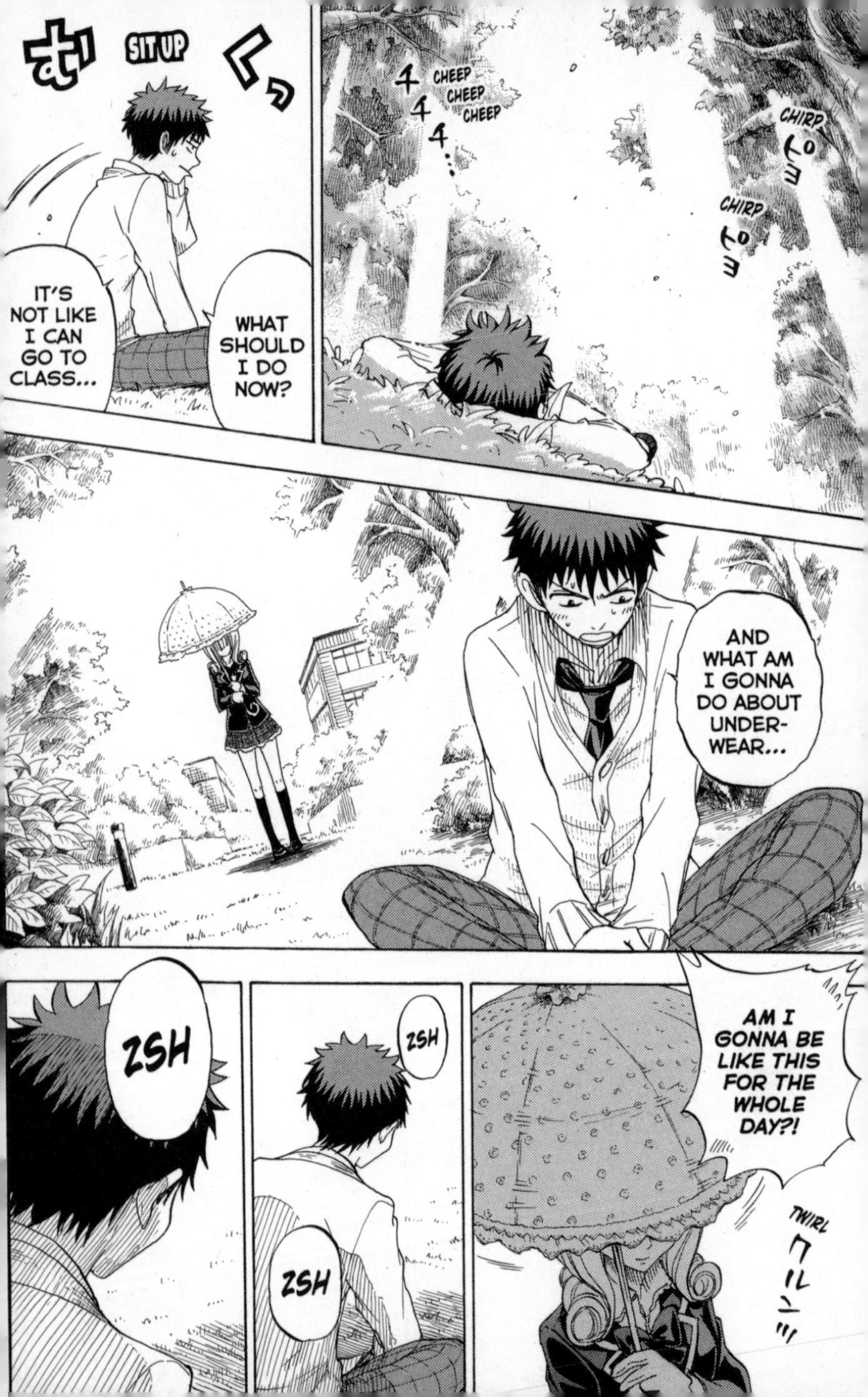
CHIRP
CHIRP
CHEEP
CHEEP
CHEEP
SIT UP
WHAT SHOULD I DO NOW?
IT'S NOT LIKE I CAN GO TO CLASS...
AND WHAT AM I GONNA DO ABOUT UNDER-WEAR...
AM I GONNA BE LIKE THIS FOR THE WHOLE DAY?!
TWIRL
ZSH
ZSH
ZSH

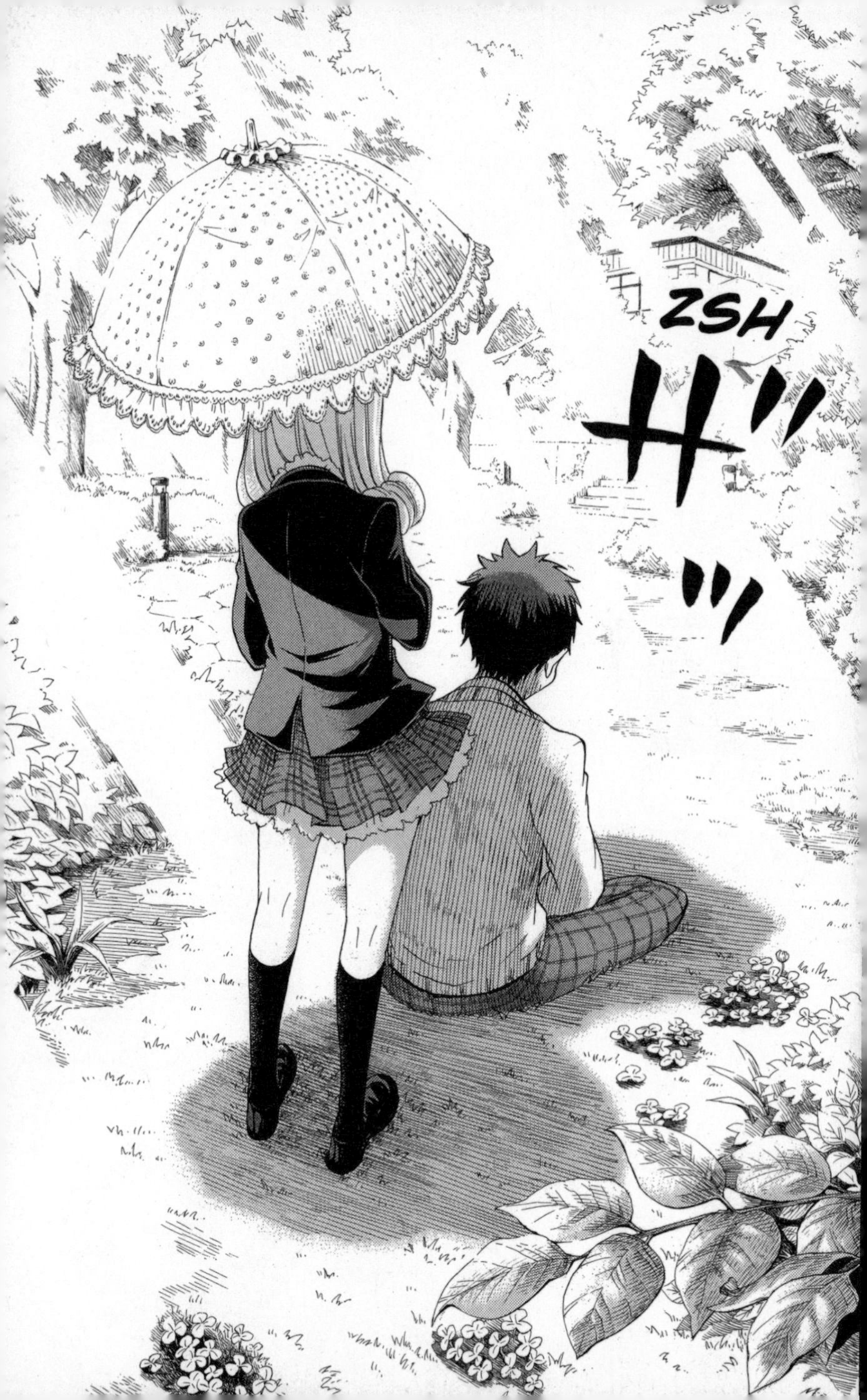
ZSH
ザッ

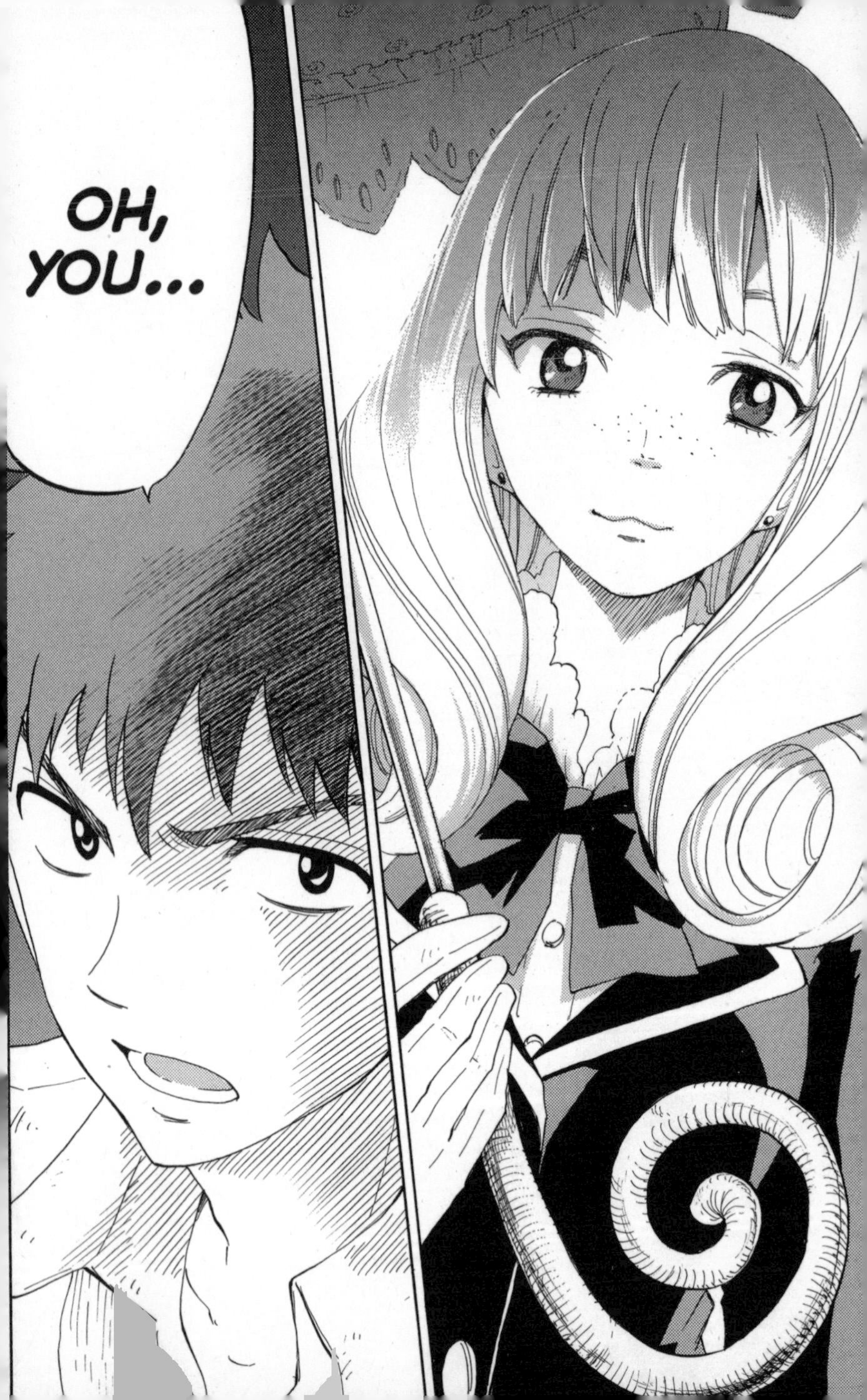
OH, YOU...

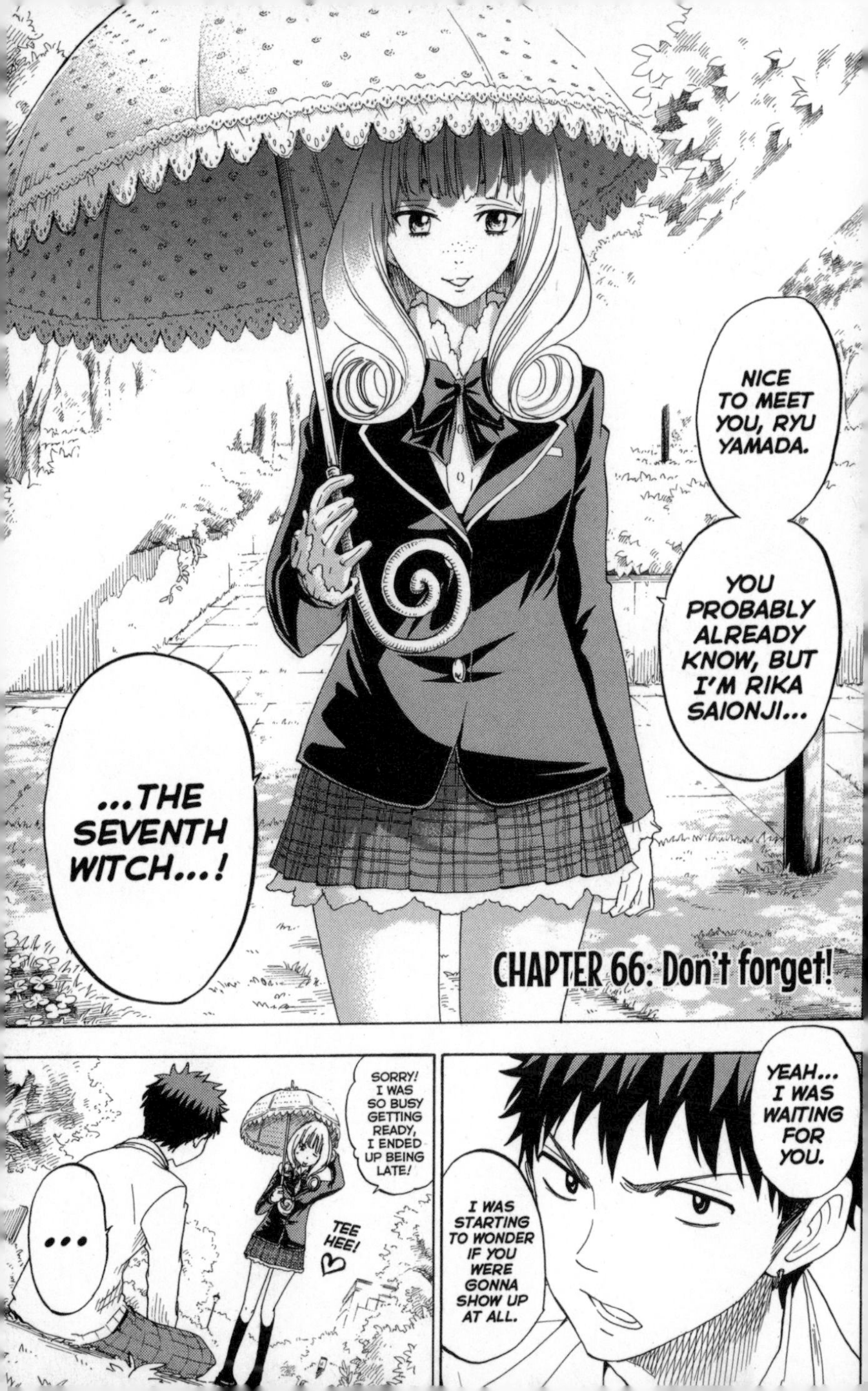
NICE TO MEET YOU, RYU YAMADA.
YOU PROBABLY ALREADY KNOW, BUT I'M RIKA SAIONJI...
...THE SEVENTH WITCH...!
CHAPTER 66: Don't forget!
YEAH... I WAS WAITING FOR YOU.
I WAS STARTING TO WONDER IF YOU WERE GONNA SHOW UP AT ALL.
SORRY! I WAS SO BUSY GETTING READY, I ENDED UP BEING LATE!
TEE HEE! ♥
...

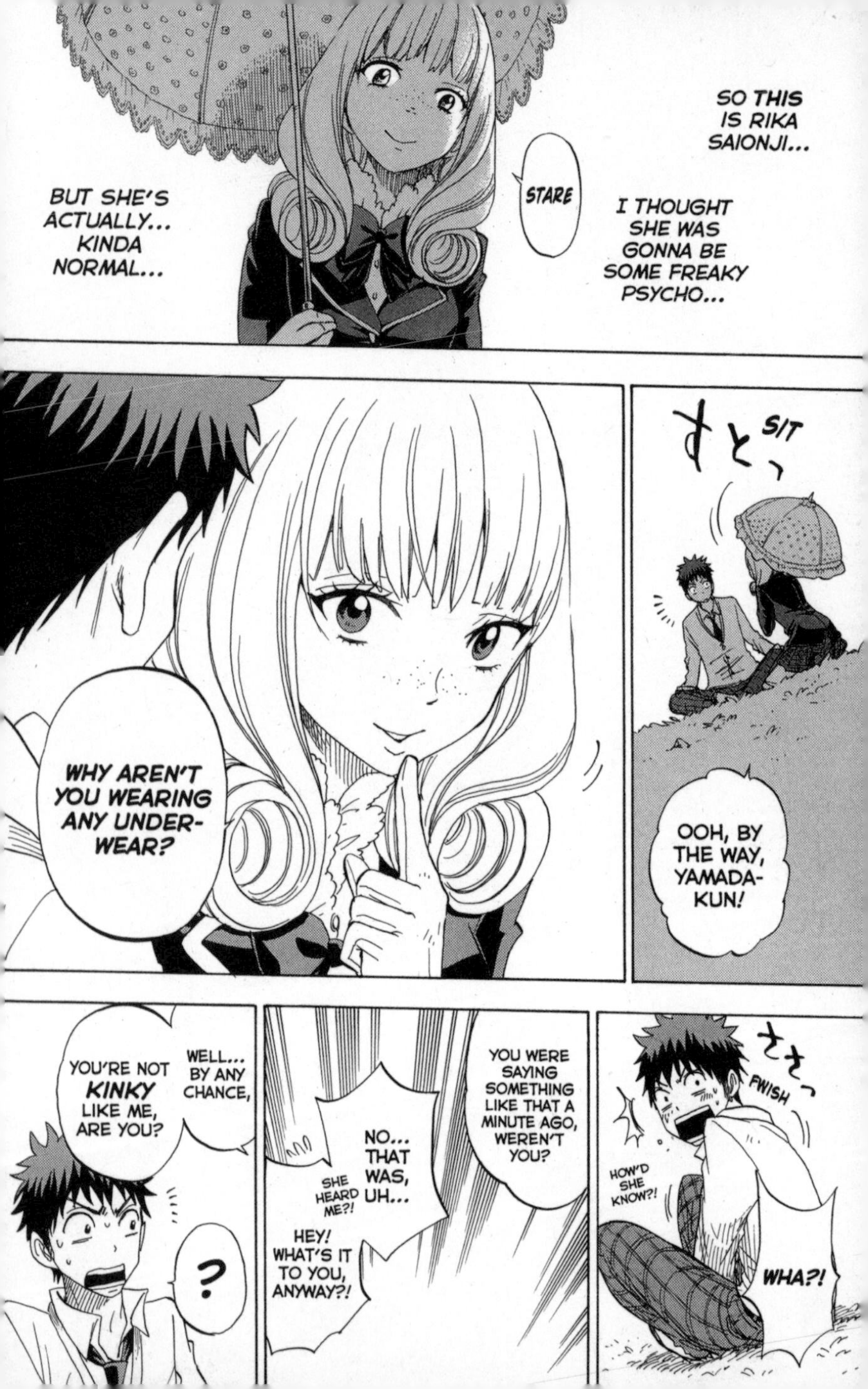
SO THIS IS RIKA SAIONJI...
I THOUGHT SHE WAS GONNA BE SOME FREAKY PSYCHO...
STARE
BUT SHE'S ACTUALLY... KINDA NORMAL...
すとっ
SIT
OOH, BY THE WAY, YAMADA-KUN!
WHY AREN'T YOU WEARING ANY UNDER-WEAR?
ささっ
FWISH
HOW'D SHE KNOW?!
WHA?!
YOU WERE SAYING SOMETHING LIKE THAT A MINUTE AGO, WEREN'T YOU?
NO... THAT WAS, UH...
SHE HEARD ME?!
HEY! WHAT'S IT TO YOU, ANYWAY?!
WELL... BY ANY CHANCE,
YOU'RE NOT KINKY LIKE ME, ARE YOU?
?

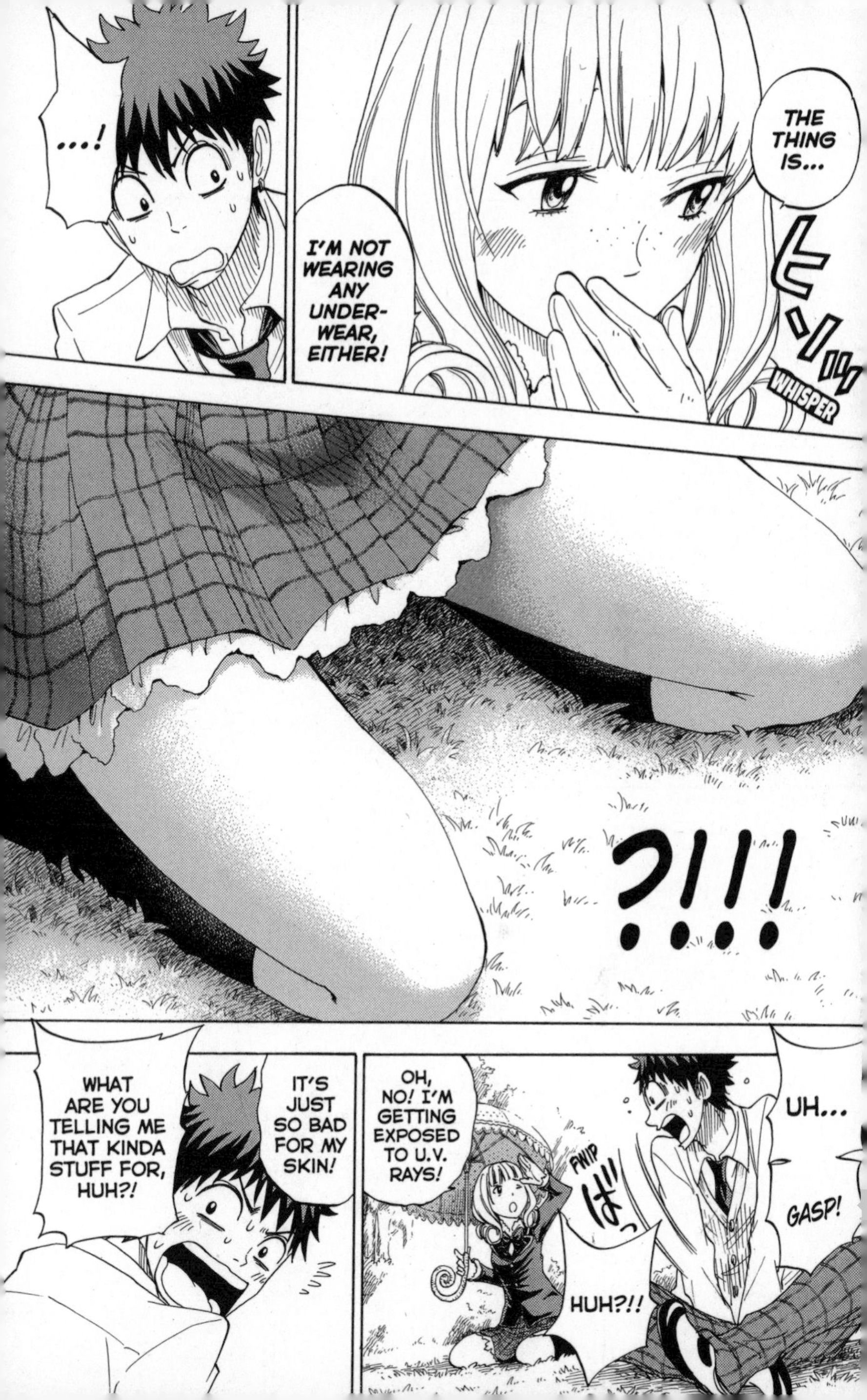
THE THING IS...
I'M NOT WEARING ANY UNDER-WEAR, EITHER!
ヒソッ
WHISPER
...!
?!!!
UH...
GASP!
HUH?!!
ばっ
FWIP
OH, NO! I'M GETTING EXPOSED TO U.V. RAYS!
IT'S JUST SO BAD FOR MY SKIN!
WHAT ARE YOU TELLING ME THAT KINDA STUFF FOR, HUH?!

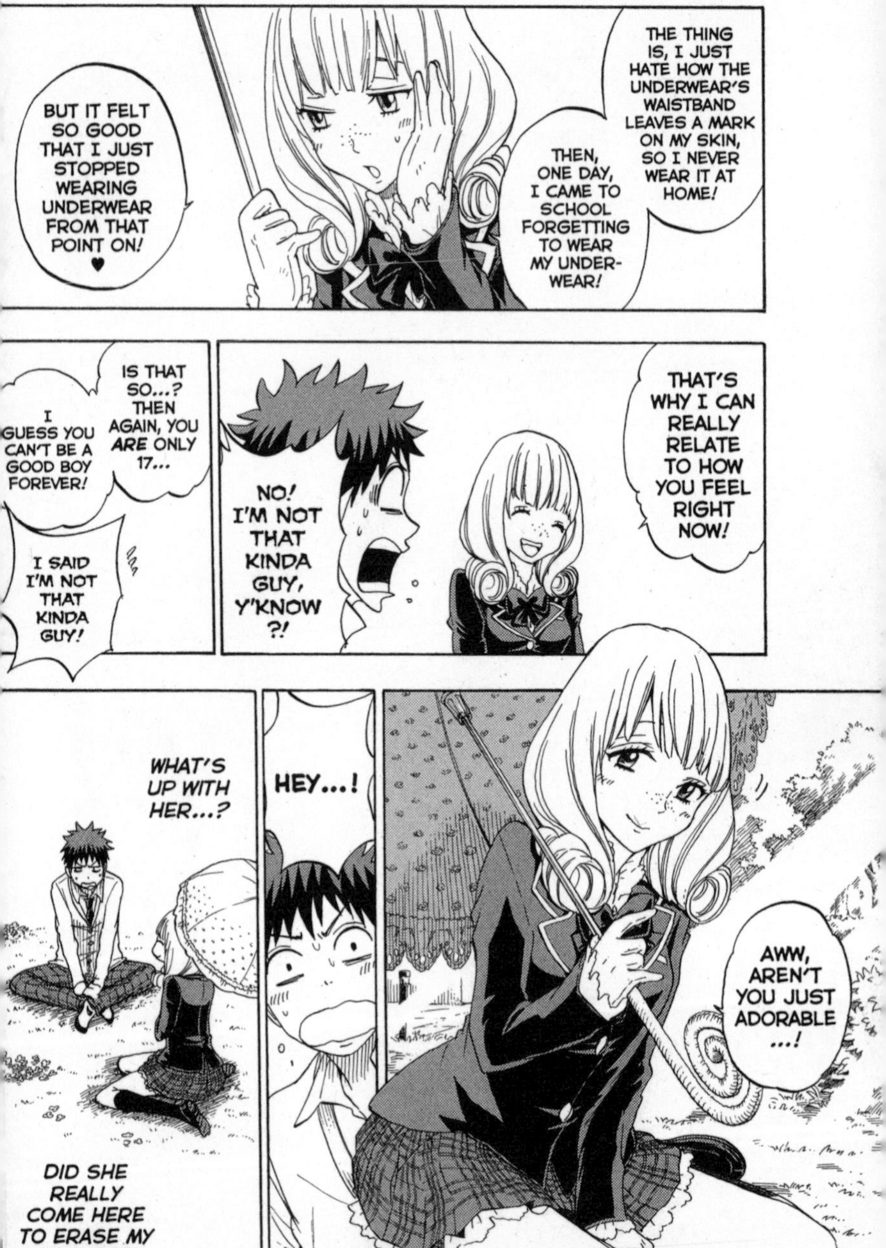
THE THING IS, I JUST HATE HOW THE UNDERWEAR'S WAISTBAND LEAVES A MARK ON MY SKIN, SO I NEVER WEAR IT AT HOME!
THEN, ONE DAY, I CAME TO SCHOOL FORGETTING TO WEAR MY UNDER-WEAR!
BUT IT FELT SO GOOD THAT I JUST STOPPED WEARING UNDERWEAR FROM THAT POINT ON! ♥
THAT'S WHY I CAN REALLY RELATE TO HOW YOU FEEL RIGHT NOW!
NO! I'M NOT THAT KINDA GUY, Y'KNOW?!
IS THAT SO...? THEN AGAIN, YOU *ARE* ONLY 17...
I GUESS YOU CAN'T BE A GOOD BOY FOREVER!
I SAID I'M NOT THAT KINDA GUY!
AWW, AREN'T YOU JUST ADORABLE ...!
HEY...!
WHAT'S UP WITH HER...?
DID SHE REALLY COME HERE TO ERASE MY MEMORY?!

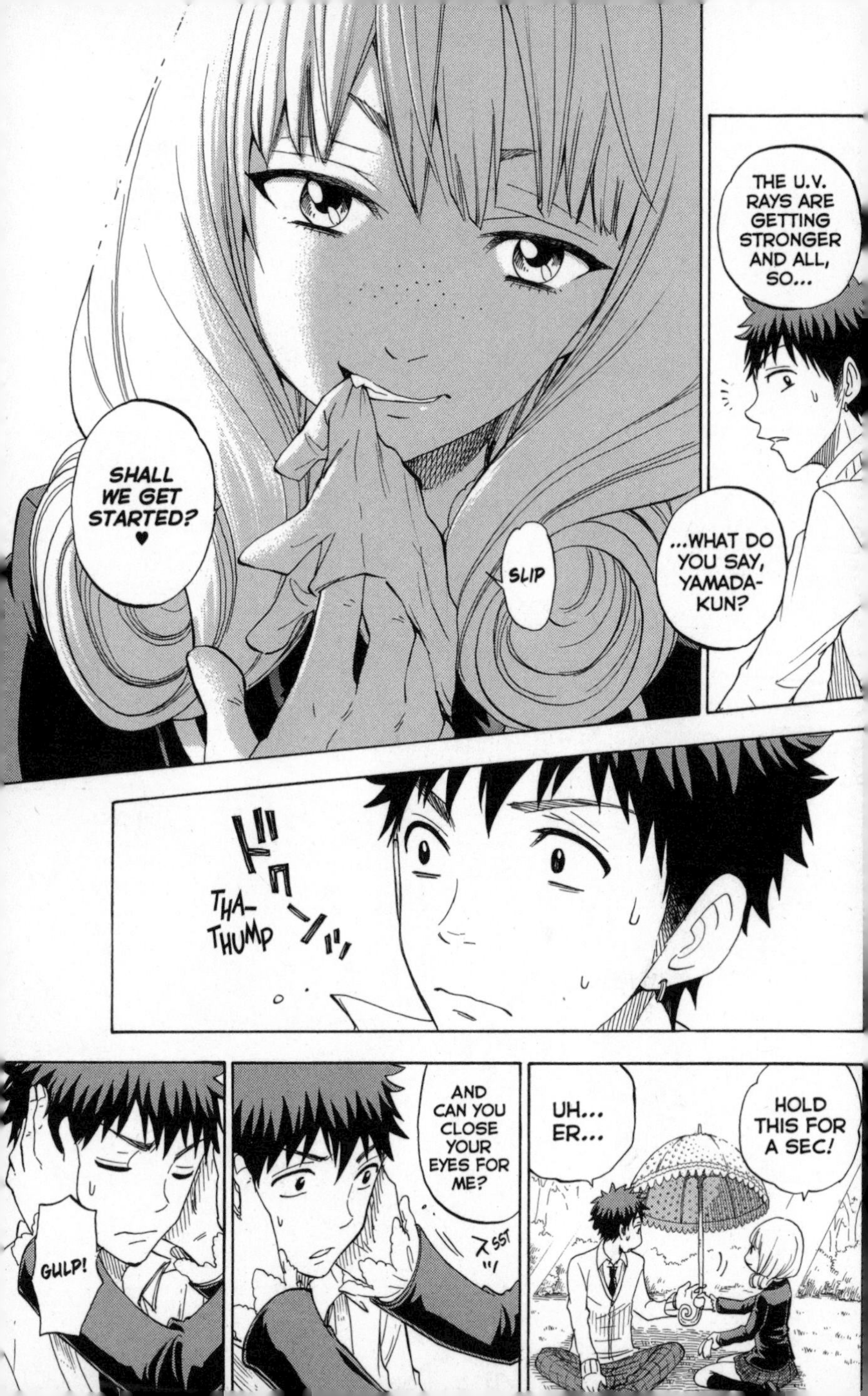
THE U.V. RAYS ARE GETTING STRONGER AND ALL, SO...
...WHAT DO YOU SAY, YAMADA-KUN?
SLIP
SHALL WE GET STARTED? ♥
THA-THUMP
HOLD THIS FOR A SEC!
UH... ER...
AND CAN YOU CLOSE YOUR EYES FOR ME?
SST
GULP!

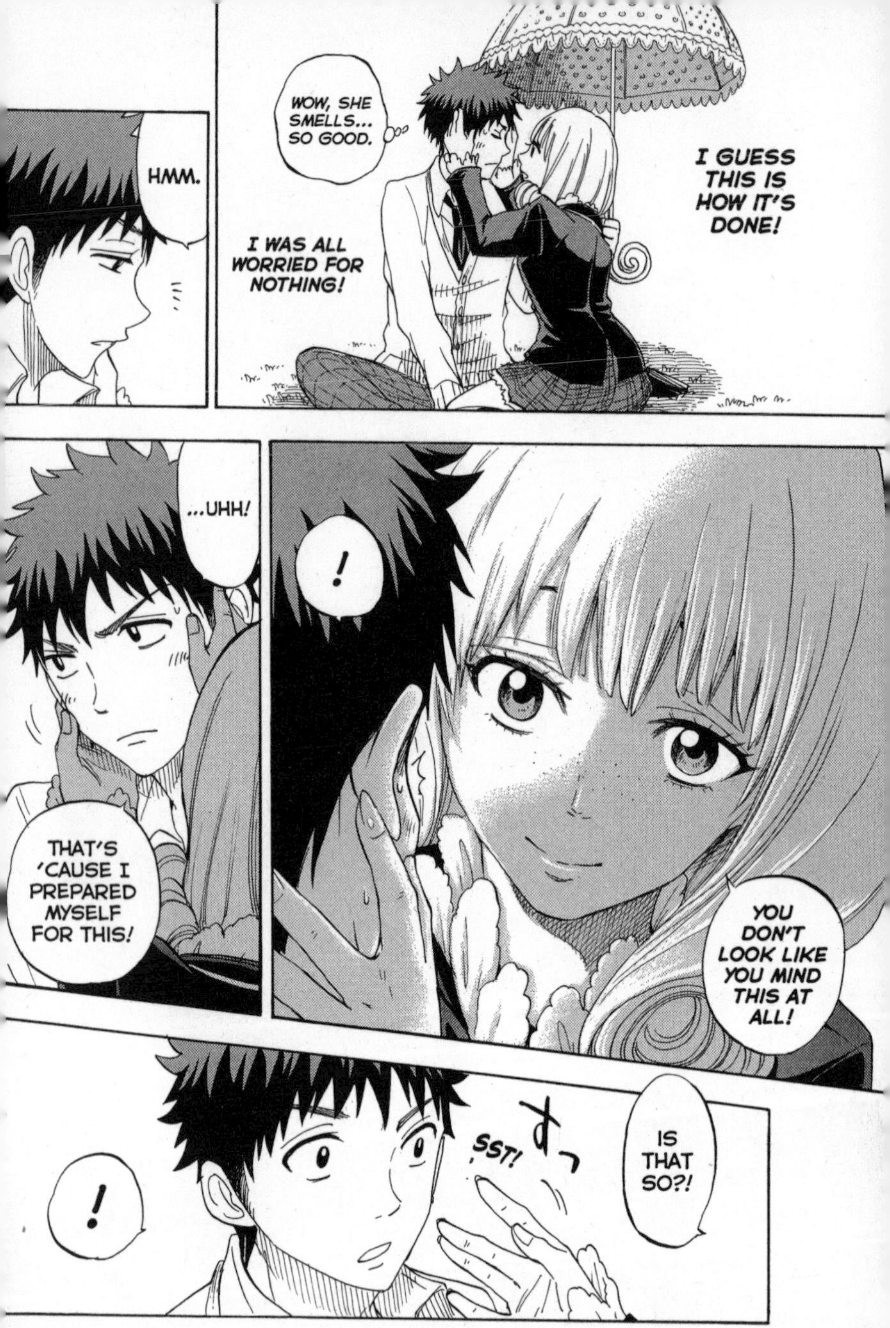
I GUESS THIS IS HOW IT'S DONE!
WOW, SHE SMELLS... SO GOOD.
I WAS ALL WORRIED FOR NOTHING!
HMM.
!
YOU DON'T LOOK LIKE YOU MIND THIS AT ALL!
...UHH!
THAT'S 'CAUSE I PREPARED MYSELF FOR THIS!
IS THAT SO?!
すっ
SST!
!

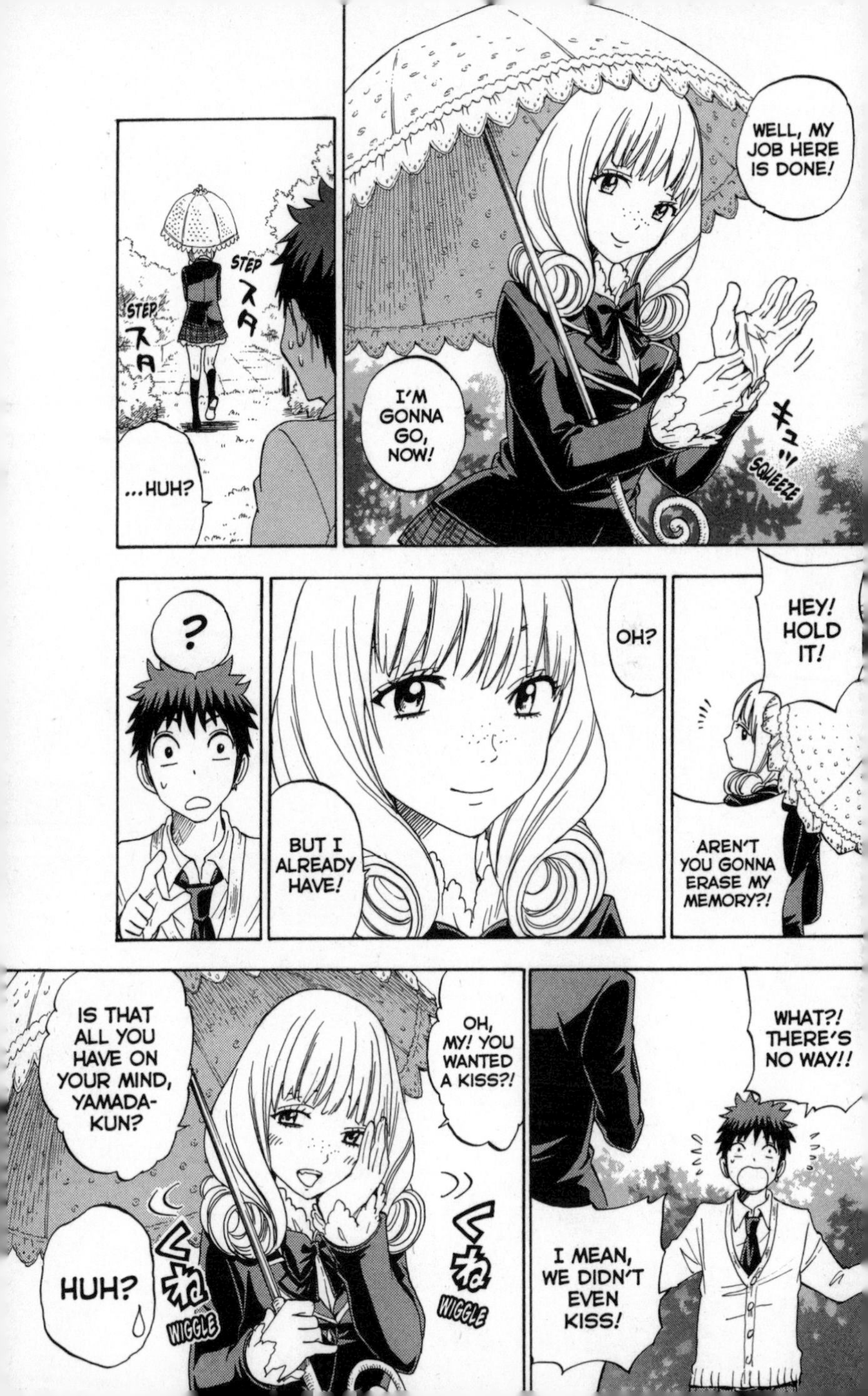
WELL, MY JOB HERE IS DONE!
I'M GONNA GO, NOW!
キュッ SQUEEZE
STEP スタ
STEP スタ
...HUH?
HEY! HOLD IT!
AREN'T YOU GONNA ERASE MY MEMORY?!
OH?
BUT I ALREADY HAVE!
?
WHAT?! THERE'S NO WAY!!
I MEAN, WE DIDN'T EVEN KISS!
OH, MY! YOU WANTED A KISS?!
IS THAT ALL YOU HAVE ON YOUR MIND, YAMADA-KUN?
くね WIGGLE
くね WIGGLE
HUH?

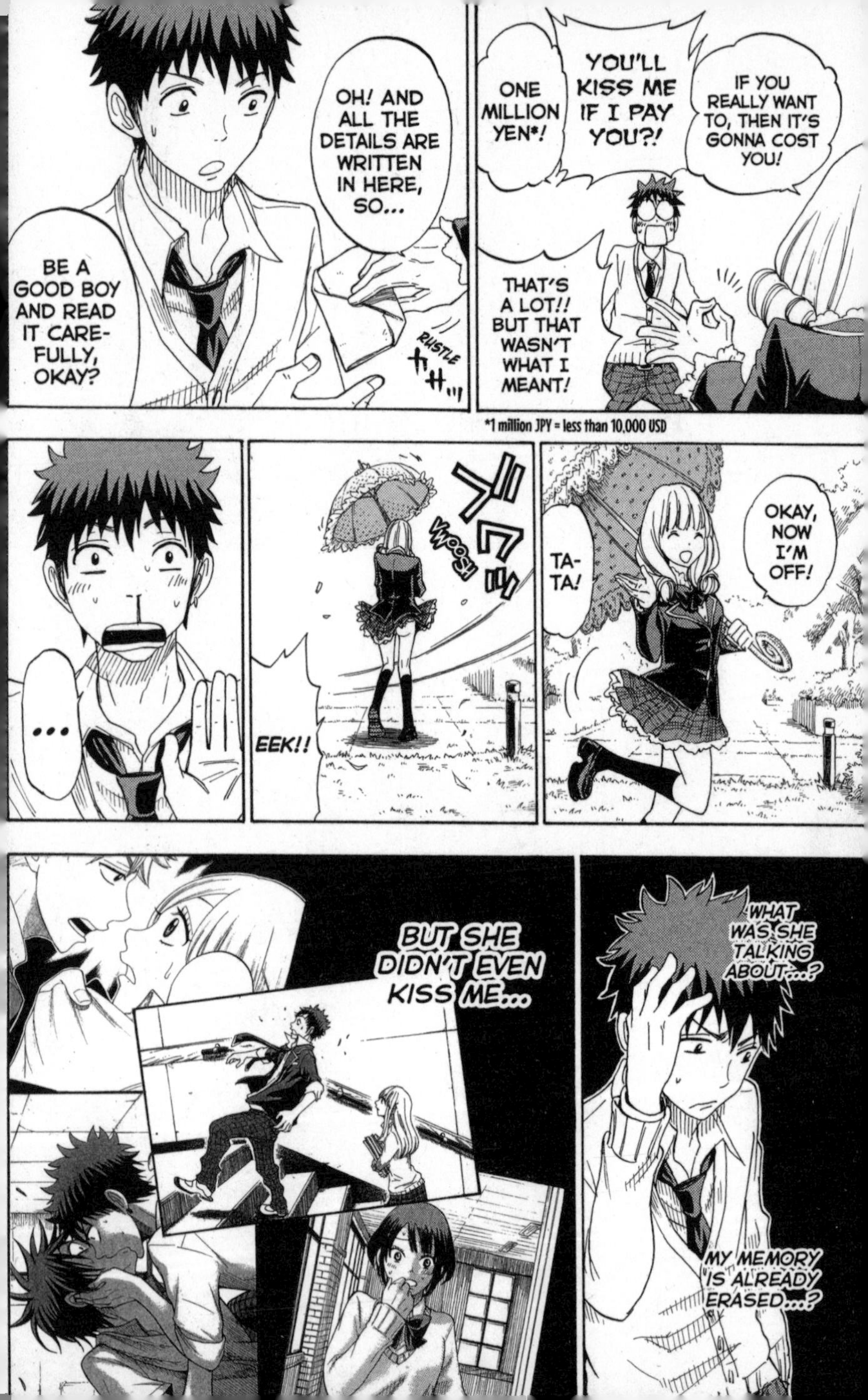
IF YOU REALLY WANT TO, THEN IT'S GONNA COST YOU!
YOU'LL KISS ME IF I PAY YOU?!
ONE MILLION YEN*!
THAT'S A LOT!! BUT THAT WASN'T WHAT I MEANT!
OH! AND ALL THE DETAILS ARE WRITTEN IN HERE, SO...
BE A GOOD BOY AND READ IT CAREFULLY, OKAY?
RUSTLE
OKAY, NOW I'M OFF!
TA-TA!
WHOOSH
EEK!!
...
WHAT WAS SHE TALKING ABOUT...?
MY MEMORY IS ALREADY ERASED...?
BUT SHE DIDN'T EVEN KISS ME...

*1 million JPY = less than 10,000 USD

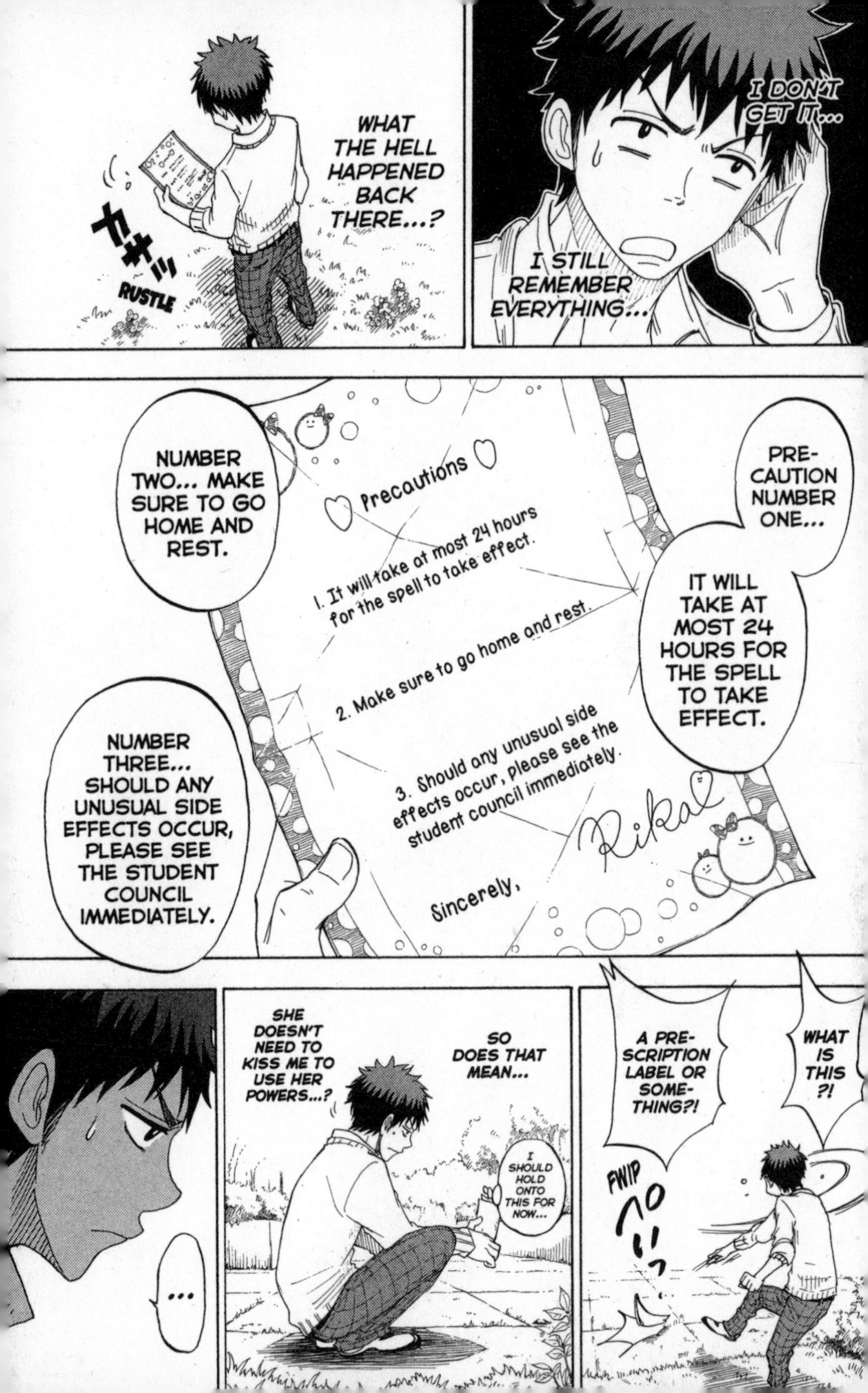

I DON'T GET IT...
I STILL REMEMBER EVERYTHING...
WHAT THE HELL HAPPENED BACK THERE...?
RUSTLE
PRE-CAUTION NUMBER ONE...
IT WILL TAKE AT MOST 24 HOURS FOR THE SPELL TO TAKE EFFECT.
Precautions
1. It will take at most 24 hours for the spell to take effect.
2. Make sure to go home and rest.
3. Should any unusual side effects occur, please see the student council immediately.
Sincerely,
Rika
NUMBER TWO... MAKE SURE TO GO HOME AND REST.
NUMBER THREE... SHOULD ANY UNUSUAL SIDE EFFECTS OCCUR, PLEASE SEE THE STUDENT COUNCIL IMMEDIATELY.
WHAT IS THIS?!
A PRE-SCRIPTION LABEL OR SOME-THING?!
FWIP
SO DOES THAT MEAN...
SHE DOESN'T NEED TO KISS ME TO USE HER POWERS...?
I SHOULD HOLD ONTO THIS FOR NOW...
...

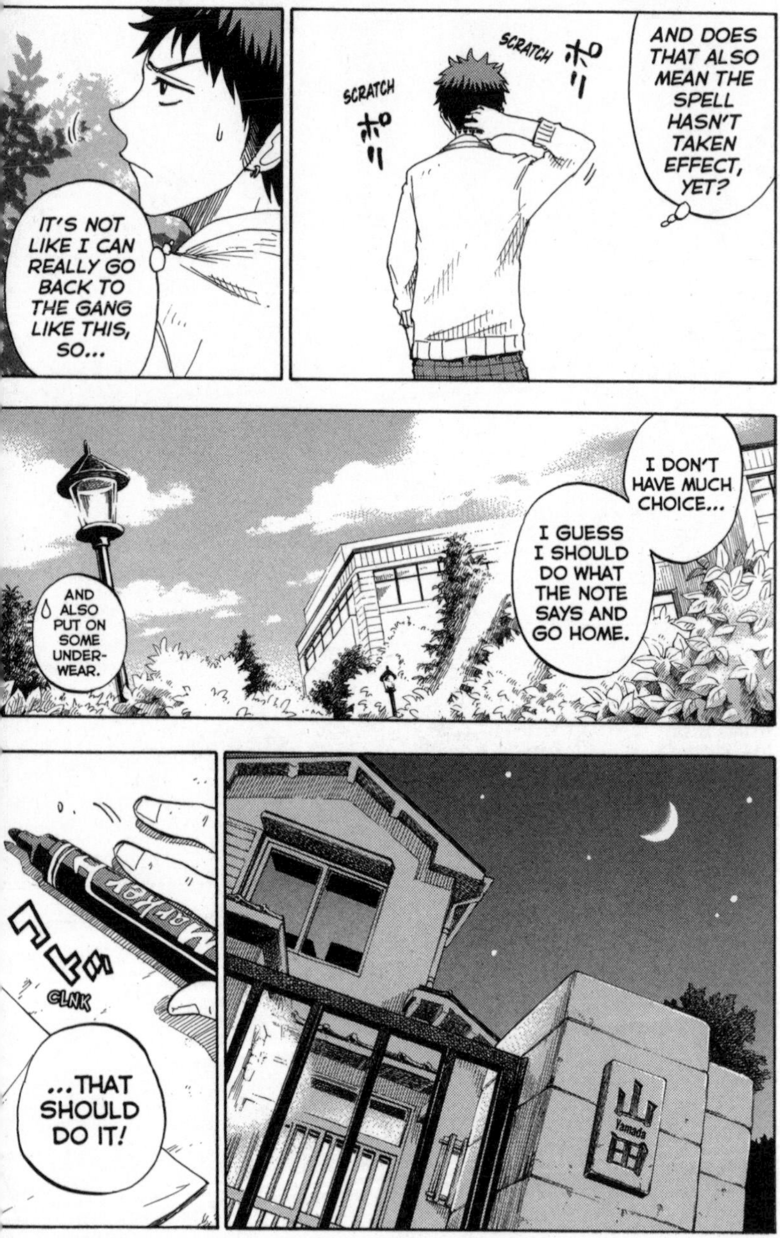
AND DOES THAT ALSO MEAN THE SPELL HASN'T TAKEN EFFECT, YET?
SCRATCH
ポリ
SCRATCH
ポリ
IT'S NOT LIKE I CAN REALLY GO BACK TO THE GANG LIKE THIS, SO...
I DON'T HAVE MUCH CHOICE...
I GUESS I SHOULD DO WHAT THE NOTE SAYS AND GO HOME.
AND ALSO PUT ON SOME UNDER-WEAR.
山
Yamada
田
CLNK
...THAT SHOULD DO IT!

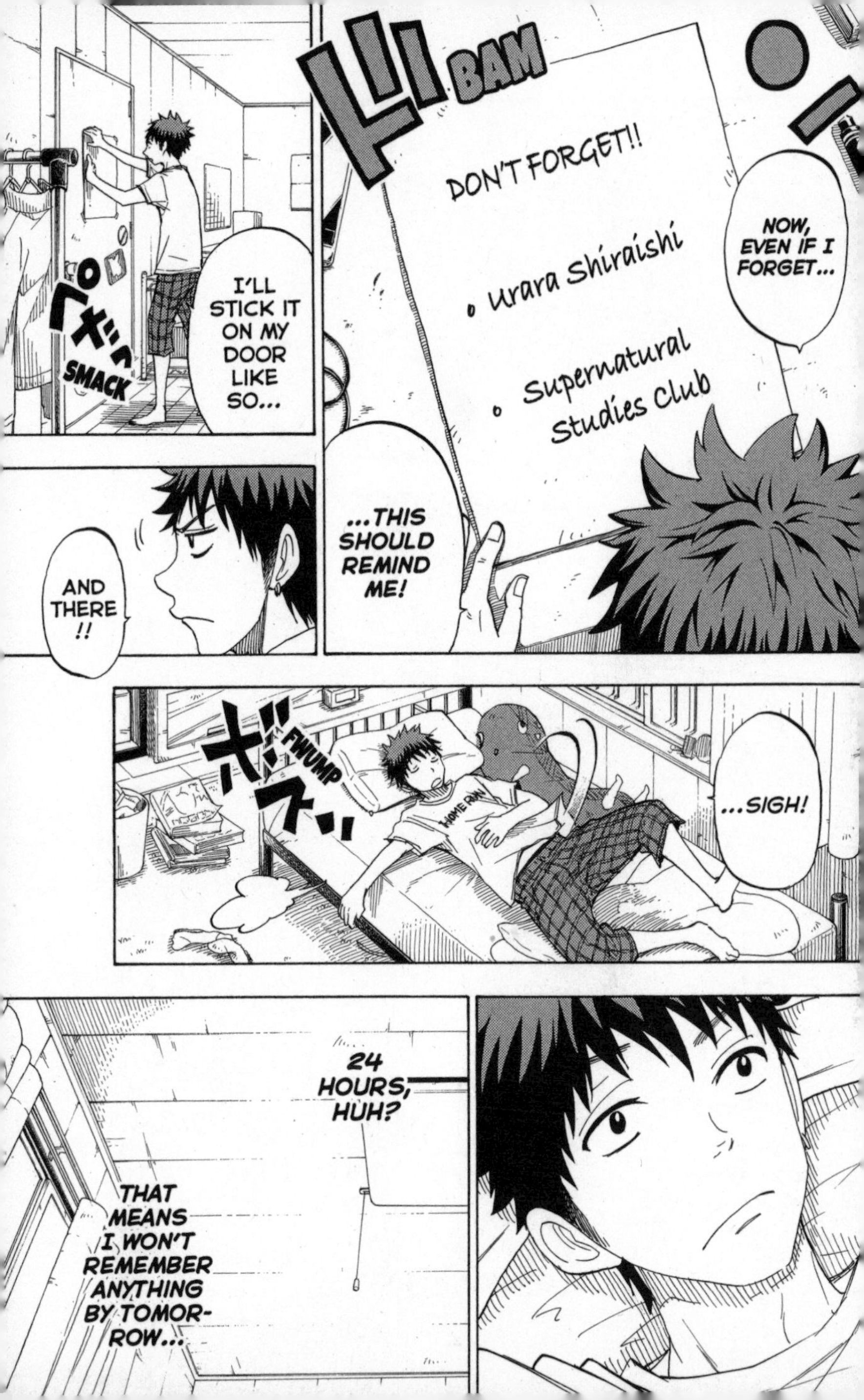
BAM
DON'T FORGET!!
Urara Shiraishi
Supernatural Studies Club
NOW, EVEN IF I FORGET...
...THIS SHOULD REMIND ME!
I'LL STICK IT ON MY DOOR LIKE SO...
SMACK
AND THERE!!
...SIGH!
FWUMP
24 HOURS, HUH?
THAT MEANS I WON'T REMEMBER ANYTHING BY TOMOR-ROW...

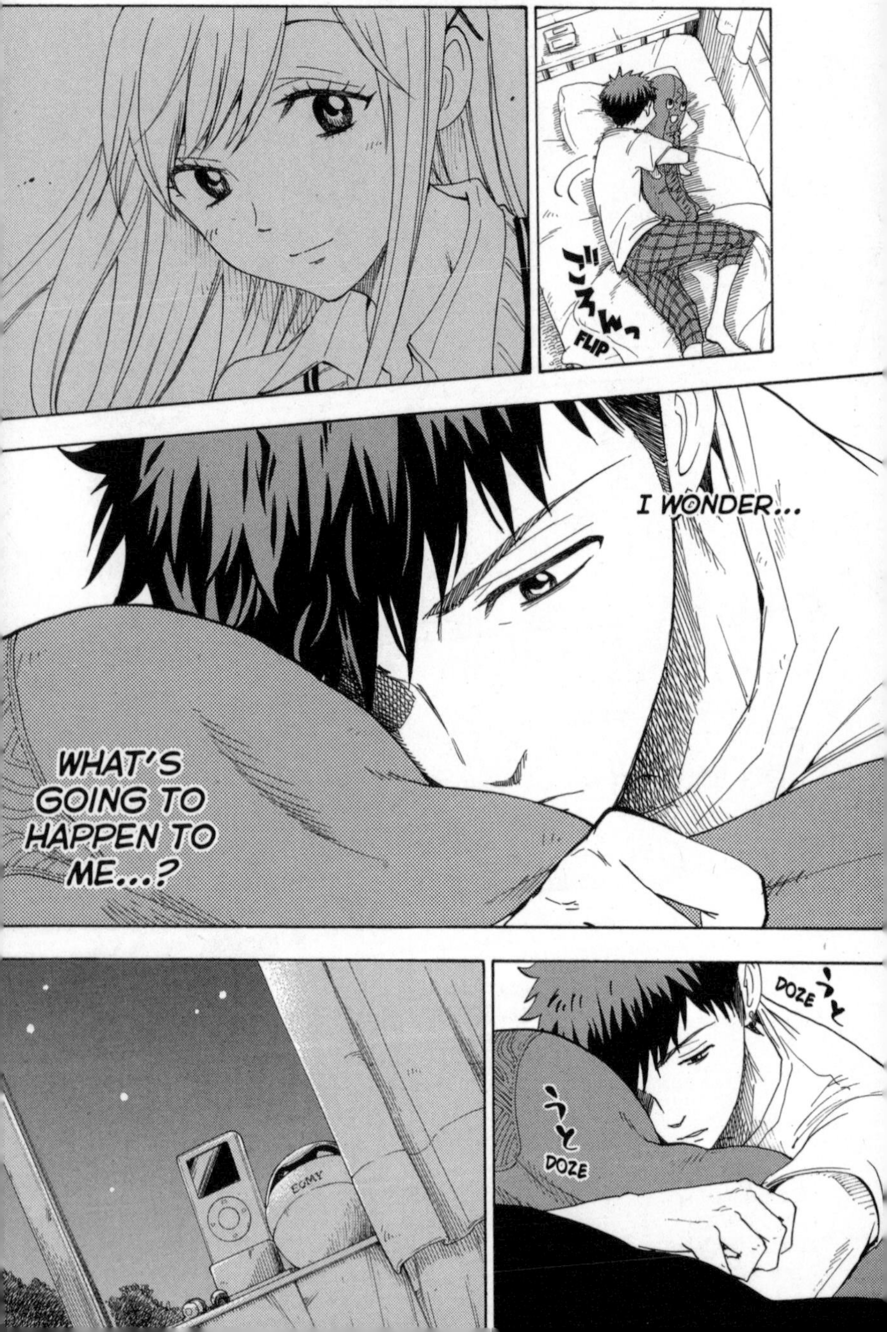
FLIP
I WONDER...
WHAT'S GOING TO HAPPEN TO ME...?
DOZE うと
うと DOZE

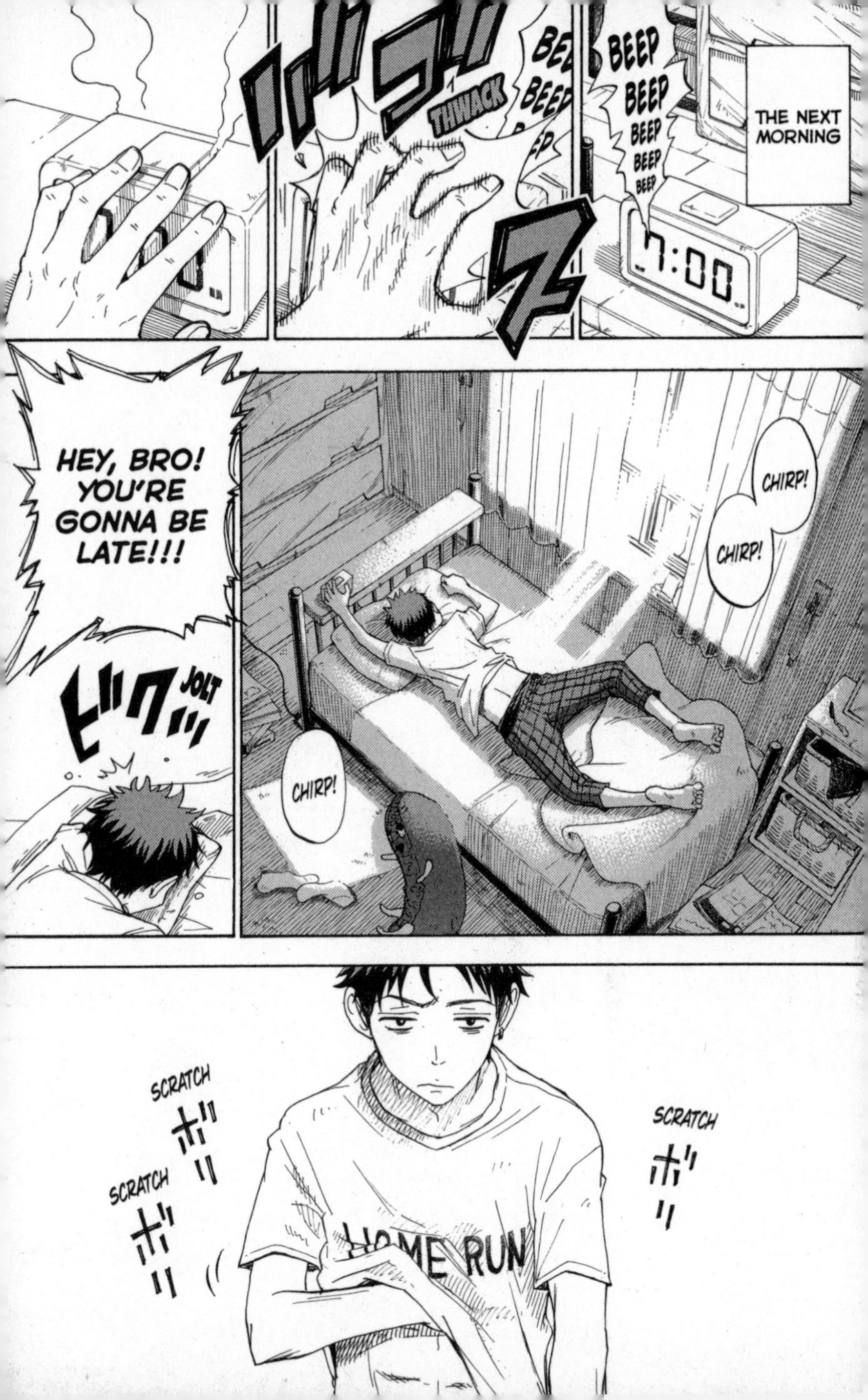
THE NEXT MORNING
BEEP BEEP BEEP BEEP BEEP
BEEP BEEP
THWACK
CHIRP!
CHIRP!
CHIRP!
HEY, BRO! YOU'RE GONNA BE LATE!!!
JOLT
SCRATCH
SCRATCH
SCRATCH
HOME RUN

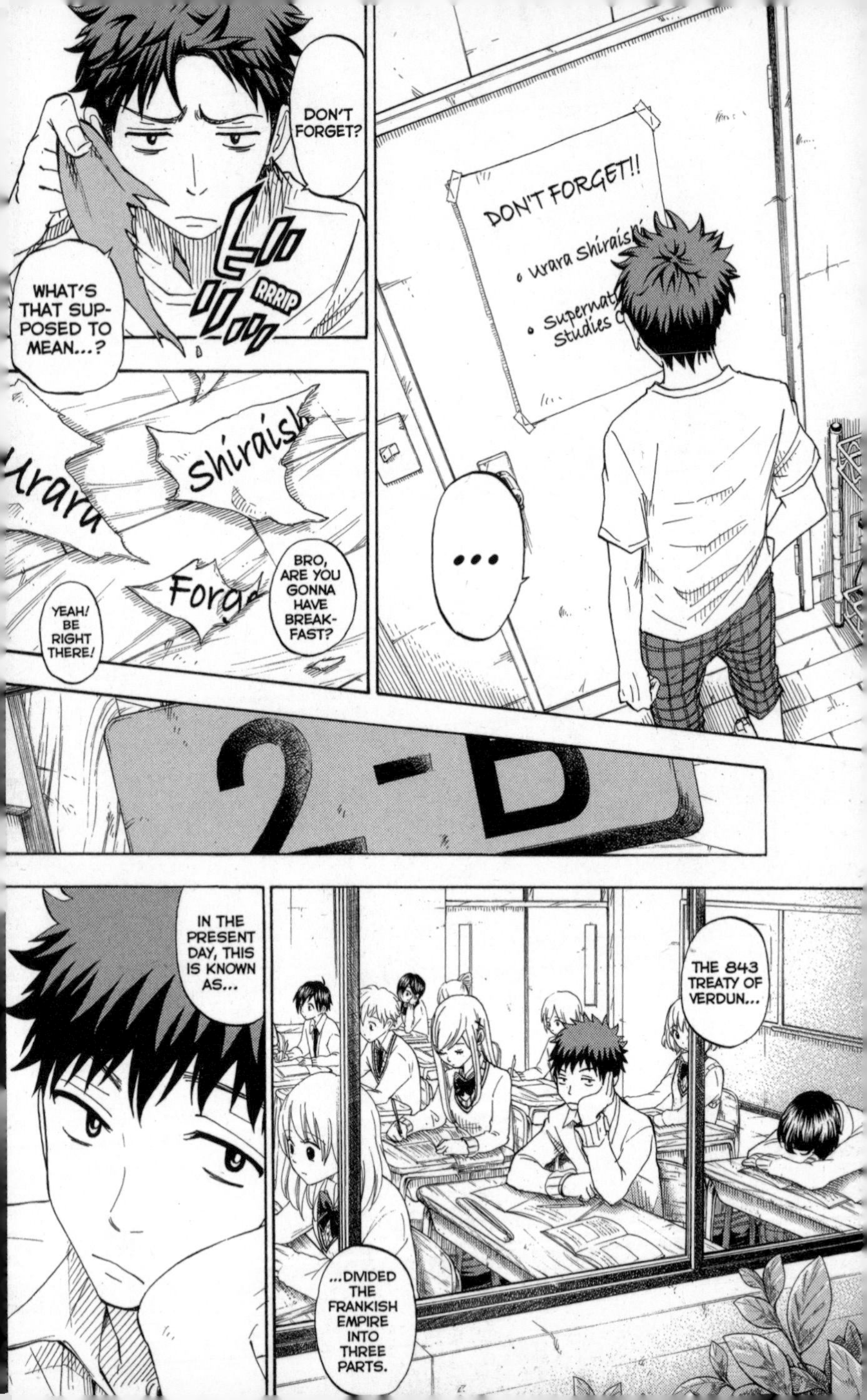
DON'T FORGET!!
Urara Shiraish
...
DON'T FORGET?
WHAT'S THAT SUP-POSED TO MEAN...?
RRRIP
Shiraish
Urara
Forg
BRO, ARE YOU GONNA HAVE BREAK-FAST?
YEAH! BE RIGHT THERE!
2-B
THE 843 TREATY OF VERDUN...
...DIVIDED THE FRANKISH EMPIRE INTO THREE PARTS.
IN THE PRESENT DAY, THIS IS KNOWN AS...

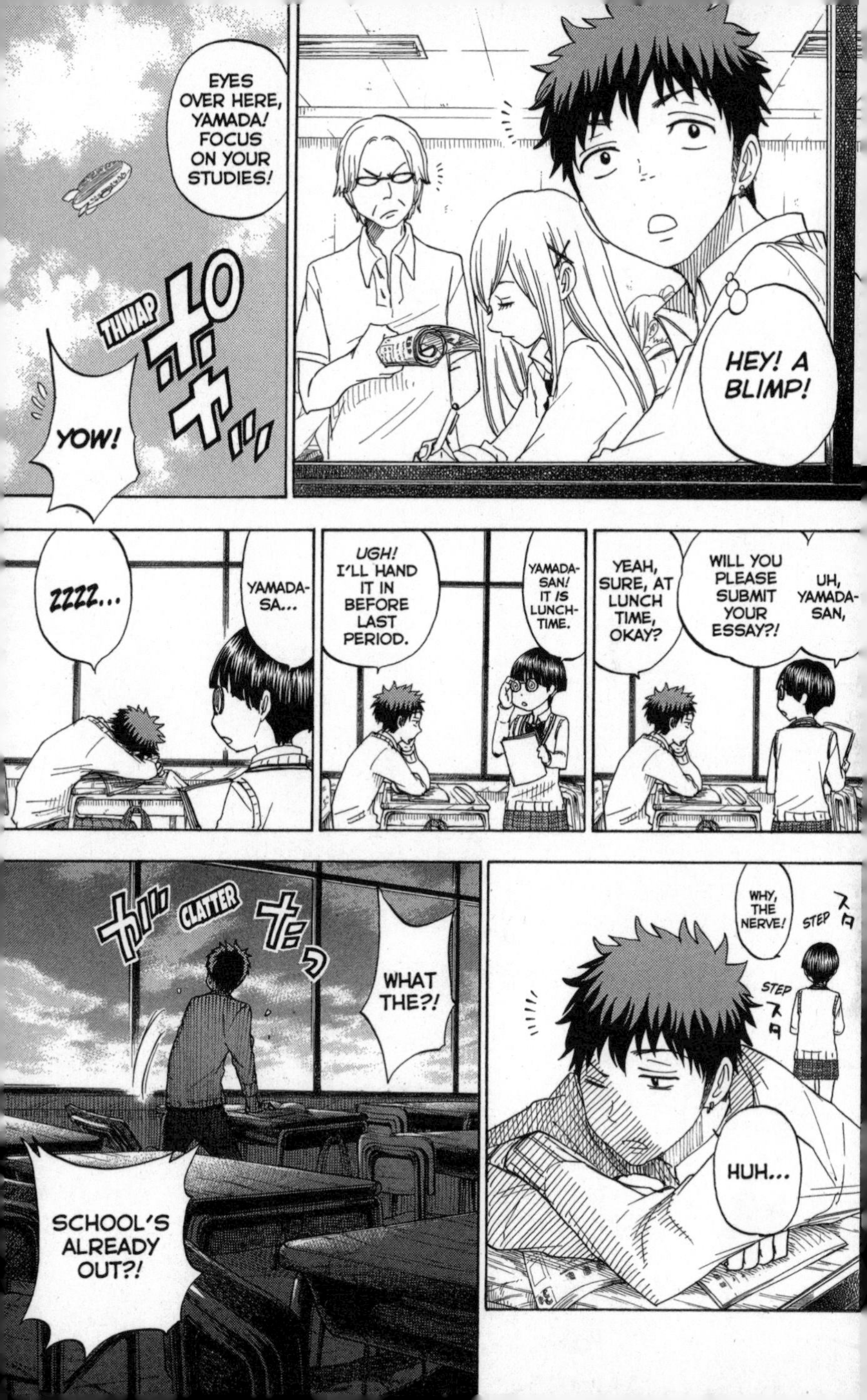
HEY! A BLIMP!
EYES OVER HERE, YAMADA! FOCUS ON YOUR STUDIES!
THWAP
YOW!
UH, YAMADA-SAN,
WILL YOU PLEASE SUBMIT YOUR ESSAY?!
YEAH, SURE, AT LUNCH TIME, OKAY?
YAMADA-SAN! IT *IS* LUNCH-TIME.
UGH! I'LL HAND IT IN BEFORE LAST PERIOD.
YAMADA-SA...
ZZZZ...
WHY, THE NERVE!
STEP
STEP
HUH...
WHAT THE?!
CLATTER
SCHOOL'S ALREADY OUT?!

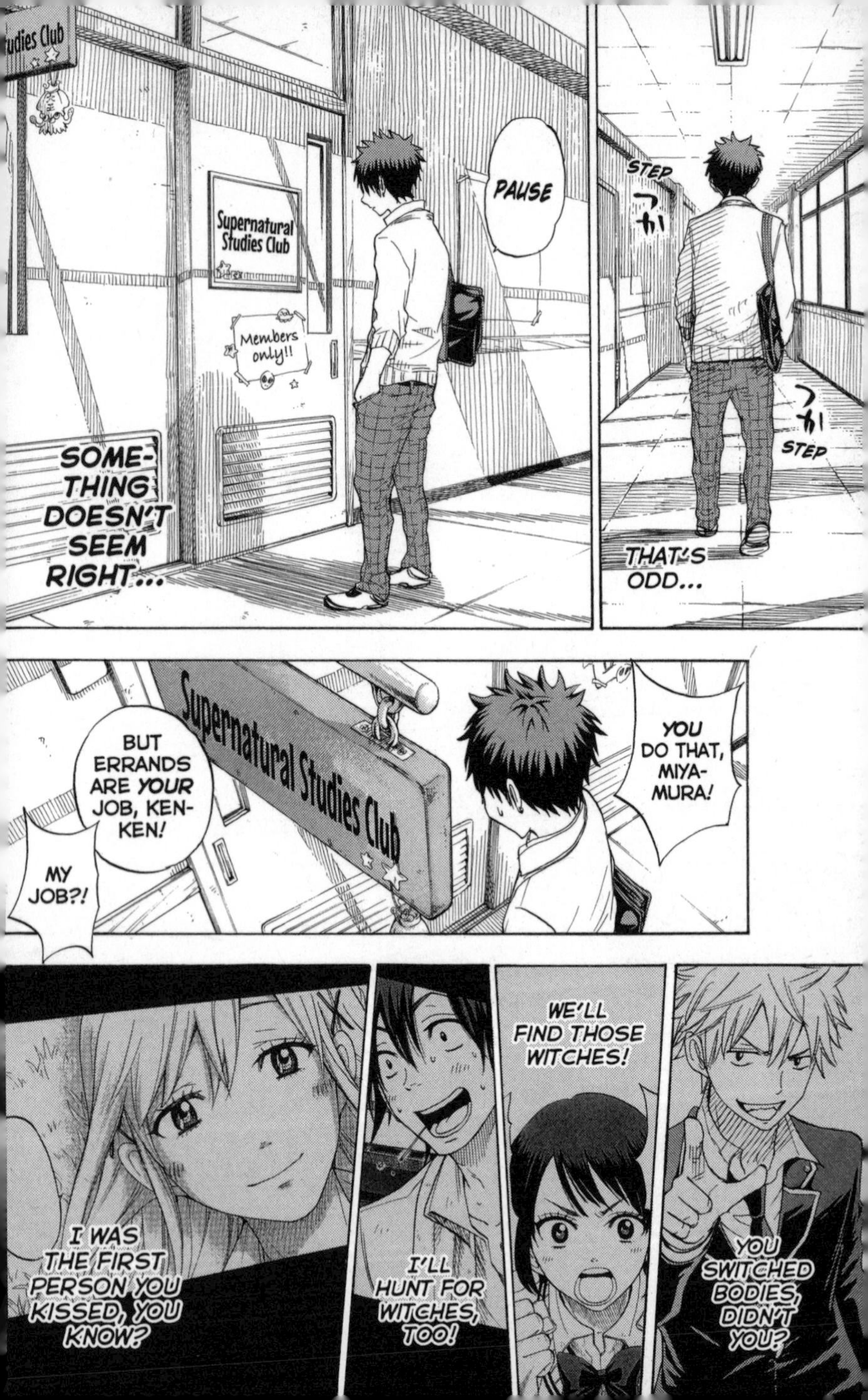
STEP
つか
つか
STEP
THAT'S ODD...
PAUSE
Supernatural Studies Club
Members only!!
SOME-THING DOESN'T SEEM RIGHT...
YOU DO THAT, MIYA-MURA!
Supernatural Studies Club
BUT ERRANDS ARE *YOUR* JOB, KEN-KEN!
MY JOB?!
YOU SWITCHED BODIES, DIDN'T YOU?
WE'LL FIND THOSE WITCHES!
I'LL HUNT FOR WITCHES, TOO!
I WAS THE FIRST PERSON YOU KISSED, YOU KNOW?

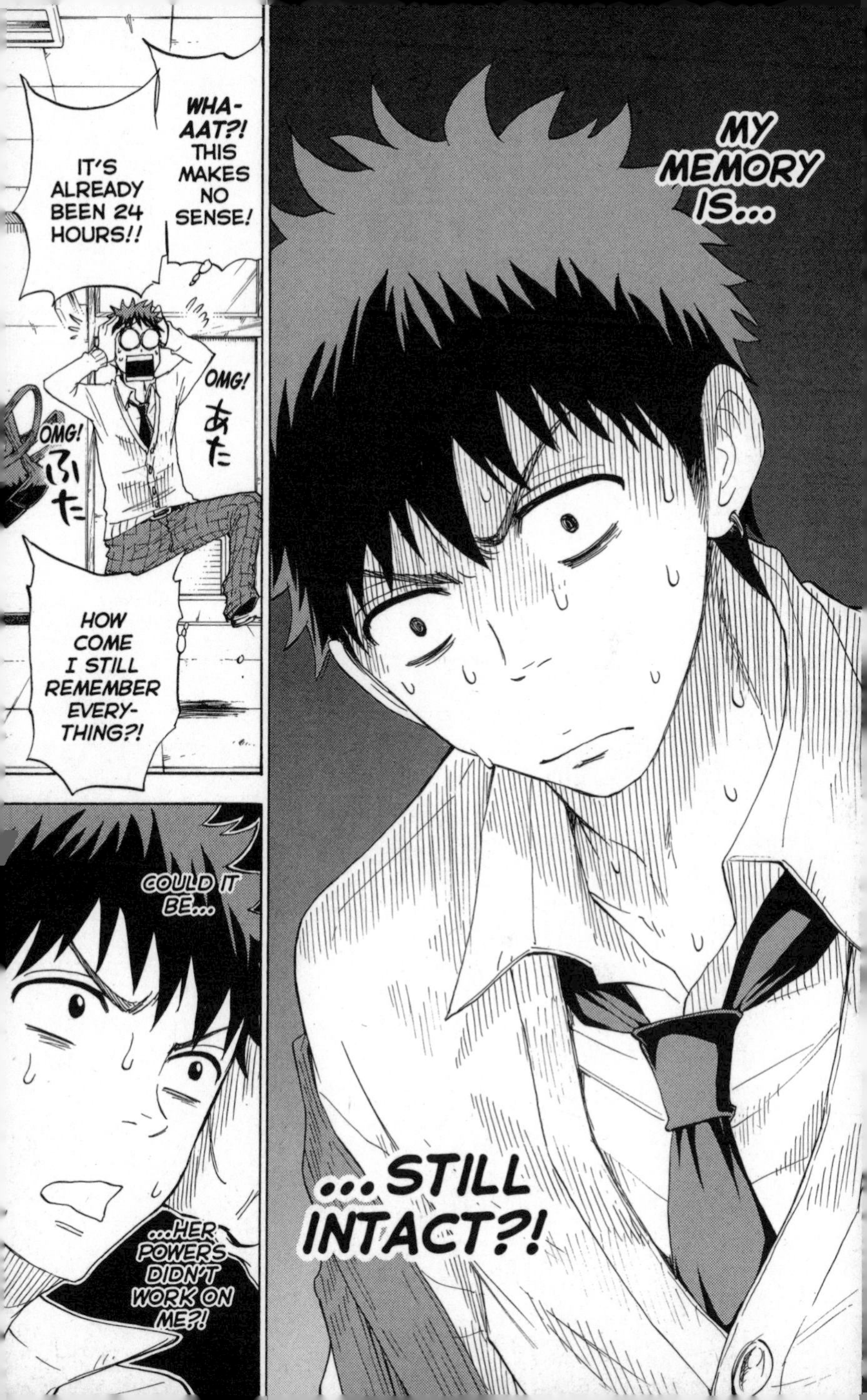
MY MEMORY IS...
...STILL INTACT?!
WHA-AAT?! THIS MAKES NO SENSE!
IT'S ALREADY BEEN 24 HOURS!!
OMG! あた
OMG! ふた
HOW COME I STILL REMEMBER EVERY-THING?!
COULD IT BE...
...HER POWERS DIDN'T WORK ON ME?!

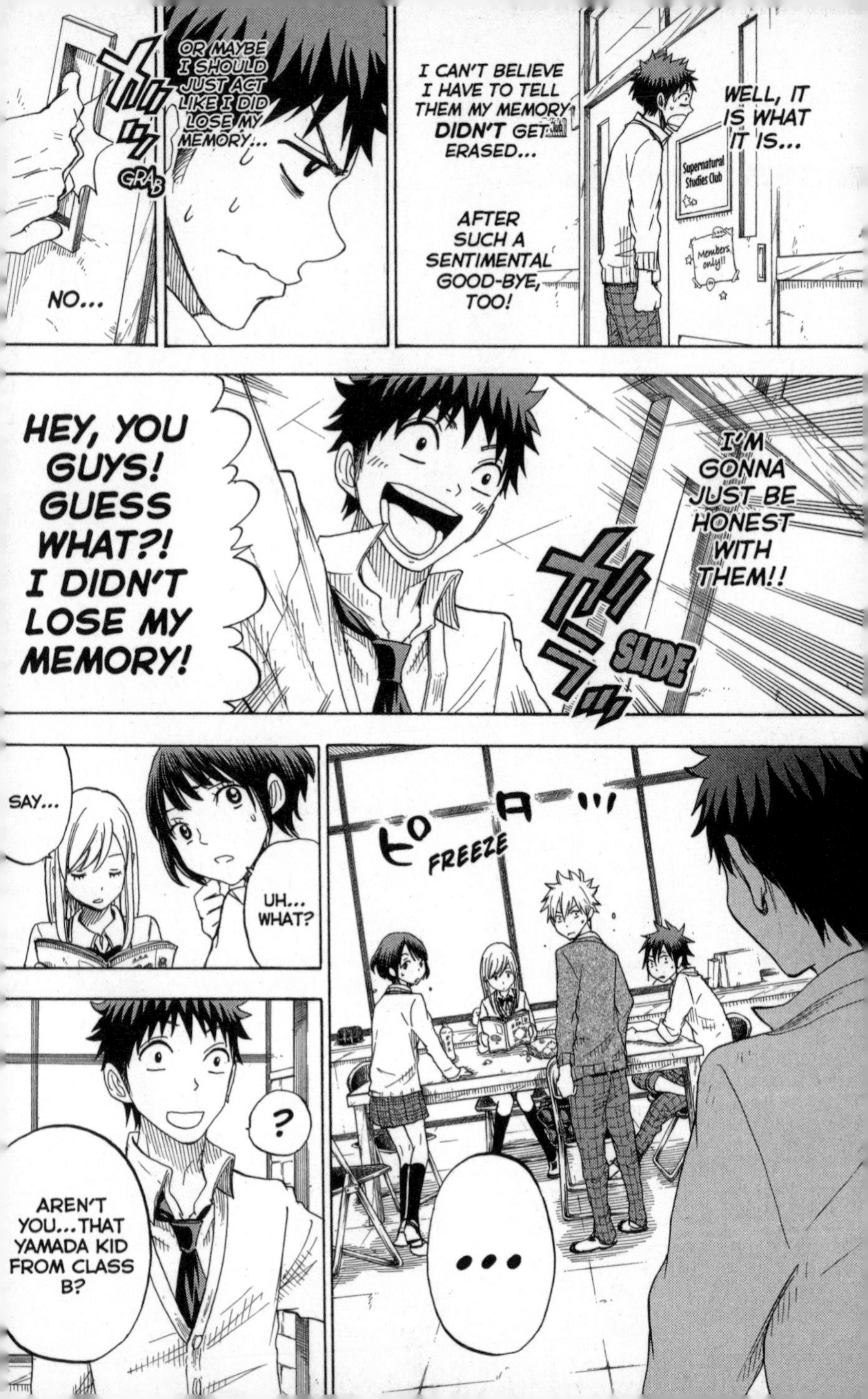
WELL, IT IS WHAT IT IS...
Supernatural Studies Club
Members only!!
I CAN'T BELIEVE I HAVE TO TELL THEM MY MEMORY DIDN'T GET ERASED...
AFTER SUCH A SENTIMENTAL GOOD-BYE, TOO!
OR MAYBE I SHOULD JUST ACT LIKE I DID LOSE MY MEMORY...
GRAB
NO...
I'M GONNA JUST BE HONEST WITH THEM!!
SLIDE
HEY, YOU GUYS! GUESS WHAT?! I DIDN'T LOSE MY MEMORY!
FREEZE
...
SAY...
UH... WHAT?
?
AREN'T YOU...THAT YAMADA KID FROM CLASS B?

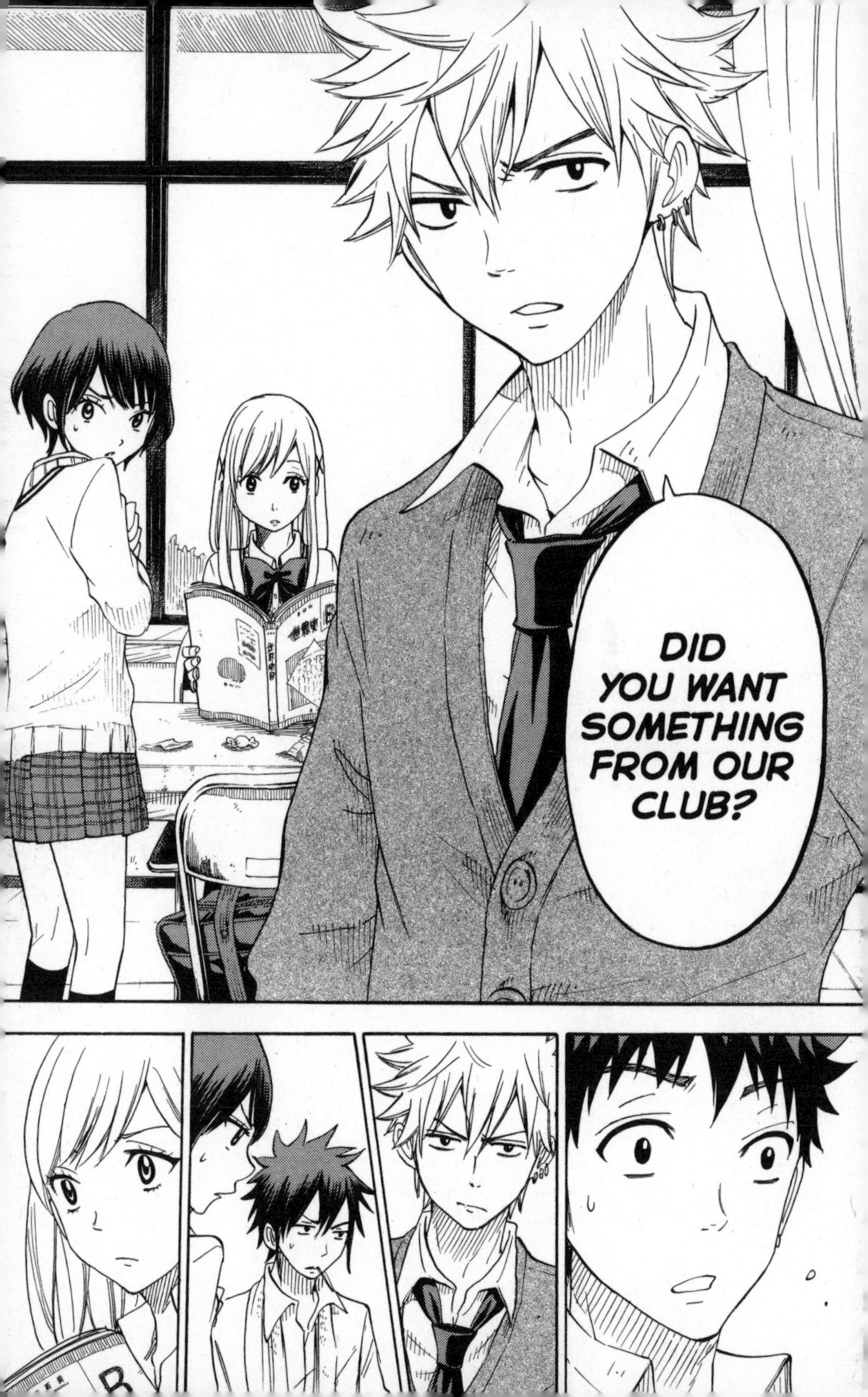
DID YOU WANT SOMETHING FROM OUR CLUB?

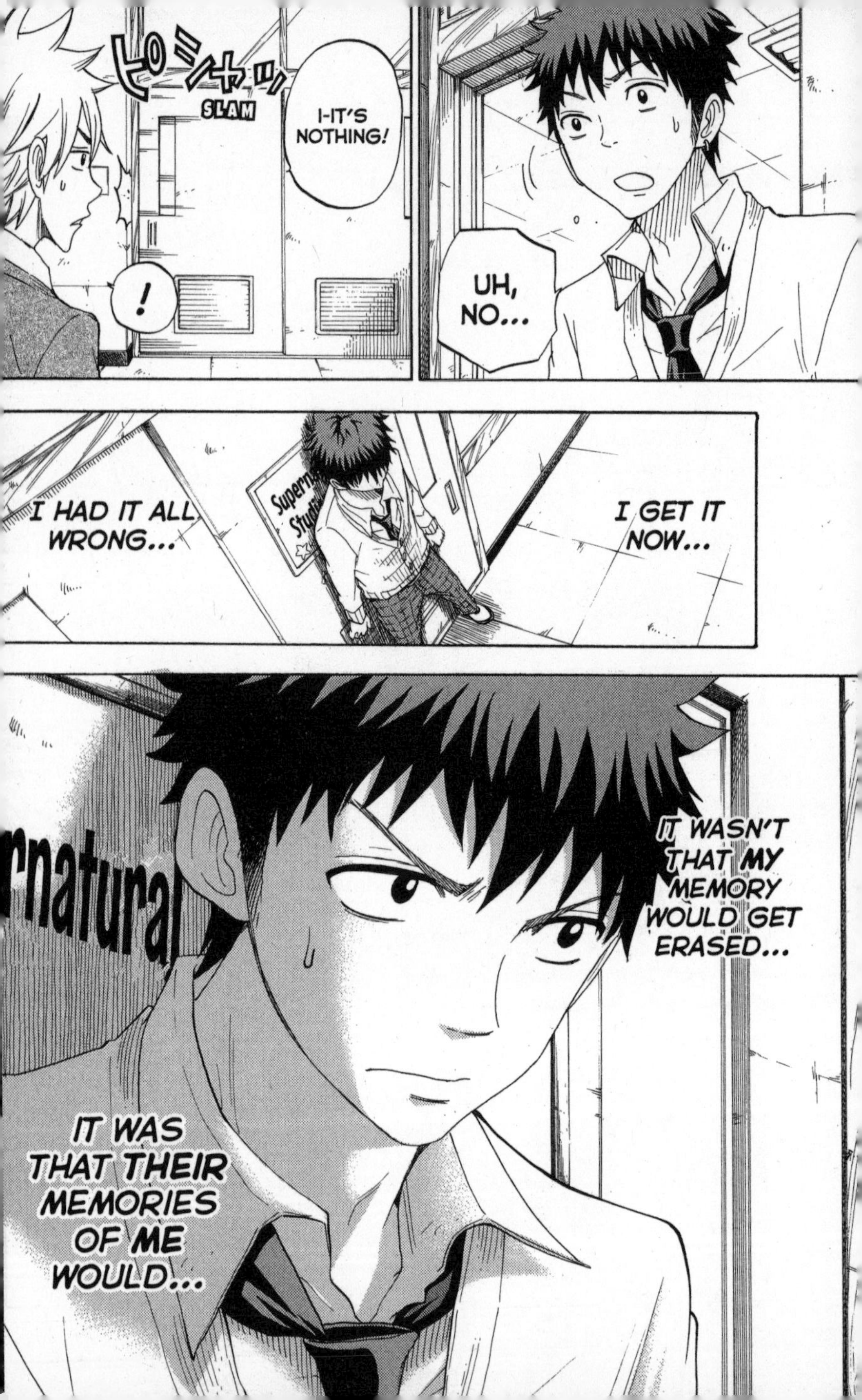
UH, NO...
SLAM
I-IT'S NOTHING!
!
I GET IT NOW...
I HAD IT ALL WRONG...
IT WASN'T THAT MY MEMORY WOULD GET ERASED...
IT WAS THAT THEIR MEMORIES OF ME WOULD...

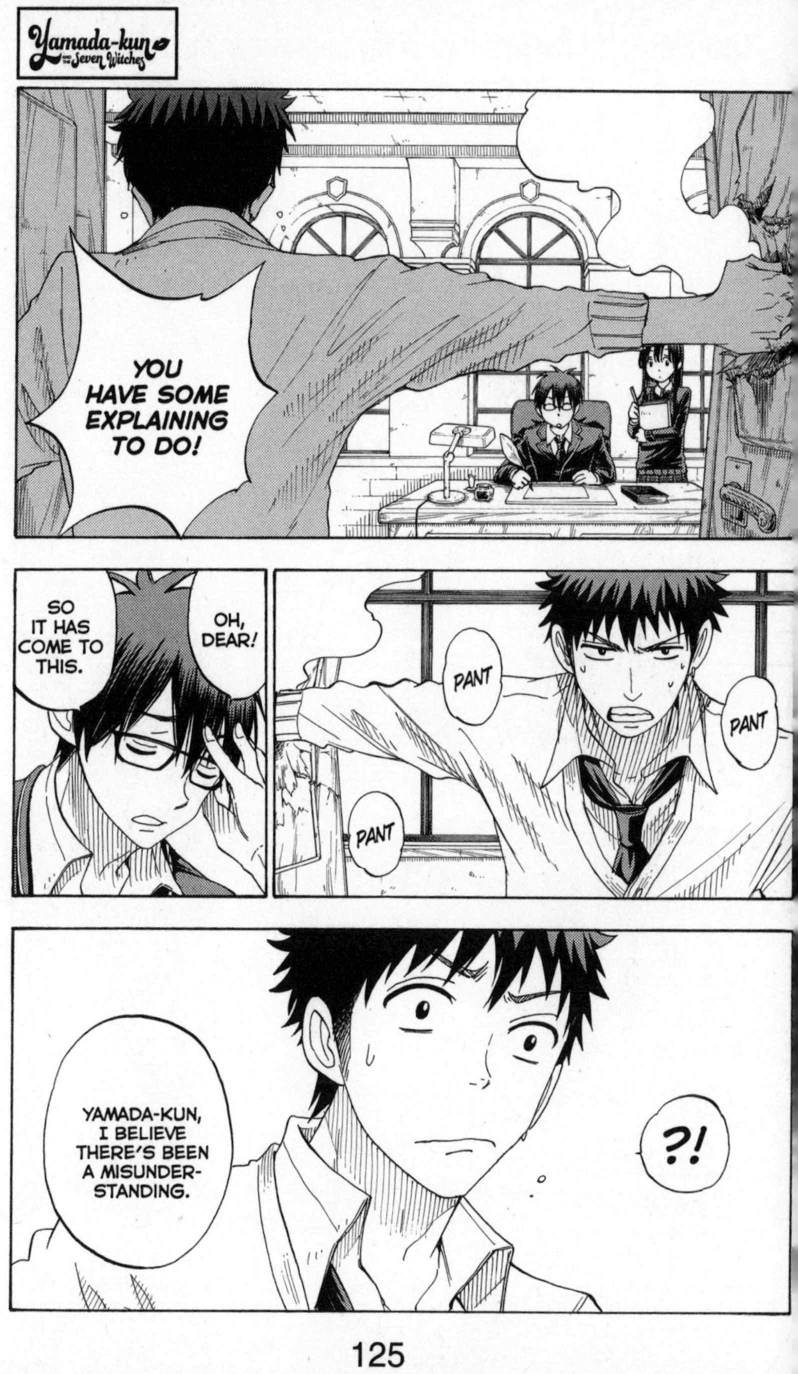
YOU HAVE SOME EXPLAINING TO DO!
PANT
PANT
PANT
OH, DEAR!
SO IT HAS COME TO THIS.
?!
YAMADA-KUN, I BELIEVE THERE'S BEEN A MISUNDER-STANDING.

CHAPTER 67: It's the material of the underwear that's important!

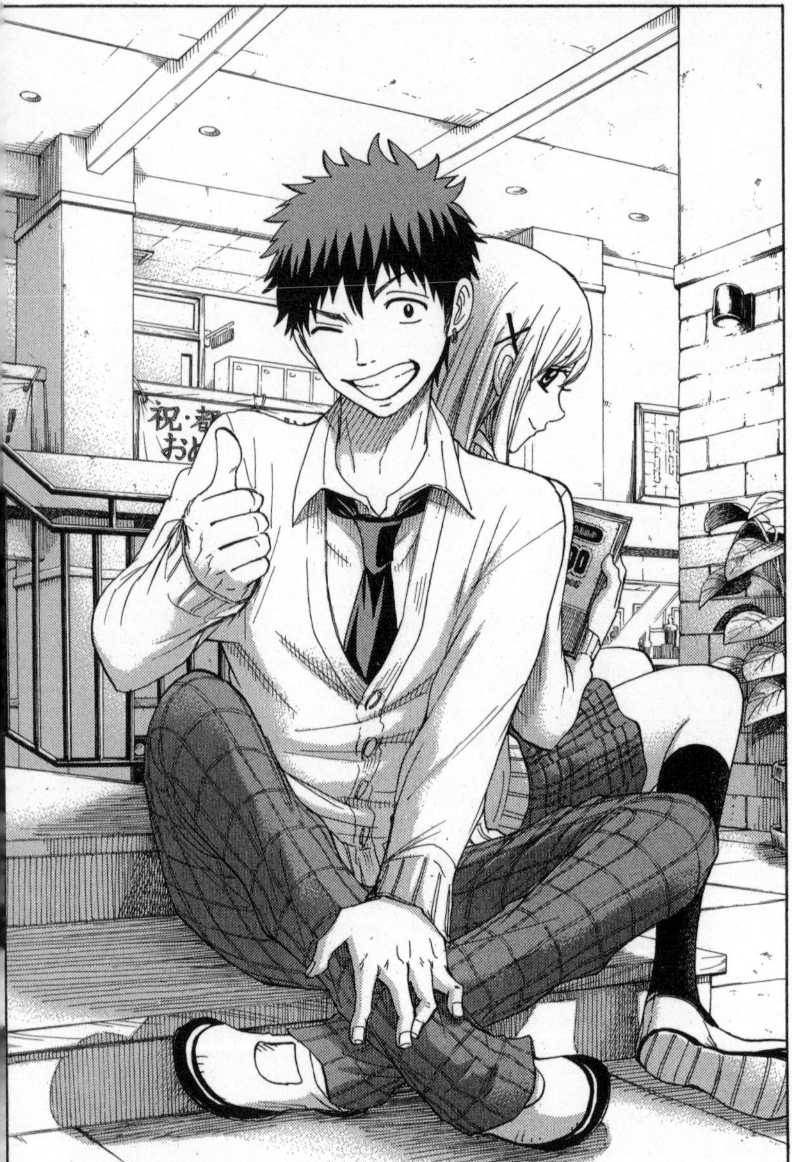

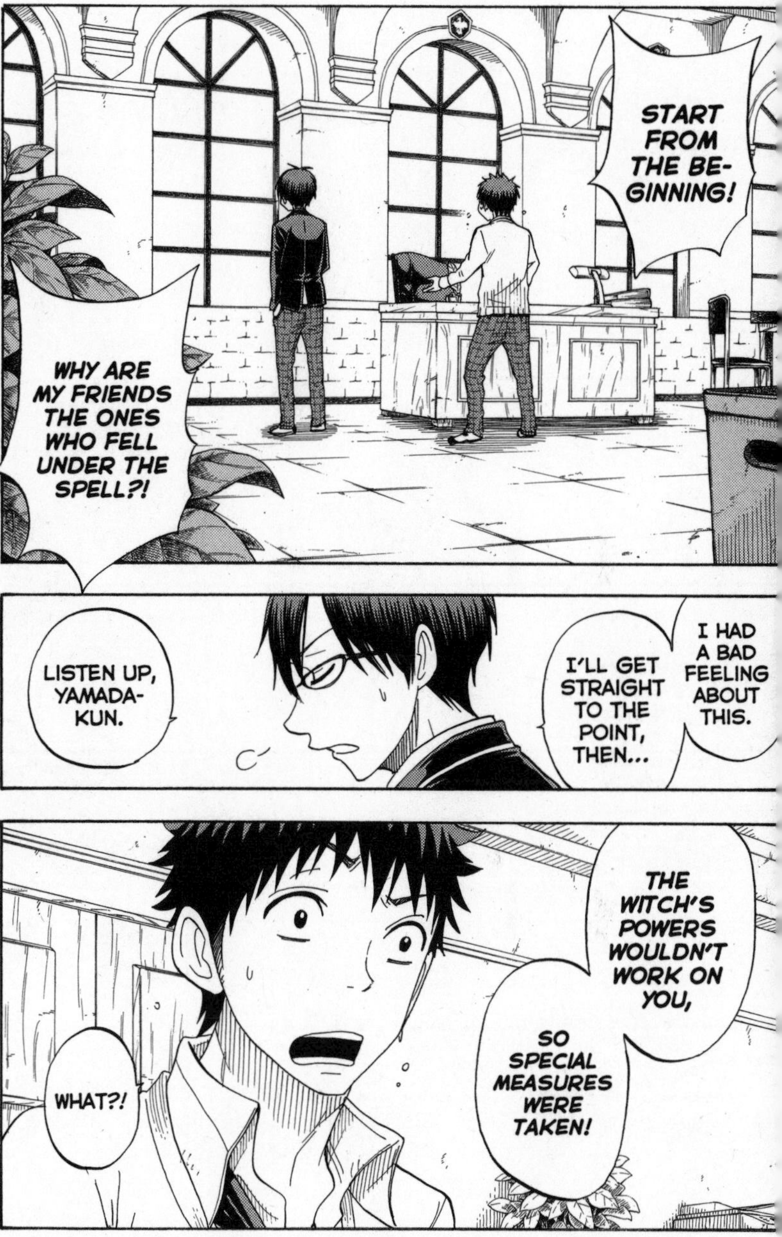
START FROM THE BE-GINNING!
WHY ARE MY FRIENDS THE ONES WHO FELL UNDER THE SPELL?!
I HAD A BAD FEELING ABOUT THIS.
I'LL GET STRAIGHT TO THE POINT, THEN...
LISTEN UP, YAMADA-KUN.
THE WITCH'S POWERS WOULDN'T WORK ON YOU,
SO SPECIAL MEASURES WERE TAKEN!
WHAT?!

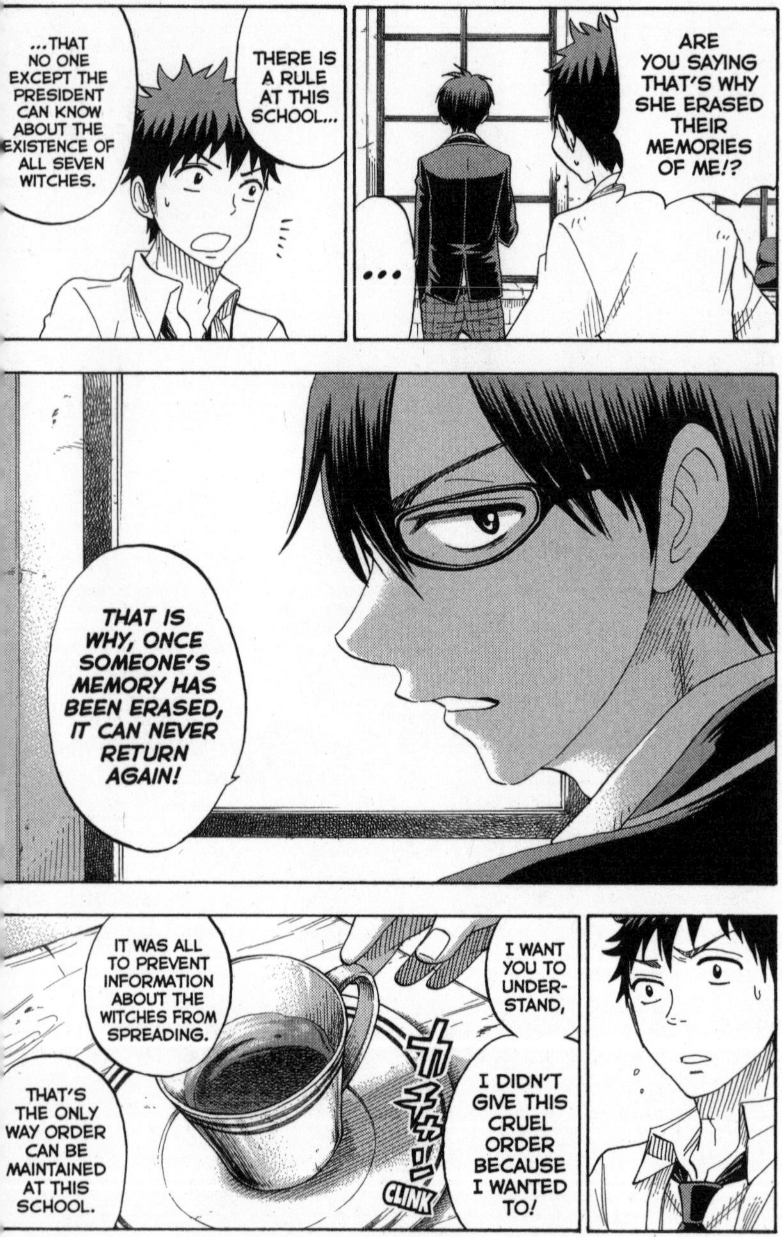
ARE YOU SAYING THAT'S WHY SHE ERASED THEIR MEMORIES OF ME!?
...
THERE IS A RULE AT THIS SCHOOL...
...THAT NO ONE EXCEPT THE PRESIDENT CAN KNOW ABOUT THE EXISTENCE OF ALL SEVEN WITCHES.
THAT IS WHY, ONCE SOMEONE'S MEMORY HAS BEEN ERASED, IT CAN NEVER RETURN AGAIN!
I WANT YOU TO UNDER-STAND,
I DIDN'T GIVE THIS CRUEL ORDER BECAUSE I WANTED TO!
CLINK
IT WAS ALL TO PREVENT INFORMATION ABOUT THE WITCHES FROM SPREADING.
THAT'S THE ONLY WAY ORDER CAN BE MAINTAINED AT THIS SCHOOL.

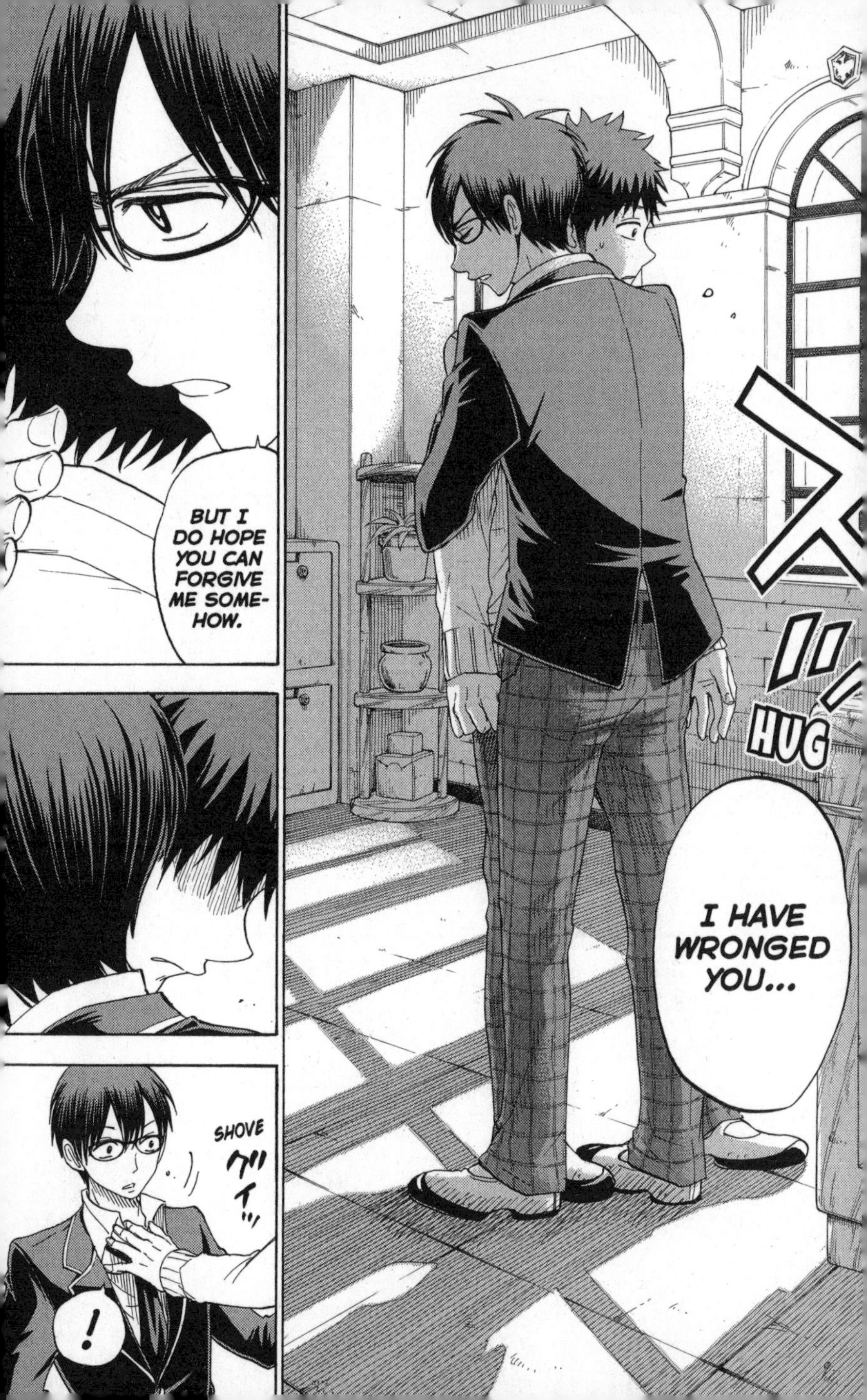
HUG
I HAVE WRONGED YOU...
BUT I DO HOPE YOU CAN FORGIVE ME SOME-HOW.
SHOVE
グイ
!

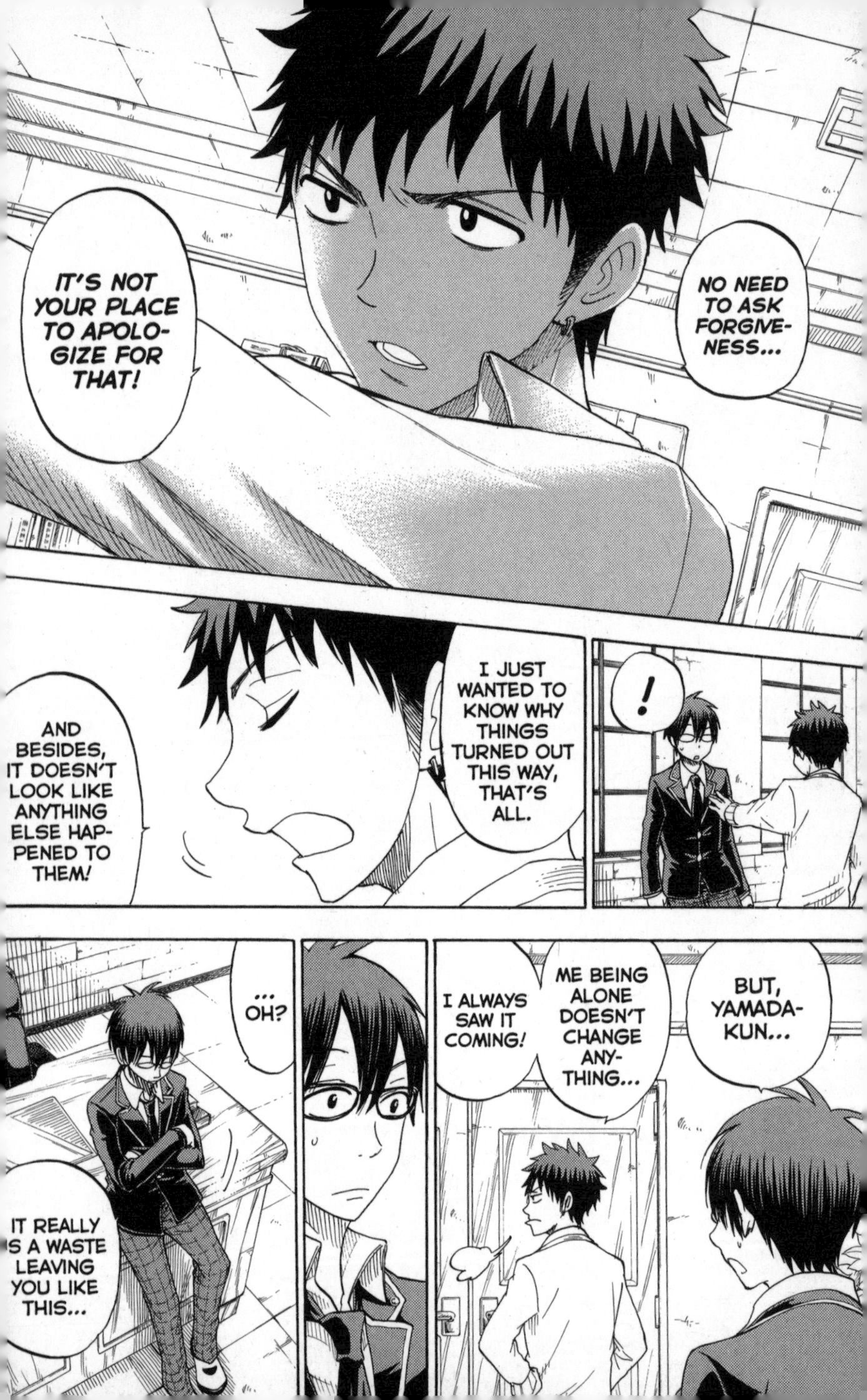
NO NEED TO ASK FORGIVE-NESS...
IT'S NOT YOUR PLACE TO APOLO-GIZE FOR THAT!
!
I JUST WANTED TO KNOW WHY THINGS TURNED OUT THIS WAY, THAT'S ALL.
AND BESIDES, IT DOESN'T LOOK LIKE ANYTHING ELSE HAP-PENED TO THEM!
BUT, YAMADA-KUN...
ME BEING ALONE DOESN'T CHANGE ANY-THING...
I ALWAYS SAW IT COMING!
... OH?
IT REALLY 'S A WASTE LEAVING YOU LIKE THIS...

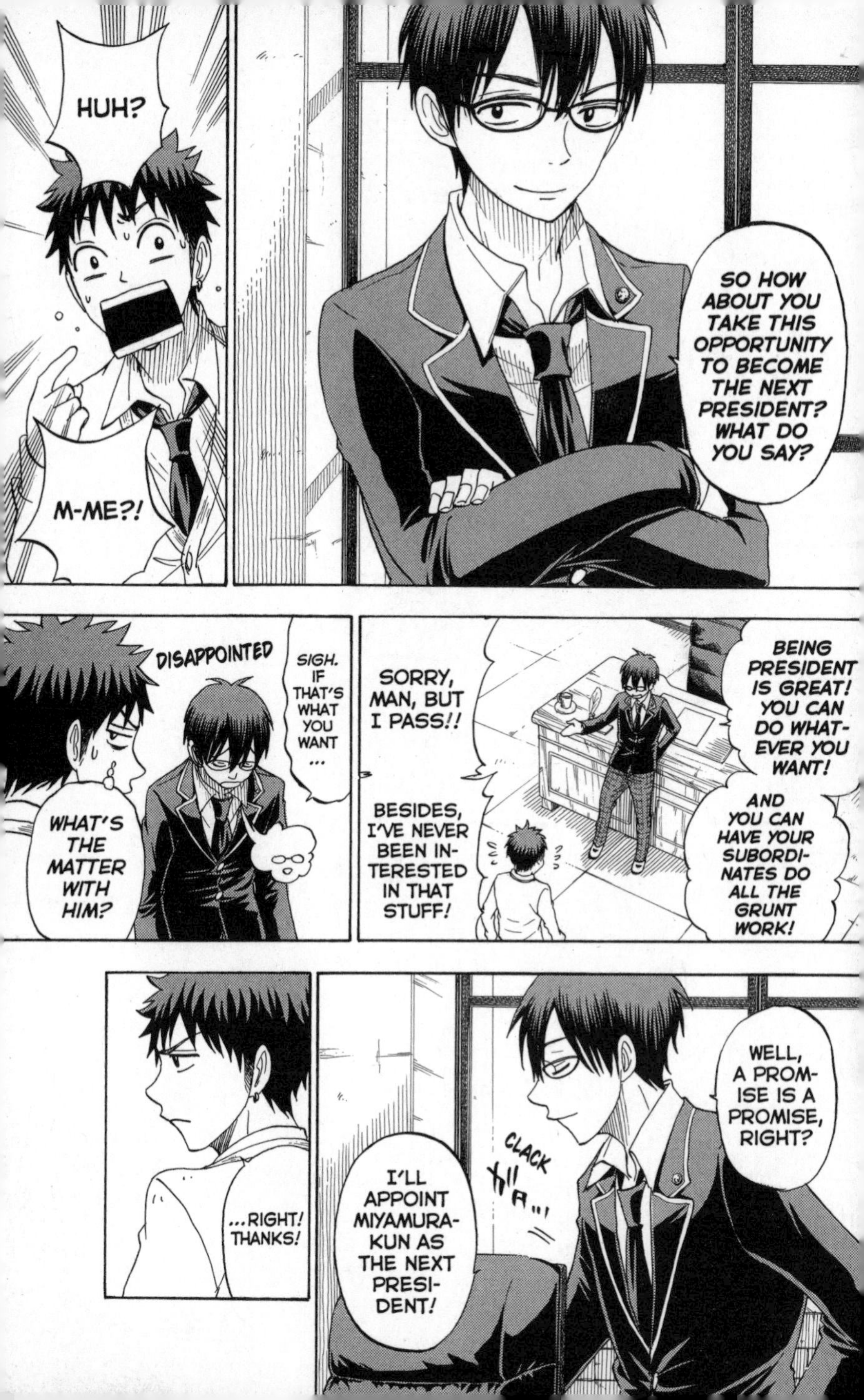
SO HOW ABOUT YOU TAKE THIS OPPORTUNITY TO BECOME THE NEXT PRESIDENT? WHAT DO YOU SAY?
HUH?
M-ME?!
BEING PRESIDENT IS GREAT! YOU CAN DO WHATEVER YOU WANT!
AND YOU CAN HAVE YOUR SUBORDINATES DO ALL THE GRUNT WORK!
SORRY, MAN, BUT I PASS!!
BESIDES, I'VE NEVER BEEN INTERESTED IN THAT STUFF!
SIGH. IF THAT'S WHAT YOU WANT...
DISAPPOINTED
WHAT'S THE MATTER WITH HIM?
WELL, A PROMISE IS A PROMISE, RIGHT?
CLACK
I'LL APPOINT MIYAMURA-KUN AS THE NEXT PRESIDENT!
...RIGHT! THANKS!

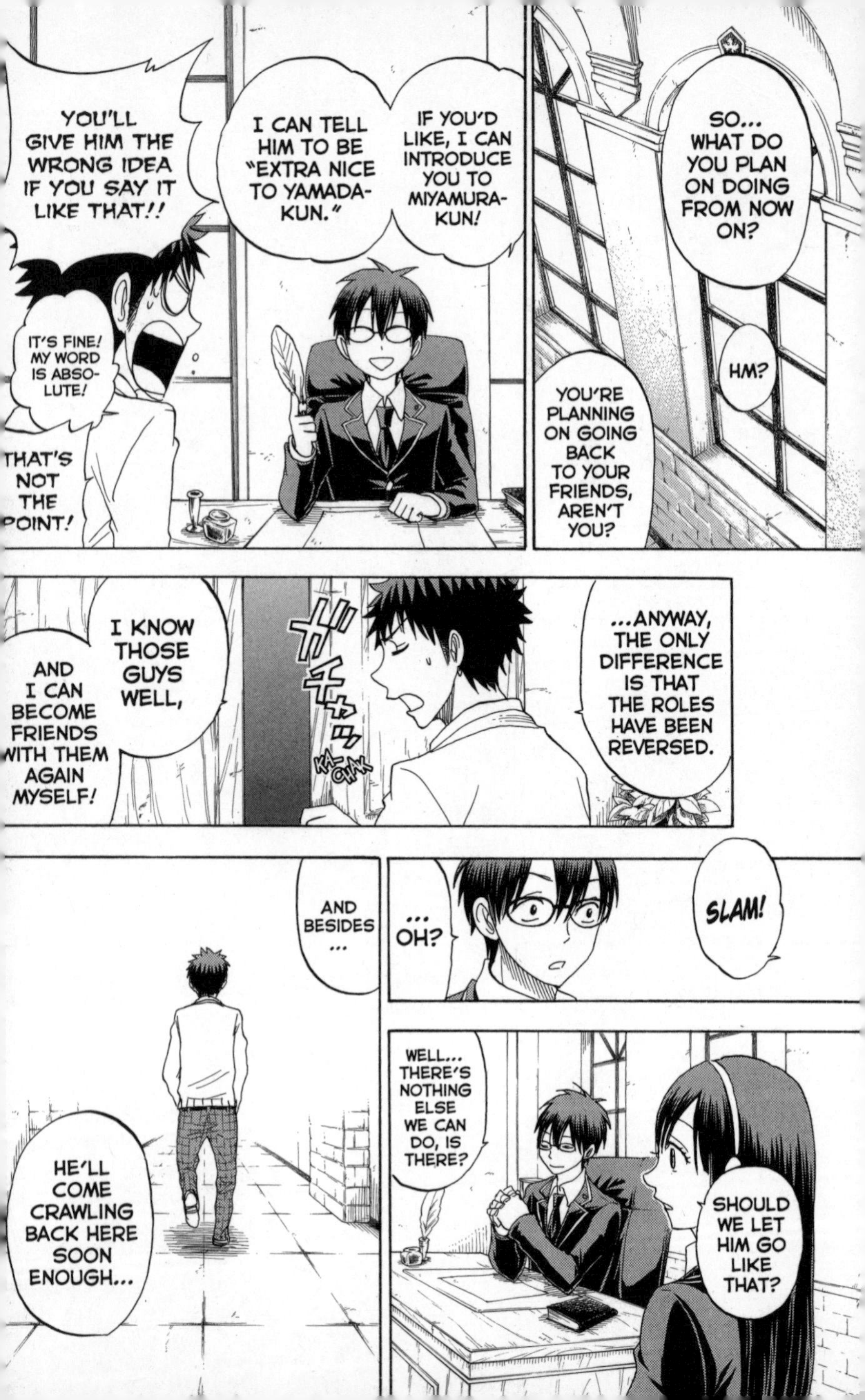
SO... WHAT DO YOU PLAN ON DOING FROM NOW ON?
HM?
YOU'RE PLANNING ON GOING BACK TO YOUR FRIENDS, AREN'T YOU?
IF YOU'D LIKE, I CAN INTRODUCE YOU TO MIYAMURA-KUN!
I CAN TELL HIM TO BE "EXTRA NICE TO YAMADA-KUN."
YOU'LL GIVE HIM THE WRONG IDEA IF YOU SAY IT LIKE THAT!!
IT'S FINE! MY WORD IS ABSOLUTE!
THAT'S NOT THE POINT!
...ANYWAY, THE ONLY DIFFERENCE IS THAT THE ROLES HAVE BEEN REVERSED.
KA-CHAK
I KNOW THOSE GUYS WELL,
AND I CAN BECOME FRIENDS WITH THEM AGAIN MYSELF!
SLAM!
...OH?
SHOULD WE LET HIM GO LIKE THAT?
WELL... THERE'S NOTHING ELSE WE CAN DO, IS THERE?
AND BESIDES...
HE'LL COME CRAWLING BACK HERE SOON ENOUGH...

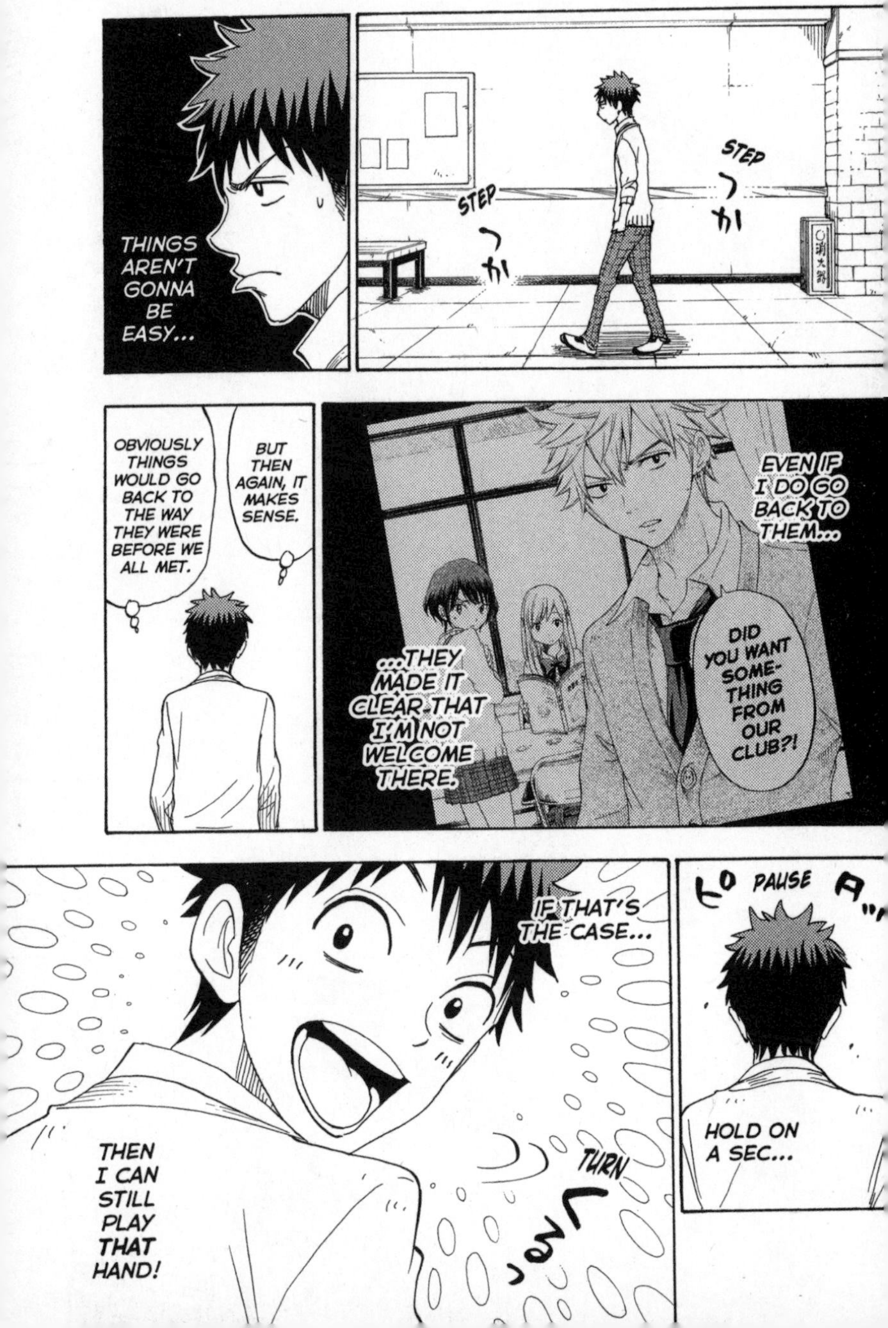
STEP
つか
STEP
つか
THINGS AREN'T GONNA BE EASY...
EVEN IF I DO GO BACK TO THEM...
DID YOU WANT SOMETHING FROM OUR CLUB?!
...THEY MADE IT CLEAR THAT I'M NOT WELCOME THERE.
BUT THEN AGAIN, IT MAKES SENSE.
OBVIOUSLY THINGS WOULD GO BACK TO THE WAY THEY WERE BEFORE WE ALL MET.
PAUSE
HOLD ON A SEC...
IF THAT'S THE CASE...
TURN
THEN I CAN STILL PLAY THAT HAND!

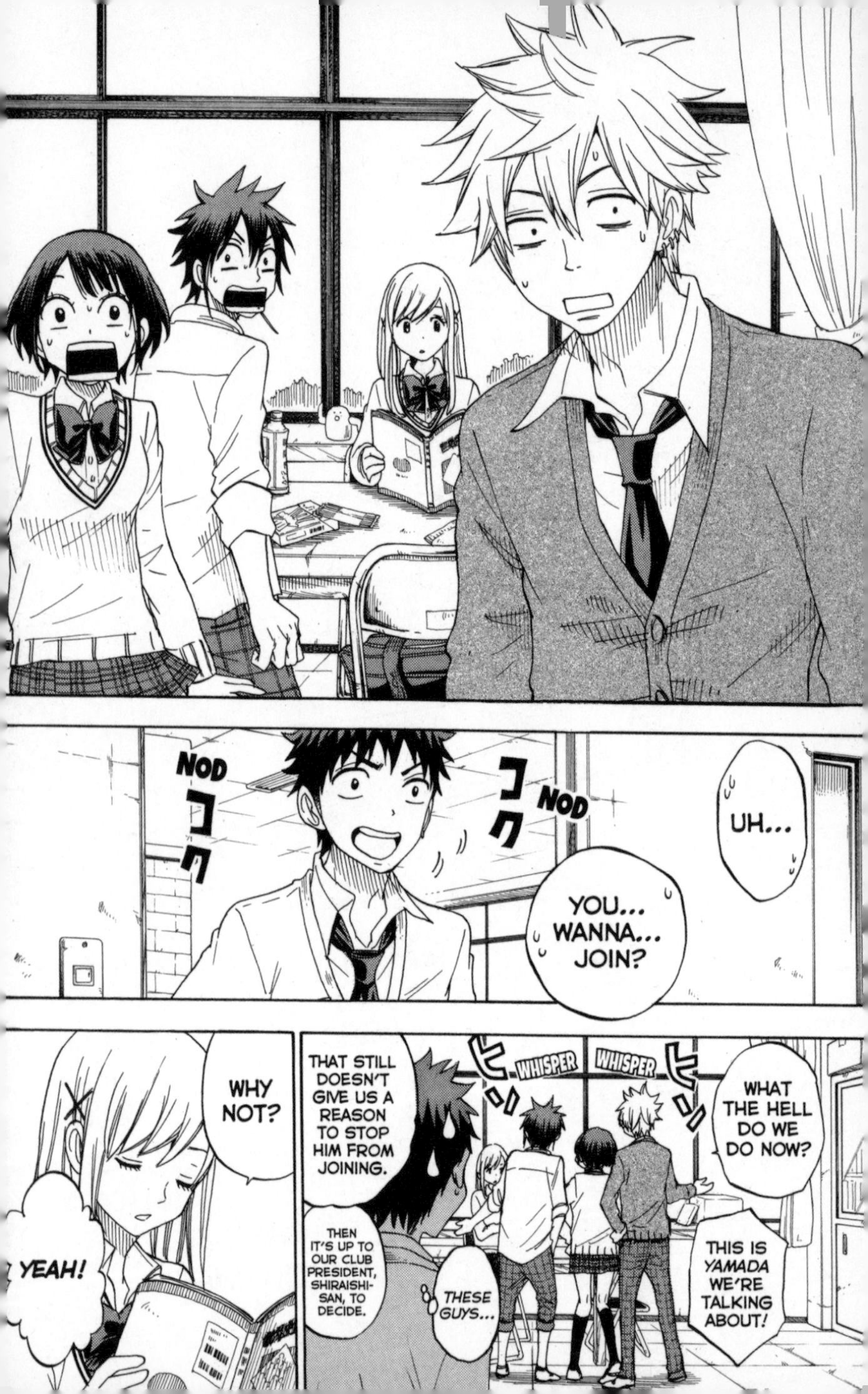
UH...
YOU... WANNA... JOIN?
NOD
コク
NOD
コク
WHAT THE HELL DO WE DO NOW?
WHISPER
ヒソ
WHISPER
ヒソ
THIS IS *YAMADA* WE'RE TALKING ABOUT!
THAT STILL DOESN'T GIVE US A REASON TO STOP HIM FROM JOINING.
THEN IT'S UP TO OUR CLUB PRESIDENT, SHIRAISHI-SAN, TO DECIDE.
THESE GUYS...
WHY NOT?
YEAH!

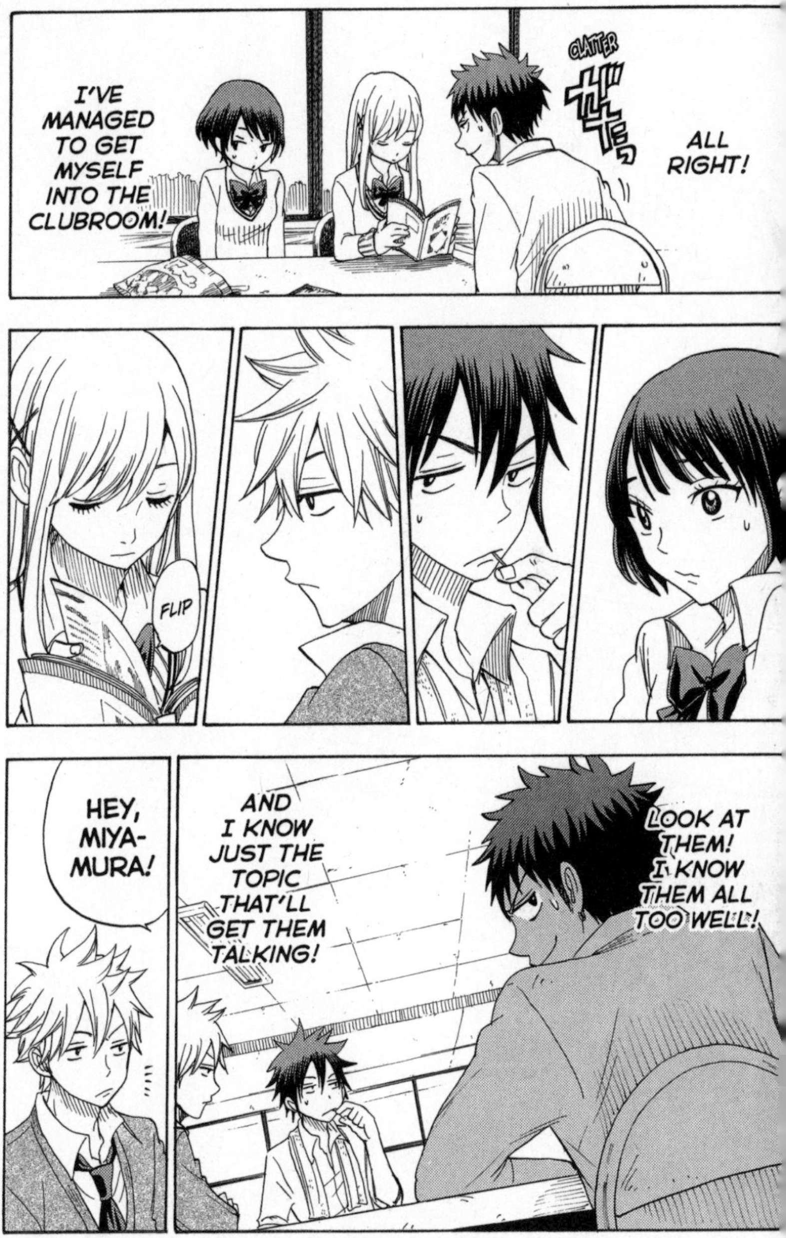
CLATTER
ALL RIGHT!
I'VE MANAGED TO GET MYSELF INTO THE CLUBROOM!
FLIP
LOOK AT THEM! I KNOW THEM ALL TOO WELL!
AND I KNOW JUST THE TOPIC THAT'LL GET THEM TALKING!
HEY, MIYA-MURA!

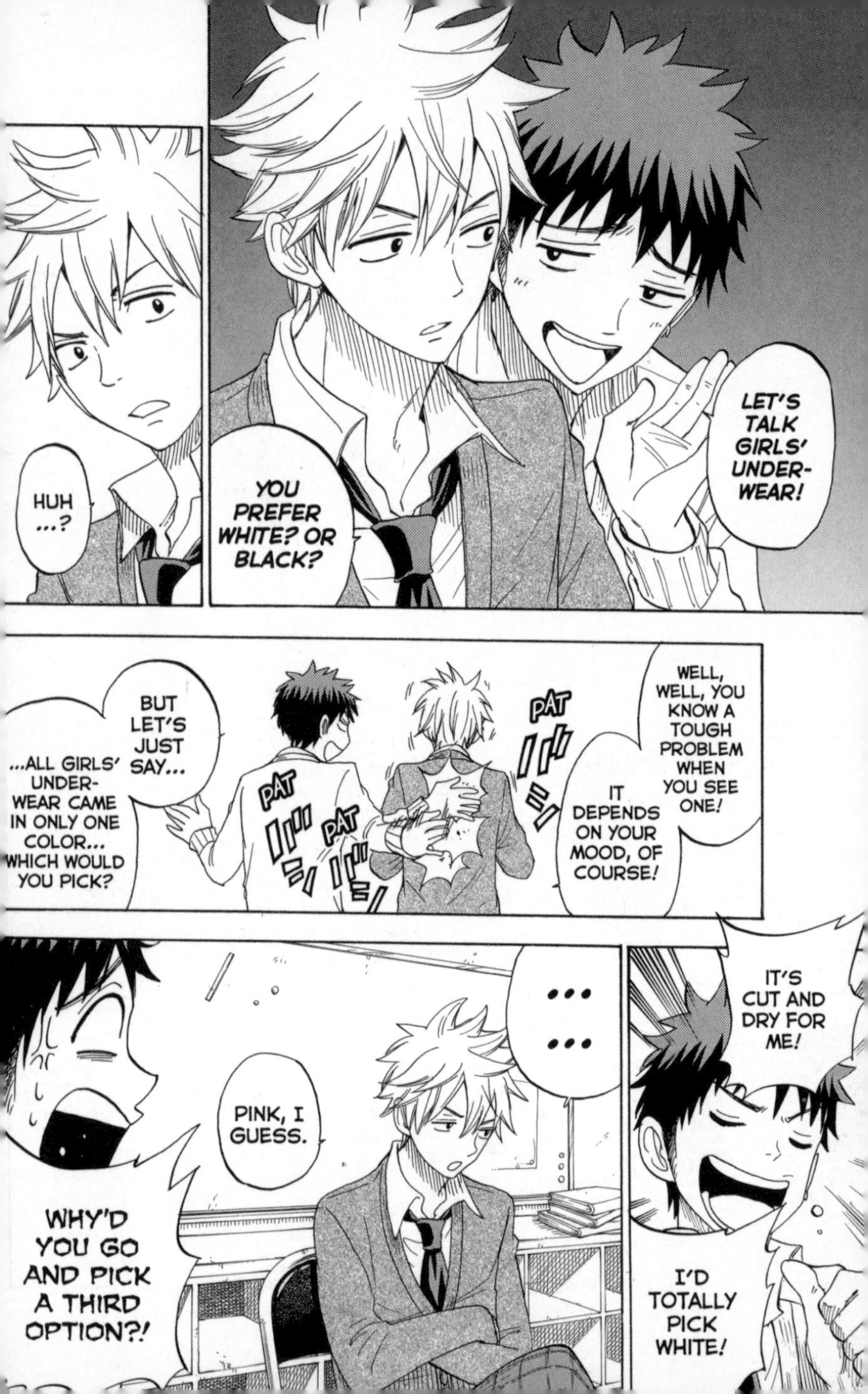
LET'S TALK GIRLS' UNDER-WEAR!
YOU PREFER WHITE? OR BLACK?
HUH ...?
WELL, WELL, YOU KNOW A TOUGH PROBLEM WHEN YOU SEE ONE!
IT DEPENDS ON YOUR MOOD, OF COURSE!
PAT
PAT
PAT
BUT LET'S JUST SAY...
...ALL GIRLS' UNDER-WEAR CAME IN ONLY ONE COLOR... WHICH WOULD YOU PICK?
IT'S CUT AND DRY FOR ME!
I'D TOTALLY PICK WHITE!
......
PINK, I GUESS.
WHY'D YOU GO AND PICK A THIRD OPTION?!

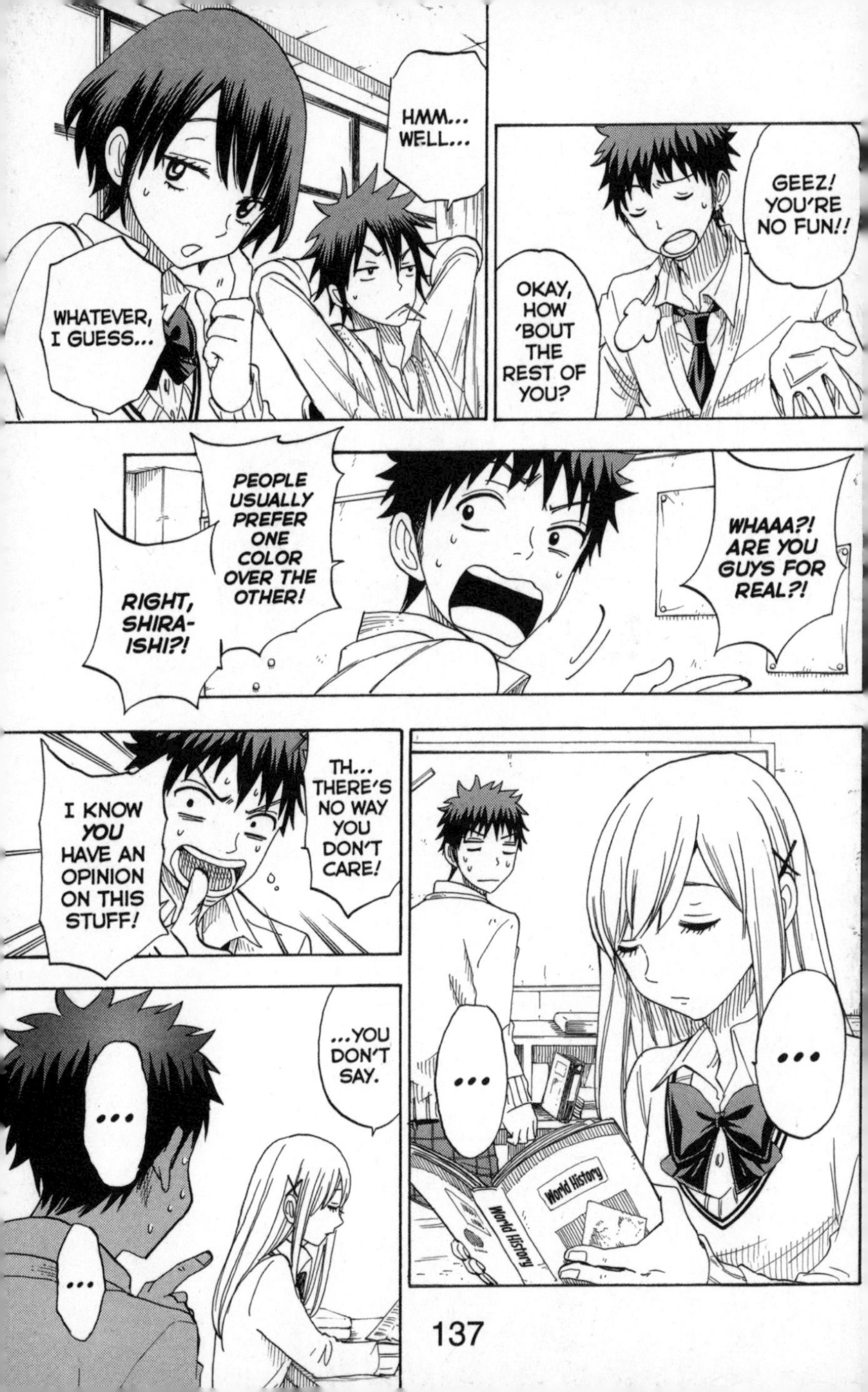
GEEZ! YOU'RE NO FUN!!
OKAY, HOW 'BOUT THE REST OF YOU?
HMM... WELL...
WHATEVER, I GUESS...
WHAAA?! ARE YOU GUYS FOR REAL?!
PEOPLE USUALLY PREFER ONE COLOR OVER THE OTHER!
RIGHT, SHIRAISHI?!
...
...
World History
World History
TH... THERE'S NO WAY YOU DON'T CARE!
I KNOW *YOU* HAVE AN OPINION ON THIS STUFF!
...YOU DON'T SAY.
...
...

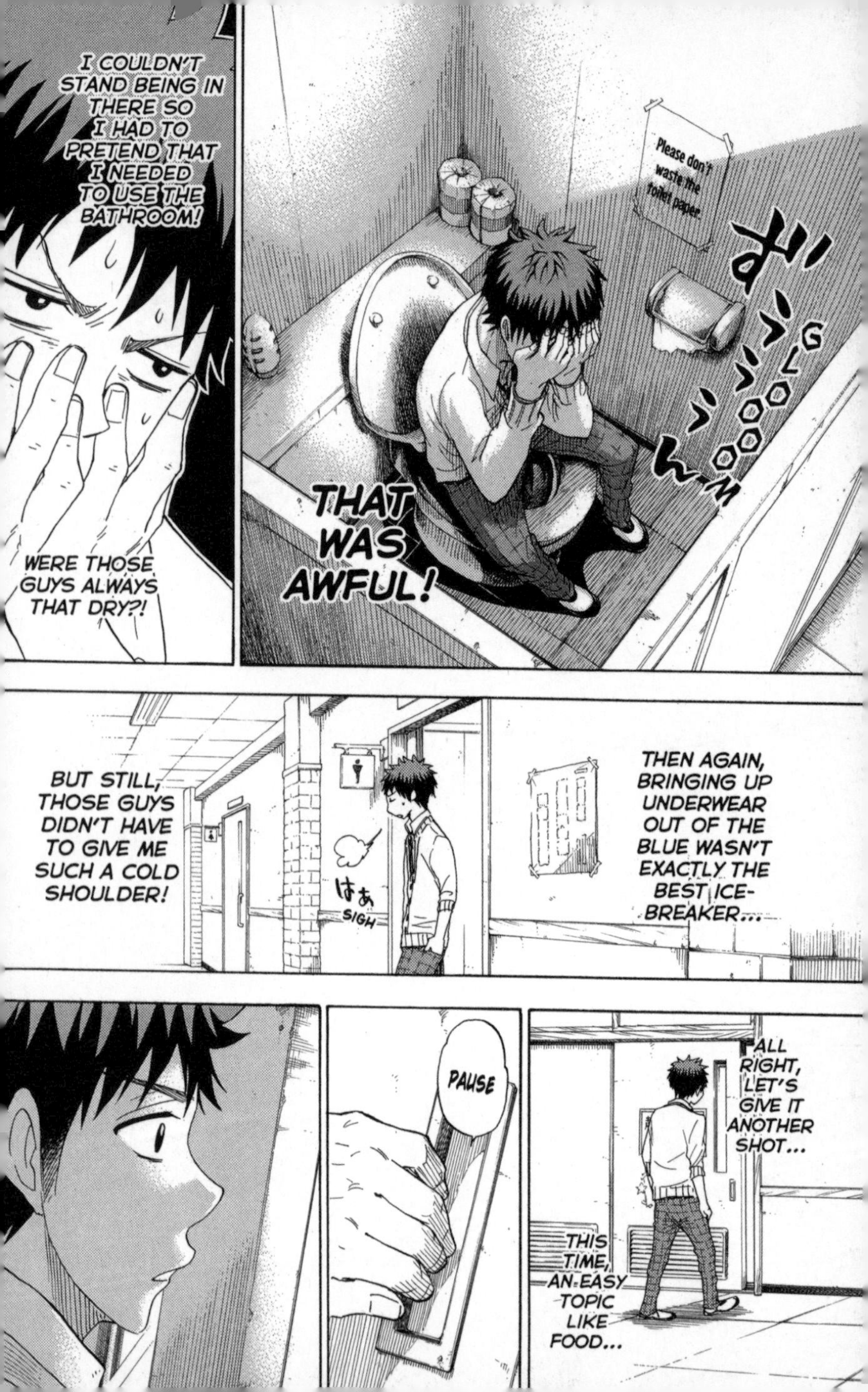
Please don't waste the toilet paper
GLOOOOOM
THAT WAS AWFUL!
I COULDN'T STAND BEING IN THERE SO I HAD TO PRETEND THAT I NEEDED TO USE THE BATHROOM!
WERE THOSE GUYS ALWAYS THAT DRY?!
THEN AGAIN, BRINGING UP UNDERWEAR OUT OF THE BLUE WASN'T EXACTLY THE BEST ICE-BREAKER...
BUT STILL, THOSE GUYS DIDN'T HAVE TO GIVE ME SUCH A COLD SHOULDER!
はぁ
SIGH
ALL RIGHT, LET'S GIVE IT ANOTHER SHOT...
THIS TIME, AN EASY TOPIC LIKE FOOD...
PAUSE

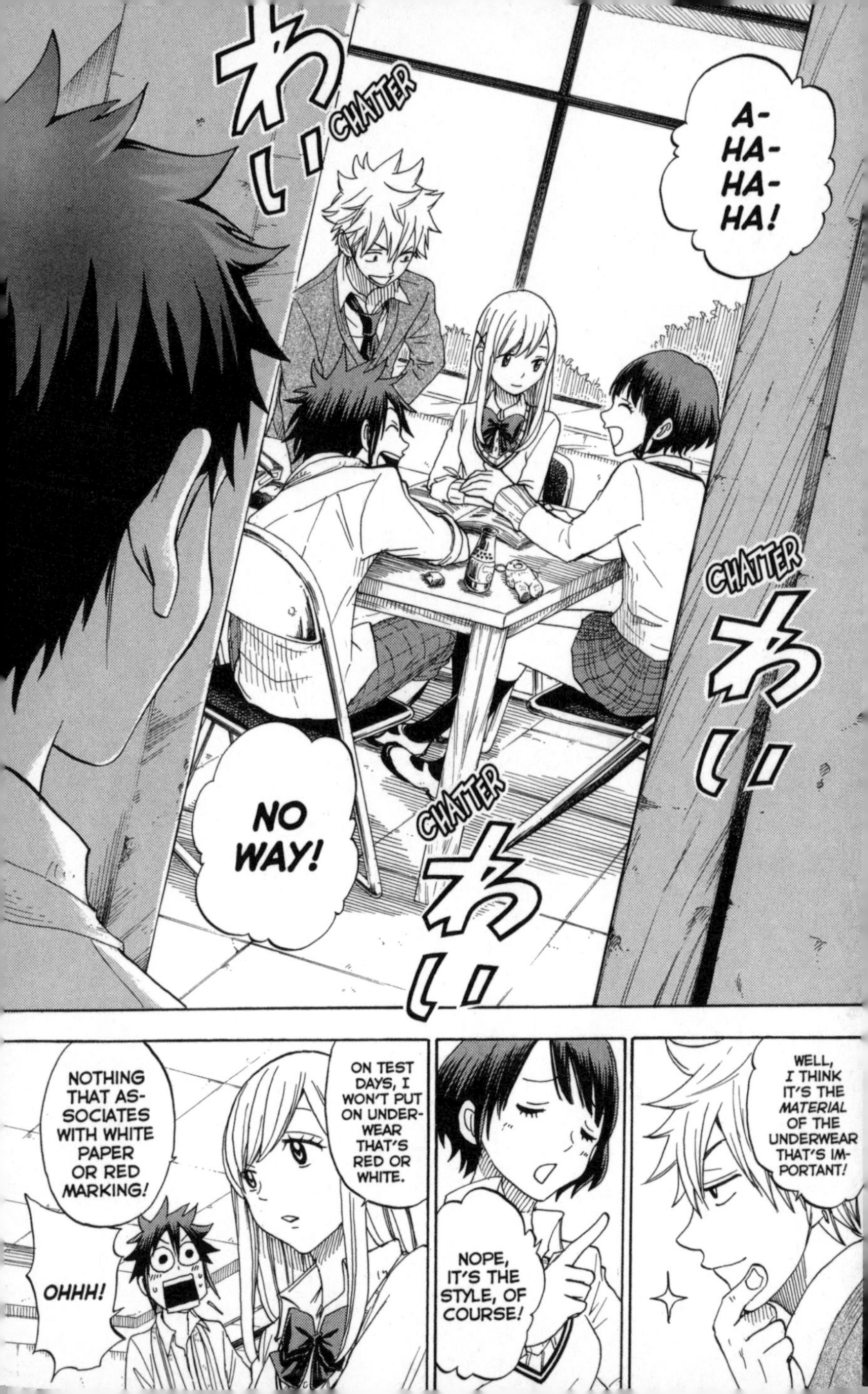
A-HA-HA-HA!
わい
CHATTER
CHATTER
わい
NO WAY!
CHATTER
わい
WELL, I THINK IT'S THE *MATERIAL* OF THE UNDERWEAR THAT'S IMPORTANT!
NOPE, IT'S THE STYLE, OF COURSE!
ON TEST DAYS, I WON'T PUT ON UNDERWEAR THAT'S RED OR WHITE.
NOTHING THAT ASSOCIATES WITH WHITE PAPER OR RED MARKING!
OHHH!

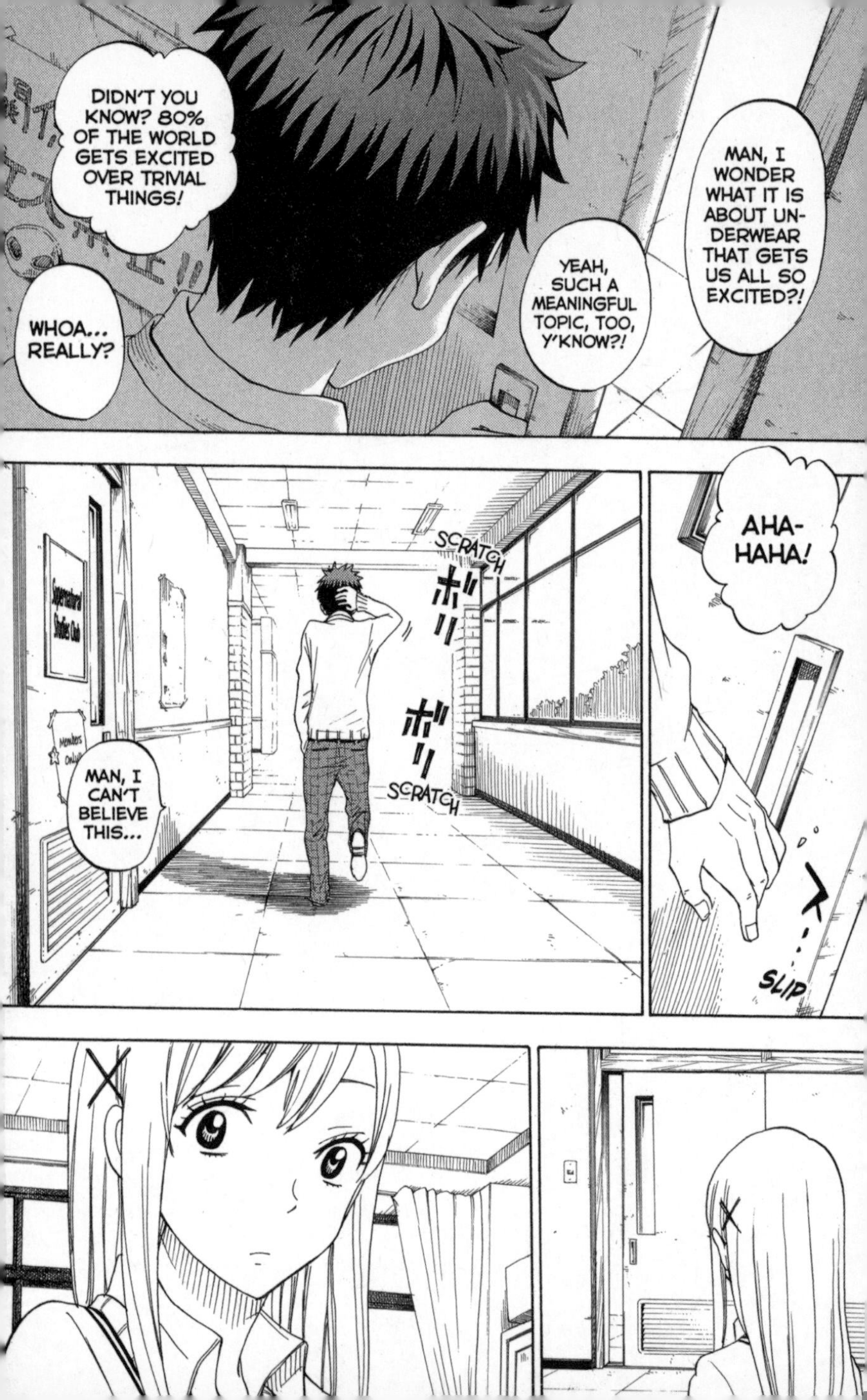
MAN, I WONDER WHAT IT IS ABOUT UNDERWEAR THAT GETS US ALL SO EXCITED?!
YEAH, SUCH A MEANINGFUL TOPIC, TOO, Y'KNOW?!
DIDN'T YOU KNOW? 80% OF THE WORLD GETS EXCITED OVER TRIVIAL THINGS!
WHOA... REALLY?
AHA-HAHA!
SLIP
SCRATCH
SCRATCH
Supernatural Studies Club
Members Only!
MAN, I CAN'T BELIEVE THIS...

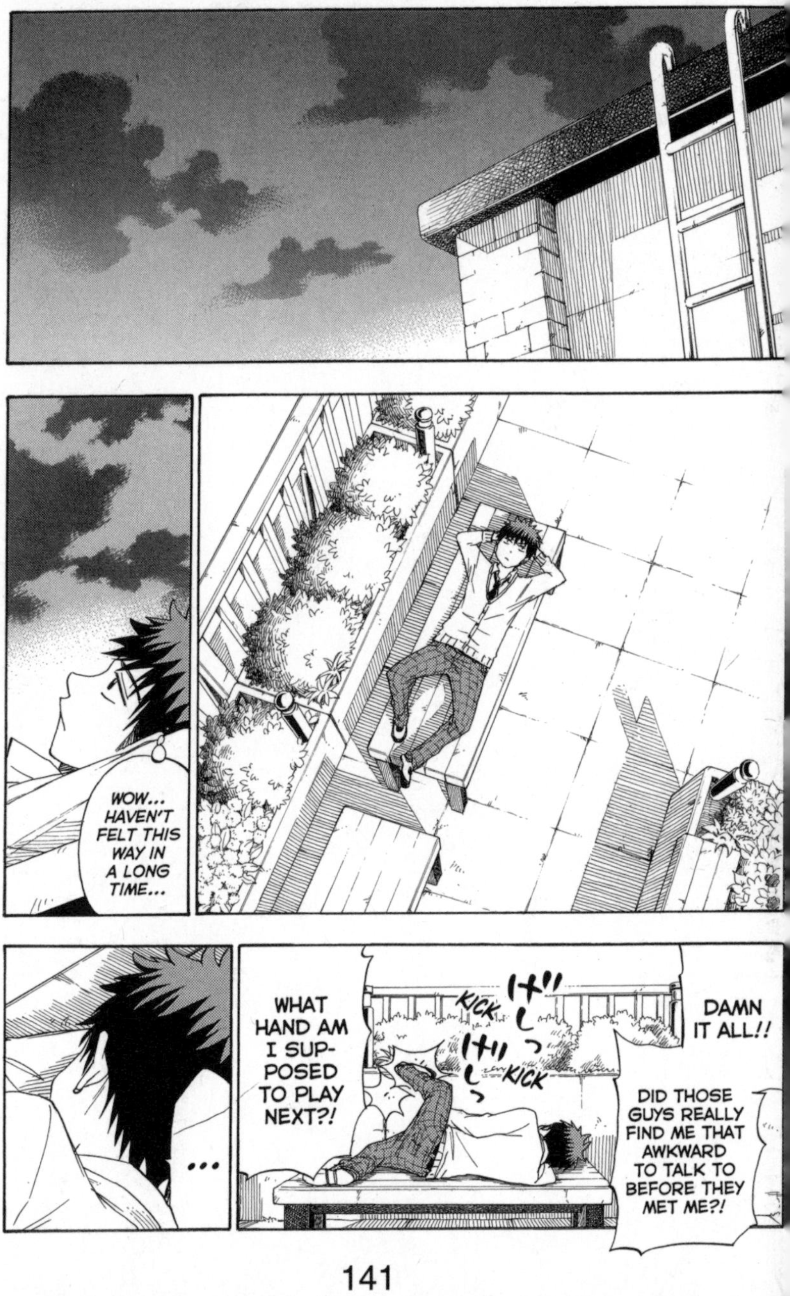
WOW... HAVEN'T FELT THIS WAY IN A LONG TIME...
DAMN IT ALL!!
DID THOSE GUYS REALLY FIND ME THAT AWKWARD TO TALK TO BEFORE THEY MET ME?!
KICK
KICK
WHAT HAND AM I SUP-POSED TO PLAY NEXT?!
...

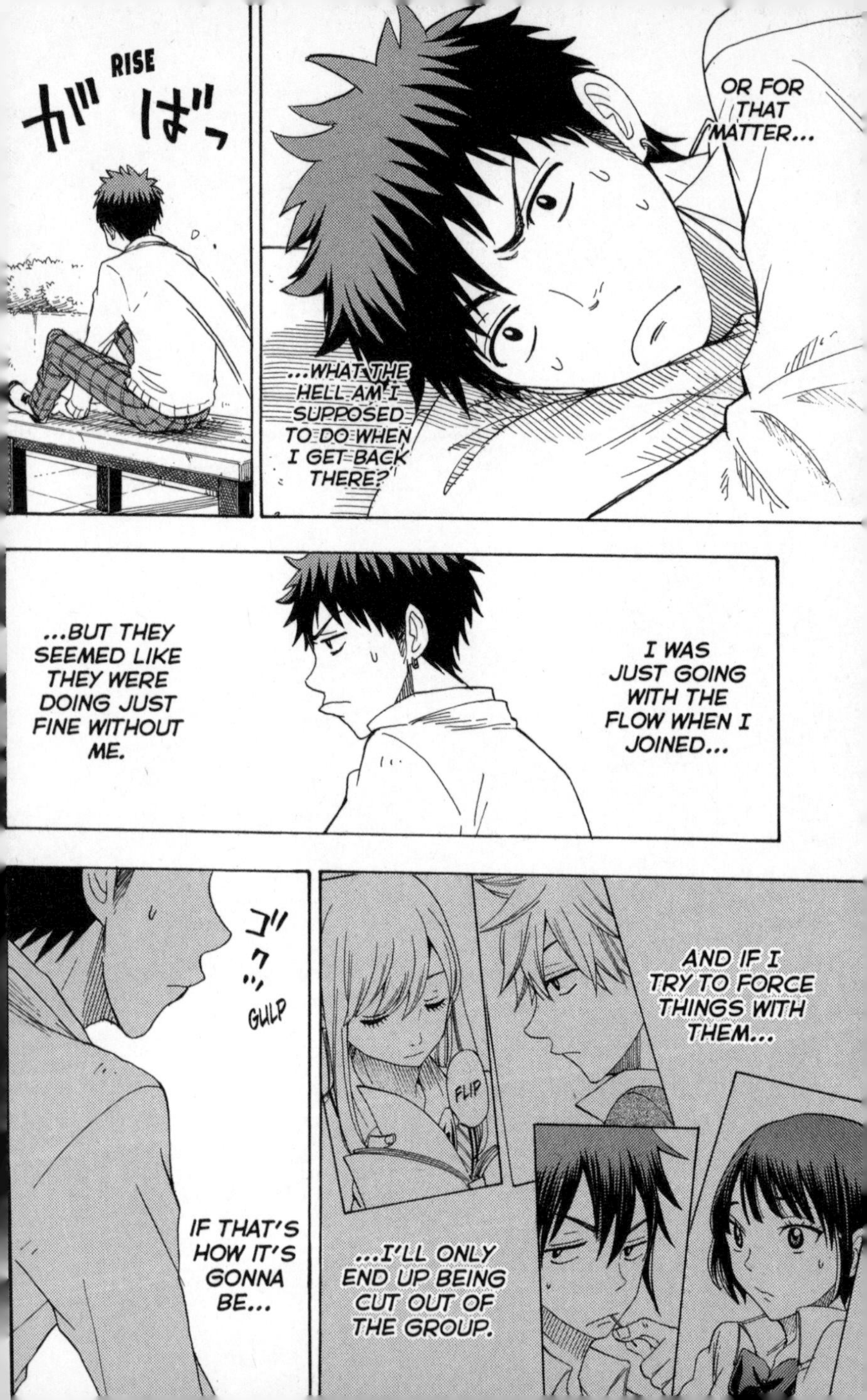
OR FOR THAT MATTER...
...WHAT THE HELL AM I SUPPOSED TO DO WHEN I GET BACK THERE?
ガばっ
RISE
I WAS JUST GOING WITH THE FLOW WHEN I JOINED...
...BUT THEY SEEMED LIKE THEY WERE DOING JUST FINE WITHOUT ME.
AND IF I TRY TO FORCE THINGS WITH THEM...
FLIP
...I'LL ONLY END UP BEING CUT OUT OF THE GROUP.
ゴクッ
GULP
IF THAT'S HOW IT'S GONNA BE...

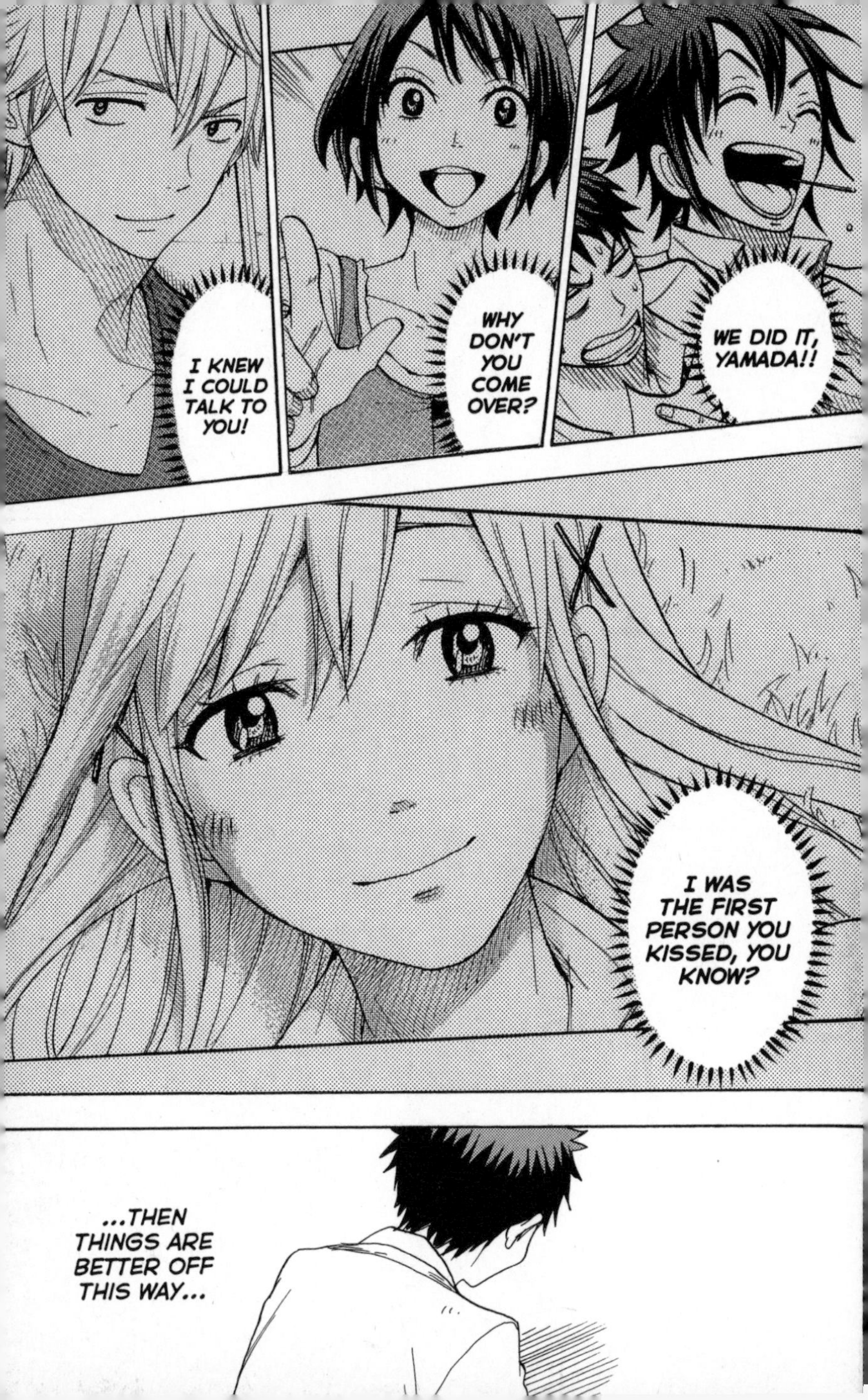
WE DID IT, YAMADA!!
WHY DON'T YOU COME OVER?
I KNEW I COULD TALK TO YOU!
I WAS THE FIRST PERSON YOU KISSED, YOU KNOW?
...THEN THINGS ARE BETTER OFF THIS WAY...

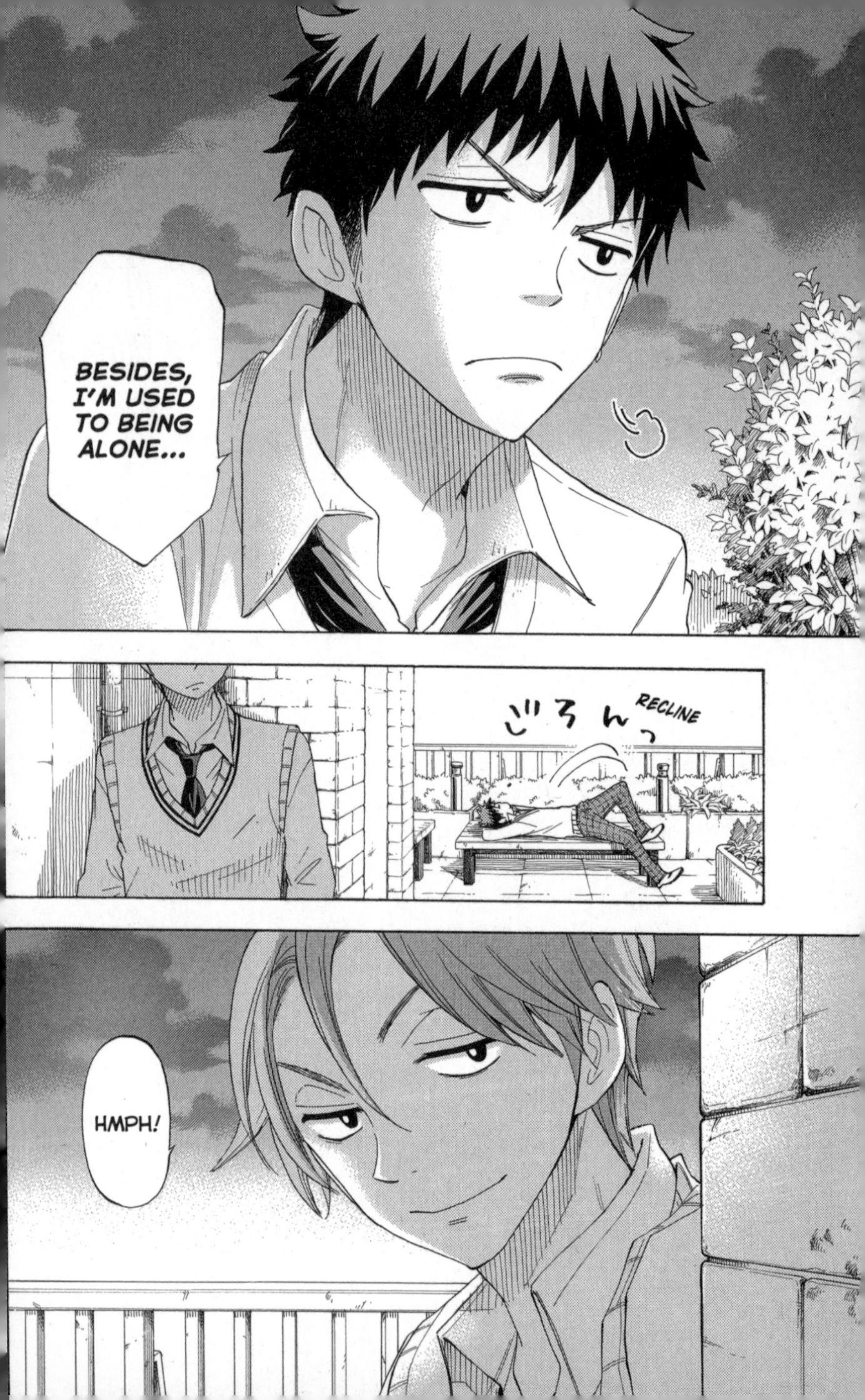
BESIDES, I'M USED TO BEING ALONE...
ごろんっ
RECLINE
HMPH!

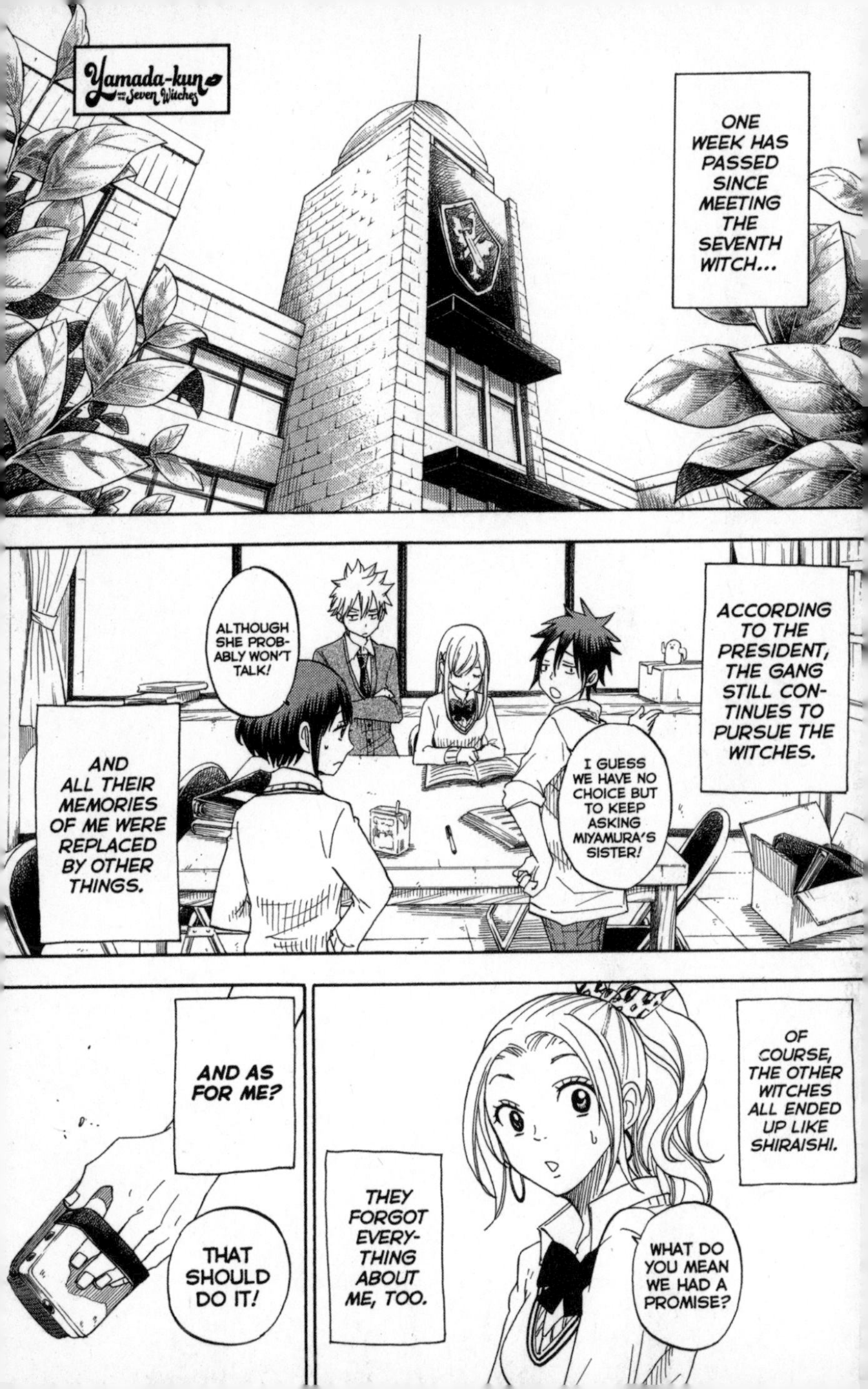
Yamada-kun and the Seven Witches
ONE WEEK HAS PASSED SINCE MEETING THE SEVENTH WITCH...
ACCORDING TO THE PRESIDENT, THE GANG STILL CONTINUES TO PURSUE THE WITCHES.
I GUESS WE HAVE NO CHOICE BUT TO KEEP ASKING MIYAMURA'S SISTER!
ALTHOUGH SHE PROBABLY WON'T TALK!
AND ALL THEIR MEMORIES OF ME WERE REPLACED BY OTHER THINGS.
OF COURSE, THE OTHER WITCHES ALL ENDED UP LIKE SHIRAISHI.
WHAT DO YOU MEAN WE HAD A PROMISE?
THEY FORGOT EVERYTHING ABOUT ME, TOO.
AND AS FOR ME?
THAT SHOULD DO IT!

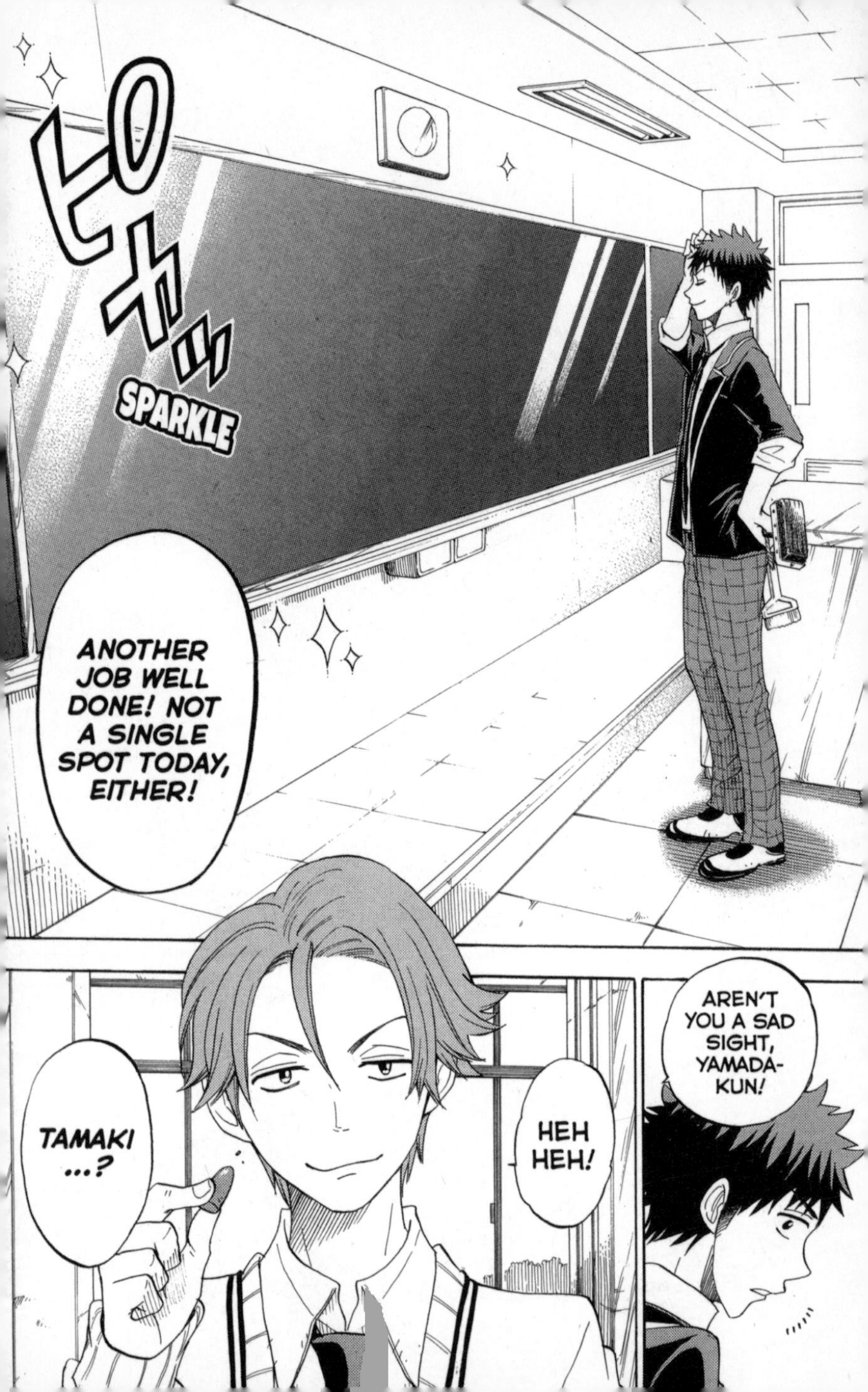
ピカッ
SPARKLE
ANOTHER JOB WELL DONE! NOT A SINGLE SPOT TODAY, EITHER!
AREN'T YOU A SAD SIGHT, YAMADA-KUN!
HEH HEH!
TAMAKI ...?

CHAPTER 68: How pathetic!

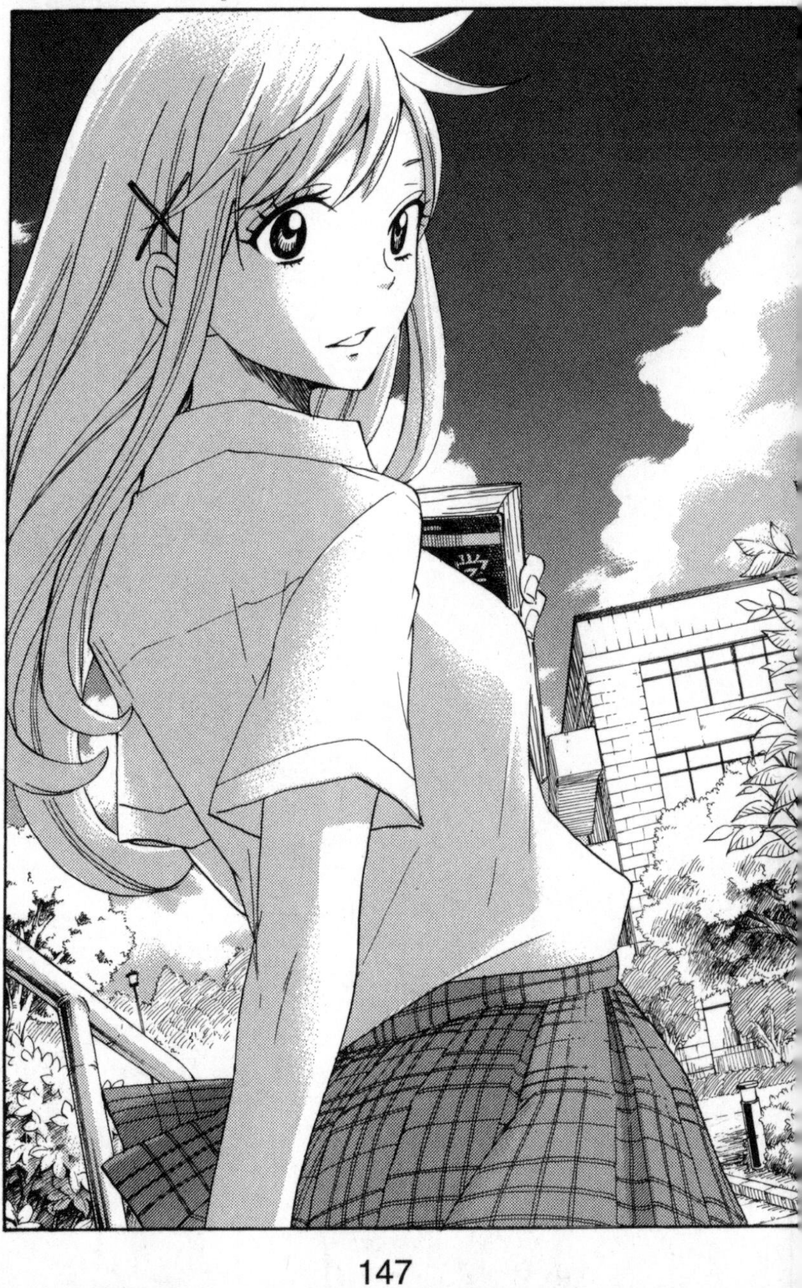

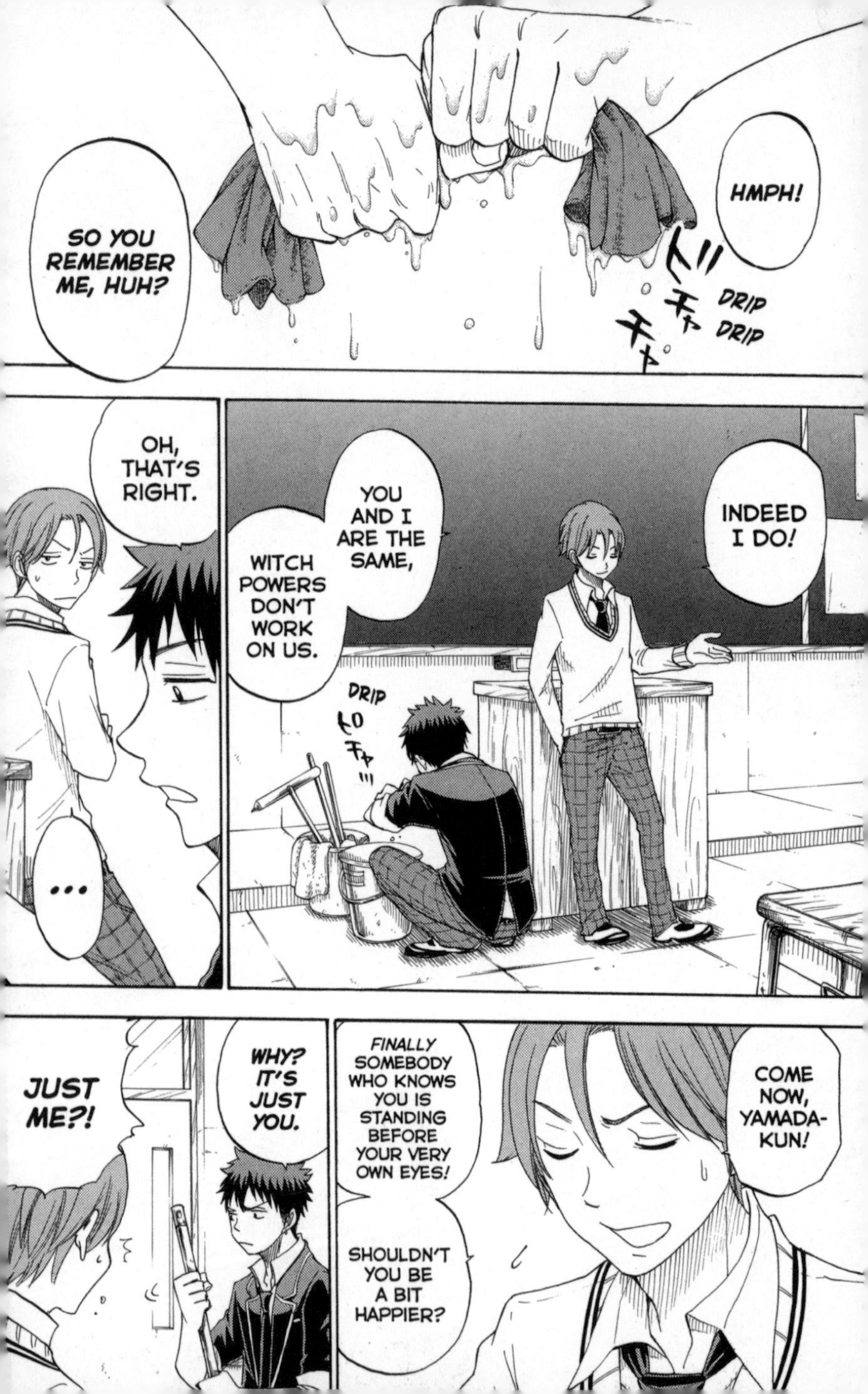
HMPH!
DRIP DRIP
SO YOU REMEMBER ME, HUH?
INDEED I DO!
YOU AND I ARE THE SAME,
WITCH POWERS DON'T WORK ON US.
DRIP
OH, THAT'S RIGHT.
...
COME NOW, YAMADA-KUN!
FINALLY SOMEBODY WHO KNOWS YOU IS STANDING BEFORE YOUR VERY OWN EYES!
SHOULDN'T YOU BE A BIT HAPPIER?
WHY? IT'S JUST YOU.
JUST ME?!

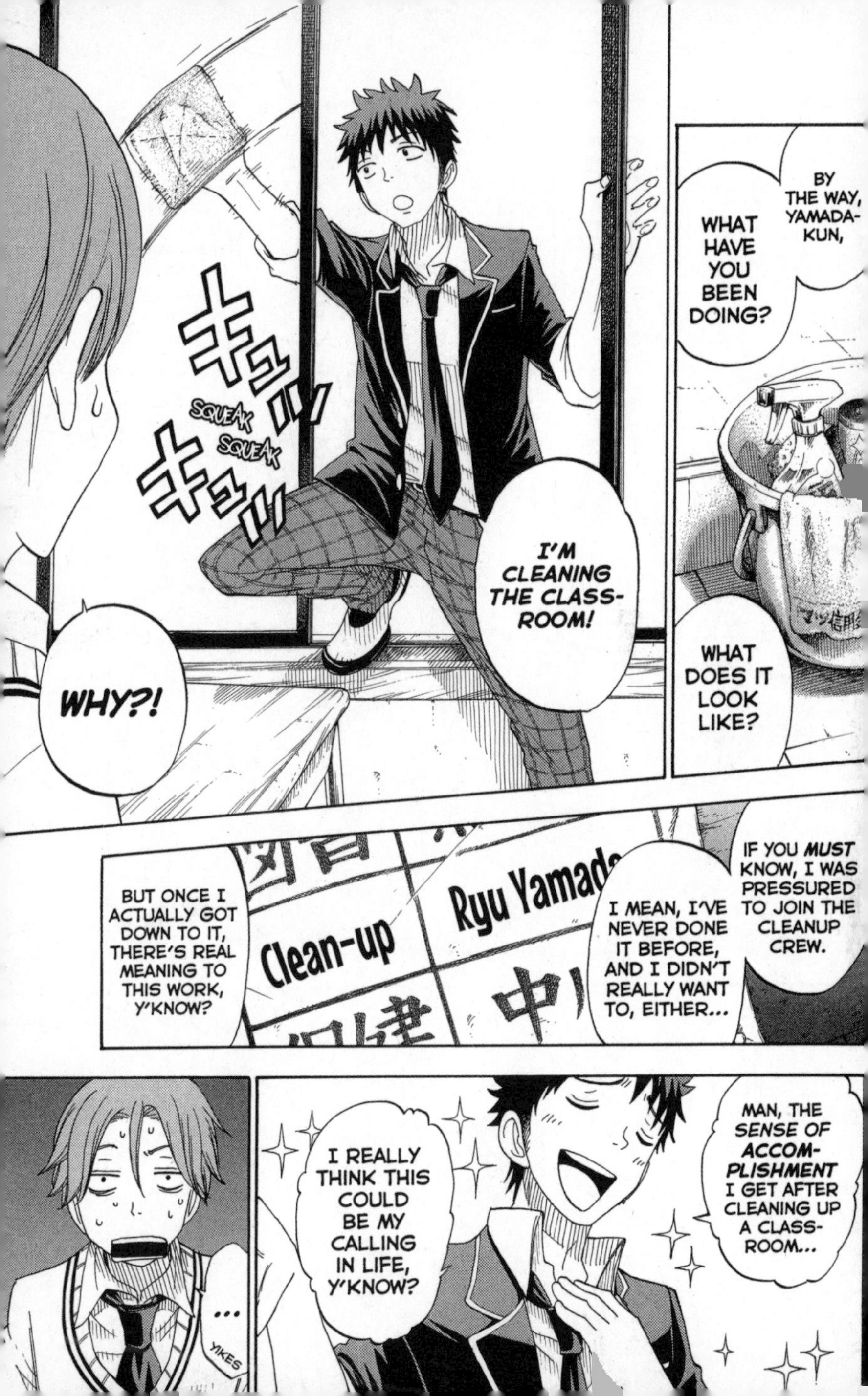
BY THE WAY, YAMADA-KUN,
WHAT HAVE YOU BEEN DOING?
WHAT DOES IT LOOK LIKE?
キュッ SQUEAK
キュッ SQUEAK
I'M CLEANING THE CLASSROOM!
WHY?!
IF YOU *MUST* KNOW, I WAS PRESSURED TO JOIN THE CLEANUP CREW.
I MEAN, I'VE NEVER DONE IT BEFORE, AND I DIDN'T REALLY WANT TO, EITHER...
Ryu Yamada
Clean-up
BUT ONCE I ACTUALLY GOT DOWN TO IT, THERE'S REAL MEANING TO THIS WORK, Y'KNOW?
MAN, THE *SENSE OF ACCOMPLISHMENT* I GET AFTER CLEANING UP A CLASSROOM...
I REALLY THINK THIS COULD BE MY CALLING IN LIFE, Y'KNOW?
...
YIKES

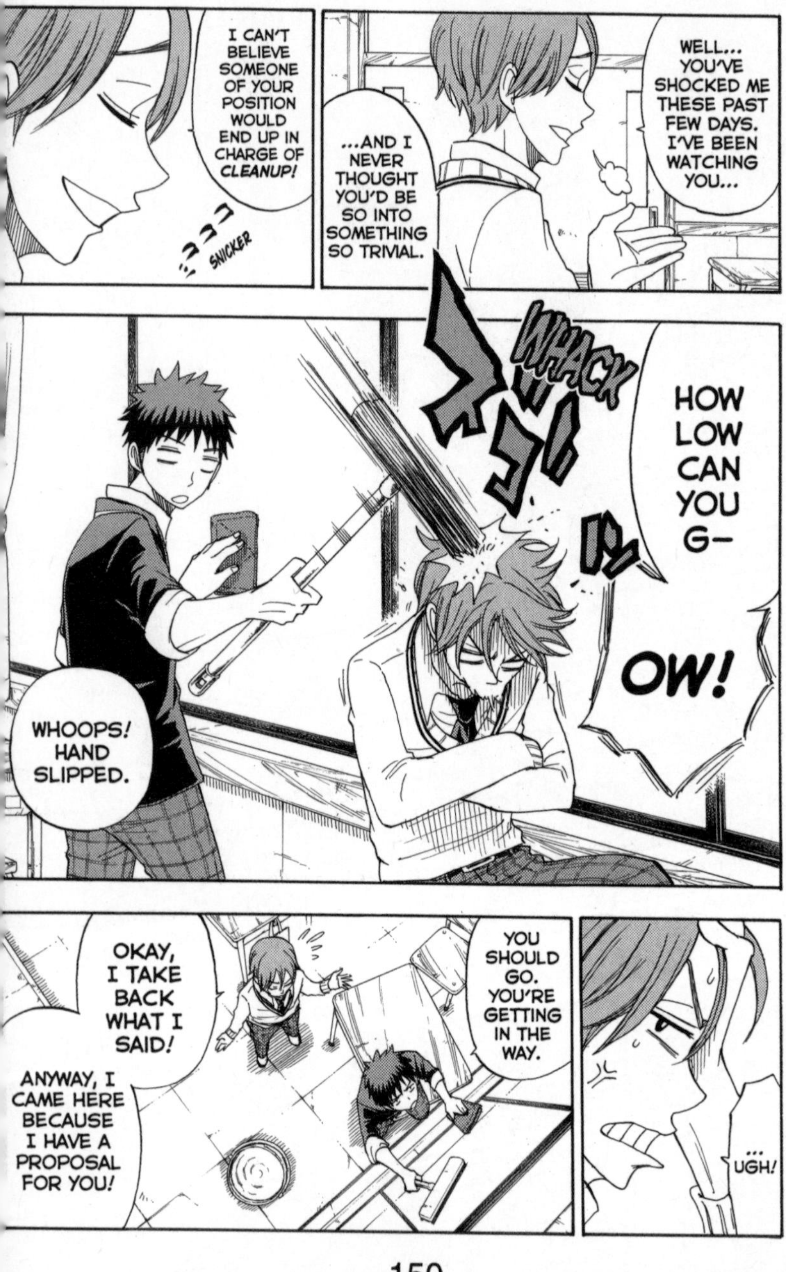
WELL... YOU'VE SHOCKED ME THESE PAST FEW DAYS. I'VE BEEN WATCHING YOU...
...AND I NEVER THOUGHT YOU'D BE SO INTO SOMETHING SO TRIVIAL.
I CAN'T BELIEVE SOMEONE OF YOUR POSITION WOULD END UP IN CHARGE OF *CLEANUP!*
SNICKER
WHACK
HOW LOW CAN YOU G—
OW!
WHOOPS! HAND SLIPPED.
...UGH!
YOU SHOULD GO. YOU'RE GETTING IN THE WAY.
OKAY, I TAKE BACK WHAT I SAID!
ANYWAY, I CAME HERE BECAUSE I HAVE A PROPOSAL FOR YOU!

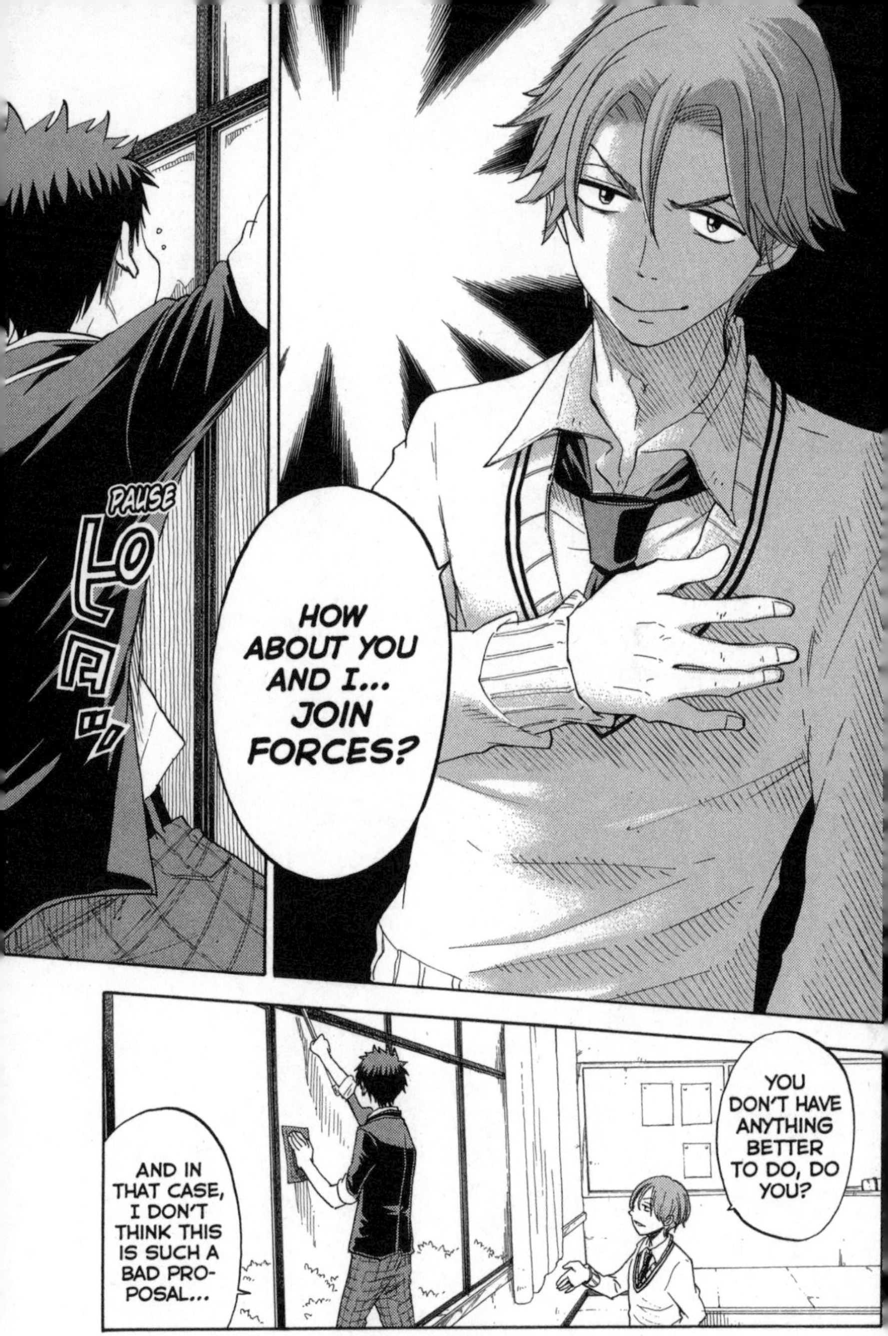
HOW ABOUT YOU AND I... JOIN FORCES?
PAUSE
YOU DON'T HAVE ANYTHING BETTER TO DO, DO YOU?
AND IN THAT CASE, I DON'T THINK THIS IS SUCH A BAD PRO-POSAL...

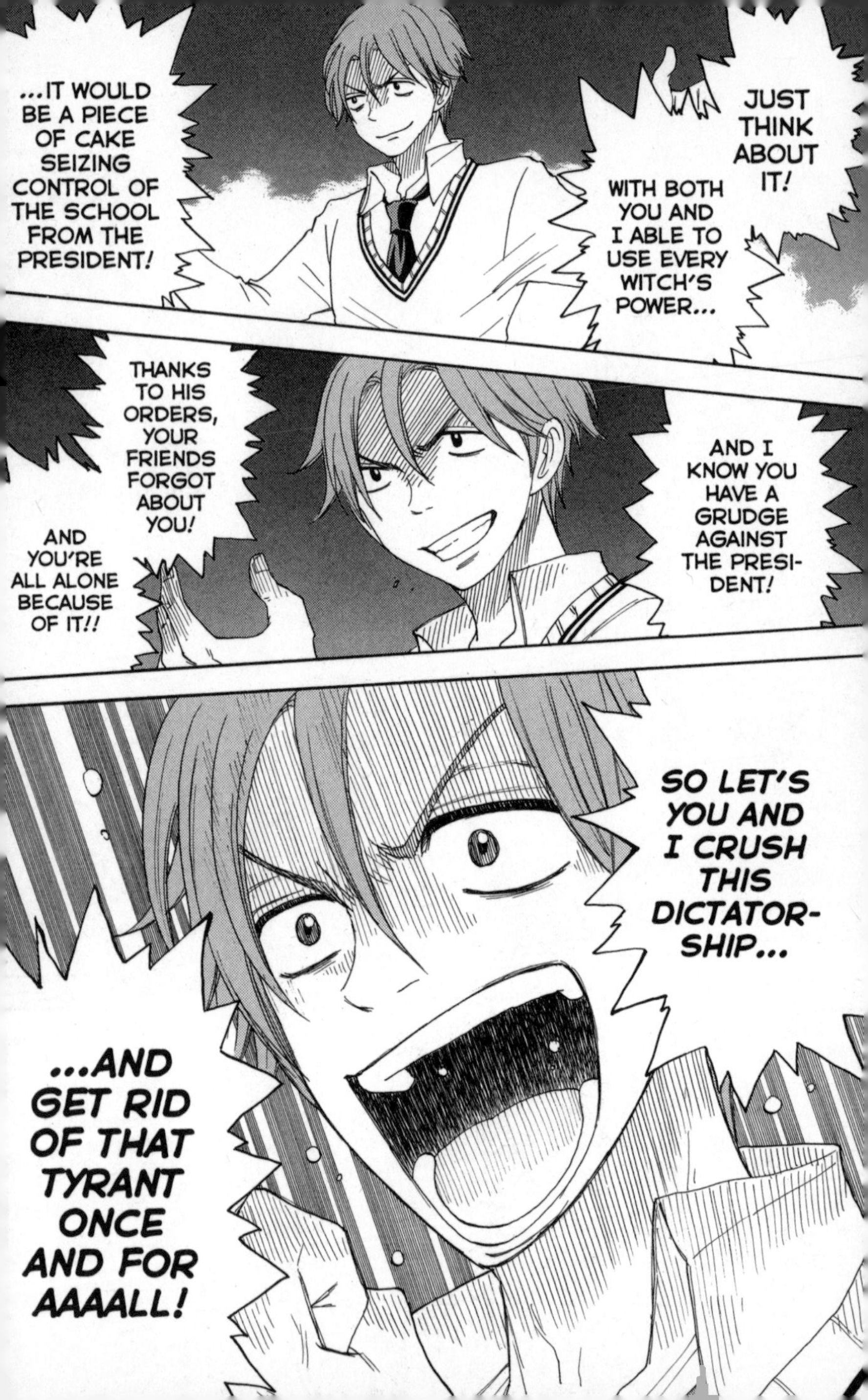
JUST THINK ABOUT IT!
WITH BOTH YOU AND I ABLE TO USE EVERY WITCH'S POWER...
...IT WOULD BE A PIECE OF CAKE SEIZING CONTROL OF THE SCHOOL FROM THE PRESIDENT!
AND I KNOW YOU HAVE A GRUDGE AGAINST THE PRESI-DENT!
THANKS TO HIS ORDERS, YOUR FRIENDS FORGOT ABOUT YOU!
AND YOU'RE ALL ALONE BECAUSE OF IT!!
SO LET'S YOU AND I CRUSH THIS DICTATOR-SHIP...
...AND GET RID OF THAT TYRANT ONCE AND FOR AAAALL!

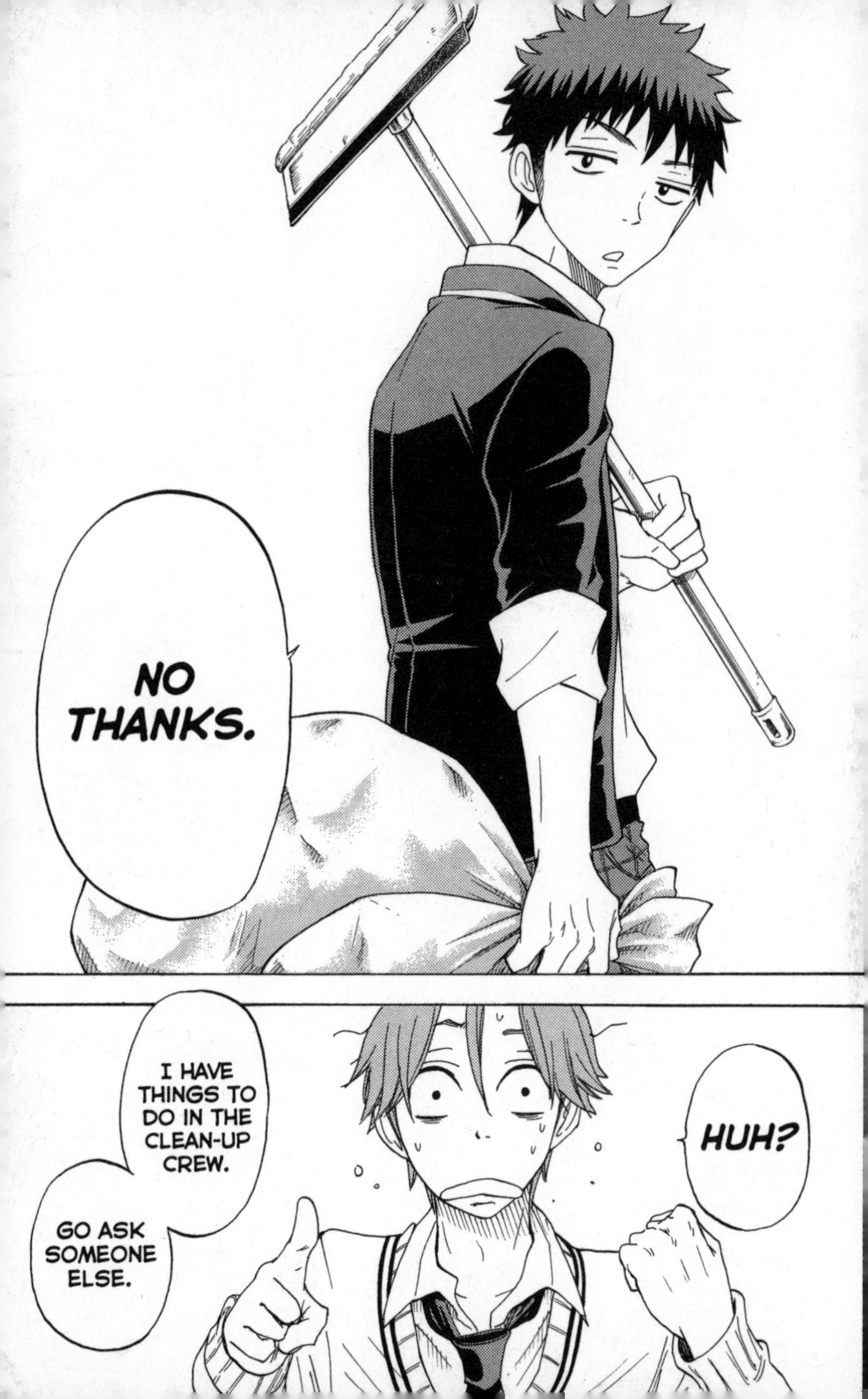
NO THANKS.
HUH?
I HAVE THINGS TO DO IN THE CLEAN-UP CREW.
GO ASK SOMEONE ELSE.

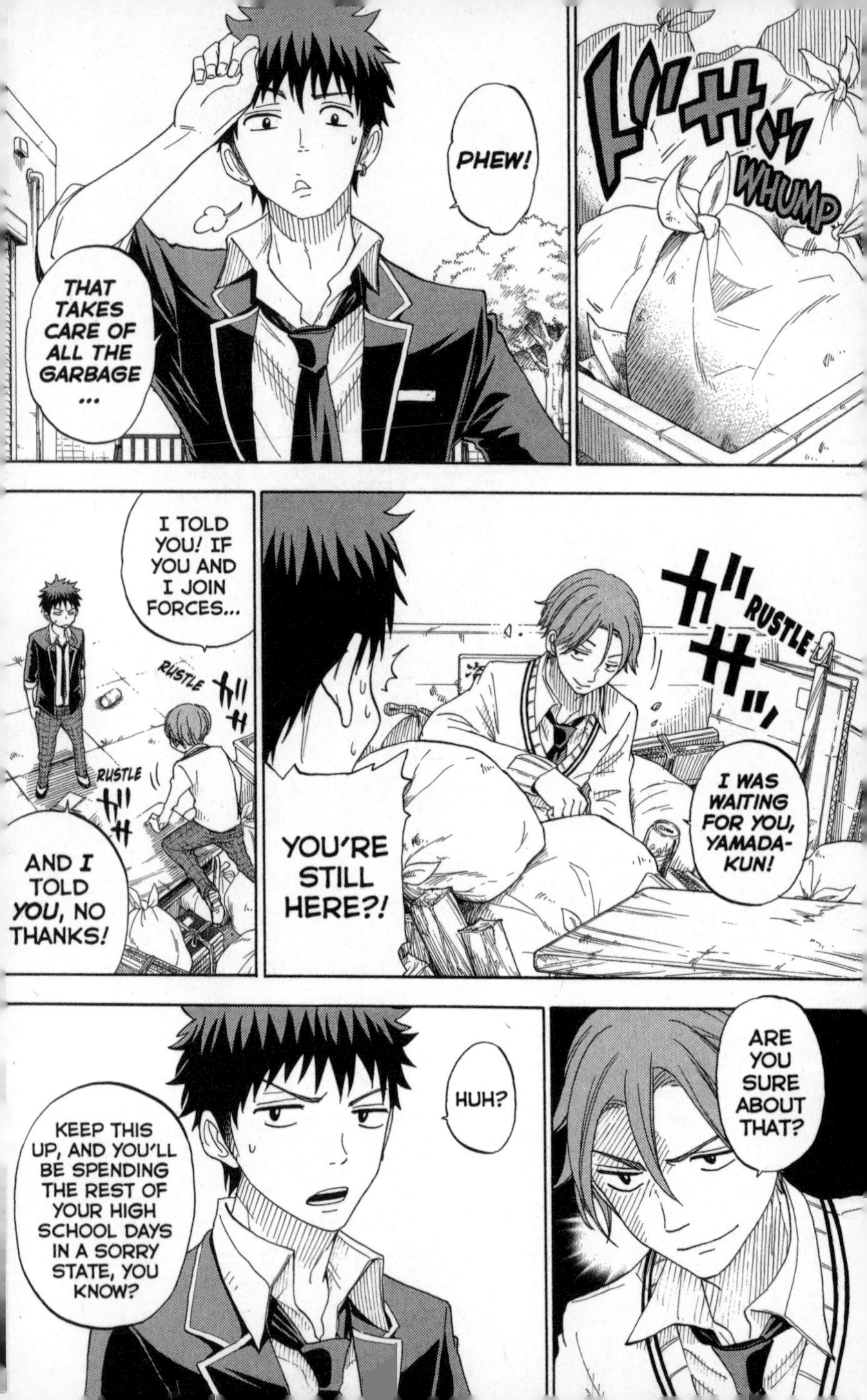
WHUMP
PHEW!
THAT TAKES CARE OF ALL THE GARBAGE...
RUSTLE
I WAS WAITING FOR YOU, YAMADA-KUN!
YOU'RE STILL HERE?!
I TOLD YOU! IF YOU AND I JOIN FORCES...
RUSTLE
RUSTLE
AND I TOLD YOU, NO THANKS!
ARE YOU SURE ABOUT THAT?
HUH?
KEEP THIS UP, AND YOU'LL BE SPENDING THE REST OF YOUR HIGH SCHOOL DAYS IN A SORRY STATE, YOU KNOW?

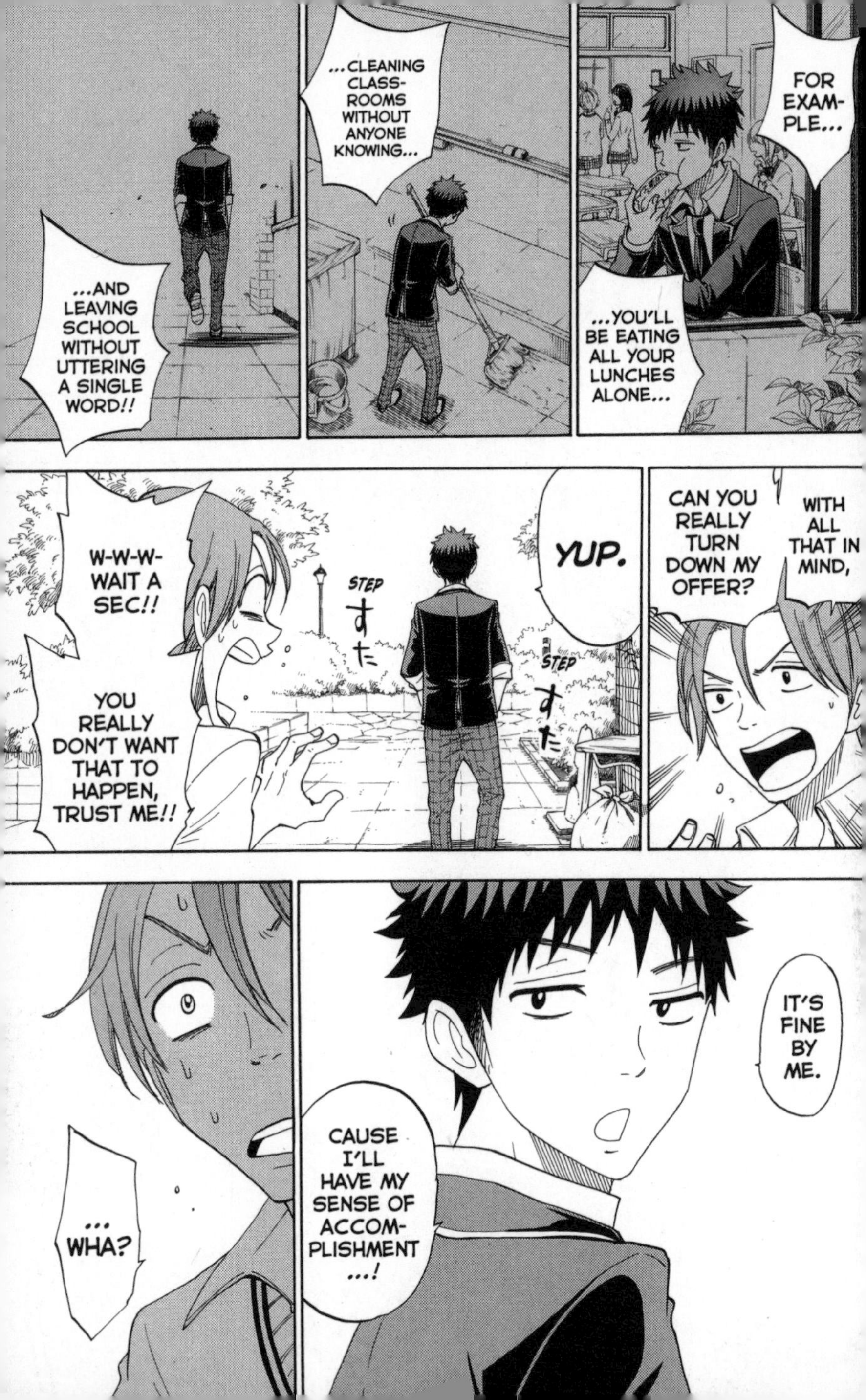
FOR EXAMPLE...
...YOU'LL BE EATING ALL YOUR LUNCHES ALONE...
...CLEANING CLASSROOMS WITHOUT ANYONE KNOWING...
...AND LEAVING SCHOOL WITHOUT UTTERING A SINGLE WORD!!
WITH ALL THAT IN MIND,
CAN YOU REALLY TURN DOWN MY OFFER?
YUP.
STEP すた
STEP すた
W-W-W-WAIT A SEC!!
YOU REALLY DON'T WANT THAT TO HAPPEN, TRUST ME!!
IT'S FINE BY ME.
CAUSE I'LL HAVE MY SENSE OF ACCOMPLISHMENT...!
...WHA?

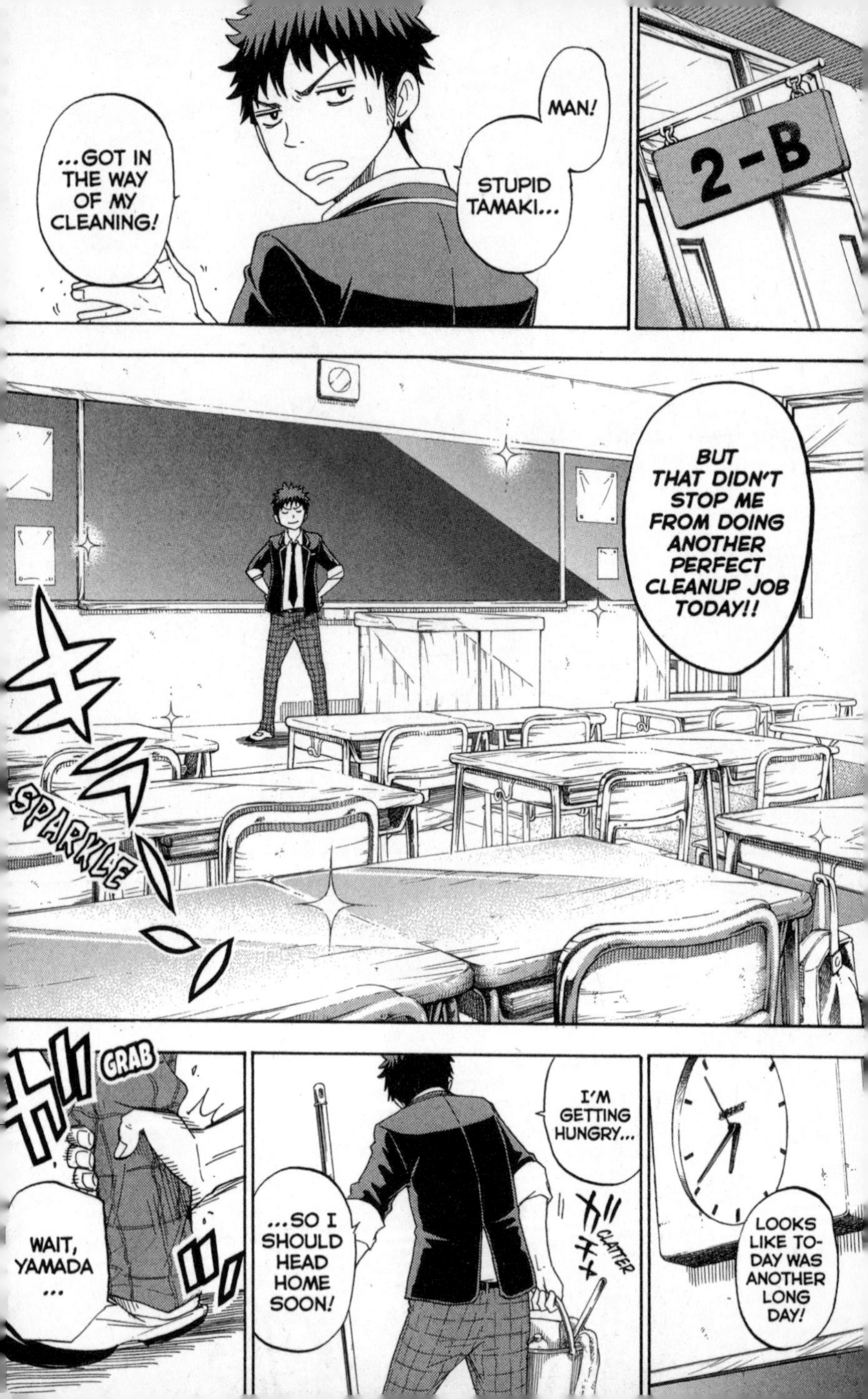
2-B
MAN!
STUPID TAMAKI...
...GOT IN THE WAY OF MY CLEANING!
BUT THAT DIDN'T STOP ME FROM DOING ANOTHER PERFECT CLEANUP JOB TODAY!!
SPARKLE
LOOKS LIKE TO-DAY WAS ANOTHER LONG DAY!
I'M GETTING HUNGRY...
...SO I SHOULD HEAD HOME SOON!
CLATTER
GRAB
WAIT, YAMADA ...

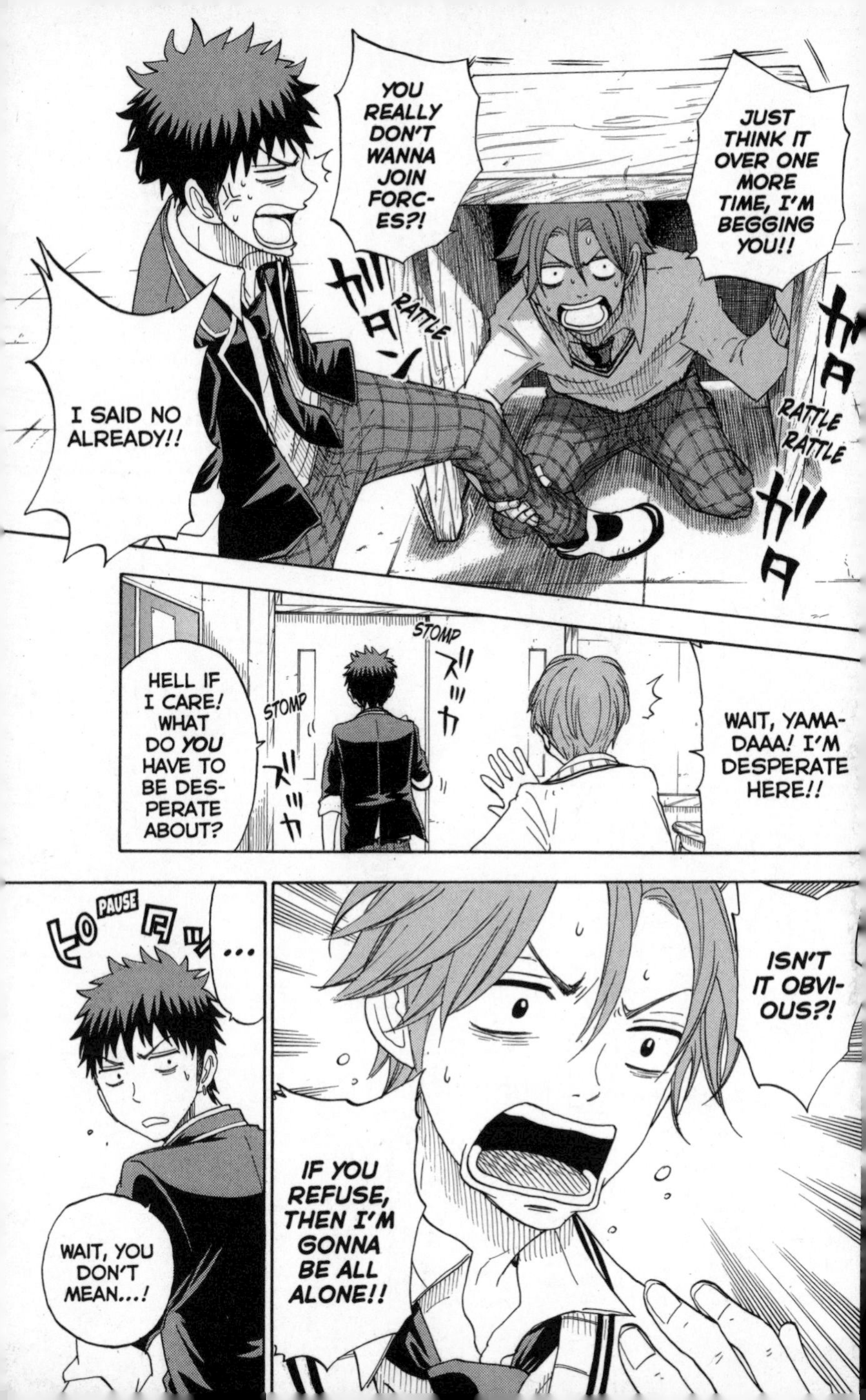
JUST THINK IT OVER ONE MORE TIME, I'M BEGGING YOU!!
RATTLE RATTLE
YOU REALLY DON'T WANNA JOIN FORC-ES?!
RATTLE
I SAID NO ALREADY!!
WAIT, YAMA-DAAA! I'M DESPERATE HERE!!
STOMP
STOMP
HELL IF I CARE! WHAT DO *YOU* HAVE TO BE DES-PERATE ABOUT?
ISN'T IT OBVI-OUS?!
IF YOU REFUSE, THEN I'M GONNA BE ALL ALONE!!
PAUSE
...
WAIT, YOU DON'T MEAN...!

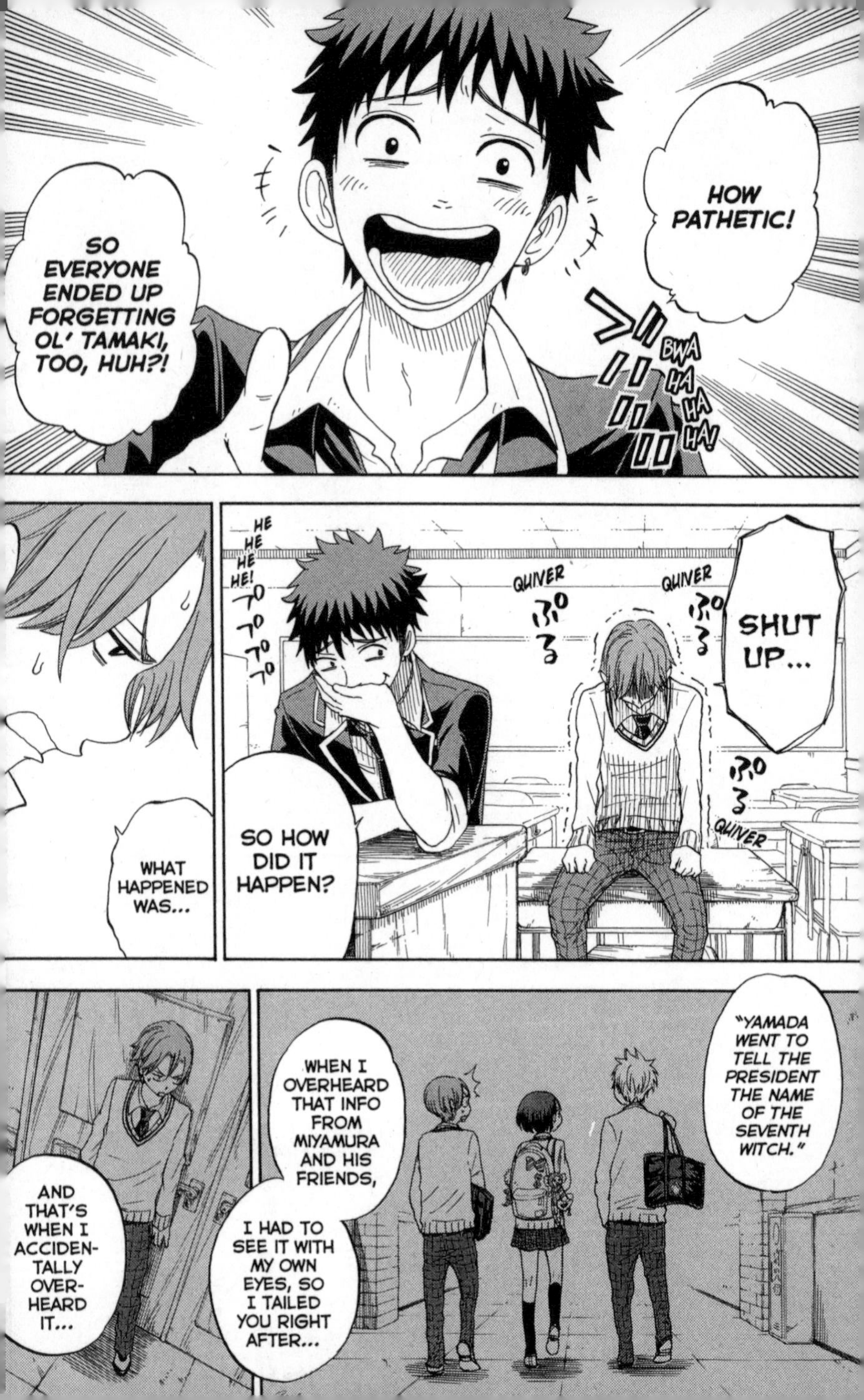
HOW PATHETIC!
BWA HA HA HA!
SO EVERYONE ENDED UP FORGETTING OL' TAMAKI, TOO, HUH?!
SHUT UP...
QUIVER
QUIVER
QUIVER
HE HE HE HE!
SO HOW DID IT HAPPEN?
WHAT HAPPENED WAS...
"YAMADA WENT TO TELL THE PRESIDENT THE NAME OF THE SEVENTH WITCH."
WHEN I OVERHEARD THAT INFO FROM MIYAMURA AND HIS FRIENDS,
I HAD TO SEE IT WITH MY OWN EYES, SO I TAILED YOU RIGHT AFTER...
AND THAT'S WHEN I ACCIDENTALLY OVERHEARD IT...

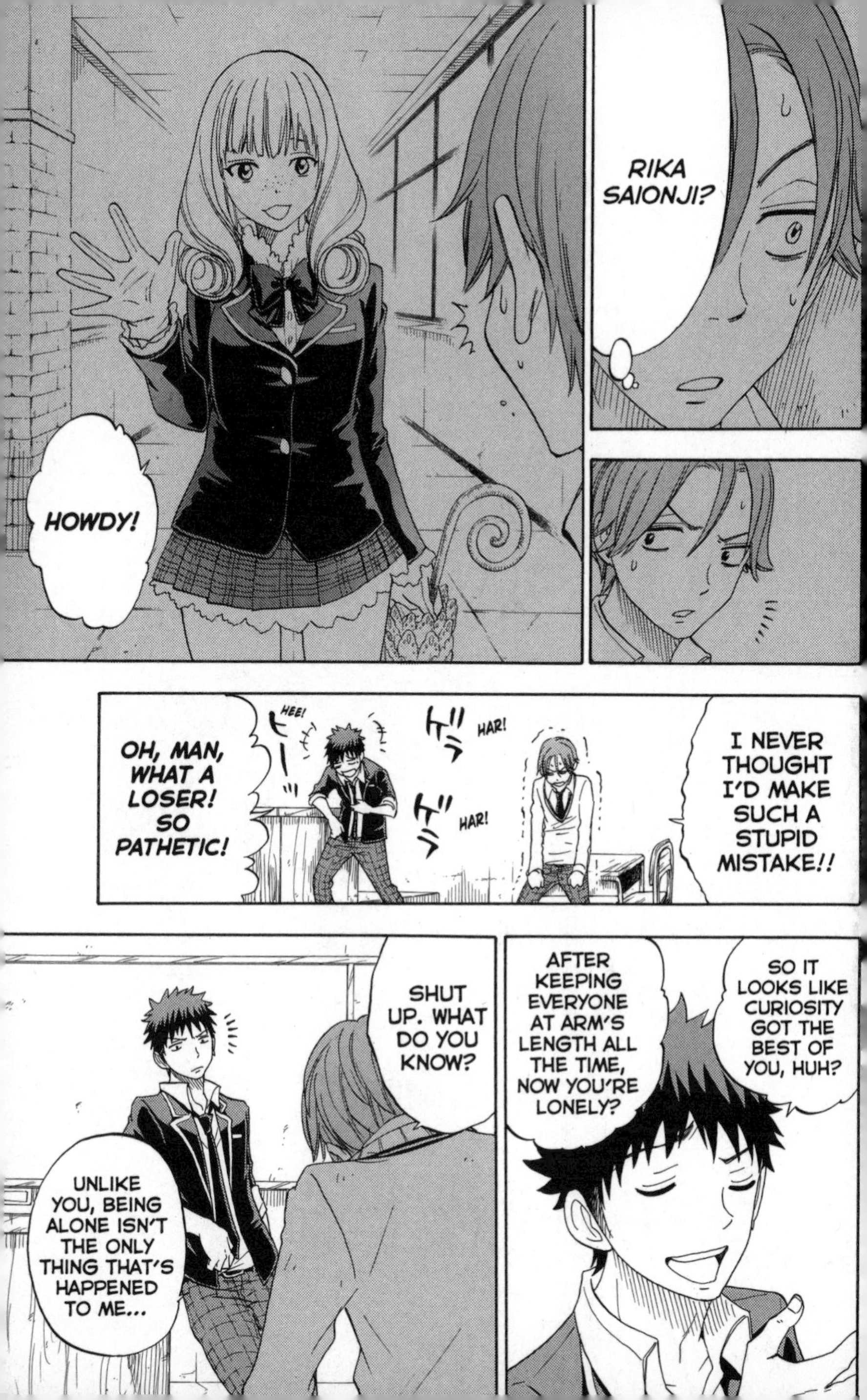
RIKA SAIONJI?
HOWDY!
I NEVER THOUGHT I'D MAKE SUCH A STUPID MISTAKE!!
HAR!
HAR!
HEE!
OH, MAN, WHAT A LOSER! SO PATHETIC!
SO IT LOOKS LIKE CURIOSITY GOT THE BEST OF YOU, HUH?
AFTER KEEPING EVERYONE AT ARM'S LENGTH ALL THE TIME, NOW YOU'RE LONELY?
SHUT UP. WHAT DO YOU KNOW?
UNLIKE YOU, BEING ALONE ISN'T THE ONLY THING THAT'S HAPPENED TO ME...

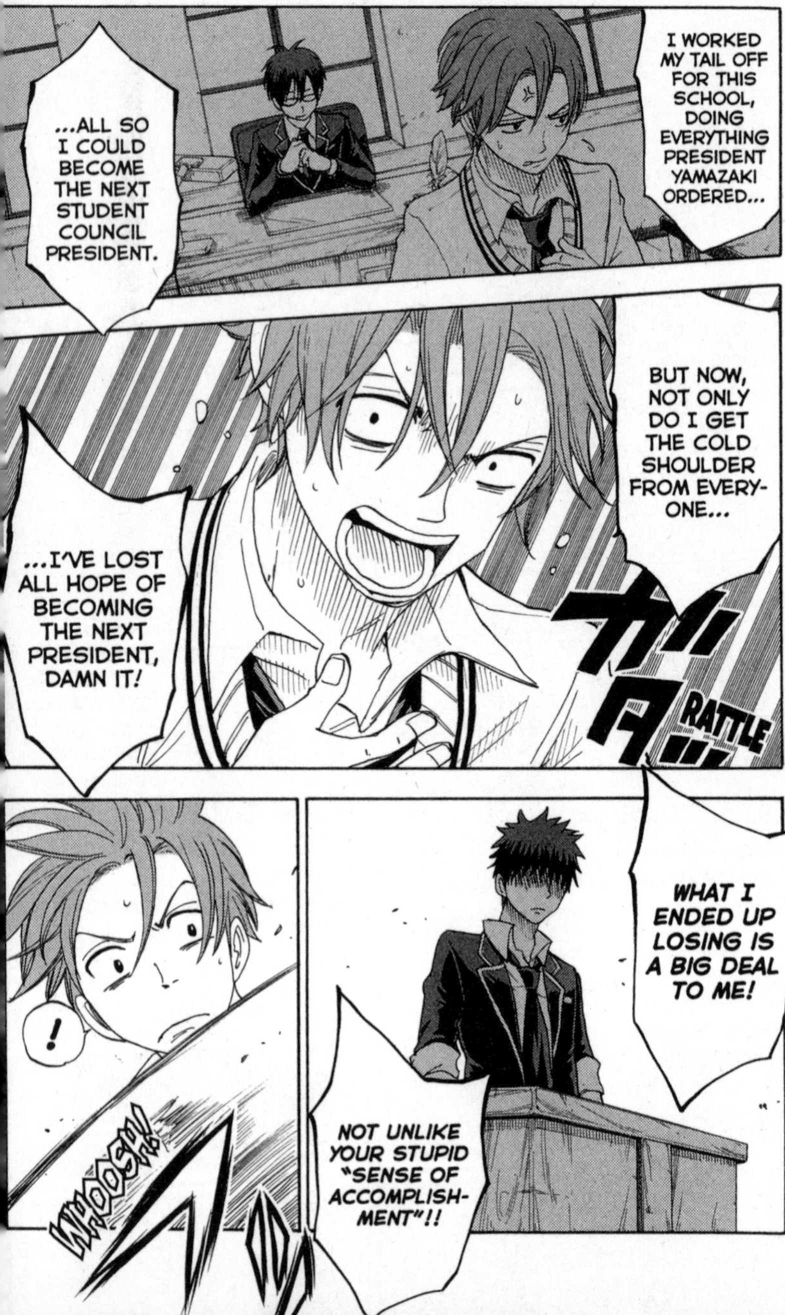
I WORKED MY TAIL OFF FOR THIS SCHOOL, DOING EVERYTHING PRESIDENT YAMAZAKI ORDERED...
...ALL SO I COULD BECOME THE NEXT STUDENT COUNCIL PRESIDENT.
BUT NOW, NOT ONLY DO I GET THE COLD SHOULDER FROM EVERY-ONE...
...I'VE LOST ALL HOPE OF BECOMING THE NEXT PRESIDENT, DAMN IT!
RATTLE
WHAT I ENDED UP LOSING IS A BIG DEAL TO ME!
NOT UNLIKE YOUR STUPID "SENSE OF ACCOMPLISH-MENT"!!
!
WHOOSH!

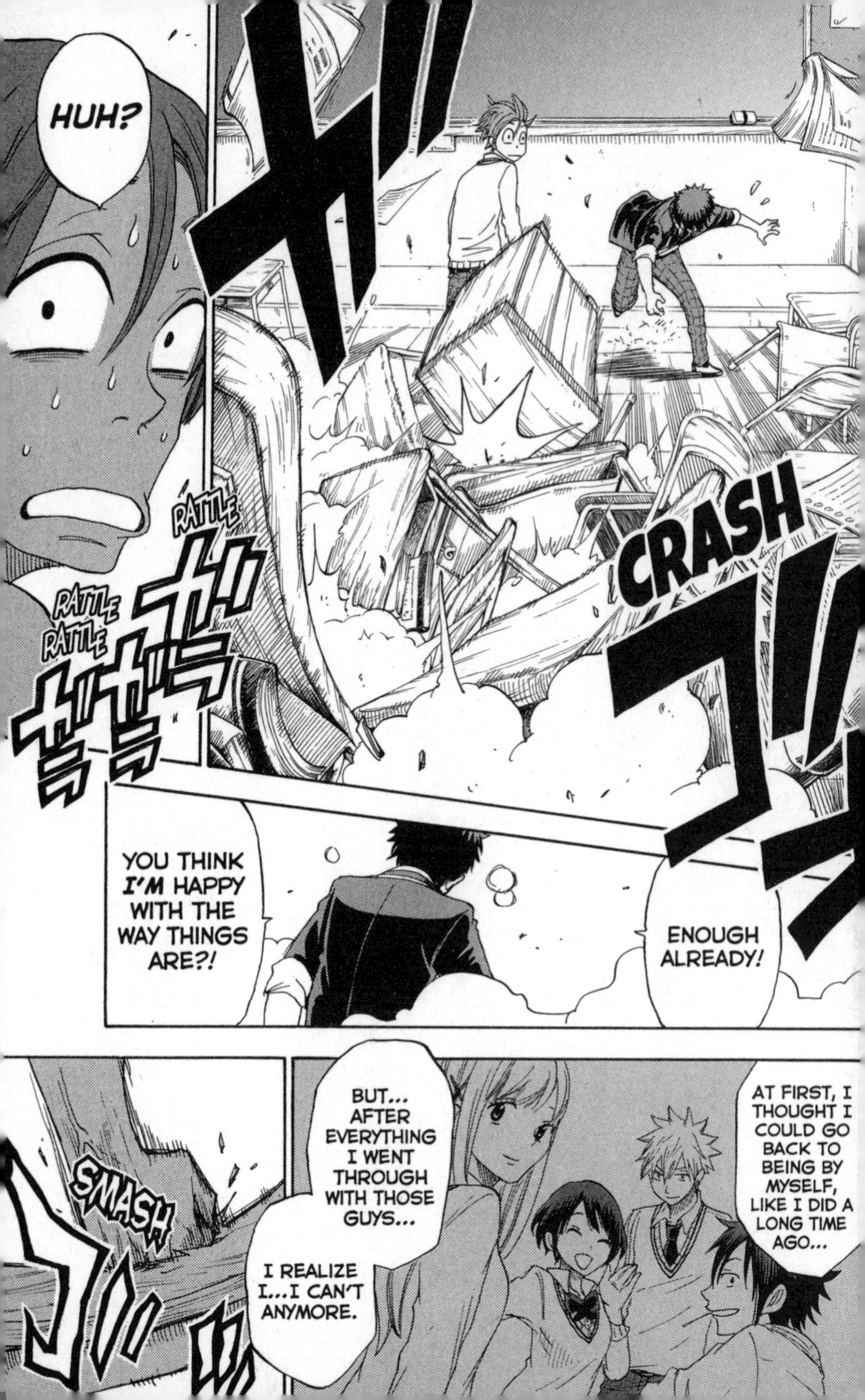
CRASH
HUH?
RATTLE
RATTLE RATTLE
ENOUGH ALREADY!
YOU THINK I'M HAPPY WITH THE WAY THINGS ARE?!
AT FIRST, I THOUGHT I COULD GO BACK TO BEING BY MYSELF, LIKE I DID A LONG TIME AGO...
BUT... AFTER EVERYTHING I WENT THROUGH WITH THOSE GUYS...
I REALIZE I...I CAN'T ANYMORE.
SMASH

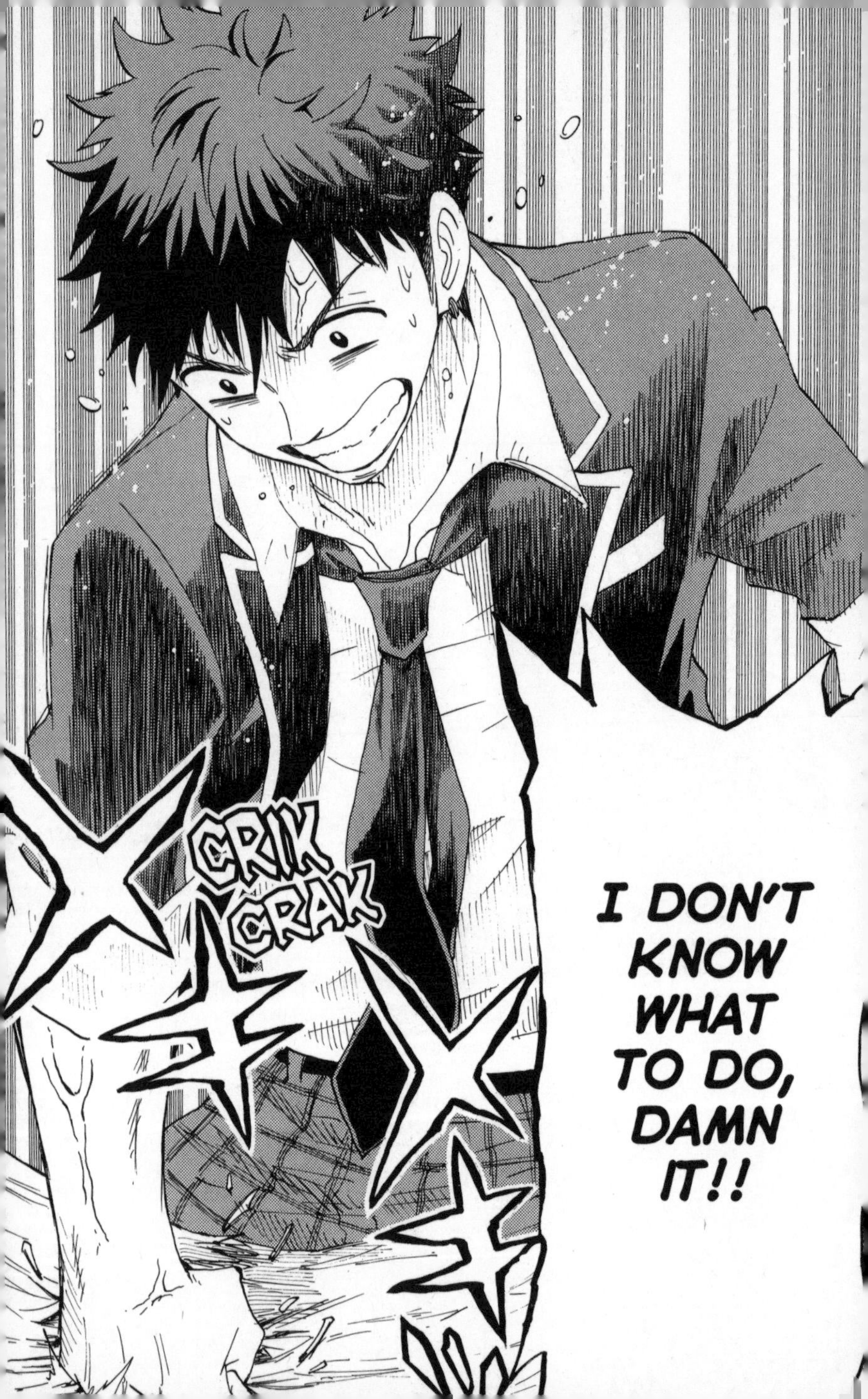
CRIK CRAK
I DON'T KNOW WHAT TO DO, DAMN IT!!

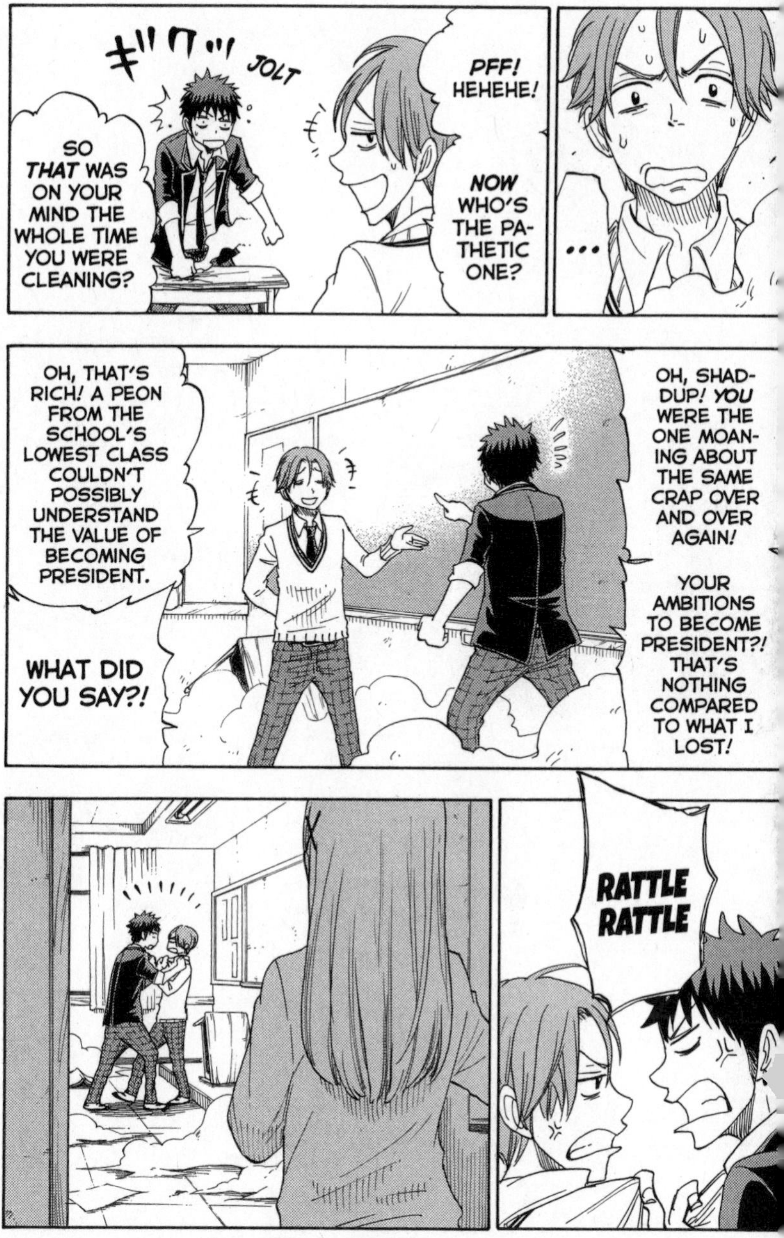
...
PFF! HEHEHE!
NOW WHO'S THE PA-THETIC ONE?
ギリッ
JOLT
SO THAT WAS ON YOUR MIND THE WHOLE TIME YOU WERE CLEANING?
OH, SHAD-DUP! YOU WERE THE ONE MOAN-ING ABOUT THE SAME CRAP OVER AND OVER AGAIN!
YOUR AMBITIONS TO BECOME PRESIDENT?! THAT'S NOTHING COMPARED TO WHAT I LOST!
OH, THAT'S RICH! A PEON FROM THE SCHOOL'S LOWEST CLASS COULDN'T POSSIBLY UNDERSTAND THE VALUE OF BECOMING PRESIDENT.
WHAT DID YOU SAY?!
RATTLE RATTLE

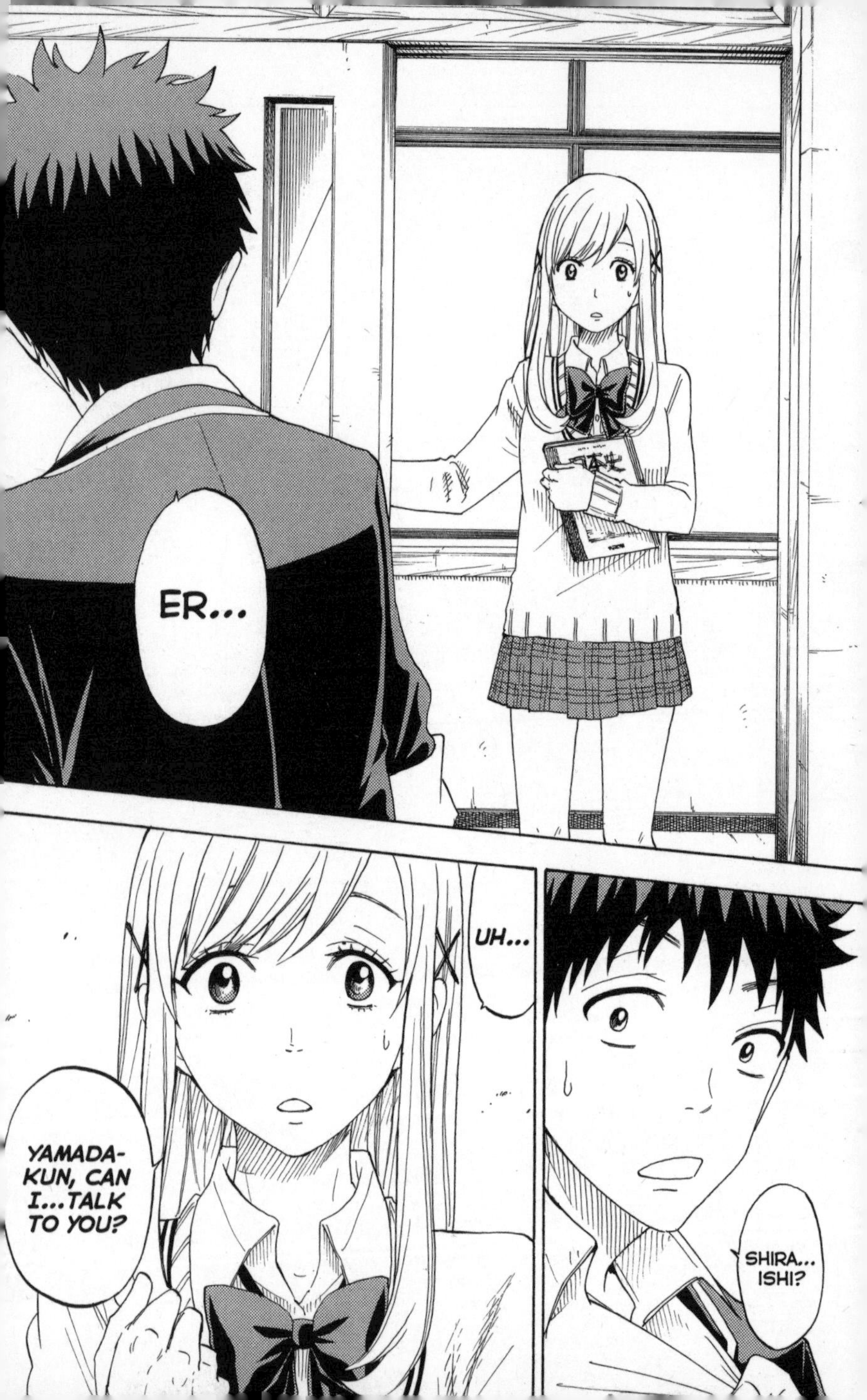
ER...
SHIRA... ISHI?
UH...
YAMADA-KUN, CAN I...TALK TO YOU?

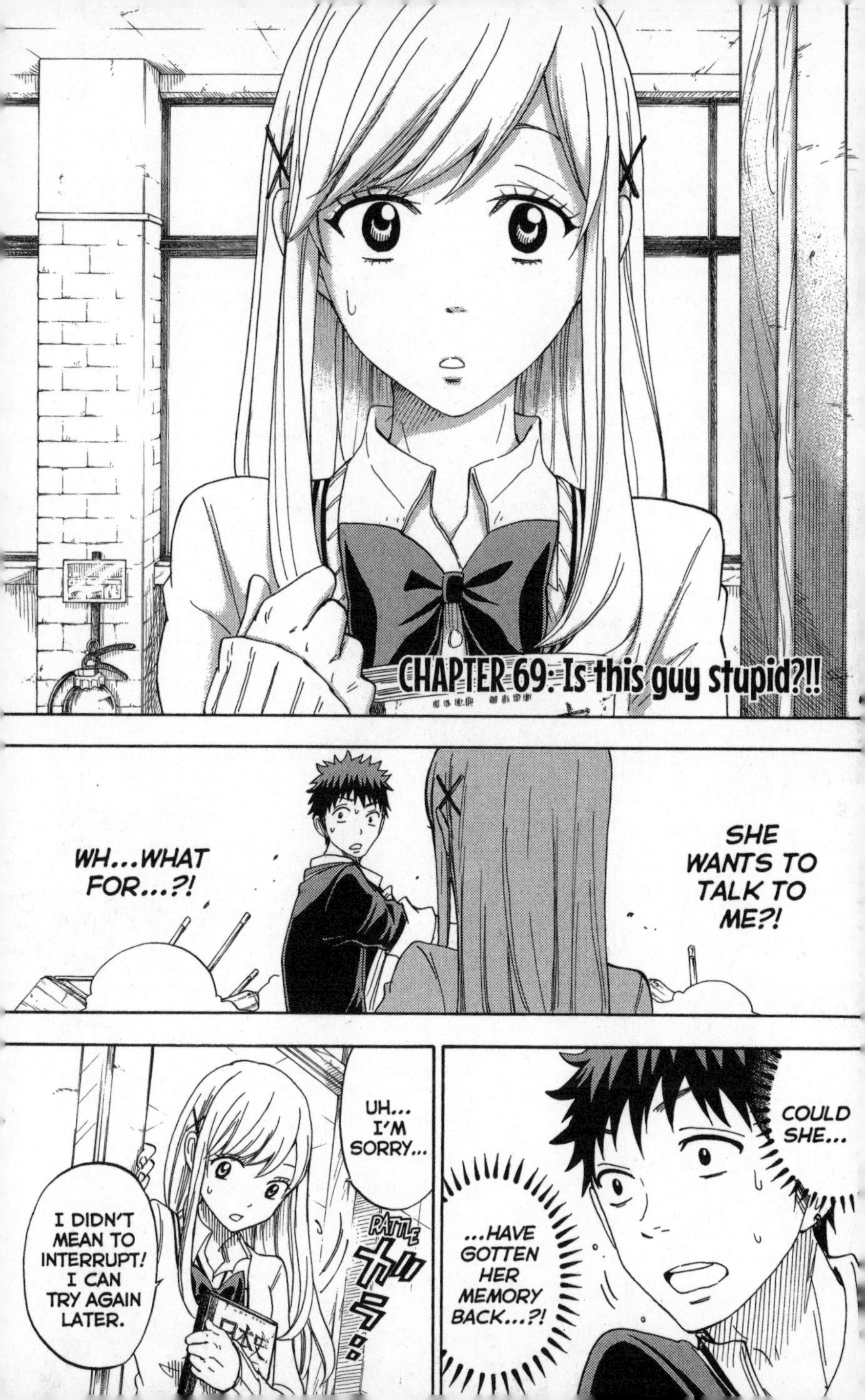
CHAPTER 69: Is this guy stupid?!!
SHE WANTS TO TALK TO ME?!
WH...WHAT FOR...?!
COULD SHE...
...HAVE GOTTEN HER MEMORY BACK...?!
UH... I'M SORRY...
RATTLE
I DIDN'T MEAN TO INTERRUPT! I CAN TRY AGAIN LATER.

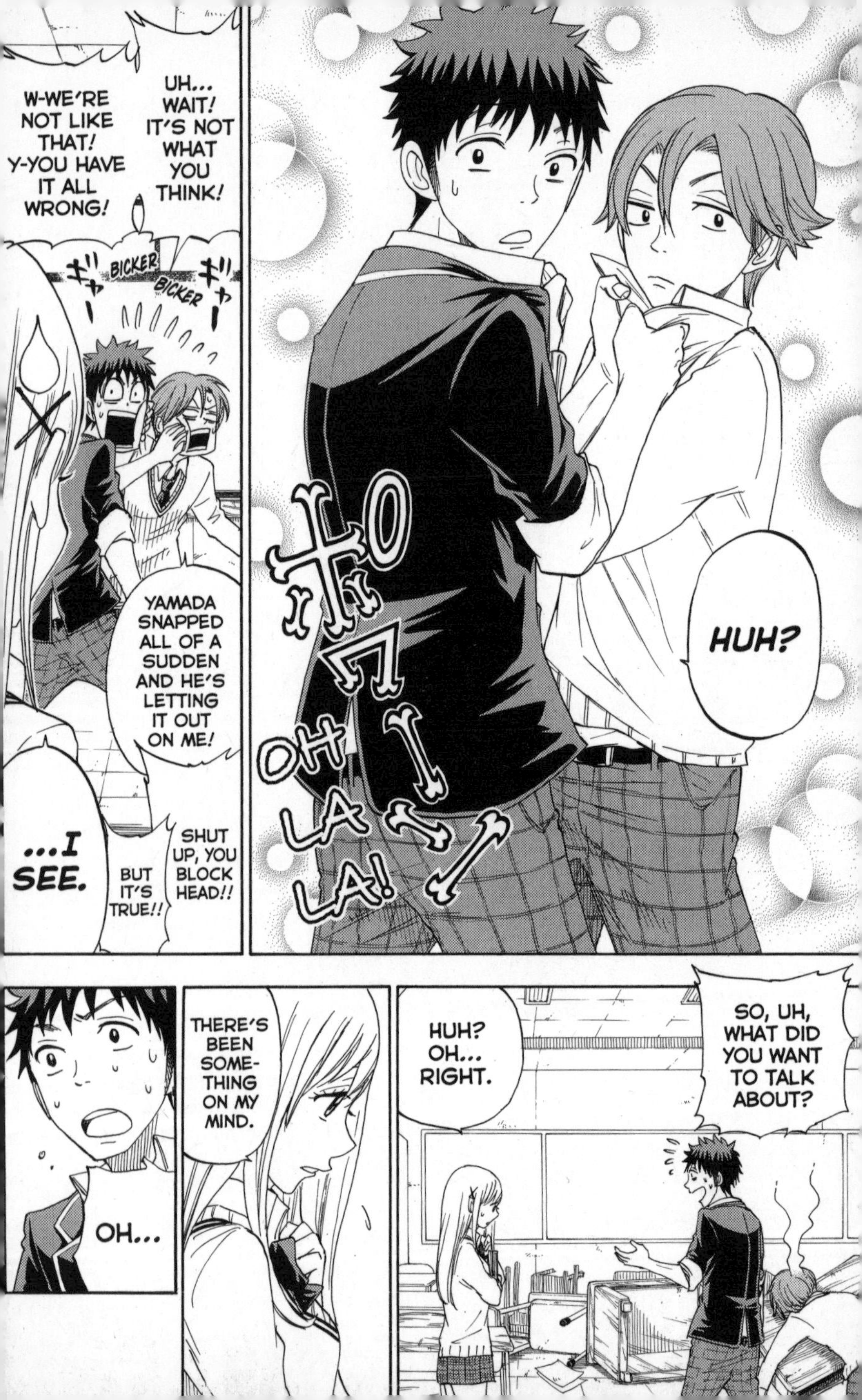
HUH?
OH LA LA!
UH... WAIT! IT'S NOT WHAT YOU THINK!
W-WE'RE NOT LIKE THAT! Y-YOU HAVE IT ALL WRONG!
BICKER BICKER
YAMADA SNAPPED ALL OF A SUDDEN AND HE'S LETTING IT OUT ON ME!
SHUT UP, YOU BLOCKHEAD!!
BUT IT'S TRUE!!
...I SEE.
SO, UH, WHAT DID YOU WANT TO TALK ABOUT?
HUH? OH... RIGHT.
THERE'S BEEN SOMETHING ON MY MIND.
OH...

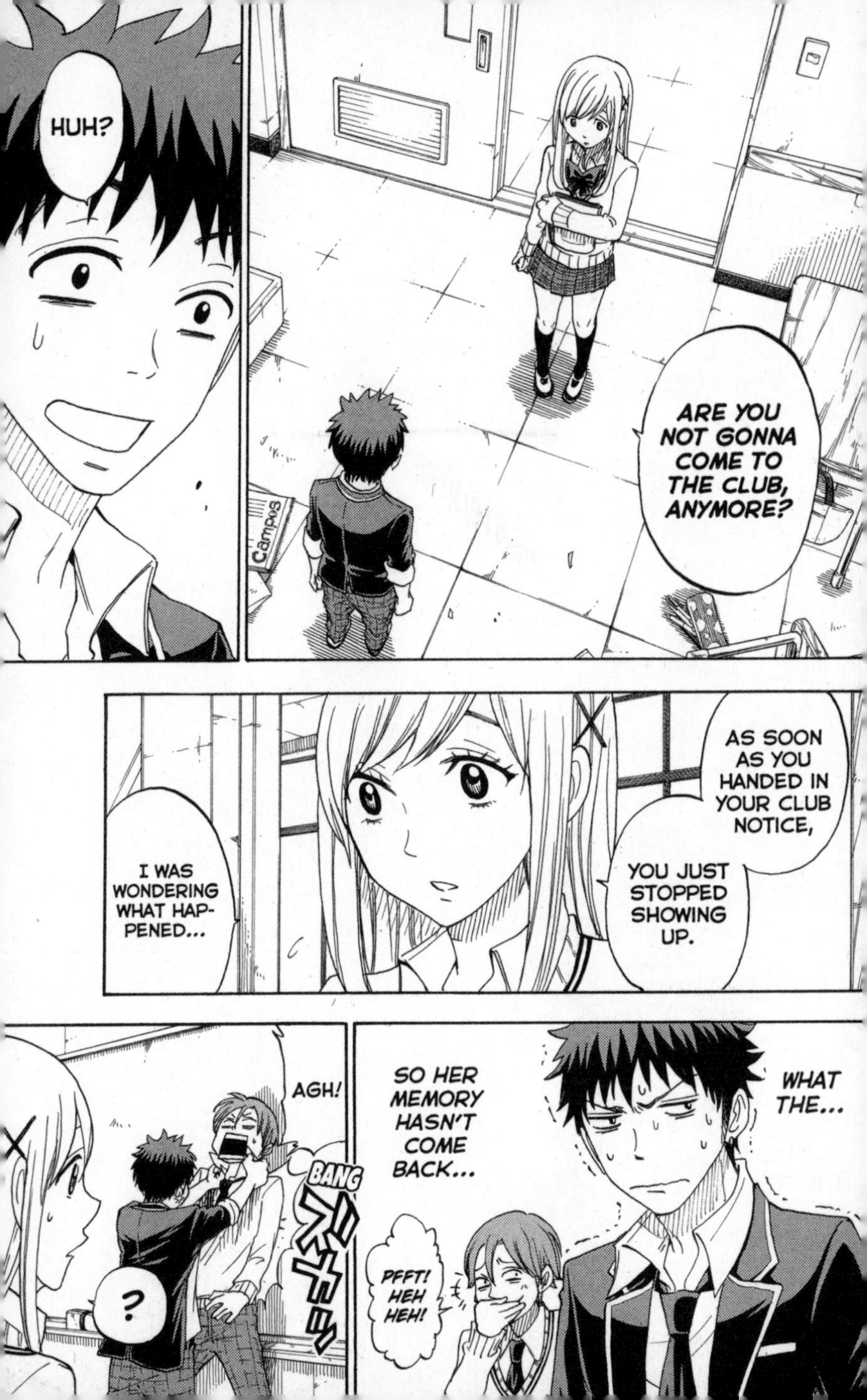

ARE YOU NOT GONNA COME TO THE CLUB, ANYMORE?
HUH?
AS SOON AS YOU HANDED IN YOUR CLUB NOTICE,
YOU JUST STOPPED SHOWING UP.
I WAS WONDERING WHAT HAPPENED...
WHAT THE...
SO HER MEMORY HASN'T COME BACK...
PFFT! HEH HEH!
AGH!
BANG
?

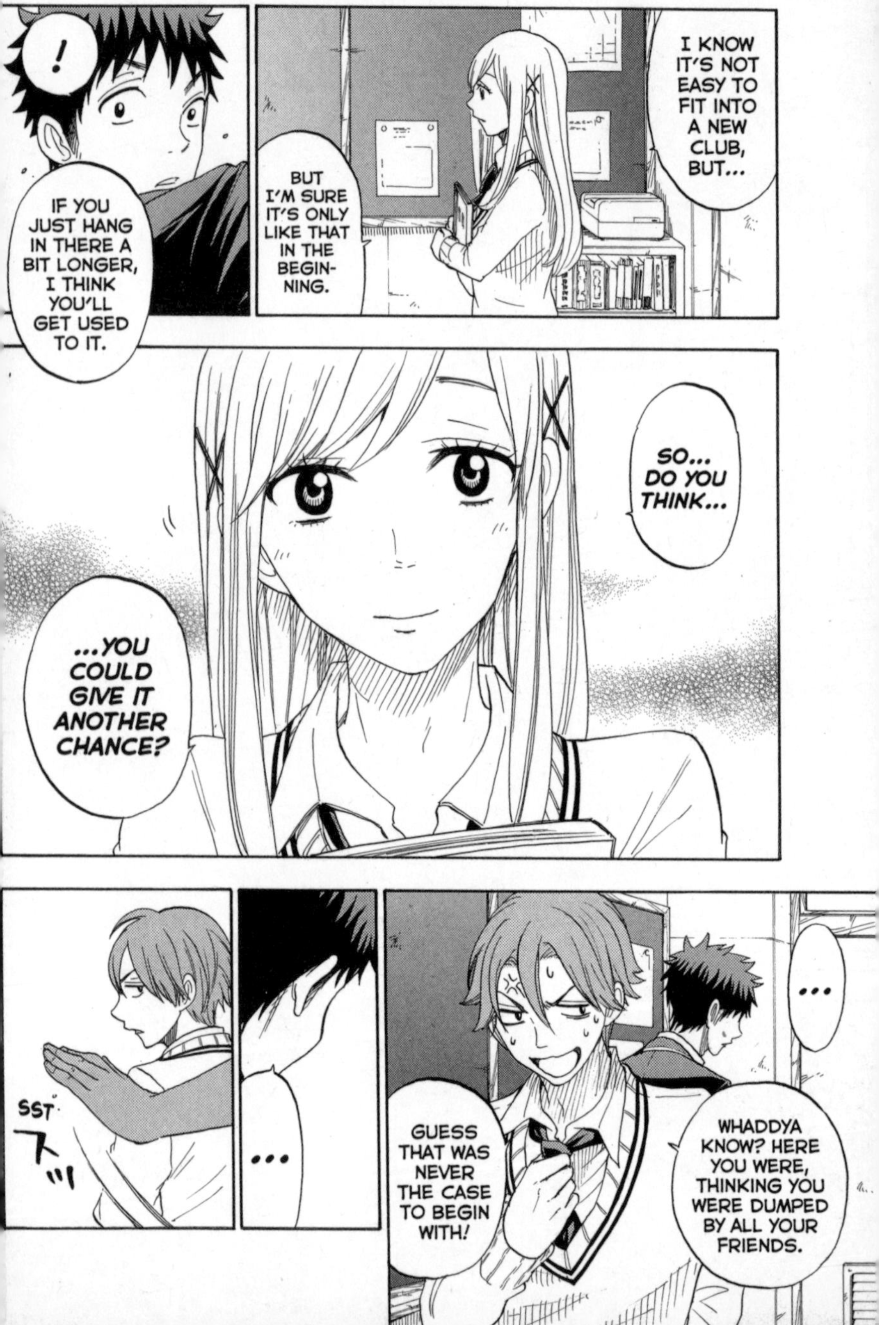
I KNOW IT'S NOT EASY TO FIT INTO A NEW CLUB, BUT...
BUT I'M SURE IT'S ONLY LIKE THAT IN THE BEGIN-NING.
!
IF YOU JUST HANG IN THERE A BIT LONGER, I THINK YOU'LL GET USED TO IT.
SO... DO YOU THINK...
...YOU COULD GIVE IT ANOTHER CHANCE?
...
WHADDYA KNOW? HERE YOU WERE, THINKING YOU WERE DUMPED BY ALL YOUR FRIENDS.
GUESS THAT WAS NEVER THE CASE TO BEGIN WITH!
...
SST
スッ

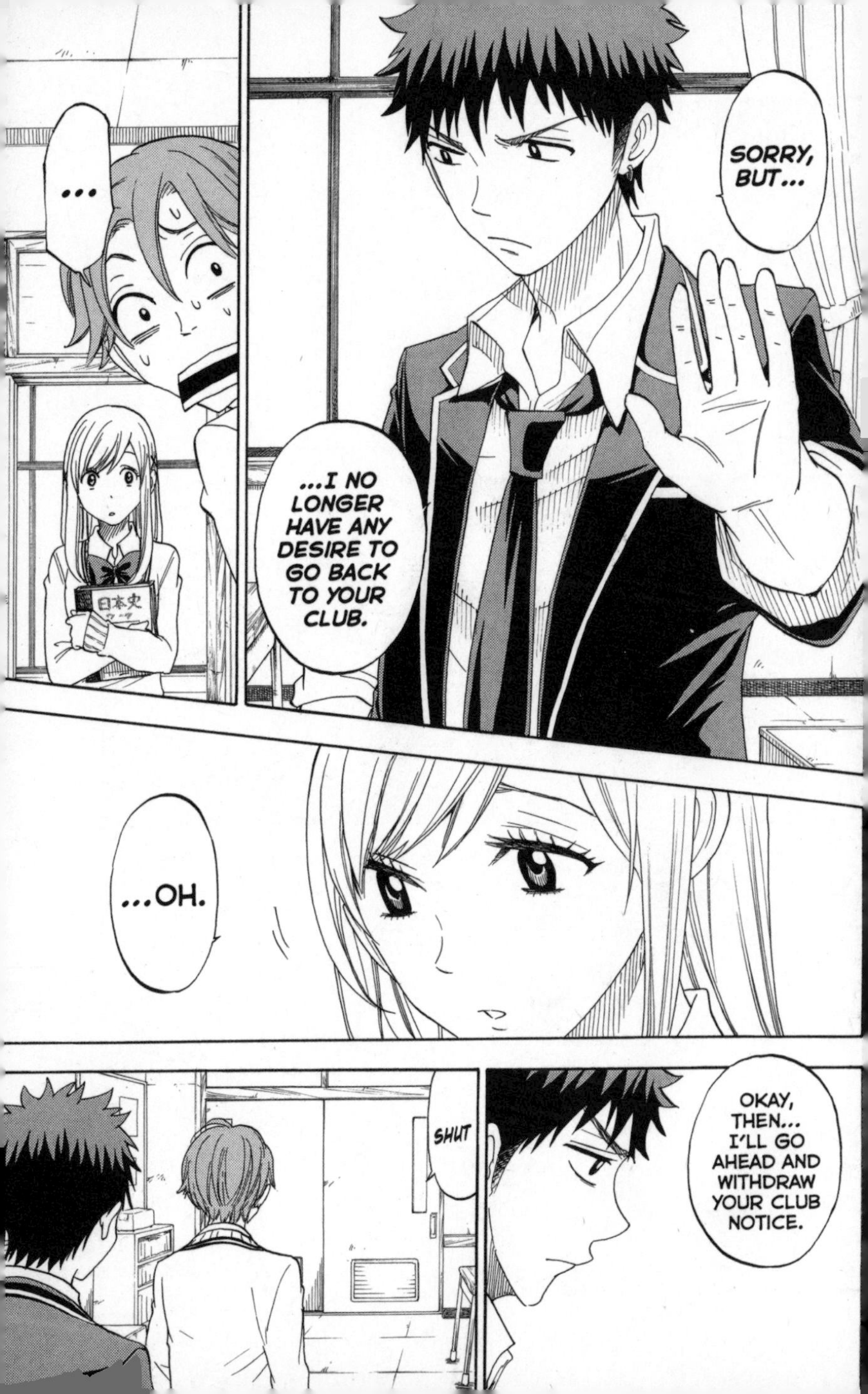
SORRY, BUT...
...I NO LONGER HAVE ANY DESIRE TO GO BACK TO YOUR CLUB.
...
...OH.
OKAY, THEN... I'LL GO AHEAD AND WITHDRAW YOUR CLUB NOTICE.
SHUT

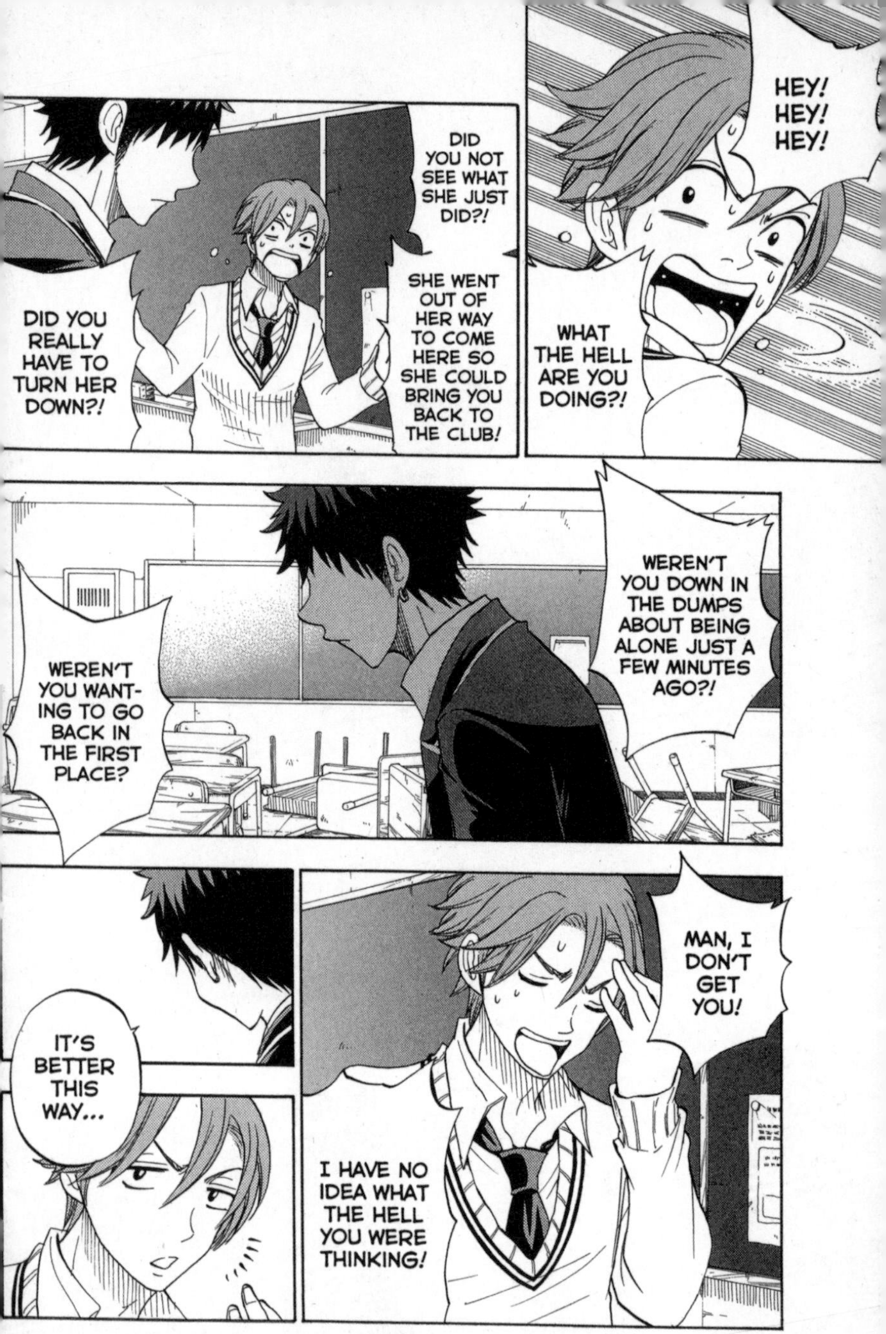

HEY! HEY! HEY!
WHAT THE HELL ARE YOU DOING?!
DID YOU NOT SEE WHAT SHE JUST DID?!
SHE WENT OUT OF HER WAY TO COME HERE SO SHE COULD BRING YOU BACK TO THE CLUB!
DID YOU REALLY HAVE TO TURN HER DOWN?!
WEREN'T YOU DOWN IN THE DUMPS ABOUT BEING ALONE JUST A FEW MINUTES AGO?!
WEREN'T YOU WANTING TO GO BACK IN THE FIRST PLACE?
MAN, I DON'T GET YOU!
I HAVE NO IDEA WHAT THE HELL YOU WERE THINKING!
IT'S BETTER THIS WAY...

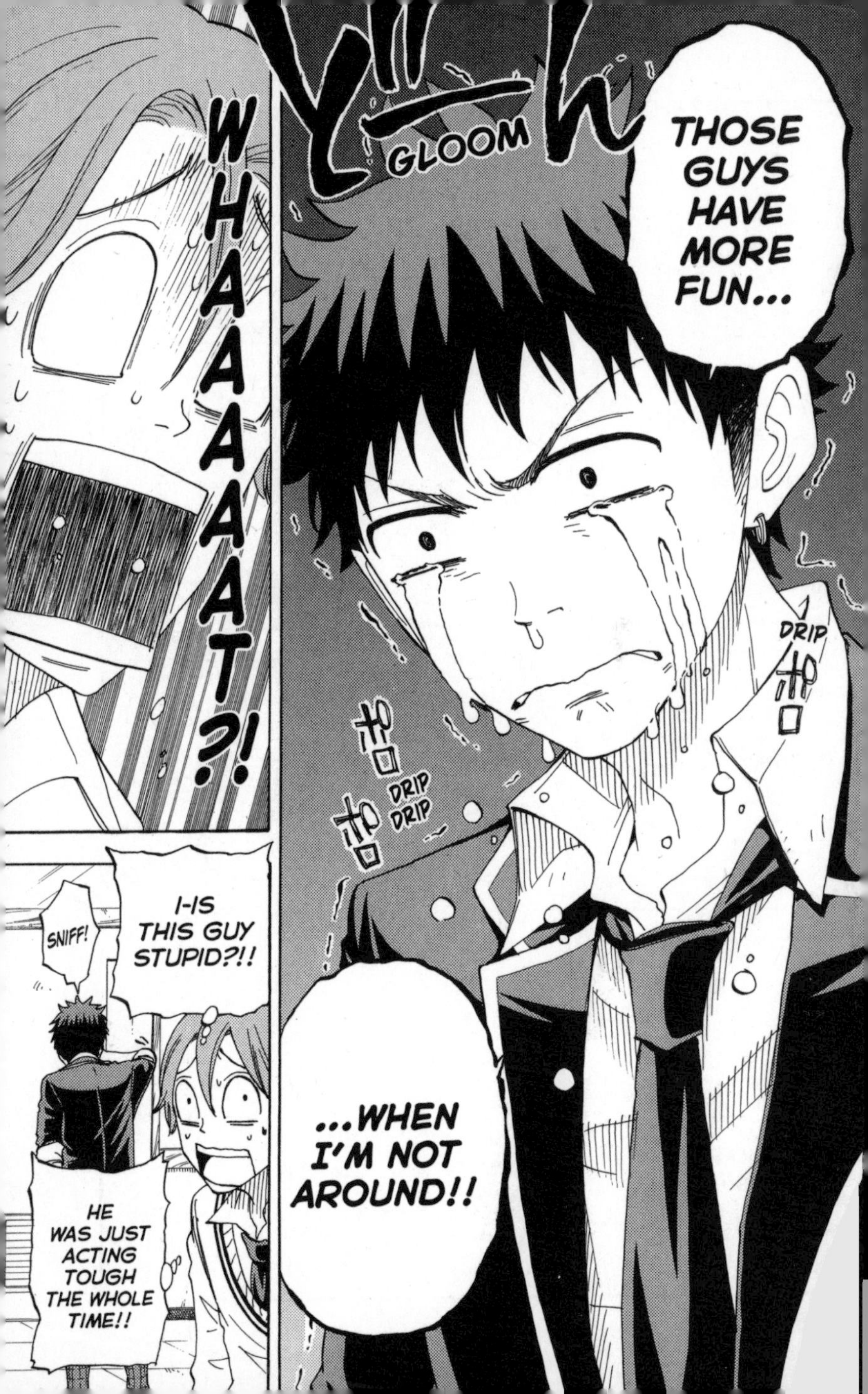
GLOOM
THOSE GUYS HAVE MORE FUN...
DRIP
DRIP DRIP
...WHEN I'M NOT AROUND!!
WHAAAAAT?!
I-IS THIS GUY STUPID?!!
SNIFF!
HE WAS JUST ACTING TOUGH THE WHOLE TIME!!

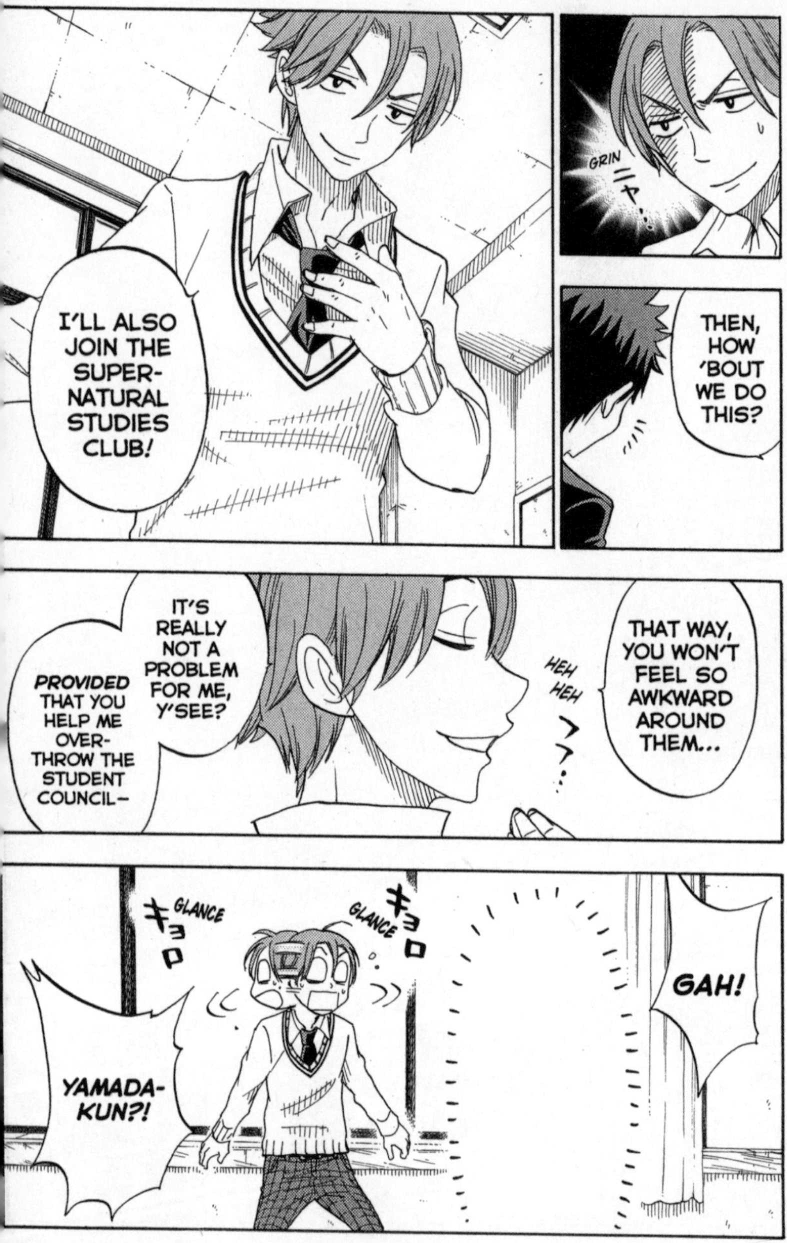
GRIN
ニヤ…
THEN, HOW 'BOUT WE DO THIS?
I'LL ALSO JOIN THE SUPER-NATURAL STUDIES CLUB!
THAT WAY, YOU WON'T FEEL SO AWKWARD AROUND THEM...
HEH HEH
IT'S REALLY NOT A PROBLEM FOR ME, Y'SEE?
PROVIDED THAT YOU HELP ME OVER-THROW THE STUDENT COUNCIL–
GAH!
キョロ GLANCE
キョロ GLANCE
YAMADA-KUN?!

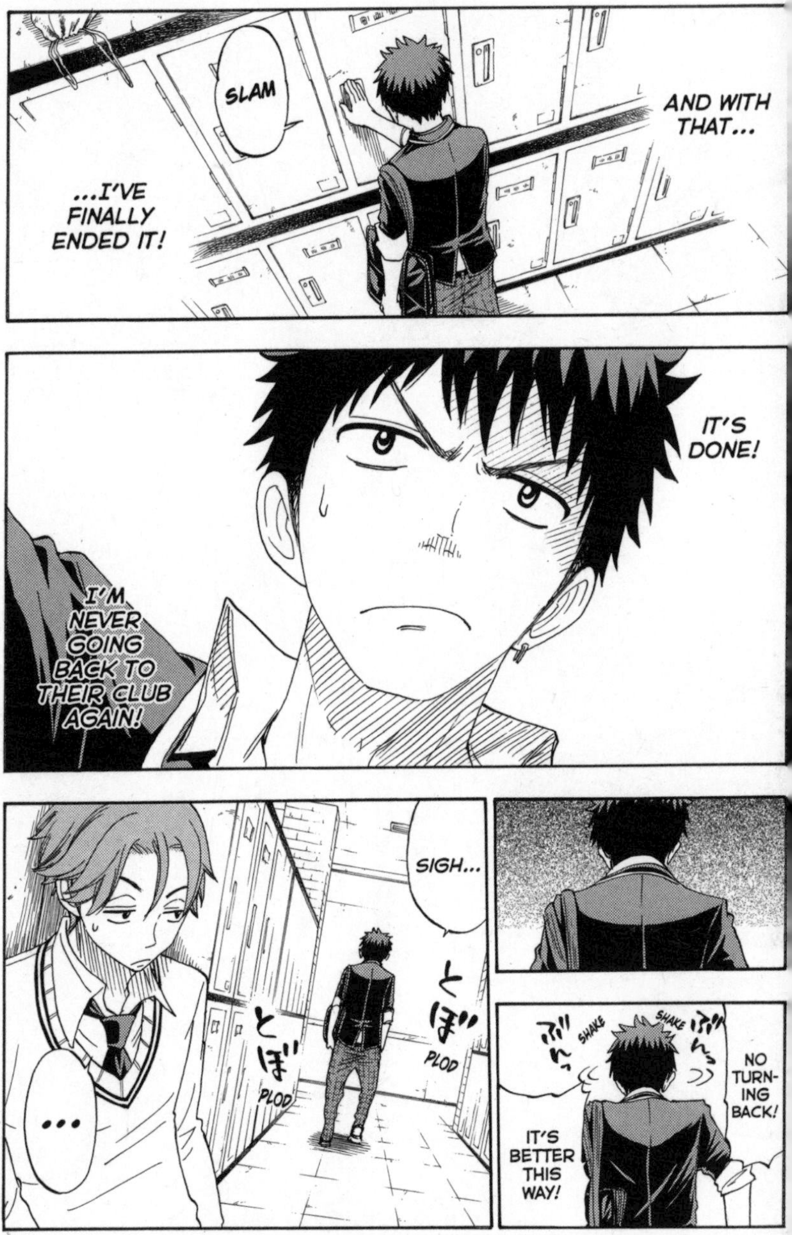
AND WITH THAT...
SLAM
...I'VE FINALLY ENDED IT!
IT'S DONE!
I'M NEVER GOING BACK TO THEIR CLUB AGAIN!
ぶんっ SHAKE
ぶんっ SHAKE
NO TURNING BACK!
IT'S BETTER THIS WAY!
SIGH...
とぼ PLOD
とぼ PLOD
...

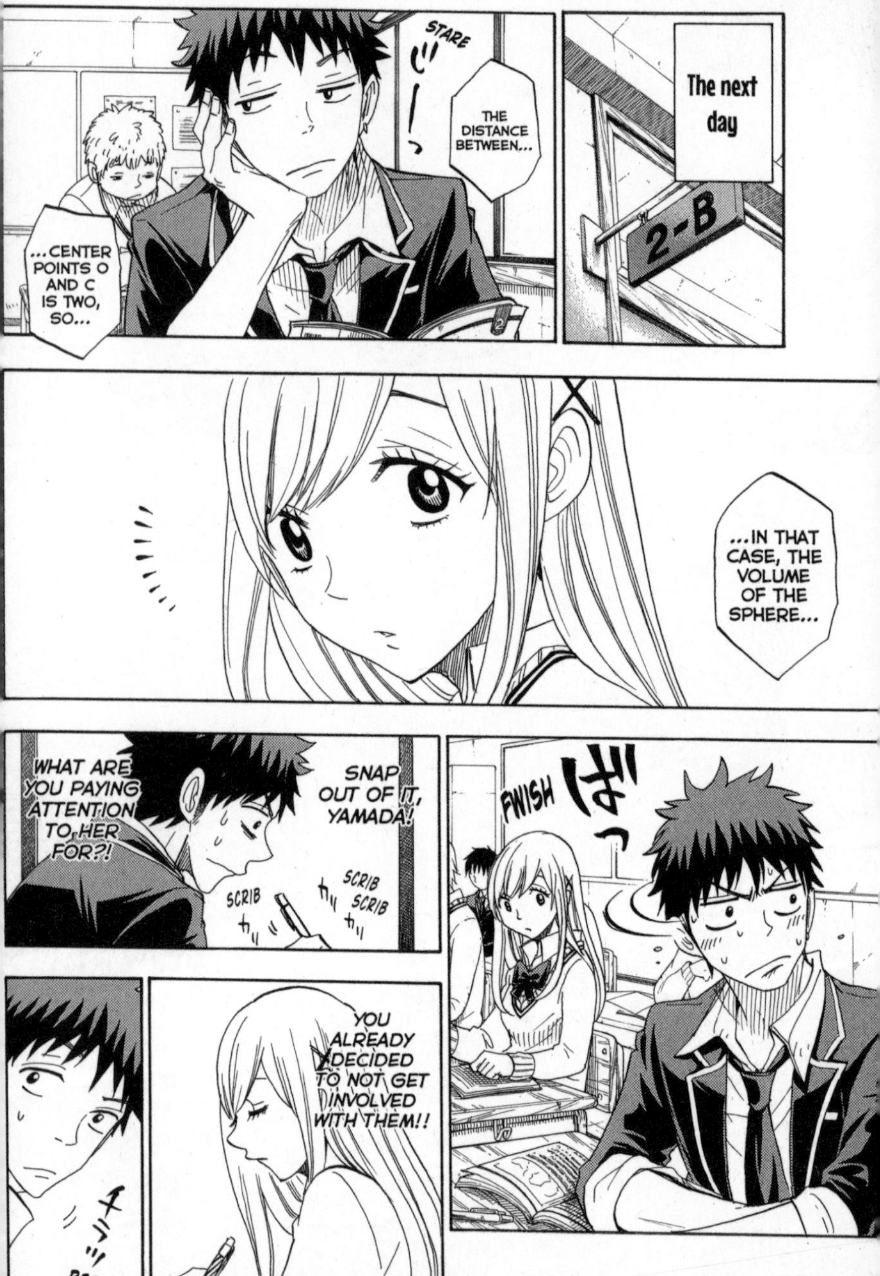
The next day
2-B
STARE
THE DISTANCE BETWEEN...
...CENTER POINTS O AND C IS TWO, SO...
...IN THAT CASE, THE VOLUME OF THE SPHERE...
FWISH
SNAP OUT OF IT, YAMADA!
WHAT ARE YOU PAYING ATTENTION TO HER FOR?!
SCRIB SCRIB
SCRIB
YOU ALREADY DECIDED TO NOT GET INVOLVED WITH THEM!!
PEEK

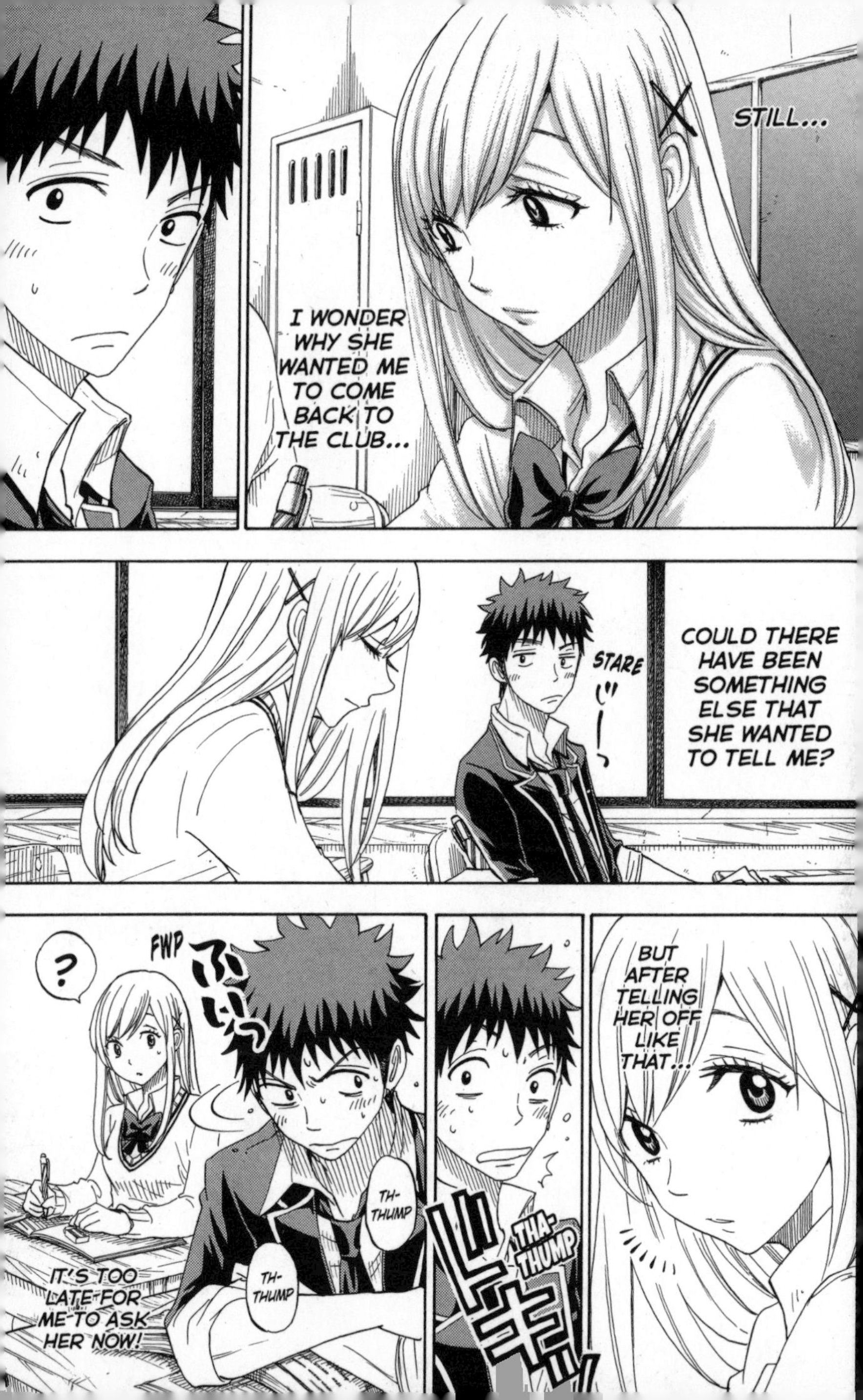
STILL...
I WONDER WHY SHE WANTED ME TO COME BACK TO THE CLUB...
COULD THERE HAVE BEEN SOMETHING ELSE THAT SHE WANTED TO TELL ME?
STARE
BUT AFTER TELLING HER OFF LIKE THAT...
THA-THUMP
?
FWP
TH-THUMP
TH-THUMP
IT'S TOO LATE FOR ME TO ASK HER NOW!

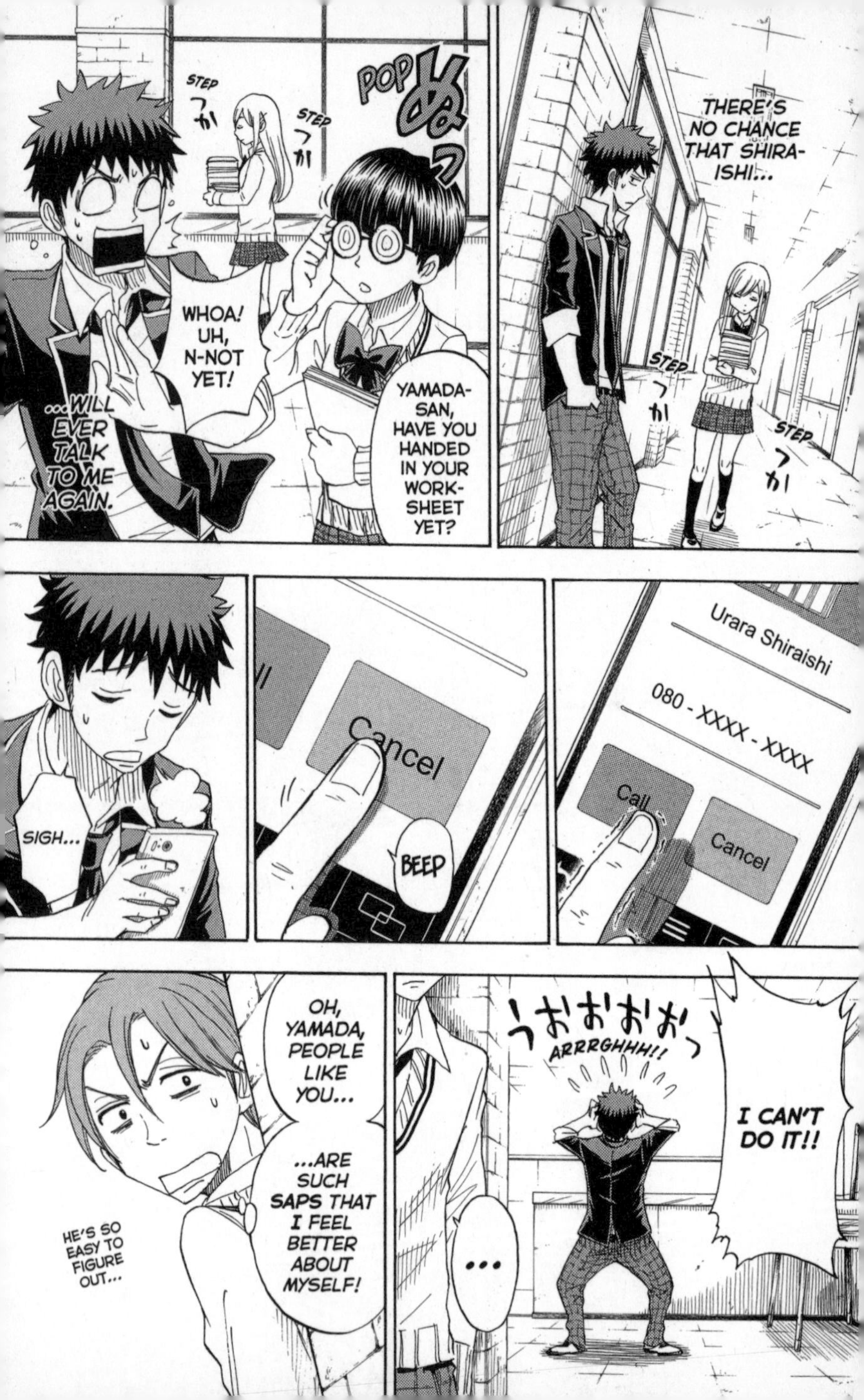
THERE'S NO CHANCE THAT SHIRA-ISHI...
STEP つか
STEP つか
POP ぬっ
STEP つか
STEP つか
YAMADA-SAN, HAVE YOU HANDED IN YOUR WORK-SHEET YET?
WHOA! UH, N-NOT YET!
...WILL EVER TALK TO ME AGAIN.
Urara Shiraishi
080 - XXXX - XXXX
Call
Cancel
Cancel
BEEP
SIGH...
うおおおおっ
ARRRGHHH!!
I CAN'T DO IT!!
OH, YAMADA, PEOPLE LIKE YOU...
...ARE SUCH SAPS THAT I FEEL BETTER ABOUT MYSELF!
...
HE'S SO EASY TO FIGURE OUT...

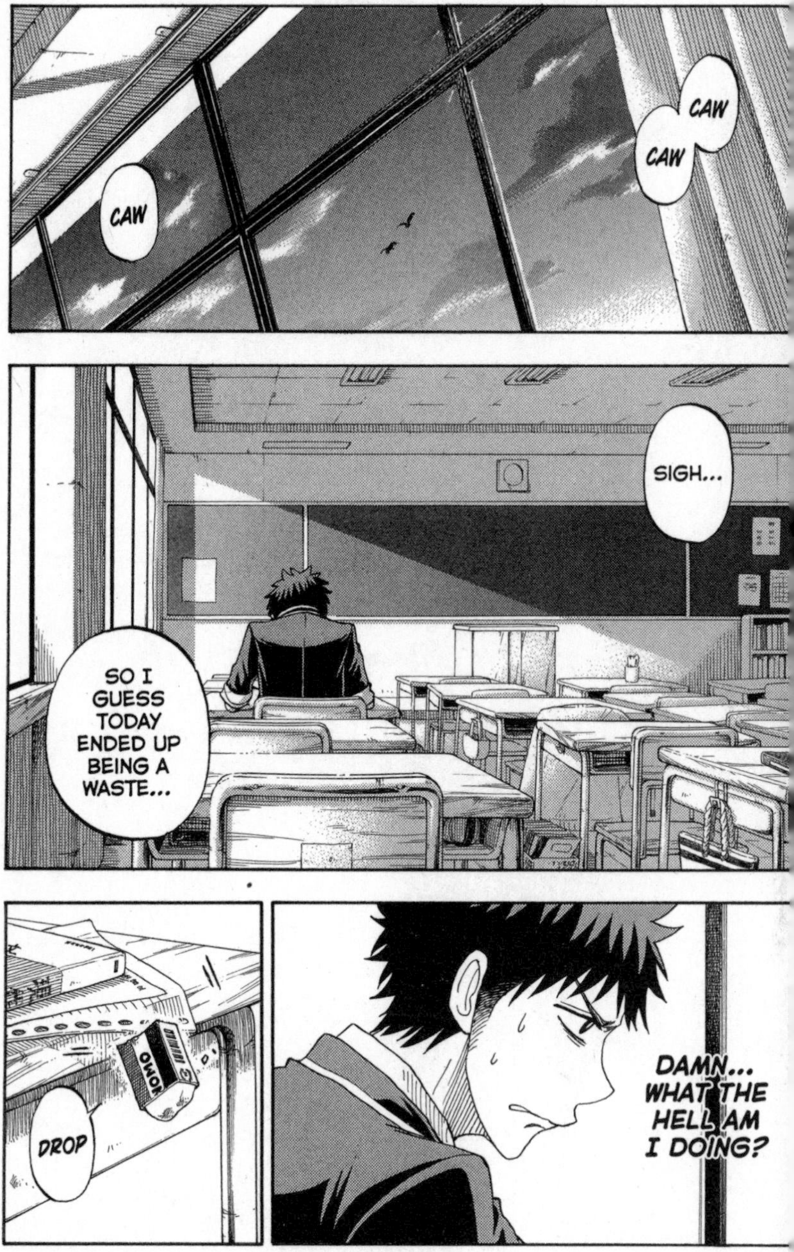
CAW
CAW
CAW
SIGH...
SO I GUESS TODAY ENDED UP BEING A WASTE...
DAMN... WHAT THE HELL AM I DOING?
DROP

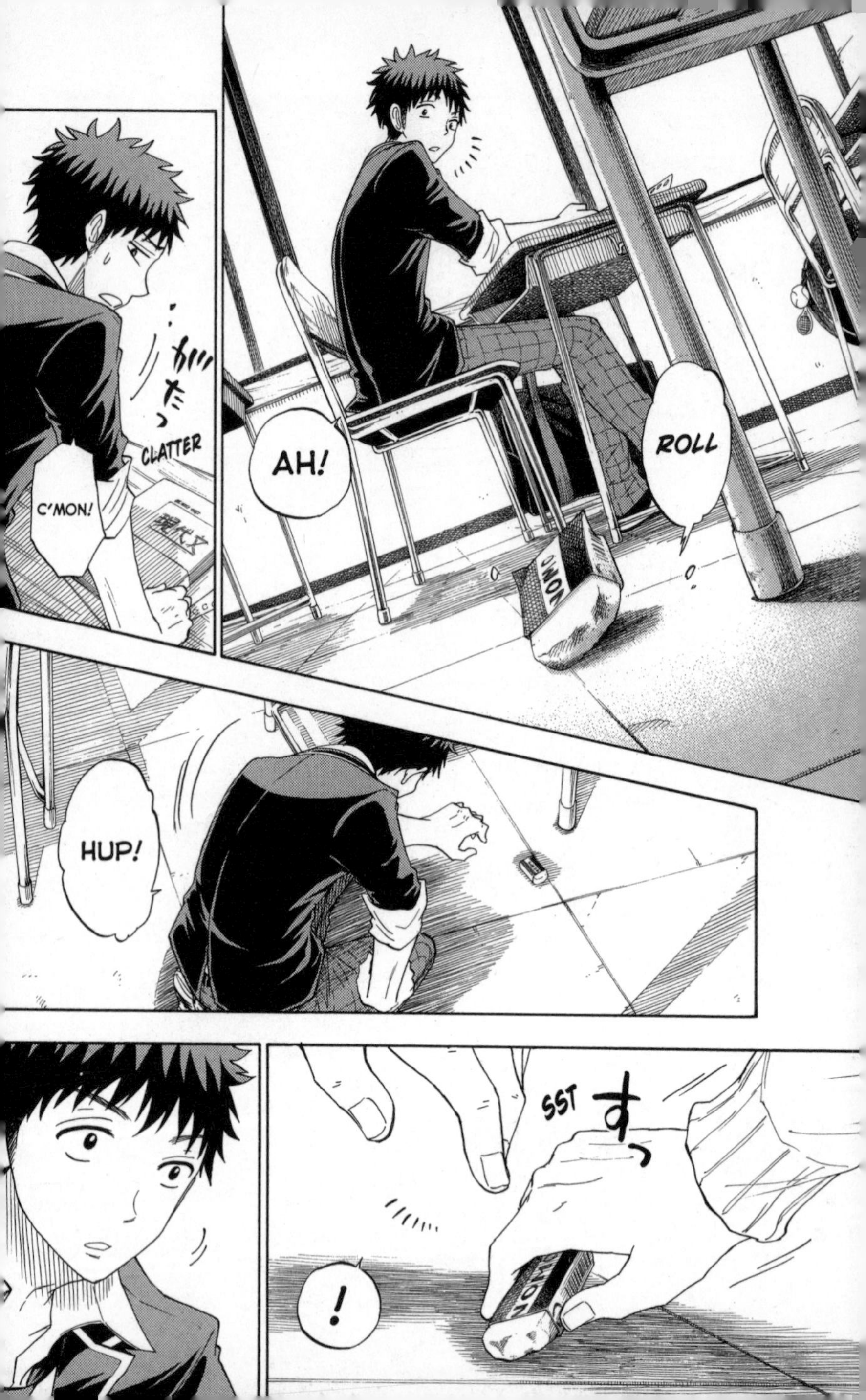
ROLL
AH!
がたっ
CLATTER
C'MON!
HUP!
SST
すっ
!

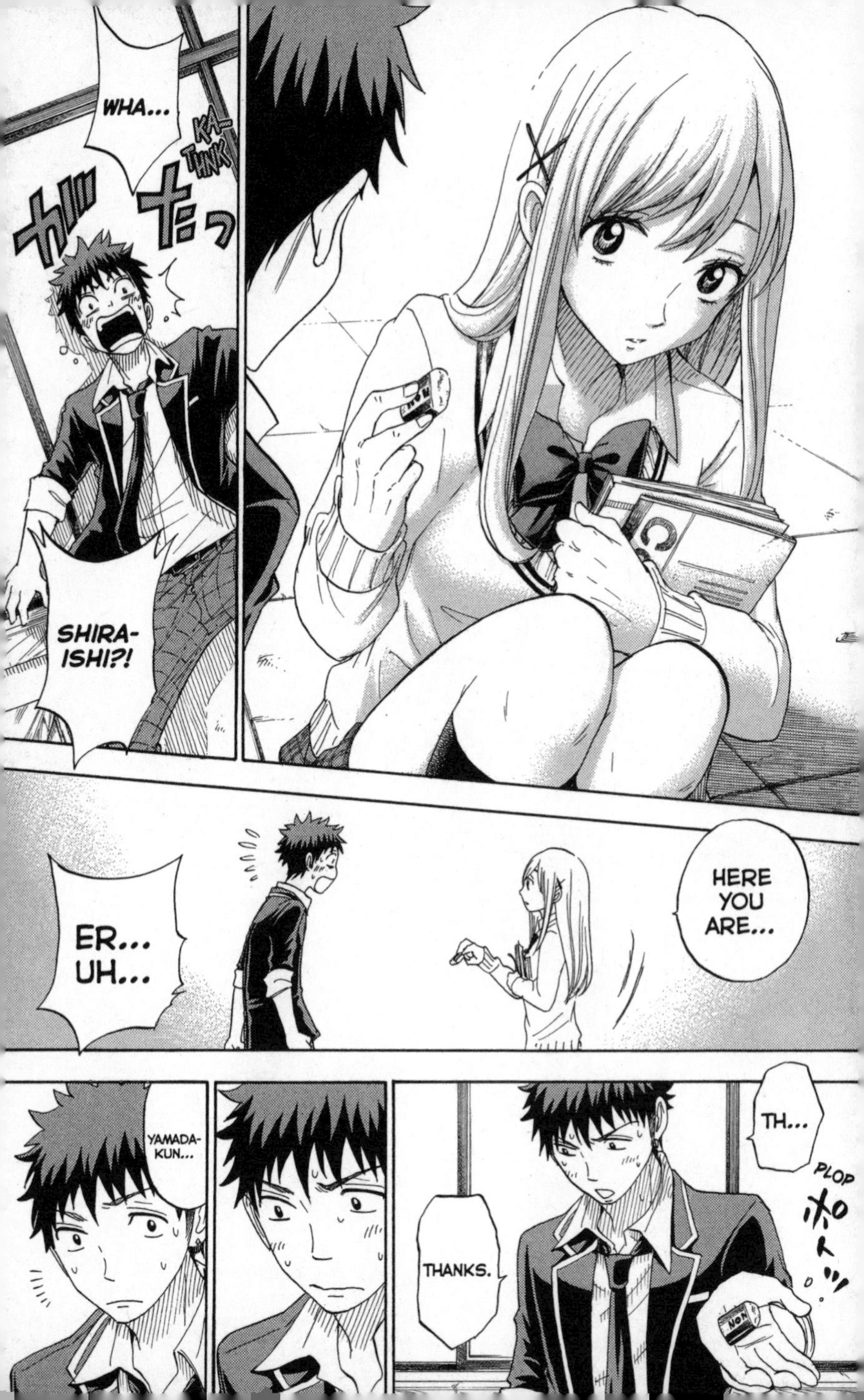
WHA...
KA-THUNK
SHIRA-ISHI?!
HERE YOU ARE...
ER... UH...
TH...
PLOP
THANKS.
YAMADA-KUN...

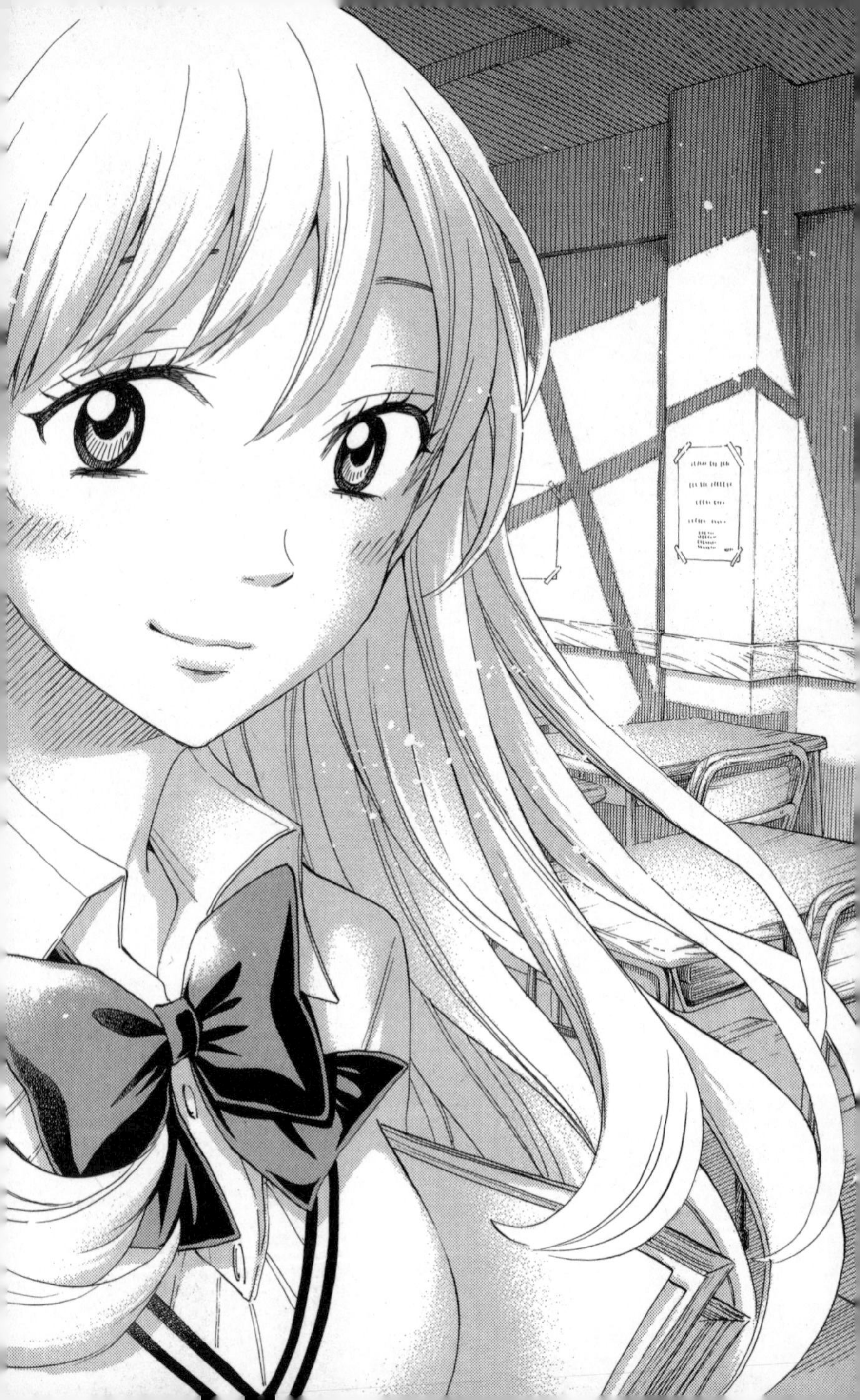

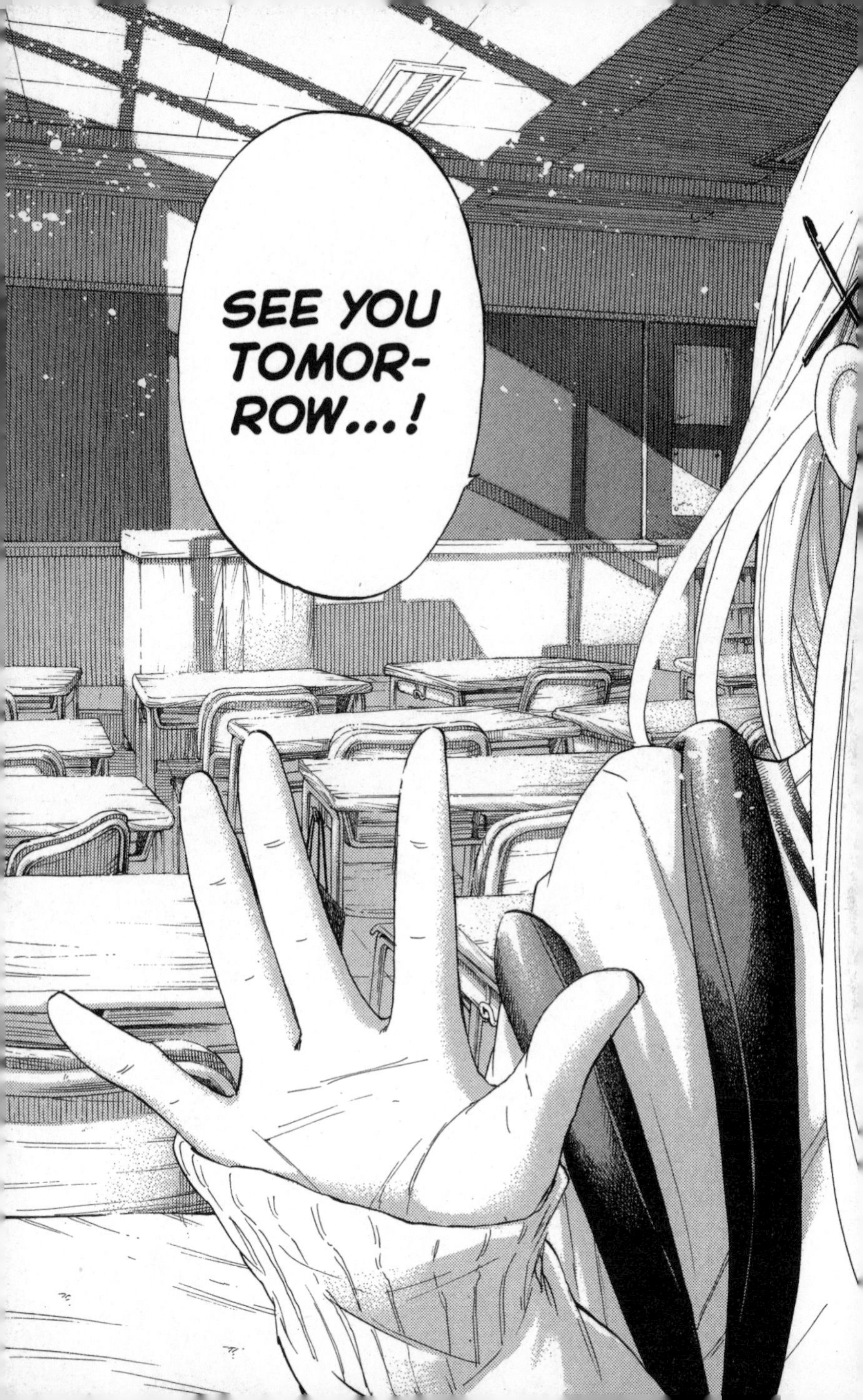
SEE YOU TOMOR-ROW...!

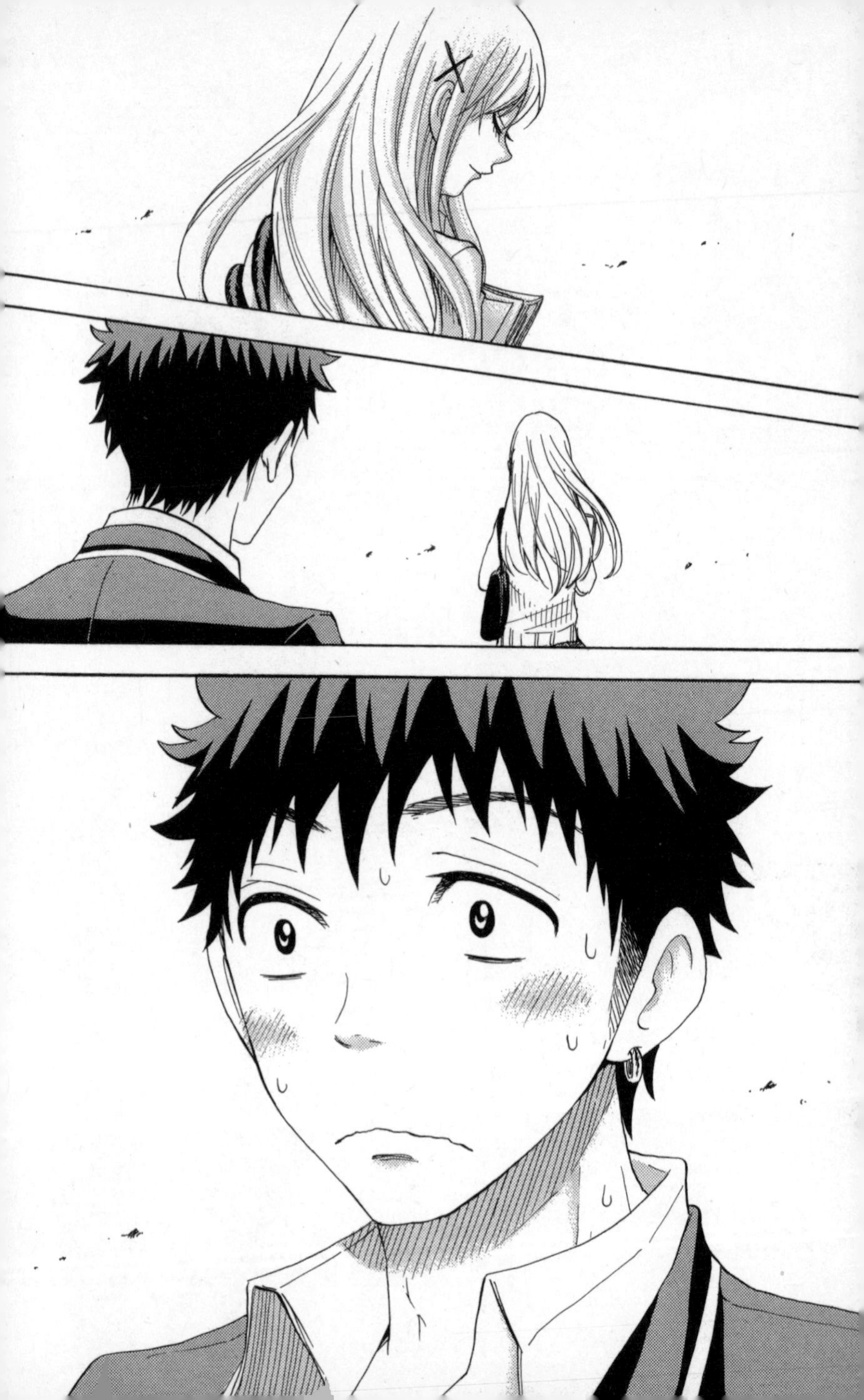

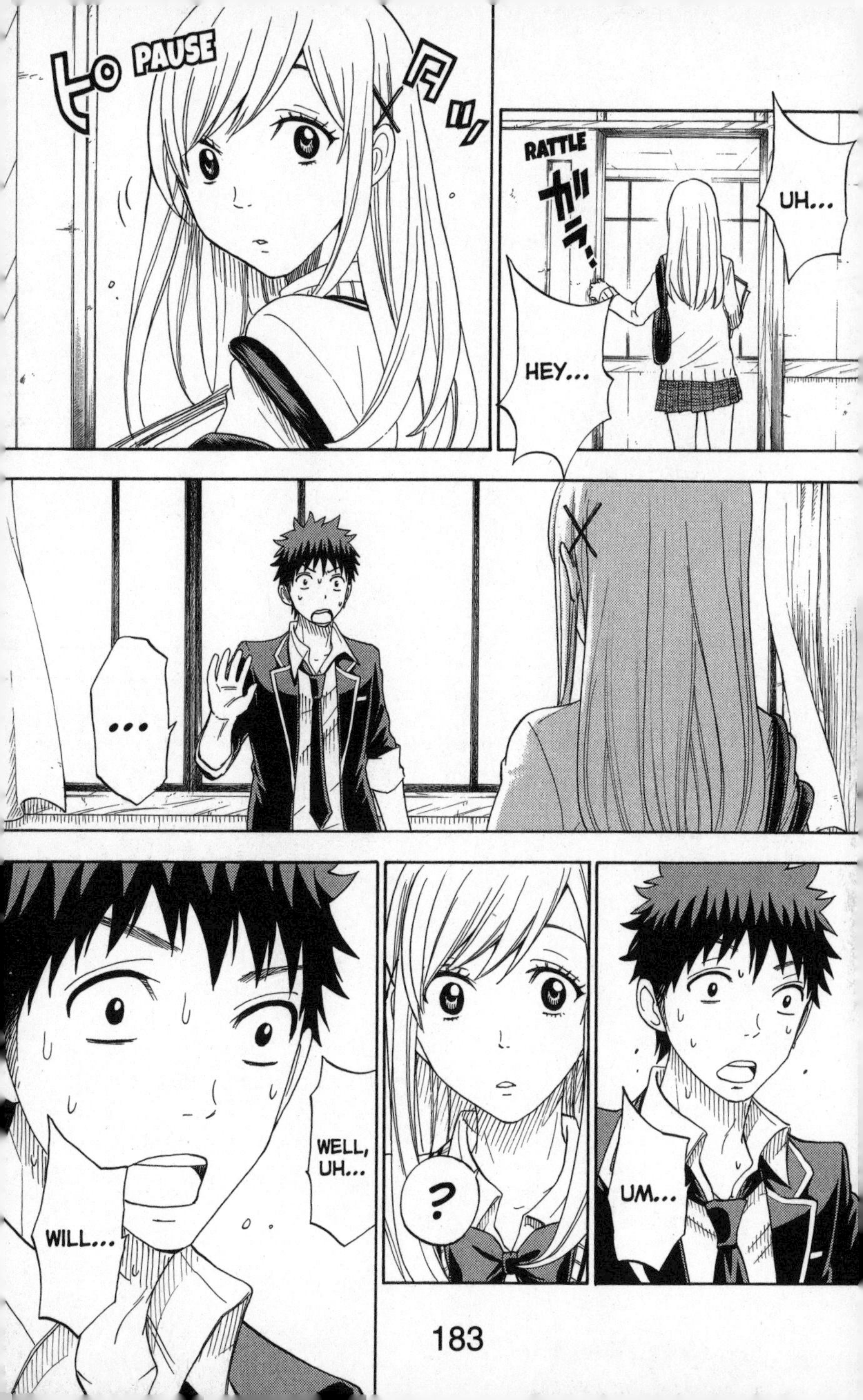

RATTLE
UH...
HEY...
PAUSE
...
UM...
?
WELL, UH...
WILL...

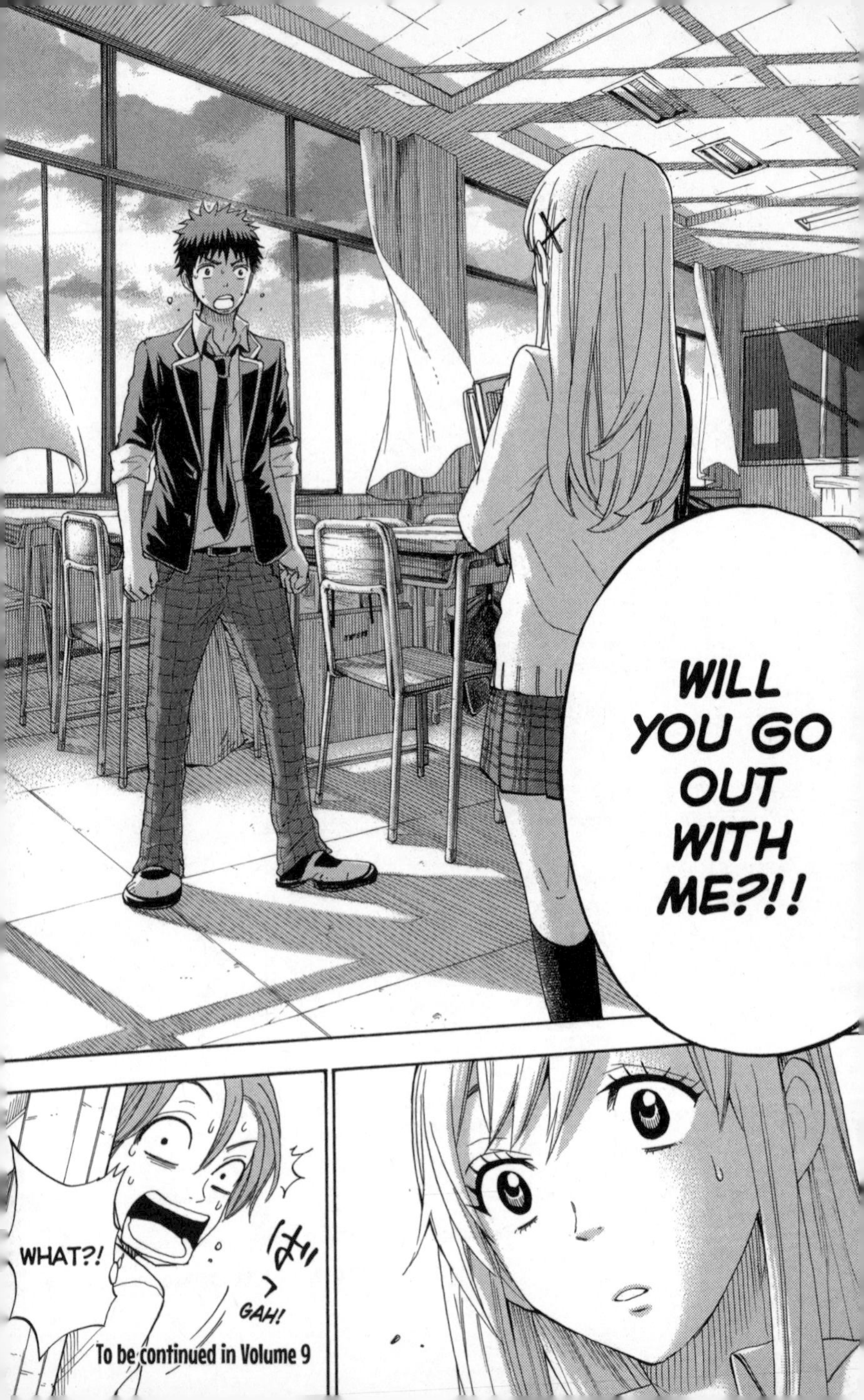
WILL YOU GO OUT WITH ME?!!
WHAT?!
はッ
GAH!
To be continued in Volume 9

Yamada's

~~Miyabi~~ Itou's Witch Research Notes

File.4

Written by: Yamada

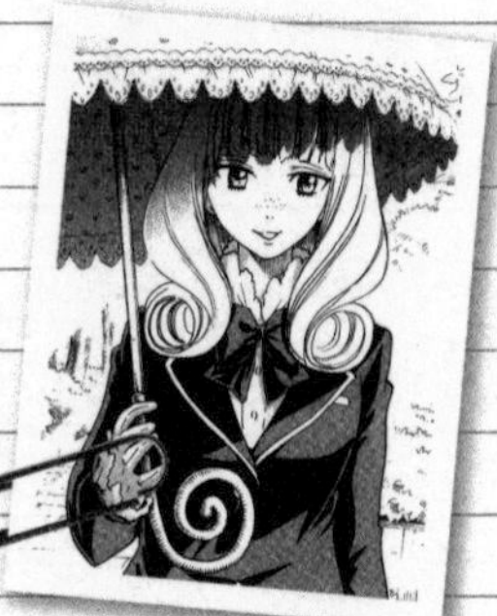

Rika Saionji

The Seventh Witch Power: ????

- Third-year student at Suzaku High School
- Appears to be taking orders from the Student Council President
- She erases "memories about the witches" from those who know the identity of the seven witches.
  In my case, her power doesn't work on me, so she erased my friends' memories (of me) instead!

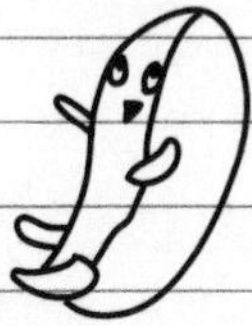

- She doesn't wear panties! For real!

★ Common rules for the witch powers that I've figured out!

- One person, one power!
- If a person under a witch's spell is kissed by another witch, the person being kissed will not be affected.

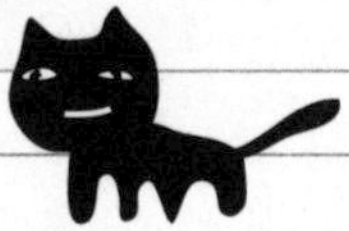

- A witch cannot put another witch under their spell.
- Tamaki and I have powers, but we don't count as witches.
- There are always seven witches.
  When a witch leaves the school and loses her power, a new witch is born in her place.

朱雀高等学校 裏ホームページ

SUZAKU HIGH SCHOOL UNDERGROUND WEBSITE

 Thanks for waiting, everyone! Let's begin the Q&A session!

 To all of you who were looking forward to this in the last volume and were disappointed to find that we couldn't include it, sorry. This time we've increased our volume to make up for things!

 All right! Continuing on from our session with Urara before, we have another guest with us today!

It's Suzaku High's very own all-powerful idiot, Yamada!

 Argh! Hey, what the hell! Why're you calling me out here now?! Hungh?!!

 Cough Cough! So much dust… Hey! You can't just kick down the door like that!

 Well, you guys called me out here last time and no one was around… Do you guys even know how long I was waiting for this?!

 You…were really looking forward to this, huh.

 ACK!

 Okay, okay. Let's just get to it then.

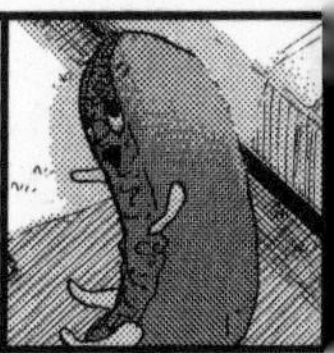

Q1. What kind of animal is the full-body pillow in your room, Yamada-kun?

Nagasaki Prefecture H.N. Suguuru-san

I was expecting that question! Nah, that's no animal.
It's the Yakisoba-pan fairy, man!
How do you not know that?! **It's Sobasshi!**

No idea what that is.

Next question!

Hey! Wait! Whaaa?!

Q2. What's you birthday, sign, and blood type?
What are everybody else's too?

Hokkaido H.N. Rina-san

I'm a Virgo born on 8/31 and I'm type-O!

Oh?! That's the end of summer!

Yup!! That's why every year, I face the fall semester tormented by the sadness of summer's end, the loneliness of having no one wish me happy birthday, and the anxiety that comes with not having my summer homework done…

Those are all your fault, Yamada… But, I do feel a little bad for you!

By the way, I'm a Leo born on 7/28 and I'm type-AB.

I'm a Gemini born on 6/6 and I'm type-B.

And I know for a fact that Urara-chan is a Capricorn born on 12/24 and she's type-A, while Tsubaki is a Scorpio born on 11/5 and a type-A.

Wow, you sure do know a lot.

Hehehe… Yeah, I guess I know a little about this and that!

Uh…there's something suspicious about this girl!

Q3. In volume 7, did Yamada-kun make the Yakisoba-pan for the cultural festival? If so, could it be that Yamada-kun has domestic skills?

Tochigi Prefecture H.N. Hoshishiho-san

Not at all! We all split the work amongst ourselves to make those! All Yamada did was watch from the sidelines and butt in with a word or two now and then. He didn't do anything else!

What the hell, Yamada? Just who do you think you are?

S-shut up!

I'm totally an **"expert eater"**!!

I have more than enough domestic-skills!!

Okay, next question!

Hey! Just wait a minute!!

Q4. Why is your sister so cute?

Tokyo H.N. Kenken-san

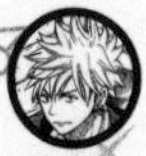

That's because they picked Yamada up by the river.

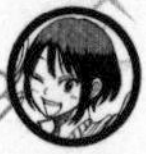

All right, next!!

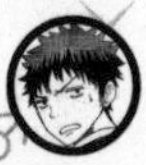

Whaaa?! I haven't even given an answer, y'know! We *do* look alike. It's like, y'know... **RIGHT?!**

Q5. Why does your house have souvenirs from all over Japan in it, Yamada-kun?

Nagano Prefecture H.N. Suguuru-san

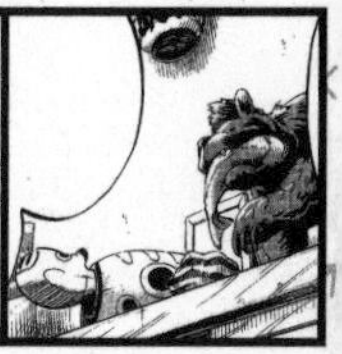

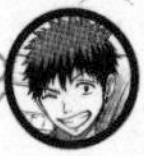

Wow! You guys were really paying attention, huh. Those are things my mom buys when she goes on group trips with her housewife friends! I guess it's what you call a hobby or whatever, but I wish she would bring back food with her!

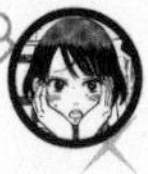

Oh yeah! So I guess that explains why Yamada's house has a real **middle-aged lady** vibe to it.

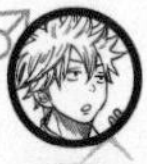

Ah, I see. So that's why I get sleepy there?

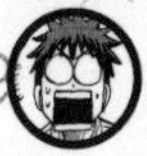

Miyamura, you always get way too comfy at my house!!

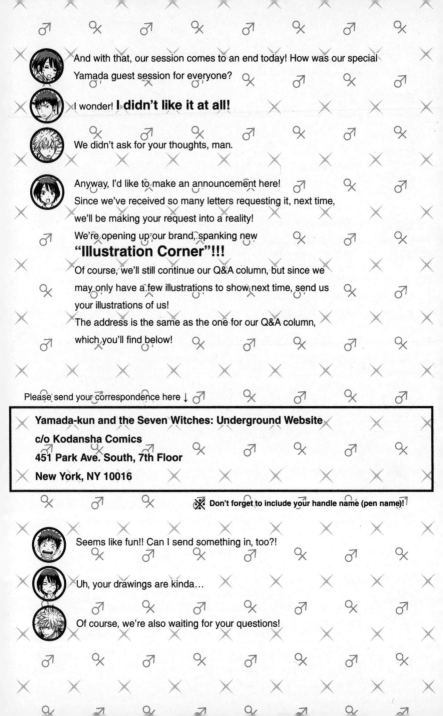

And with that, our session comes to an end today! How was our special Yamada guest session for everyone?

I wonder! **I didn't like it at all!**

We didn't ask for your thoughts, man.

Anyway, I'd like to make an announcement here!
Since we've received so many letters requesting it, next time, we'll be making your request into a reality!
We're opening up our brand, spanking new **"Illustration Corner"!!!**
Of course, we'll still continue our Q&A column, but since we may only have a few illustrations to show next time, send us your illustrations of us!
The address is the same as the one for our Q&A column, which you'll find below!

Please send your correspondence here ↓

Yamada-kun and the Seven Witches: Underground Website
c/o Kodansha Comics
451 Park Ave. South, 7th Floor
New York, NY 10016

Don't forget to include your handle name (pen name)!

Seems like fun!! Can I send something in, too?!

Uh, your drawings are kinda…

Of course, we're also waiting for your questions!

Translation Notes

Sobasshi, page 117

As Yamada explains in his Q&A, Sobasshi is the *yakisoba-pan* (fried chow-mein-style noodles in a bun) fairy, but this is actually a parody of another well-known character named Funassyi (pronounced *foo-na-shee*). Funassyi is a pear-fairy and the unofficial mascot of Funabashi, Chiba Prefecture, an area known for its quality pears. The character exploded in popularity shortly after its debut and has been featured in everything from comics to TV shows, where it is represented in *kigurumi* form (i.e. someone in a costume).

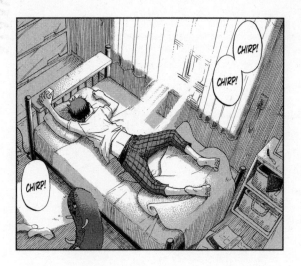

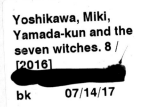

Yamada-kun and the Seven Witches volume 8 is a work of fiction. Names, characters, places, and incidents are the products of the author's imagination or are used fictitiously. Any resemblance to actual events, locales, or persons, living or dead, is entirely coincidental.

A Kodansha Comics Trade Paperback Original.

Published in the United States by Kodansha Comics, an imprint of Kodansha USA Publishing, LLC, New York.

Publication rights for this English edition arranged through Kodansha Ltd., Tokyo.

First published in Japan in 2013 by Kodansha Ltd., Tokyo, as *Yamada-kun to Nananin no Majo* volume 8.

ISBN 978-1-63236-137-0

Printed in the United States of America.

www.kodanshacomics.com

9 8 7 6 5 4 3 2 1

Translation: David Rhie
Lettering: Sara Linsley
Editing: Ajani Oloye
Kodansha Comics Edition Cover Design: Phil Balsman